'AIRDRIE,

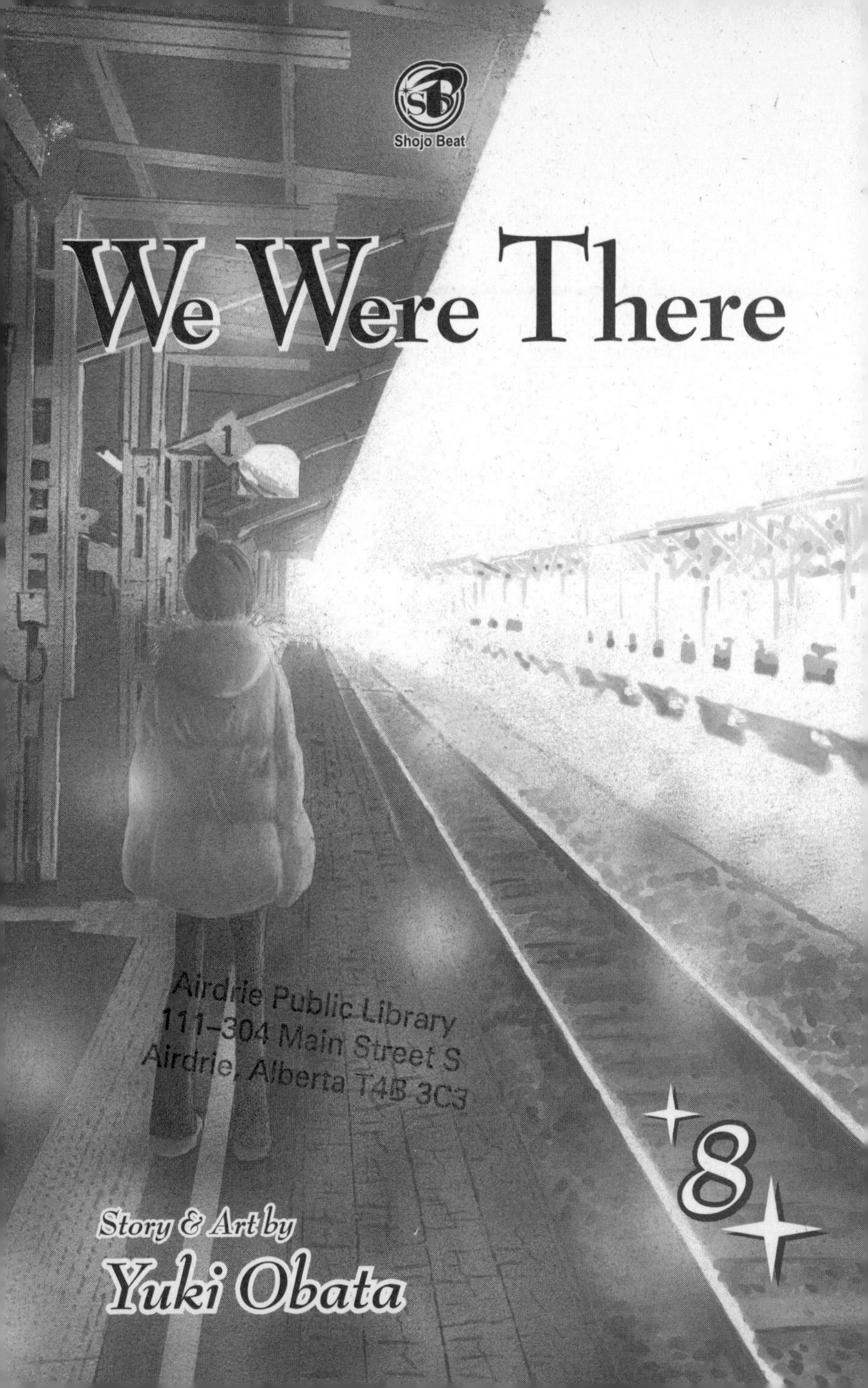
Shojo Beat
1

We Were There

8

Story & Art by
Yuki Obata

Contents

Characters

Masafumi Takeuchi
*Yano's childhood friend.
He's kinder and more
modest than Yano.*

Nanami Takahashi
*She's earnest but a bit
forgetful at times.*

Motoharu Yano
*Nanami's popular classmate.
His girlfriend Nana-san died.*

Story

Yano did not show up for his date with Nanami. Instead
he was with Yuri, to the shock and dismay of Nanami.
Seeing Nanami in despair, Takeuchi finally tells her his
feelings for her. And just when it looks like Nanami
and Yano's relationship couldn't get any more difficult,
Yano's mother decides to get a divorce and move...

Chapter 28

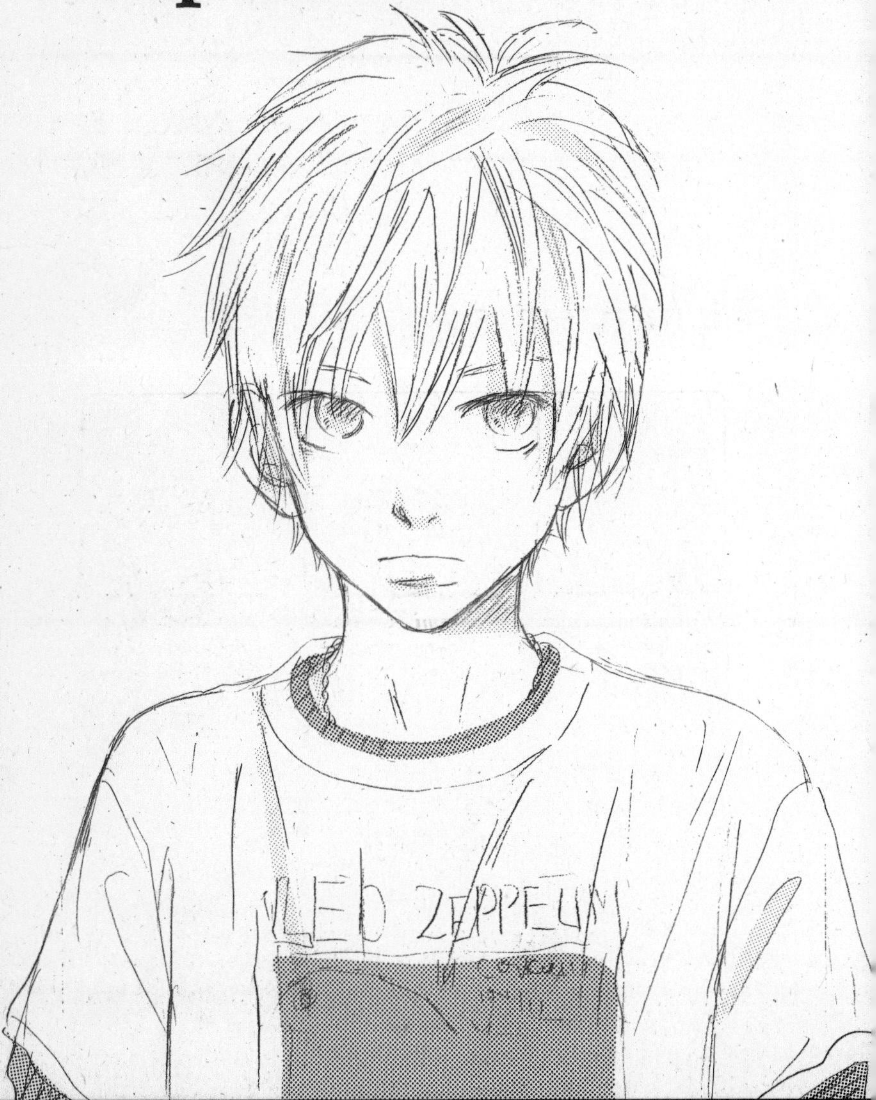
LED ZEPPELIN

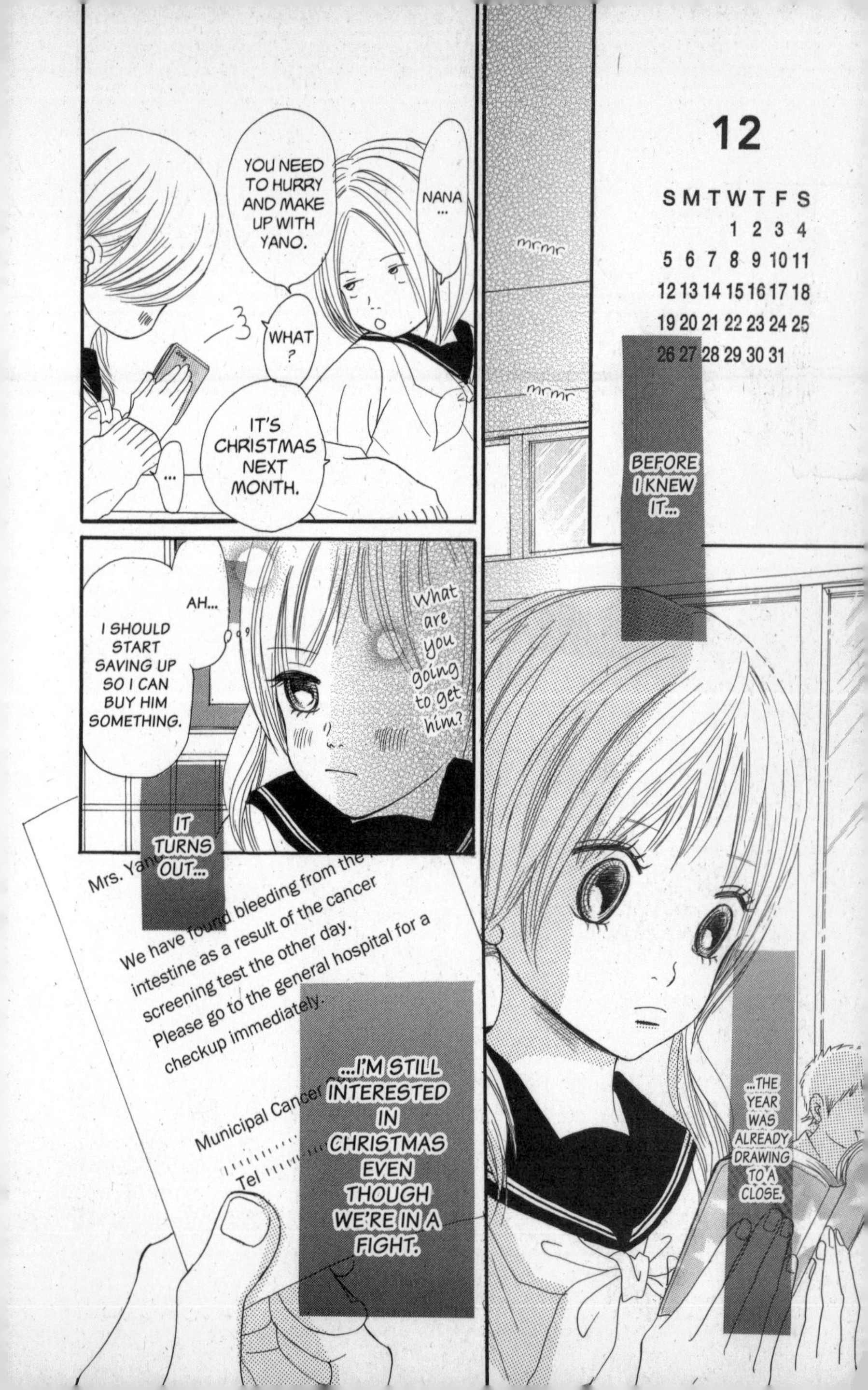
12
S M T W T F S
1 2 3 4
5 6 7 8 9 10 11
12 13 14 15 16 17 18
19 20 21 22 23 24 25
26 27 28 29 30 31
mrmr
mrmr
BEFORE I KNEW IT...
...THE YEAR WAS ALREADY DRAWING TO A CLOSE.
NANA...
YOU NEED TO HURRY AND MAKE UP WITH YANO.
WHAT?
IT'S CHRISTMAS NEXT MONTH.
...
What are you going to get him?
AH...
I SHOULD START SAVING UP SO I CAN BUY HIM SOMETHING.
IT TURNS OUT...
Mrs. Yan
We have found bleeding from the
intestine as a result of the cancer
screening test the other day.
Please go to the general hospital for a
checkup immediately.
Municipal Cancer
Tel
...I'M STILL INTERESTED IN CHRISTMAS EVEN THOUGH WE'RE IN A FIGHT.

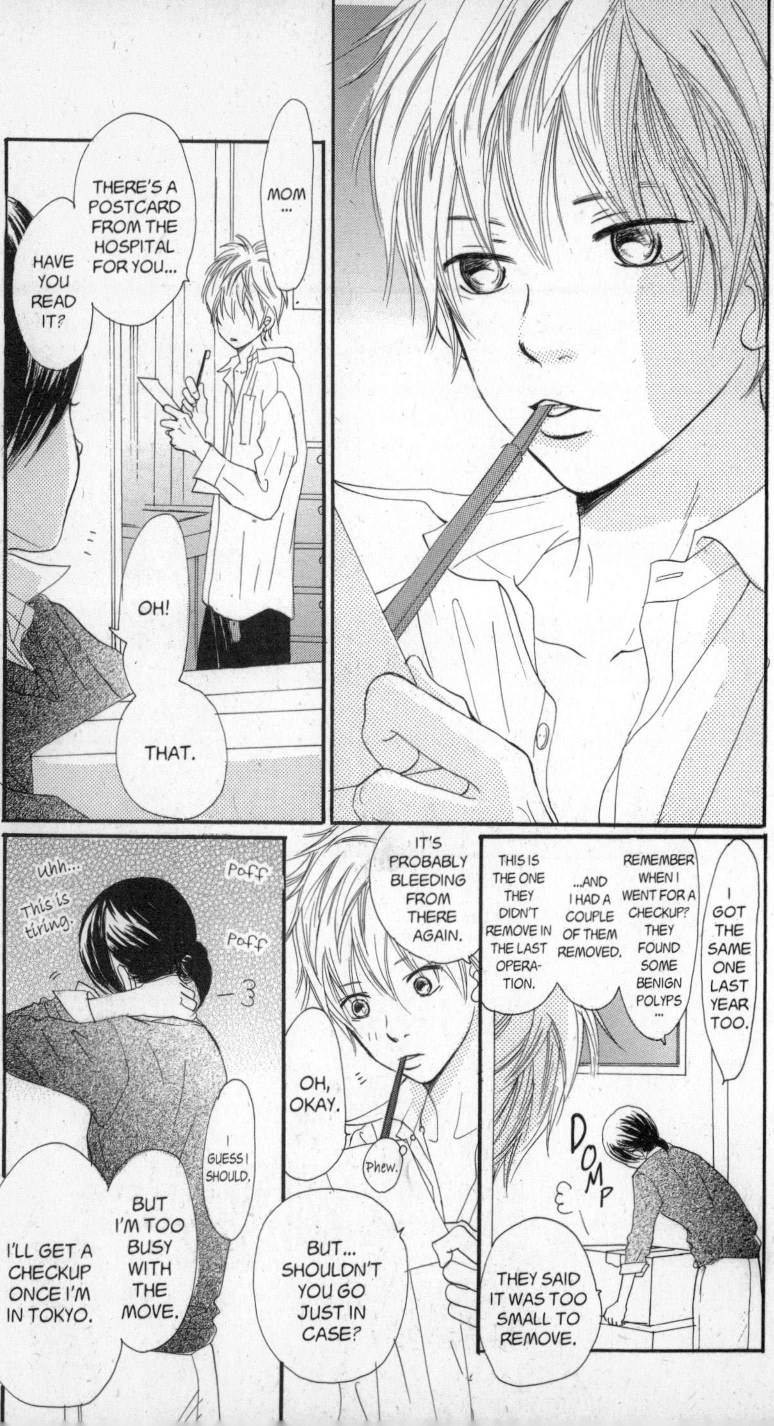
MOM ...
THERE'S A POSTCARD FROM THE HOSPITAL FOR YOU...
HAVE YOU READ IT?
OH!
THAT.
I GOT THE SAME ONE LAST YEAR TOO.
REMEMBER WHEN I WENT FOR A CHECKUP? THEY FOUND SOME BENIGN POLYPS ...
...AND I HAD A COUPLE OF THEM REMOVED.
THIS IS THE ONE THEY DIDN'T REMOVE IN THE LAST OPERA-TION.
DOMP
THEY SAID IT WAS TOO SMALL TO REMOVE.
IT'S PROBABLY BLEEDING FROM THERE AGAIN.
OH, OKAY.
Phew.
BUT... SHOULDN'T YOU GO JUST IN CASE?
Poff
Poff
Uhh... This is tiring.
I GUESS I SHOULD.
BUT I'M TOO BUSY WITH THE MOVE.
I'LL GET A CHECKUP ONCE I'M IN TOKYO.

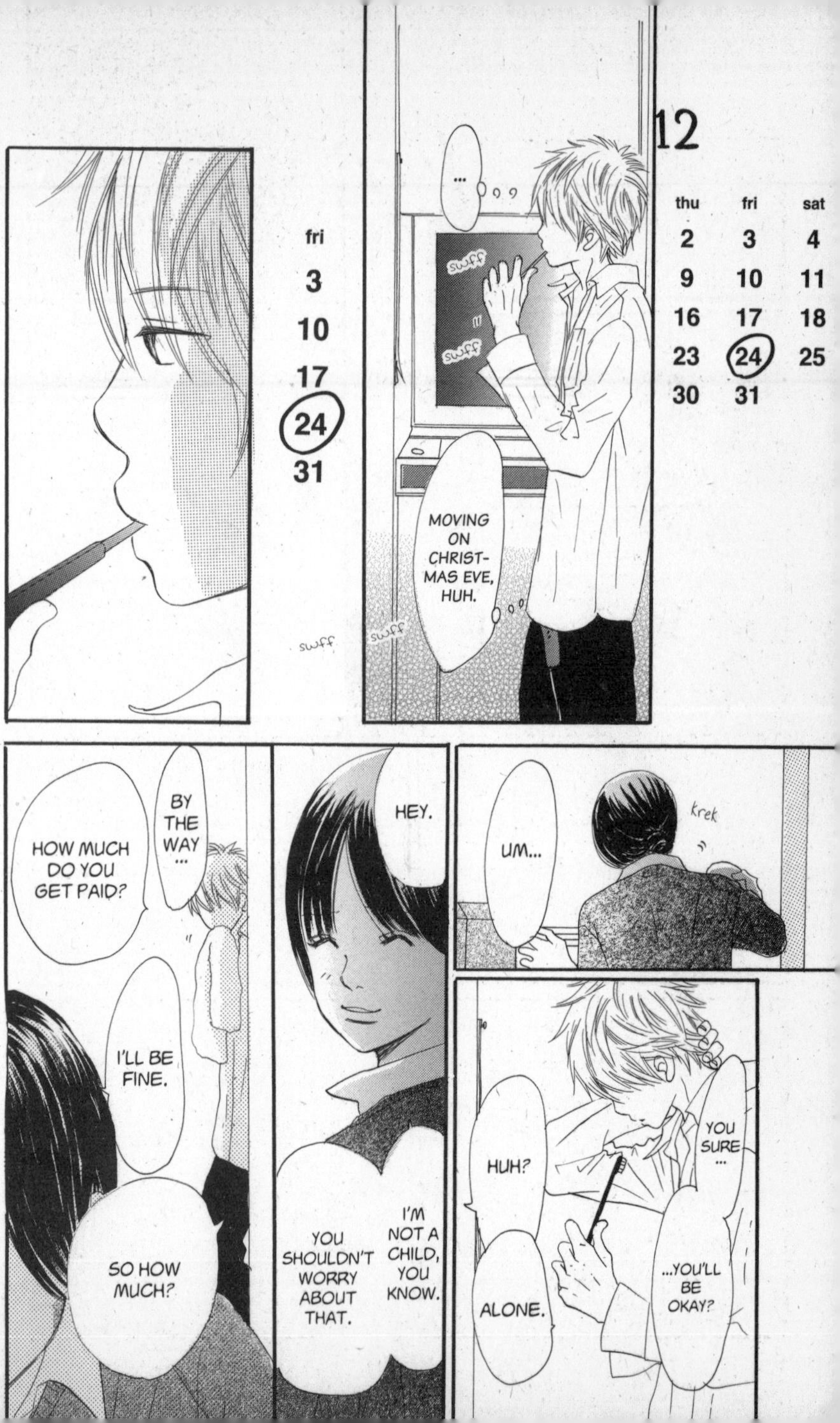
12
thu fri sat
2 3 4
9 10 11
16 17 18
23 24 25
30 31
...
swff
swff
MOVING ON CHRISTMAS EVE, HUH.
swff
fri
3
10
17
24
31
swff
UM...
krek
YOU SURE...
...YOU'LL BE OKAY?
ALONE.
HUH?
HEY.
I'M NOT A CHILD, YOU KNOW.
YOU SHOULDN'T WORRY ABOUT THAT.
BY THE WAY...
HOW MUCH DO YOU GET PAID?
I'LL BE FINE.
SO HOW MUCH?

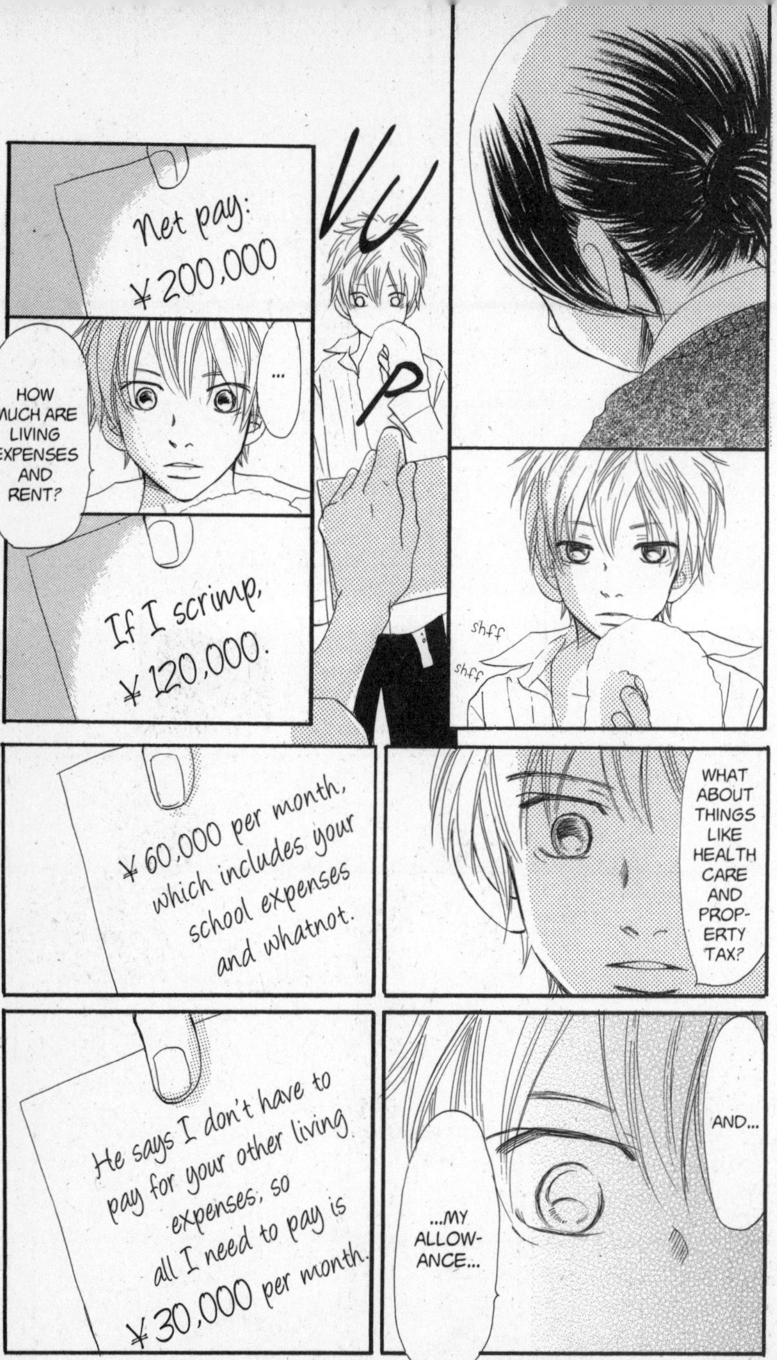

shff
shff
Net pay: ¥200,000
...
HOW MUCH ARE LIVING EXPENSES AND RENT?
If I scrimp, ¥120,000.
WHAT ABOUT THINGS LIKE HEALTH CARE AND PROP-ERTY TAX?
¥60,000 per month, which includes your school expenses and whatnot.
AND...
...MY ALLOW-ANCE...
He says I don't have to pay for your other living expenses, so all I need to pay is ¥30,000 per month.

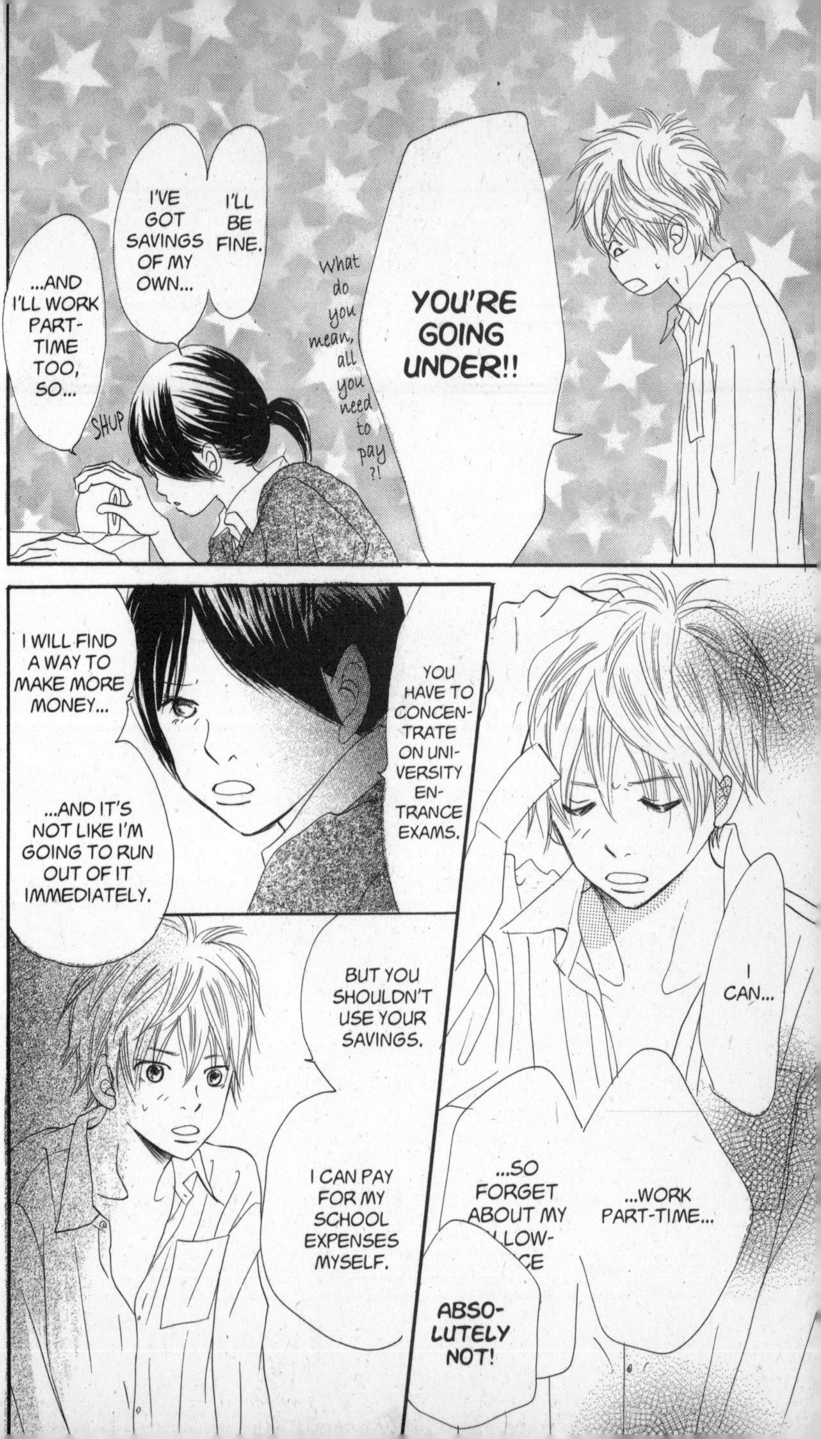

YOU'RE GOING UNDER!!
What do you mean, all you need to pay?!
I'LL BE FINE.
I'VE GOT SAVINGS OF MY OWN...
...AND I'LL WORK PART-TIME TOO, SO...
SHUP
I CAN...
...WORK PART-TIME...
...SO FORGET ABOUT MY
ABSOLUTELY NOT!
YOU HAVE TO CONCENTRATE ON UNIVERSITY ENTRANCE EXAMS.
I WILL FIND A WAY TO MAKE MORE MONEY...
...AND IT'S NOT LIKE I'M GOING TO RUN OUT OF IT IMMEDIATELY.
BUT YOU SHOULDN'T USE YOUR SAVINGS.
I CAN PAY FOR MY SCHOOL EXPENSES MYSELF.

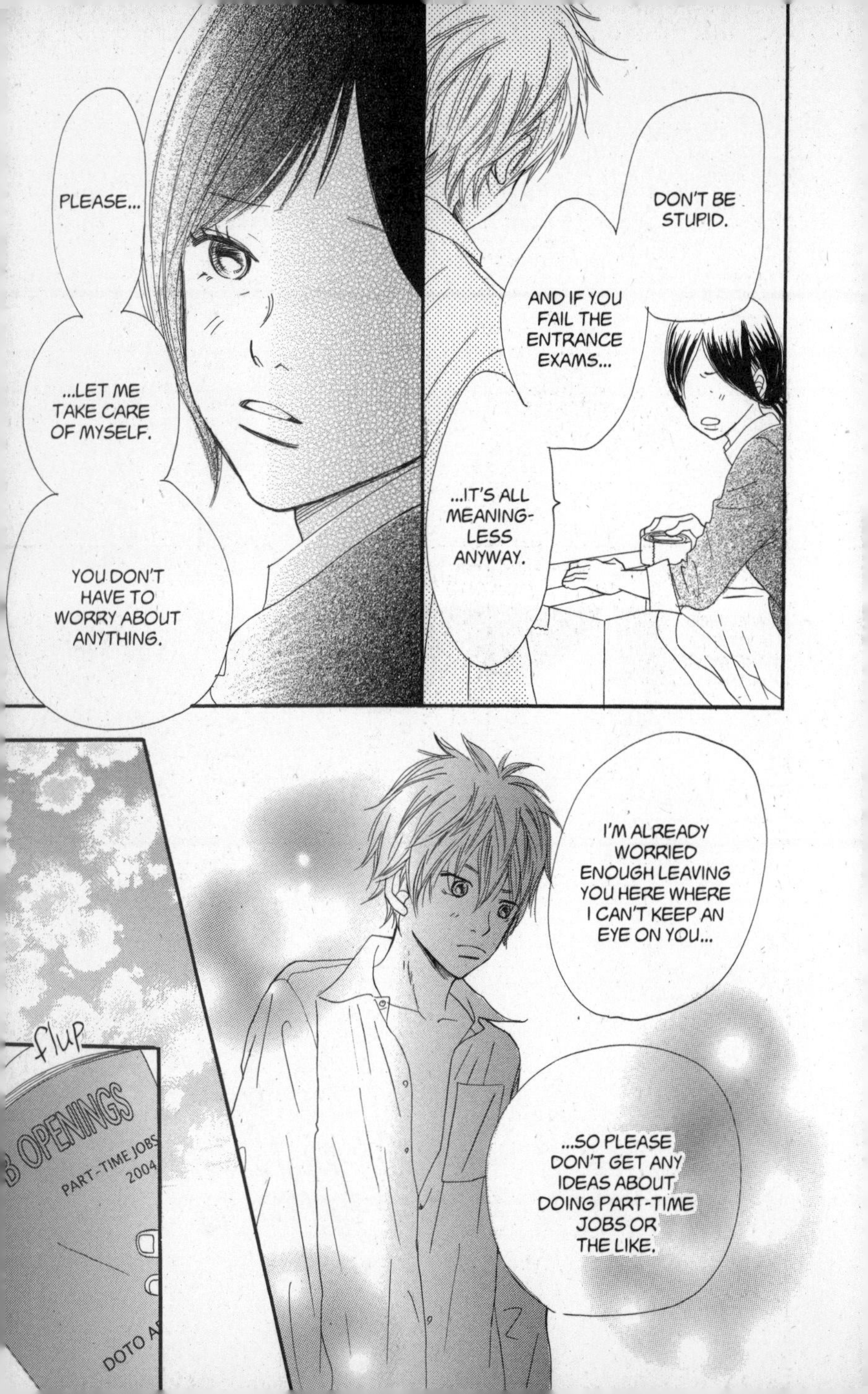
DON'T BE STUPID.
AND IF YOU FAIL THE ENTRANCE EXAMS...
...IT'S ALL MEANING-LESS ANYWAY.
PLEASE...
...LET ME TAKE CARE OF MYSELF.
YOU DON'T HAVE TO WORRY ABOUT ANYTHING.
I'M ALREADY WORRIED ENOUGH LEAVING YOU HERE WHERE I CAN'T KEEP AN EYE ON YOU...
...SO PLEASE DON'T GET ANY IDEAS ABOUT DOING PART-TIME JOBS OR THE LIKE.
flup
OPENINGS
PART-TIME JOBS
2004

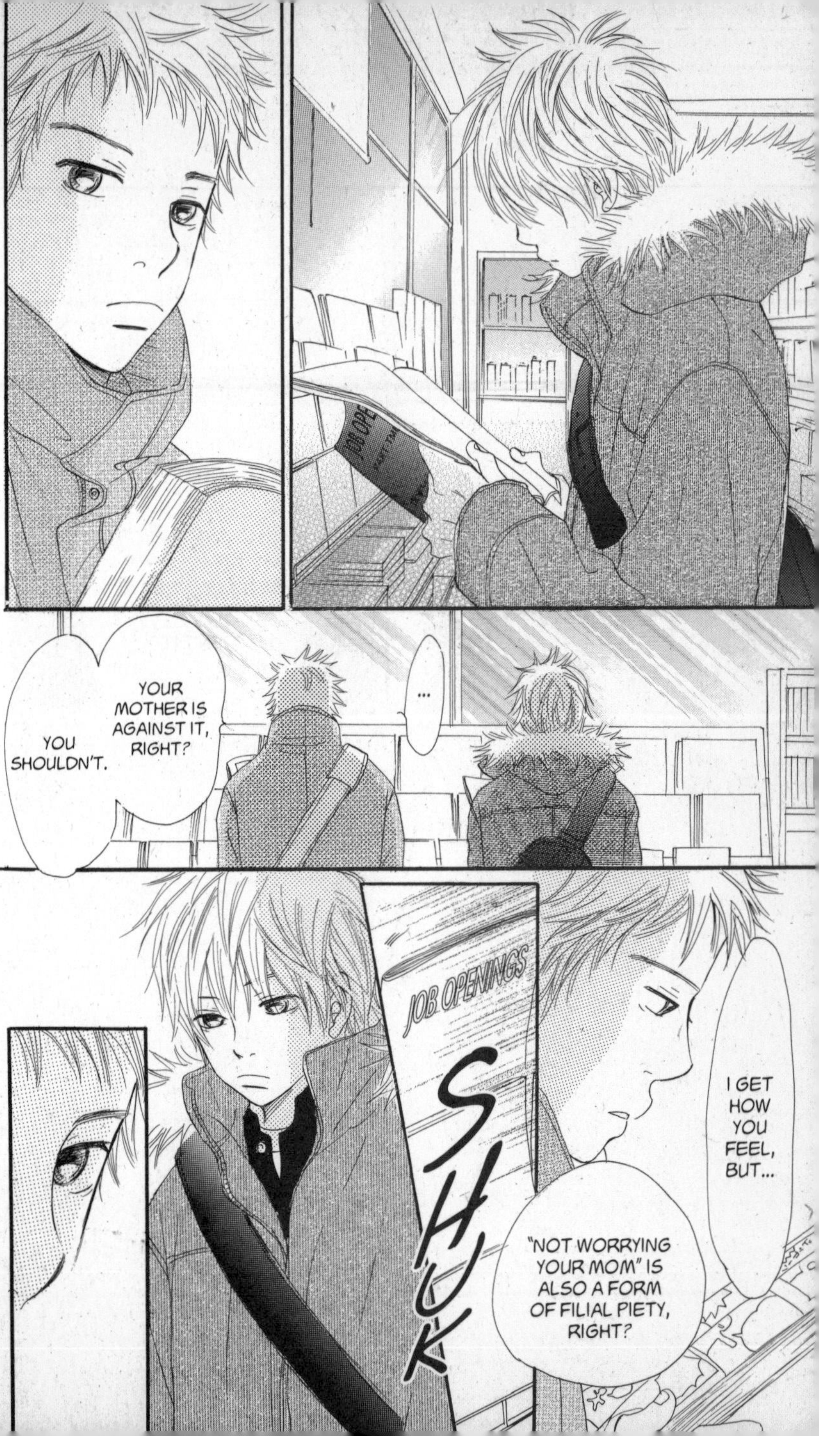
...
YOUR MOTHER IS AGAINST IT, RIGHT?
YOU SHOULDN'T.
I GET HOW YOU FEEL, BUT...
JOB. OPENINGS
SHUK
"NOT WORRYING YOUR MOM" IS ALSO A FORM OF FILIAL PIETY, RIGHT?

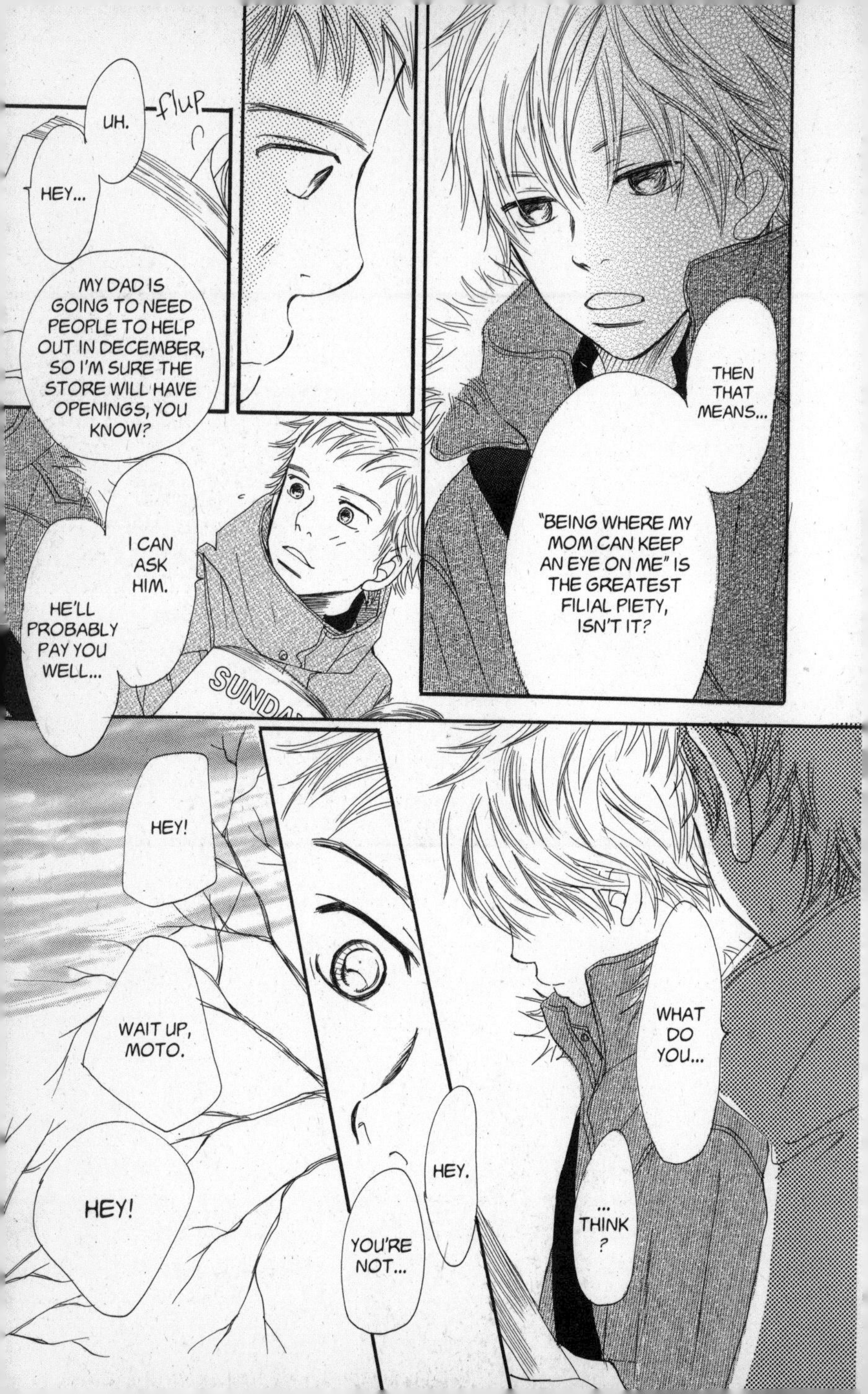
THEN THAT MEANS...
"BEING WHERE MY MOM CAN KEEP AN EYE ON ME" IS THE GREATEST FILIAL PIETY, ISN'T IT?
UH.
flup
HEY...
MY DAD IS GOING TO NEED PEOPLE TO HELP OUT IN DECEMBER, SO I'M SURE THE STORE WILL HAVE OPENINGS, YOU KNOW?
I CAN ASK HIM.
HE'LL PROBABLY PAY YOU WELL...
SUNDA
WHAT DO YOU...
...THINK?
HEY.
YOU'RE NOT...
HEY!
WAIT UP, MOTO.
HEY!

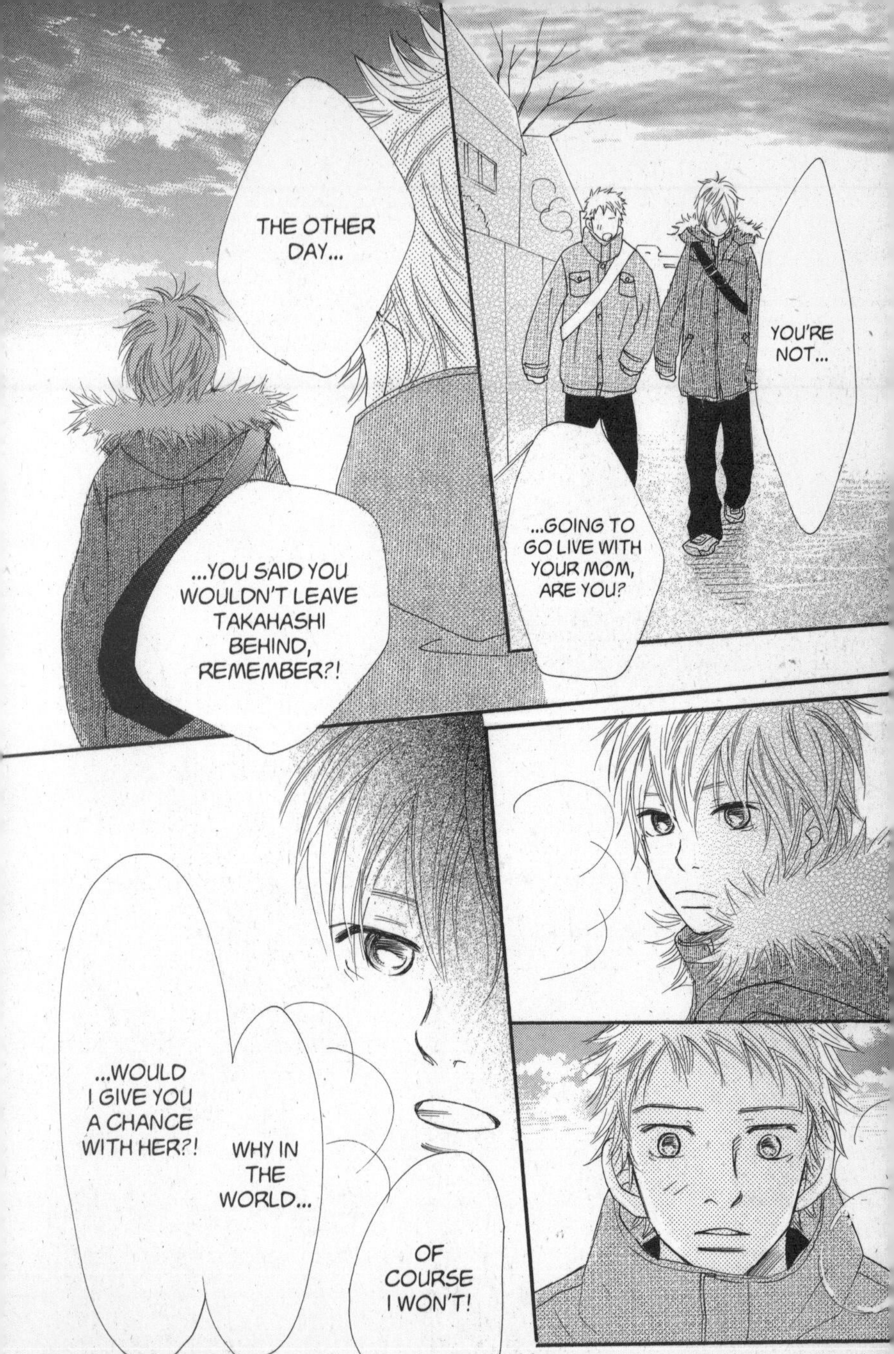
YOU'RE NOT...
...GOING TO GO LIVE WITH YOUR MOM, ARE YOU?
THE OTHER DAY...
...YOU SAID YOU WOULDN'T LEAVE TAKAHASHI BEHIND, REMEMBER?!
OF COURSE I WON'T!
WHY IN THE WORLD...
...WOULD I GIVE YOU A CHANCE WITH HER?!

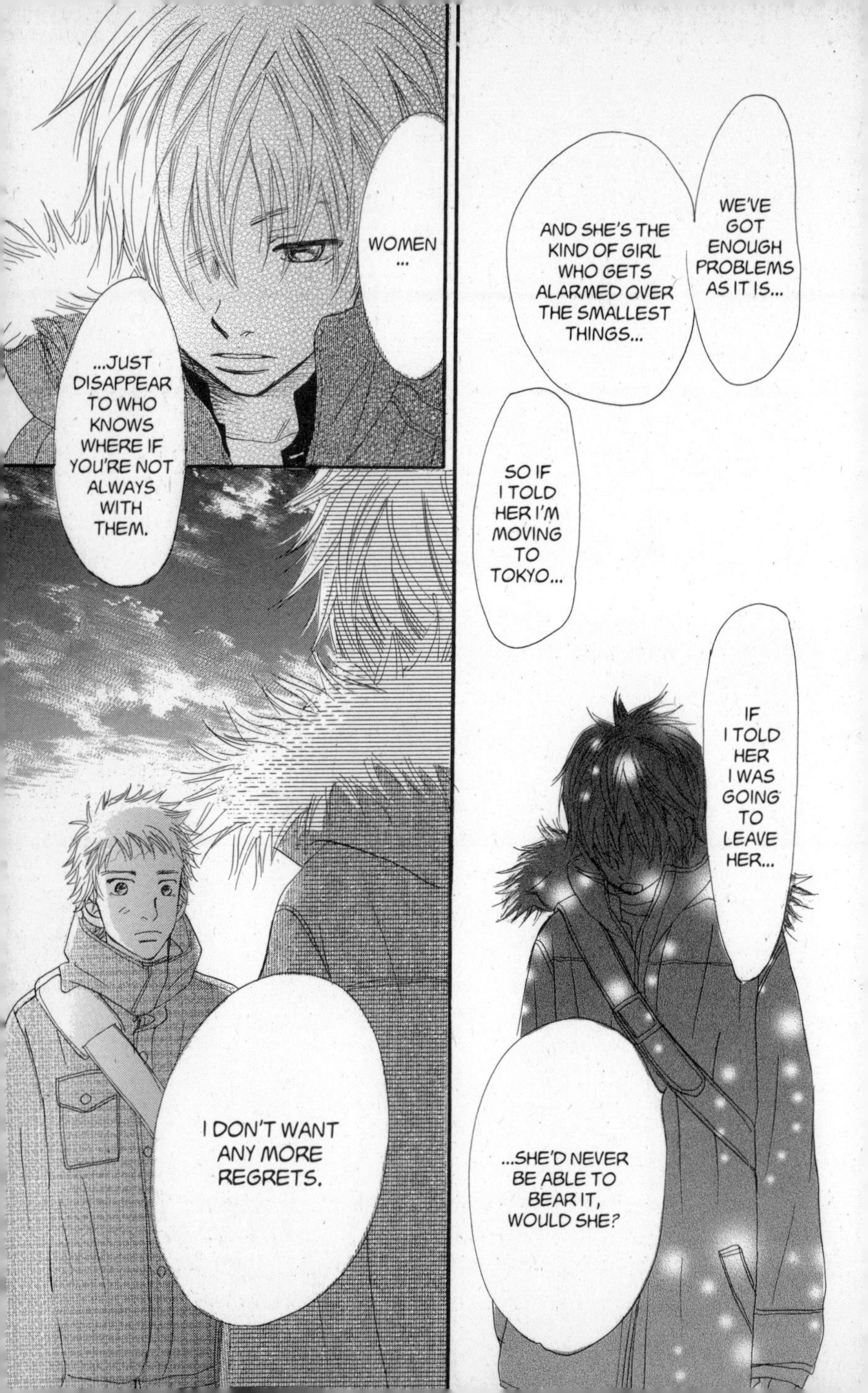
WE'VE GOT ENOUGH PROBLEMS AS IT IS...
AND SHE'S THE KIND OF GIRL WHO GETS ALARMED OVER THE SMALLEST THINGS...
SO IF I TOLD HER I'M MOVING TO TOKYO...
IF I TOLD HER I WAS GOING TO LEAVE HER...
...SHE'D NEVER BE ABLE TO BEAR IT, WOULD SHE?
WOMEN ...
...JUST DISAPPEAR TO WHO KNOWS WHERE IF YOU'RE NOT ALWAYS WITH THEM.
I DON'T WANT ANY MORE REGRETS.

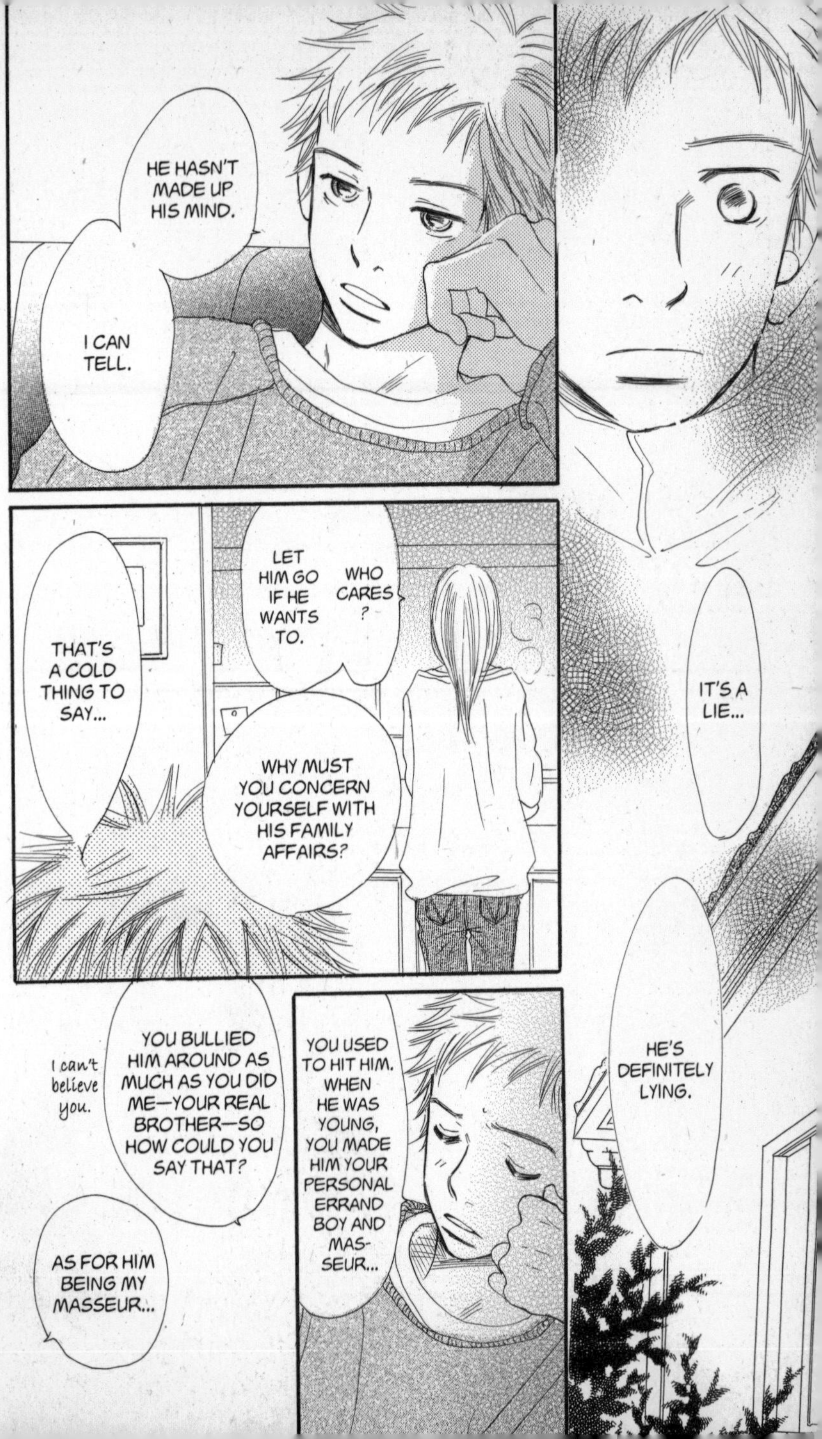
IT'S A LIE...
HE'S DEFINITELY LYING.
HE HASN'T MADE UP HIS MIND.
I CAN TELL.
WHO CARES?
LET HIM GO IF HE WANTS TO.
WHY MUST YOU CONCERN YOURSELF WITH HIS FAMILY AFFAIRS?
THAT'S A COLD THING TO SAY...
YOU USED TO HIT HIM. WHEN HE WAS YOUNG, YOU MADE HIM YOUR PERSONAL ERRAND BOY AND MAS-SEUR...
YOU BULLIED HIM AROUND AS MUCH AS YOU DID ME—YOUR REAL BROTHER—SO HOW COULD YOU SAY THAT?
I can't believe you.
AS FOR HIM BEING MY MASSEUR...

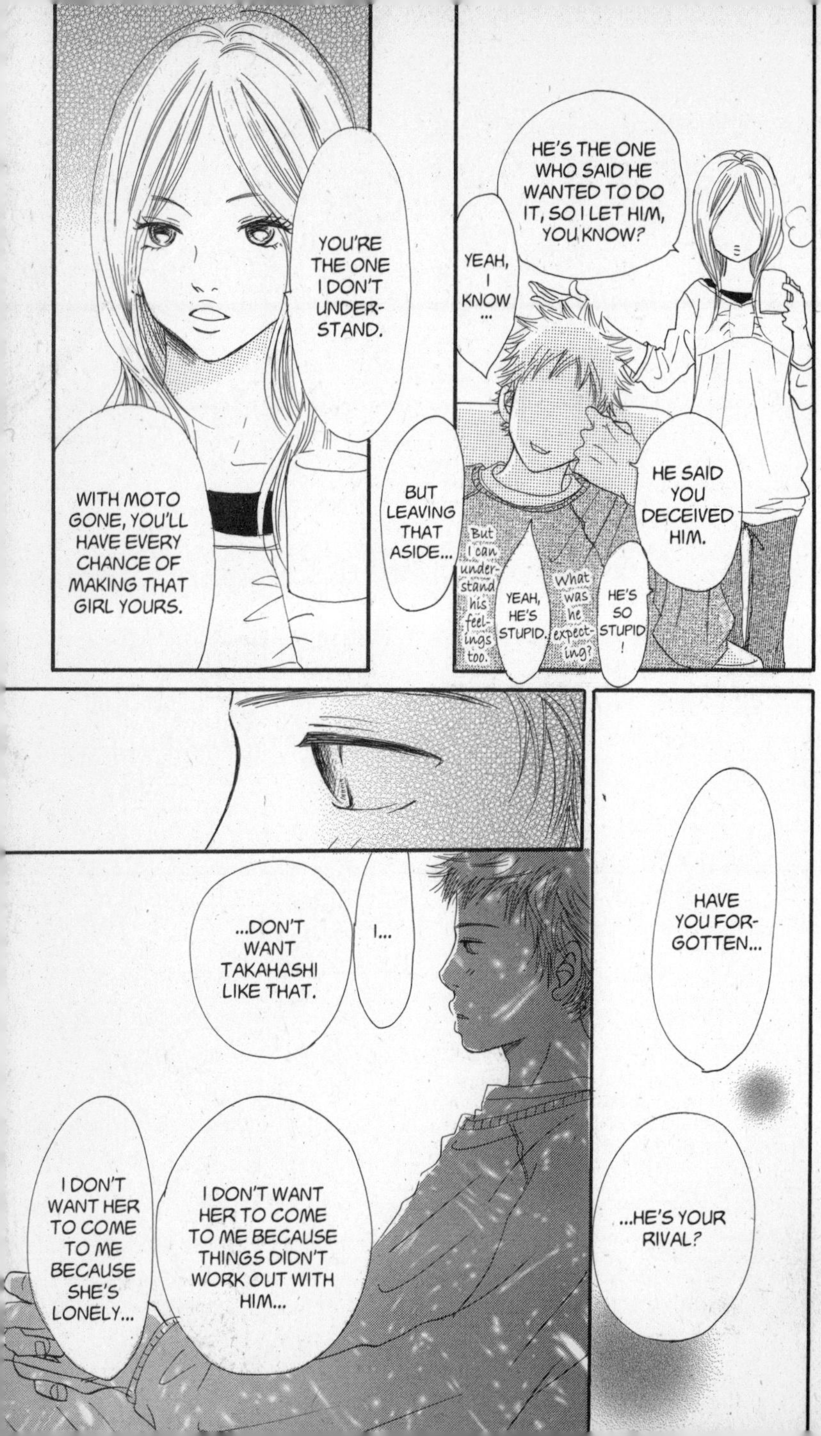
HE'S THE ONE WHO SAID HE WANTED TO DO IT, SO I LET HIM, YOU KNOW?
YEAH, I KNOW...
HE SAID YOU DECEIVED HIM.
HE'S SO STUPID!
What was he expecting?
YEAH, HE'S STUPID.
But I can understand his feelings too.
BUT LEAVING THAT ASIDE...
YOU'RE THE ONE I DON'T UNDERSTAND.
WITH MOTO GONE, YOU'LL HAVE EVERY CHANCE OF MAKING THAT GIRL YOURS.
HAVE YOU FORGOTTEN...
...HE'S YOUR RIVAL?
I...
...DON'T WANT TAKAHASHI LIKE THAT.
I DON'T WANT HER TO COME TO ME BECAUSE THINGS DIDN'T WORK OUT WITH HIM...
I DON'T WANT HER TO COME TO ME BECAUSE SHE'S LONELY...

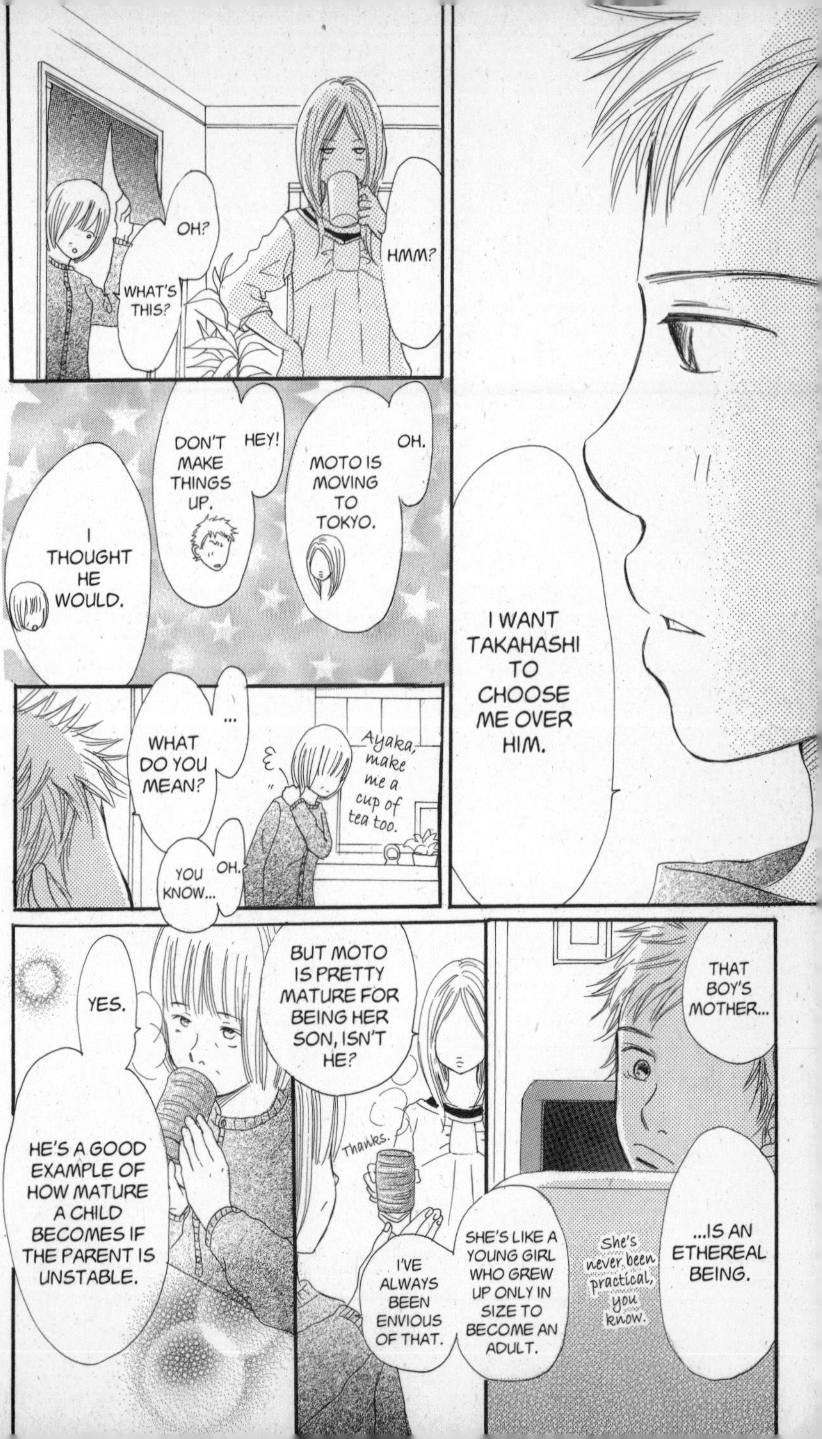

I WANT TAKAHASHI TO CHOOSE ME OVER HIM.
HMM?
OH?
WHAT'S THIS?
OH.
MOTO IS MOVING TO TOKYO.
HEY!
DON'T MAKE THINGS UP.
I THOUGHT HE WOULD.
... WHAT DO YOU MEAN?
Ayaka, make me a cup of tea too.
OH.
YOU KNOW...
THAT BOY'S MOTHER...
...IS AN ETHEREAL BEING.
She's never been practical, you know.
SHE'S LIKE A YOUNG GIRL WHO GREW UP ONLY IN SIZE TO BECOME AN ADULT.
BUT MOTO IS PRETTY MATURE FOR BEING HER SON, ISN'T HE?
Thanks.
I'VE ALWAYS BEEN ENVIOUS OF THAT.
YES.
HE'S A GOOD EXAMPLE OF HOW MATURE A CHILD BECOMES IF THE PARENT IS UNSTABLE.

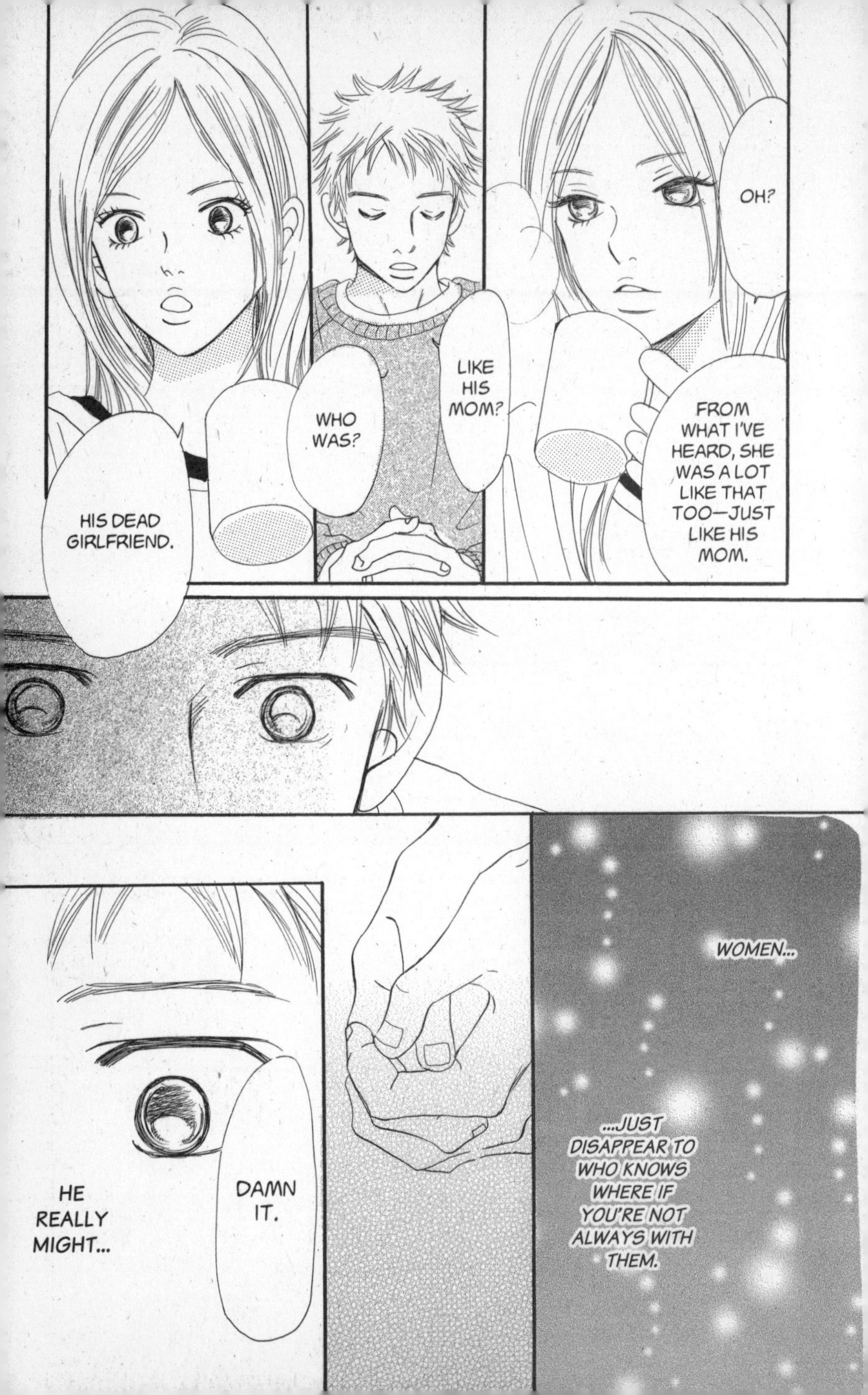
OH?
FROM WHAT I'VE HEARD, SHE WAS A LOT LIKE THAT TOO—JUST LIKE HIS MOM.
LIKE HIS MOM?
WHO WAS?
HIS DEAD GIRLFRIEND.
WOMEN...
...JUST DISAPPEAR TO WHO KNOWS WHERE IF YOU'RE NOT ALWAYS WITH THEM.
DAMN IT.
HE REALLY MIGHT...

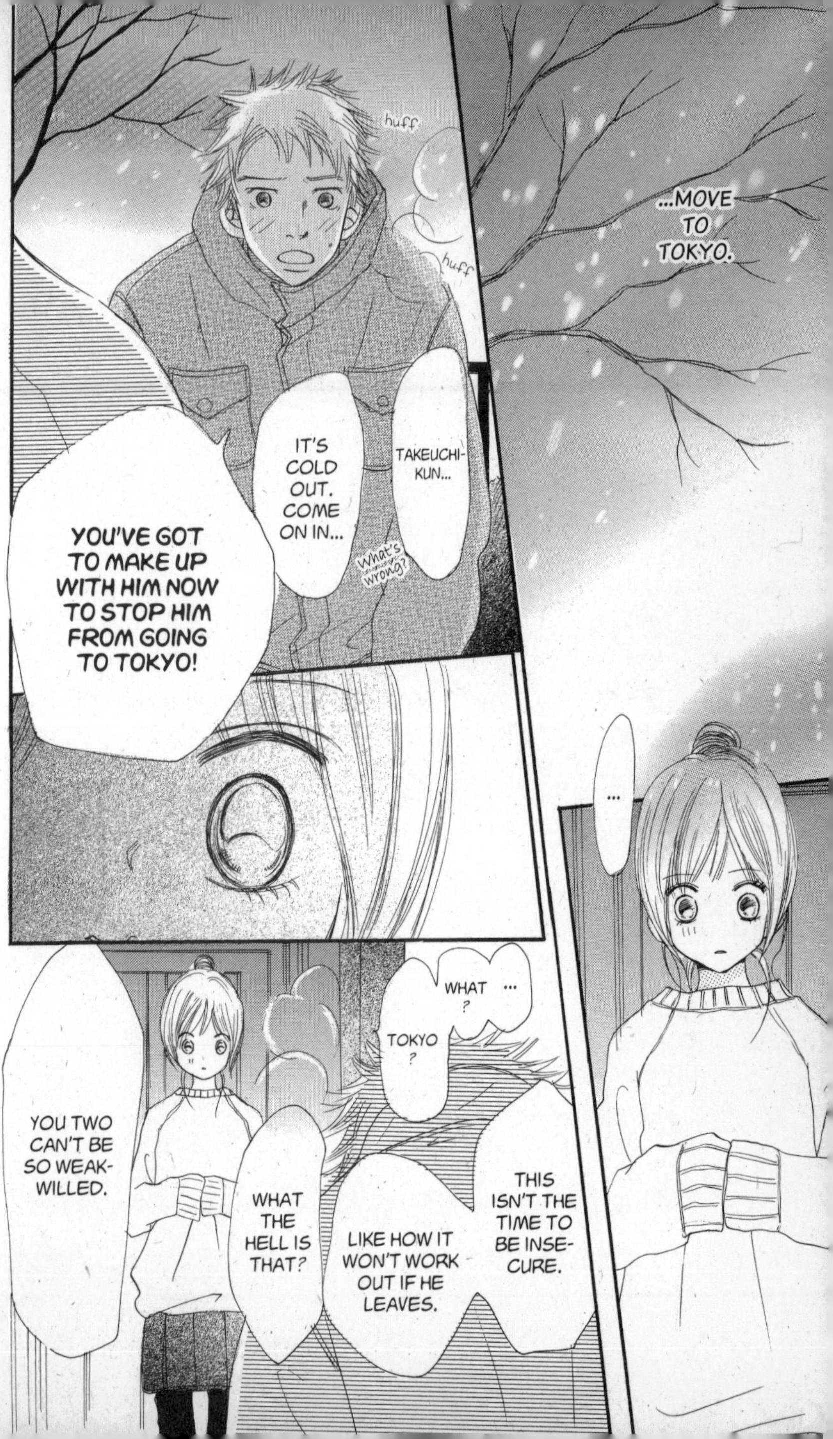
...MOVE TO TOKYO.
huff
huff
TAKEUCHI-KUN...
IT'S COLD OUT. COME ON IN...
What's wrong?
YOU'VE GOT TO MAKE UP WITH HIM NOW TO STOP HIM FROM GOING TO TOKYO!
...
WHAT ...?
TOKYO?
THIS ISN'T THE TIME TO BE INSE-CURE.
LIKE HOW IT WON'T WORK OUT IF HE LEAVES.
WHAT THE HELL IS THAT?
YOU TWO CAN'T BE SO WEAK-WILLED.

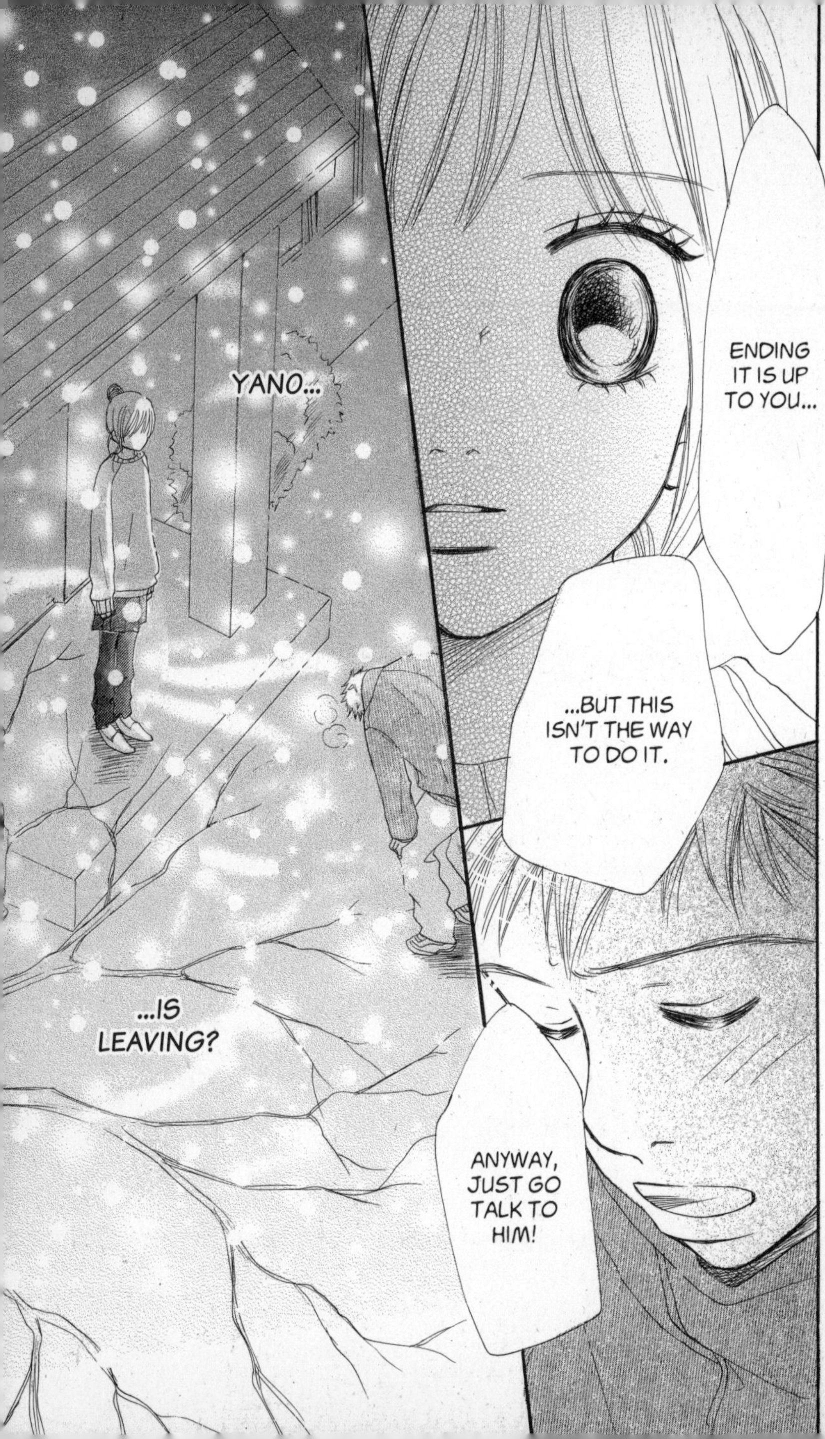
ENDING IT IS UP TO YOU...
...BUT THIS ISN'T THE WAY TO DO IT.
ANYWAY, JUST GO TALK TO HIM!
YANO...
...IS LEAVING?

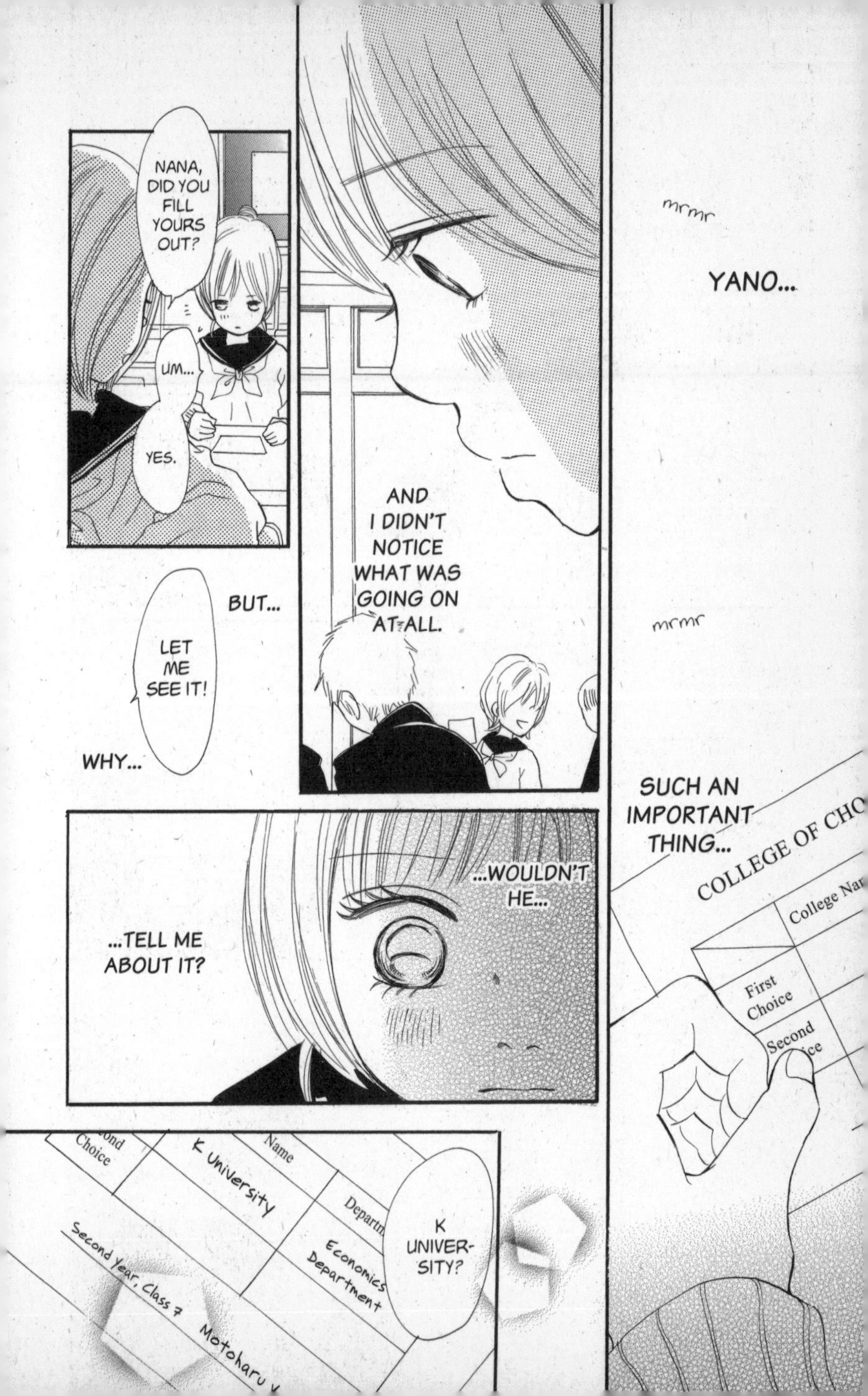
mrmr
YANO...
mrmr
SUCH AN IMPORTANT THING...
First Choice
AND I DIDN'T NOTICE WHAT WAS GOING ON AT ALL.
NANA, DID YOU FILL YOURS OUT?
UM...
YES.
BUT...
LET ME SEE IT!
WHY...
...WOULDN'T HE...
...TELL ME ABOUT IT?
K UNIVERSITY?
K University
Name
Economics Department
Second Year, Class 7
Choice

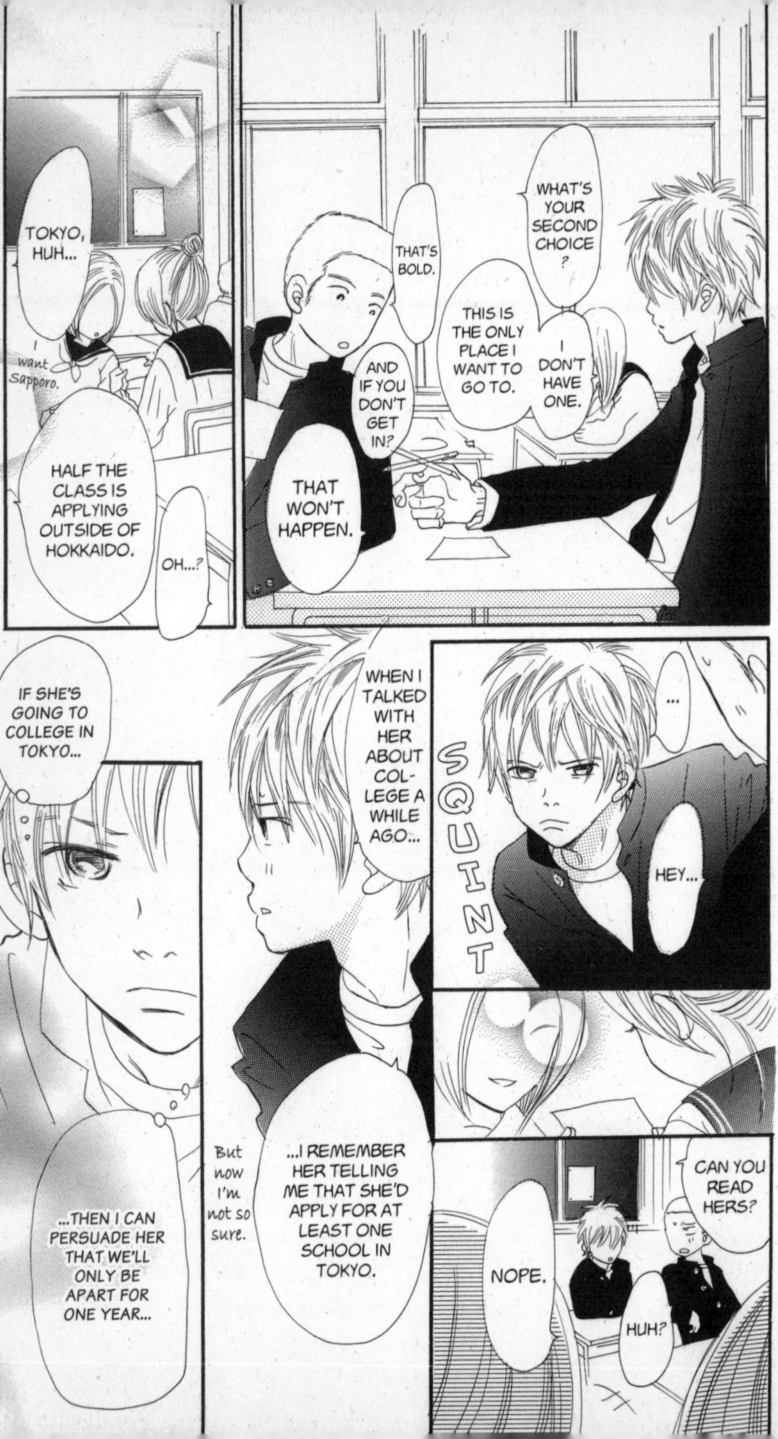
WHAT'S YOUR SECOND CHOICE?
I DON'T HAVE ONE.
THIS IS THE ONLY PLACE I WANT TO GO TO.
THAT'S BOLD.
AND IF YOU DON'T GET IN?
THAT WON'T HAPPEN.
TOKYO, HUH...
I want Sapporo.
HALF THE CLASS IS APPLYING OUTSIDE OF HOKKAIDO.
OH...?
...
HEY...
SQUINT
CAN YOU READ HERS?
NOPE.
HUH?
WHEN I TALKED WITH HER ABOUT COL-LEGE A WHILE AGO...
...I REMEMBER HER TELLING ME THAT SHE'D APPLY FOR AT LEAST ONE SCHOOL IN TOKYO.
But now I'm not so sure.
IF SHE'S GOING TO COLLEGE IN TOKYO...
...THEN I CAN PERSUADE HER THAT WE'LL ONLY BE APART FOR ONE YEAR...

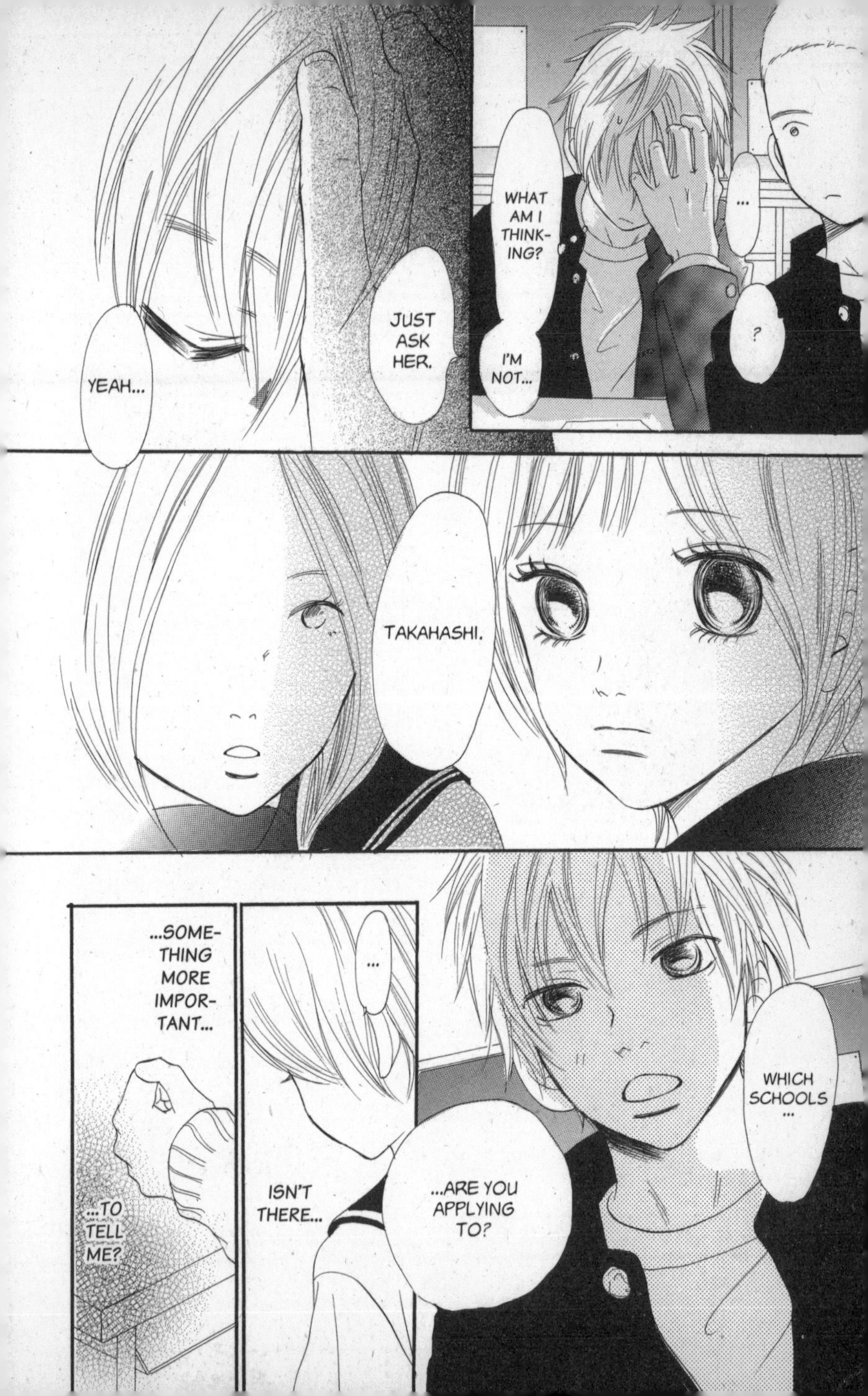
...
WHAT AM I THINKING?
?
I'M NOT...
JUST ASK HER.
YEAH...
TAKAHASHI.
WHICH SCHOOLS ...
...ARE YOU APPLYING TO?
...
ISN'T THERE...
...SOMETHING MORE IMPORTANT...
...TO TELL ME?

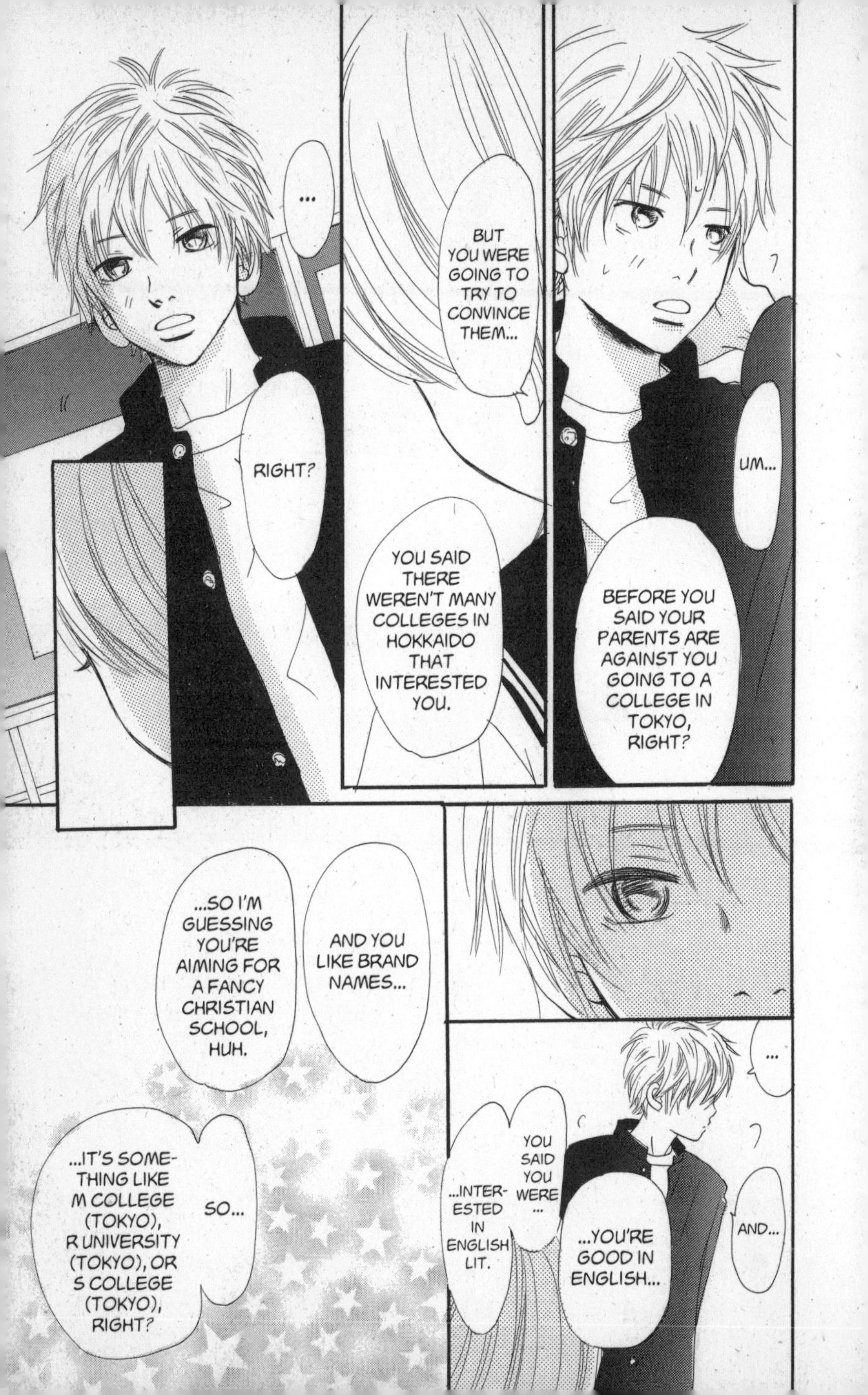
UM...
BEFORE YOU SAID YOUR PARENTS ARE AGAINST YOU GOING TO A COLLEGE IN TOKYO, RIGHT?
BUT YOU WERE GOING TO TRY TO CONVINCE THEM...
YOU SAID THERE WEREN'T MANY COLLEGES IN HOKKAIDO THAT INTERESTED YOU.
...
RIGHT?
...
AND...
...YOU'RE GOOD IN ENGLISH...
YOU SAID YOU WERE ...
...INTER-ESTED IN ENGLISH LIT.
AND YOU LIKE BRAND NAMES...
...SO I'M GUESSING YOU'RE AIMING FOR A FANCY CHRISTIAN SCHOOL, HUH.
SO...
...IT'S SOME-THING LIKE M COLLEGE (TOKYO), R UNIVERSITY (TOKYO), OR S COLLEGE (TOKYO), RIGHT?

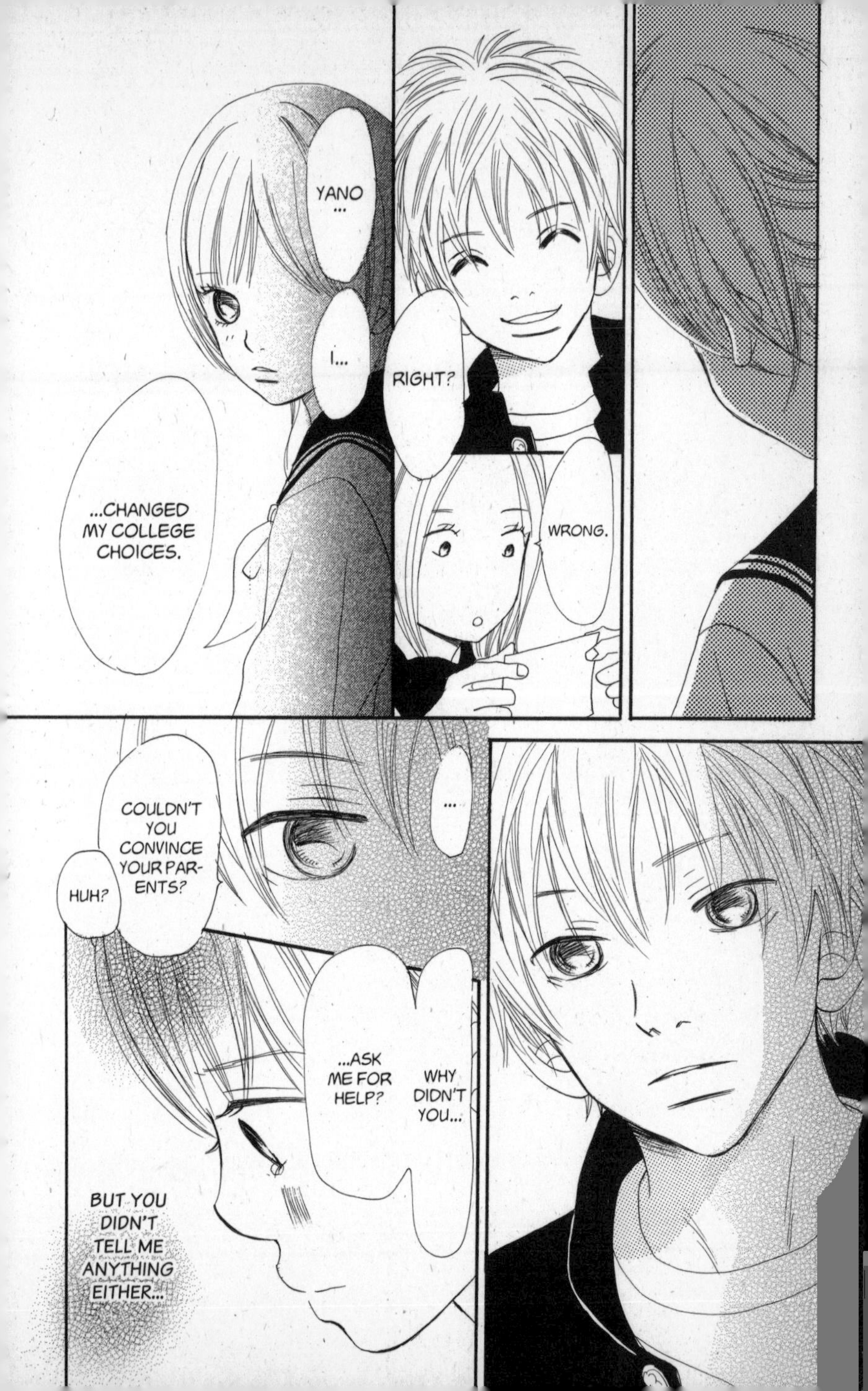
RIGHT?
WRONG.
YANO...
I...
...CHANGED MY COLLEGE CHOICES.
...
COULDN'T YOU CONVINCE YOUR PAR-ENTS?
HUH?
WHY DIDN'T YOU...
...ASK ME FOR HELP?
BUT YOU DIDN'T TELL ME ANYTHING EITHER...

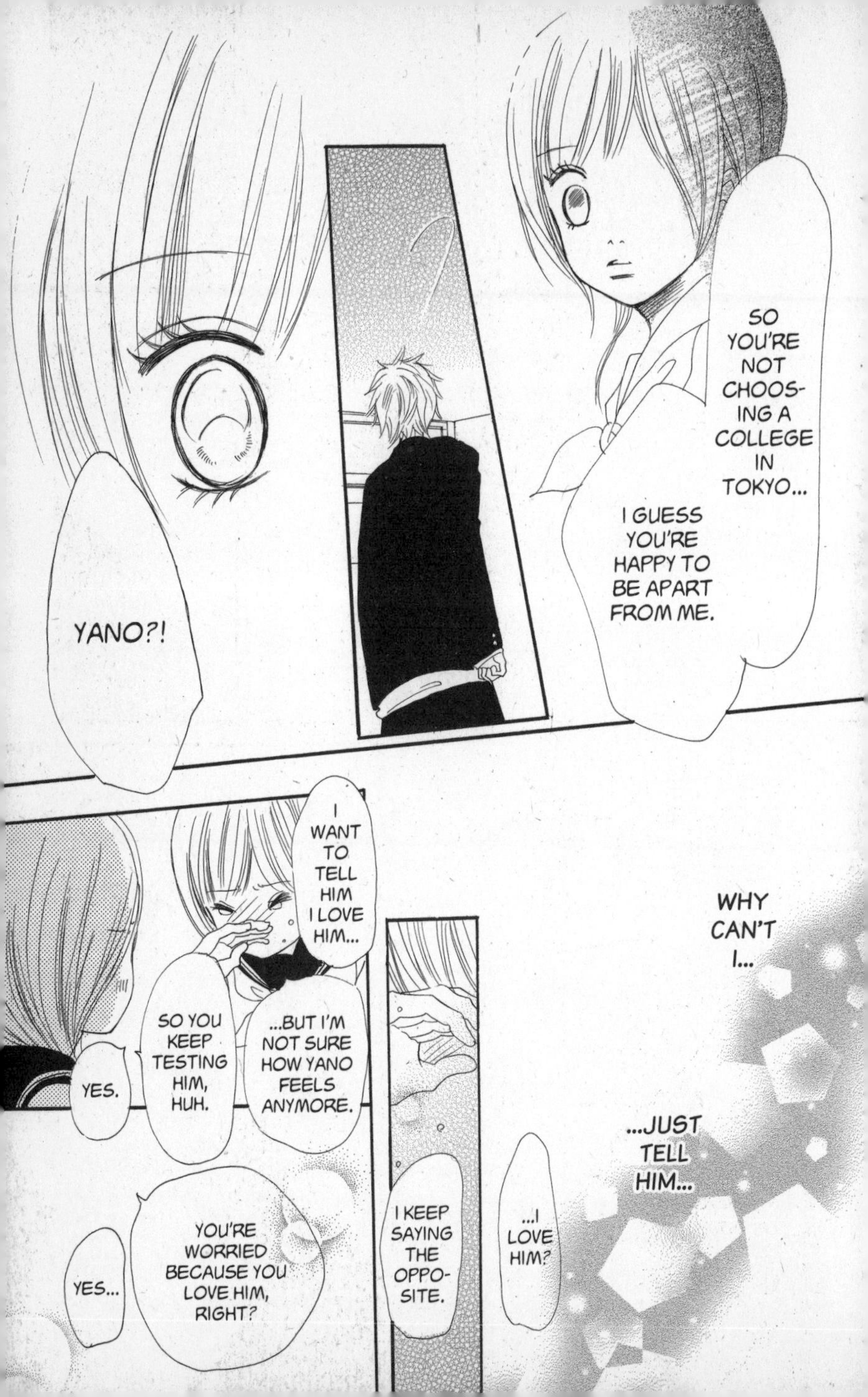

SO YOU'RE NOT CHOOSING A COLLEGE IN TOKYO...
I GUESS YOU'RE HAPPY TO BE APART FROM ME.
YANO?!
WHY CAN'T I...
...JUST TELL HIM...
...I LOVE HIM?
I KEEP SAYING THE OPPOSITE.
I WANT TO TELL HIM I LOVE HIM...
...BUT I'M NOT SURE HOW YANO FEELS ANYMORE.
SO YOU KEEP TESTING HIM, HUH.
YES.
YOU'RE WORRIED BECAUSE YOU LOVE HIM, RIGHT?
YES...

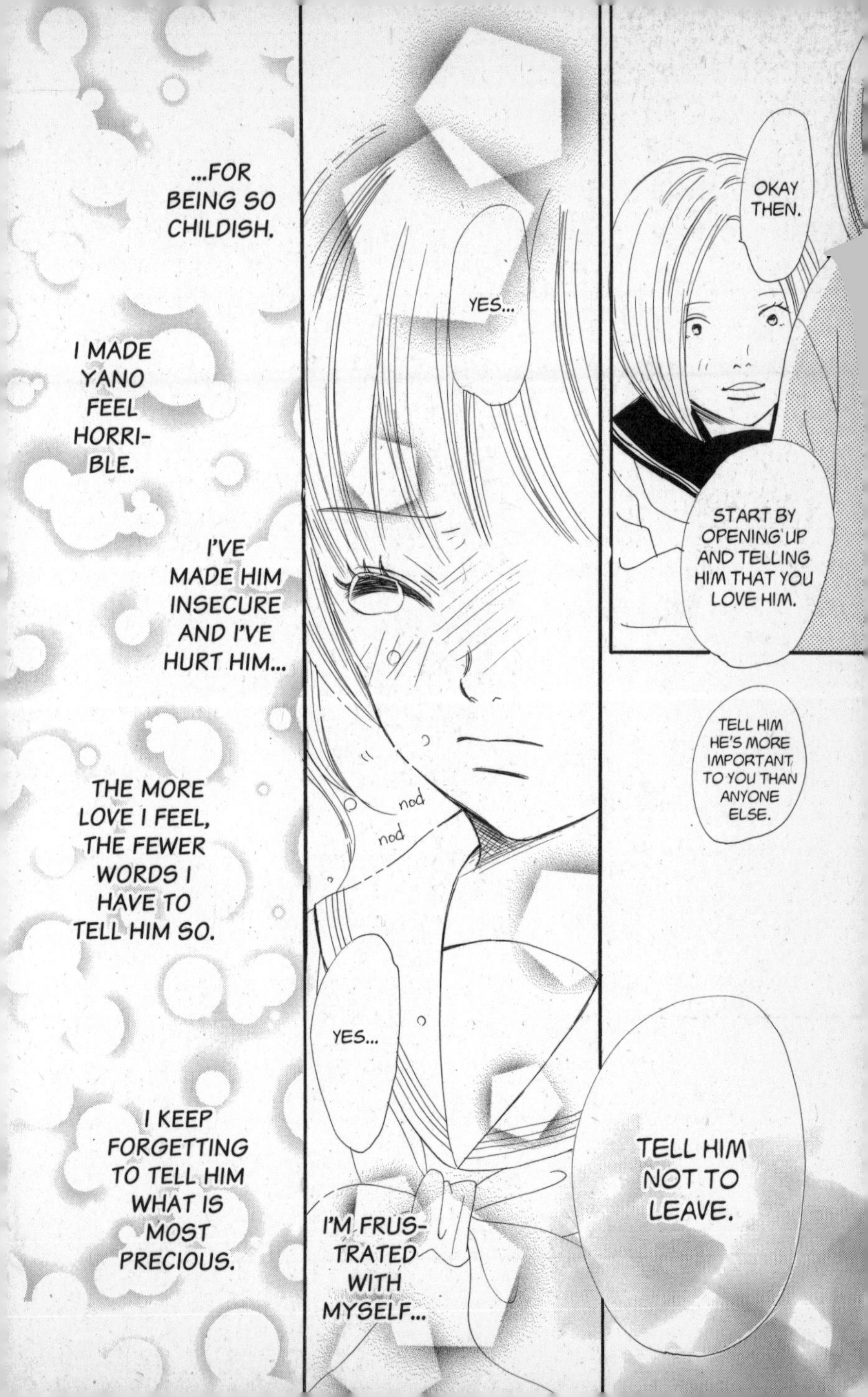
OKAY THEN.
START BY OPENING UP AND TELLING HIM THAT YOU LOVE HIM.
TELL HIM HE'S MORE IMPORTANT TO YOU THAN ANYONE ELSE.
TELL HIM NOT TO LEAVE.
YES...
nod
nod
YES...
I'M FRUSTRATED WITH MYSELF...
...FOR BEING SO CHILDISH.
I MADE YANO FEEL HORRIBLE.
I'VE MADE HIM INSECURE AND I'VE HURT HIM...
THE MORE LOVE I FEEL, THE FEWER WORDS I HAVE TO TELL HIM SO.
I KEEP FORGETTING TO TELL HIM WHAT IS MOST PRECIOUS.

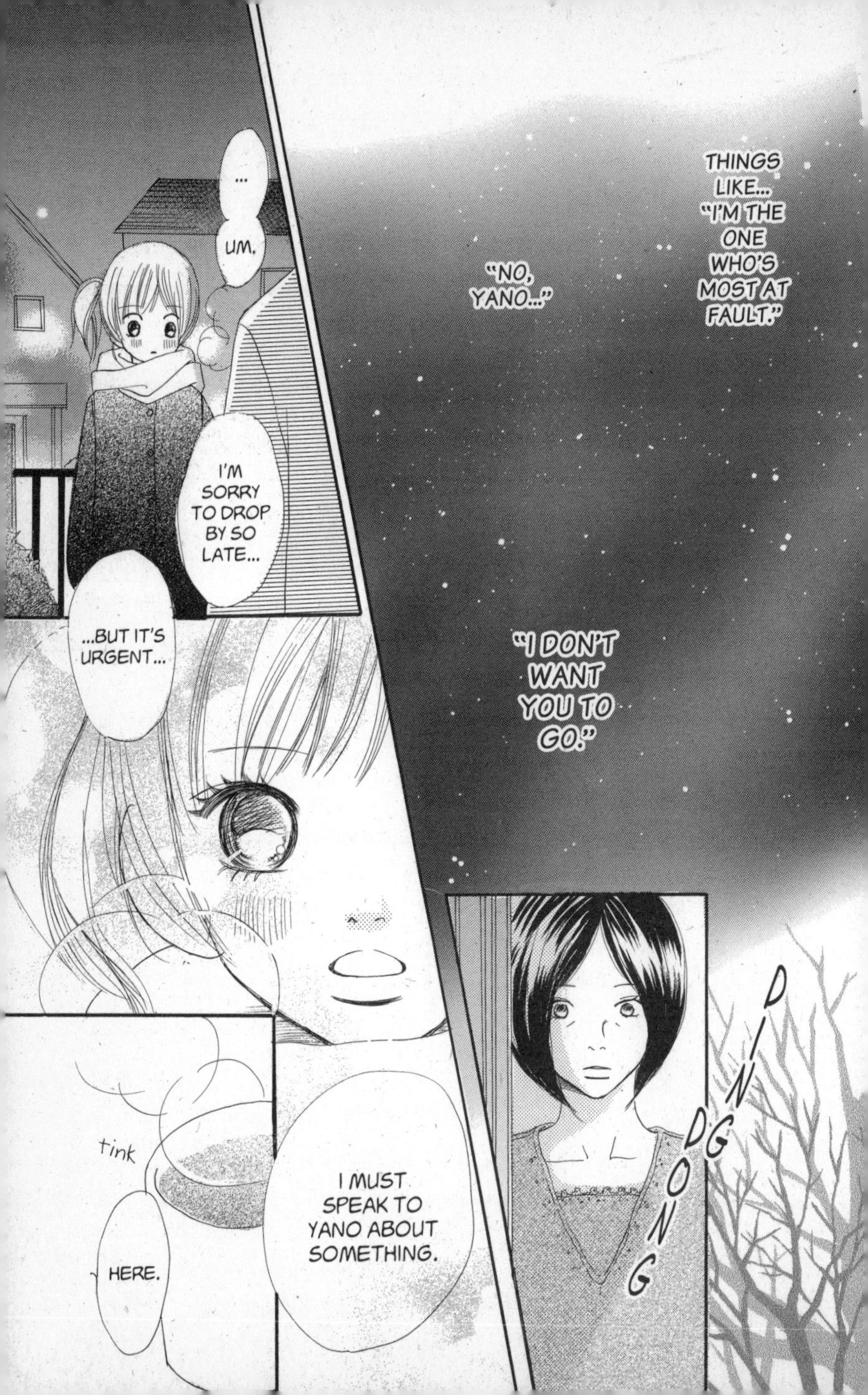
THINGS LIKE... "I'M THE ONE WHO'S MOST AT FAULT."
"NO, YANO..."
"I DON'T WANT YOU TO GO."
DING DONG
...
UM.
I'M SORRY TO DROP BY SO LATE...
...BUT IT'S URGENT...
I MUST SPEAK TO YANO ABOUT SOMETHING.
tink
HERE.

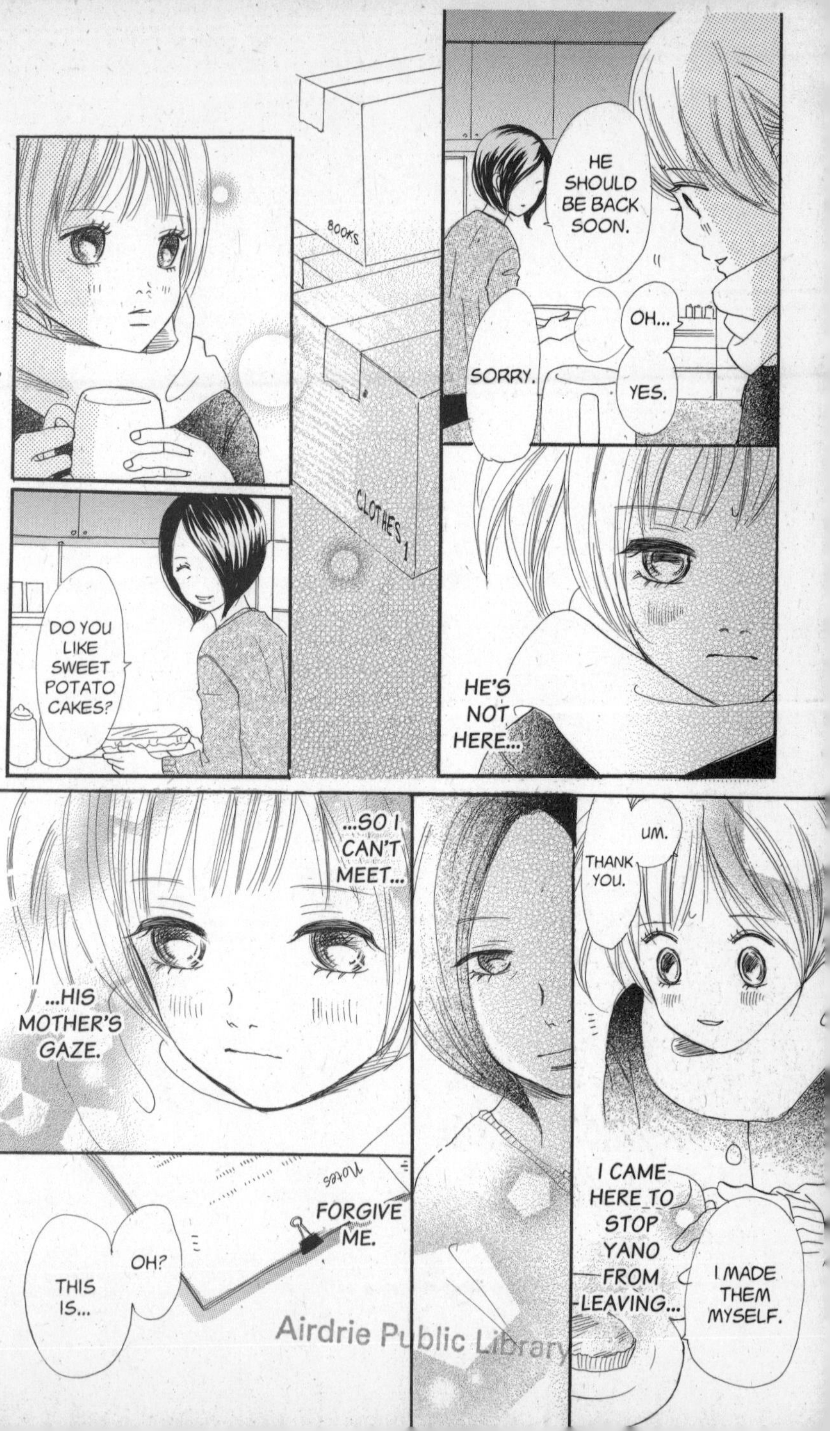
HE SHOULD BE BACK SOON.
OH...
YES.
SORRY.
BOOKS
CLOTHES 1
HE'S NOT HERE...
DO YOU LIKE SWEET POTATO CAKES?
UM.
THANK YOU.
I MADE THEM MYSELF.
I CAME HERE TO STOP YANO FROM LEAVING...
...SO I CAN'T MEET...
...HIS MOTHER'S GAZE.
Notes
FORGIVE ME.
OH?
THIS IS...

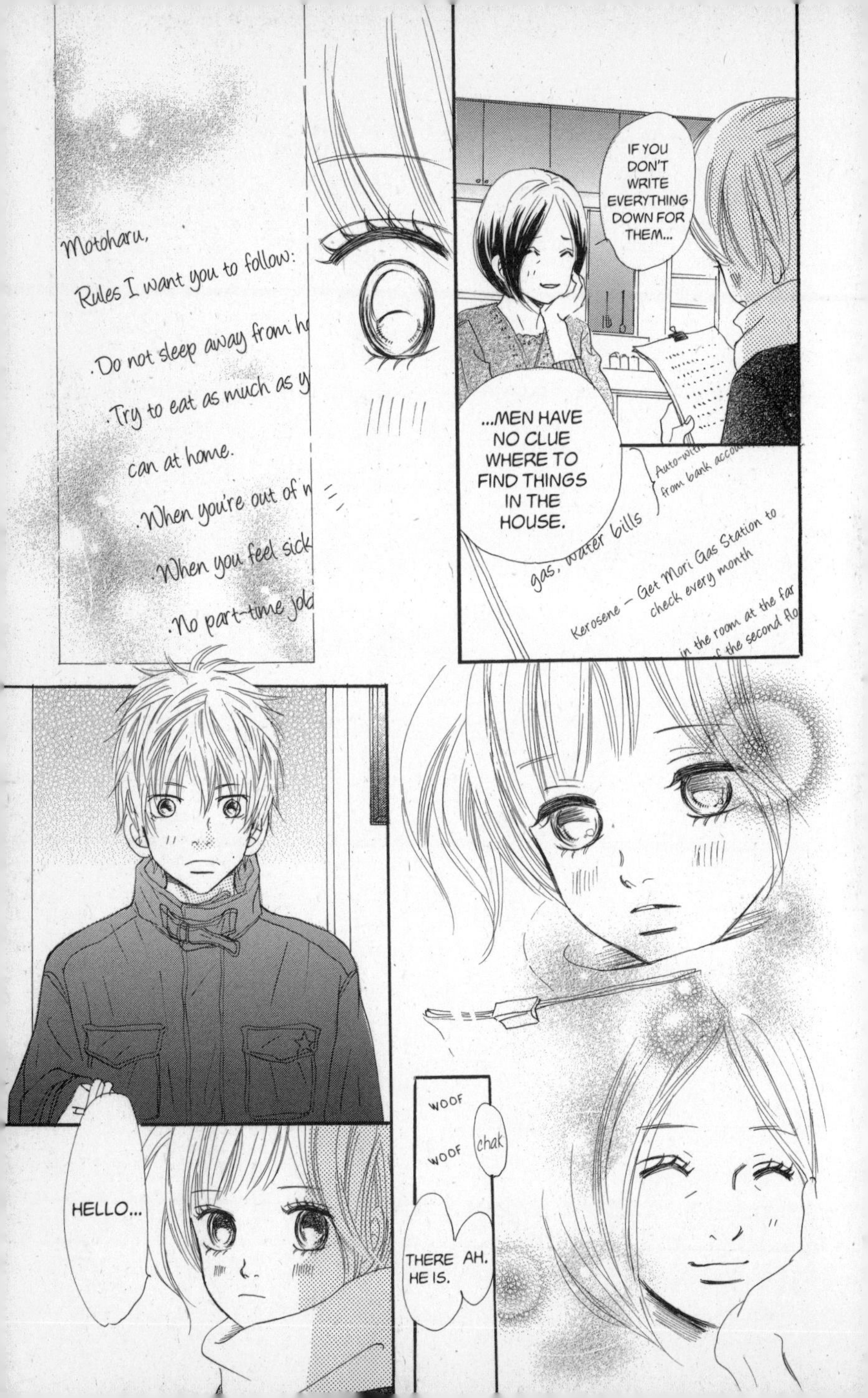
IF YOU DON'T WRITE EVERYTHING DOWN FOR THEM...
...MEN HAVE NO CLUE WHERE TO FIND THINGS IN THE HOUSE.
from bank acco
gas, water bills
Kerosene – Get Mori Gas Station to check every month
in the room at the far
f the second flo
Motoharu,
Rules I want you to follow:
.Do not sleep away from h
.Try to eat as much as y
can at home.
.When you're out of n
.When you feel sick
.No part-time job
WOOF
WOOF
chak
AH.
THERE HE IS.
HELLO...

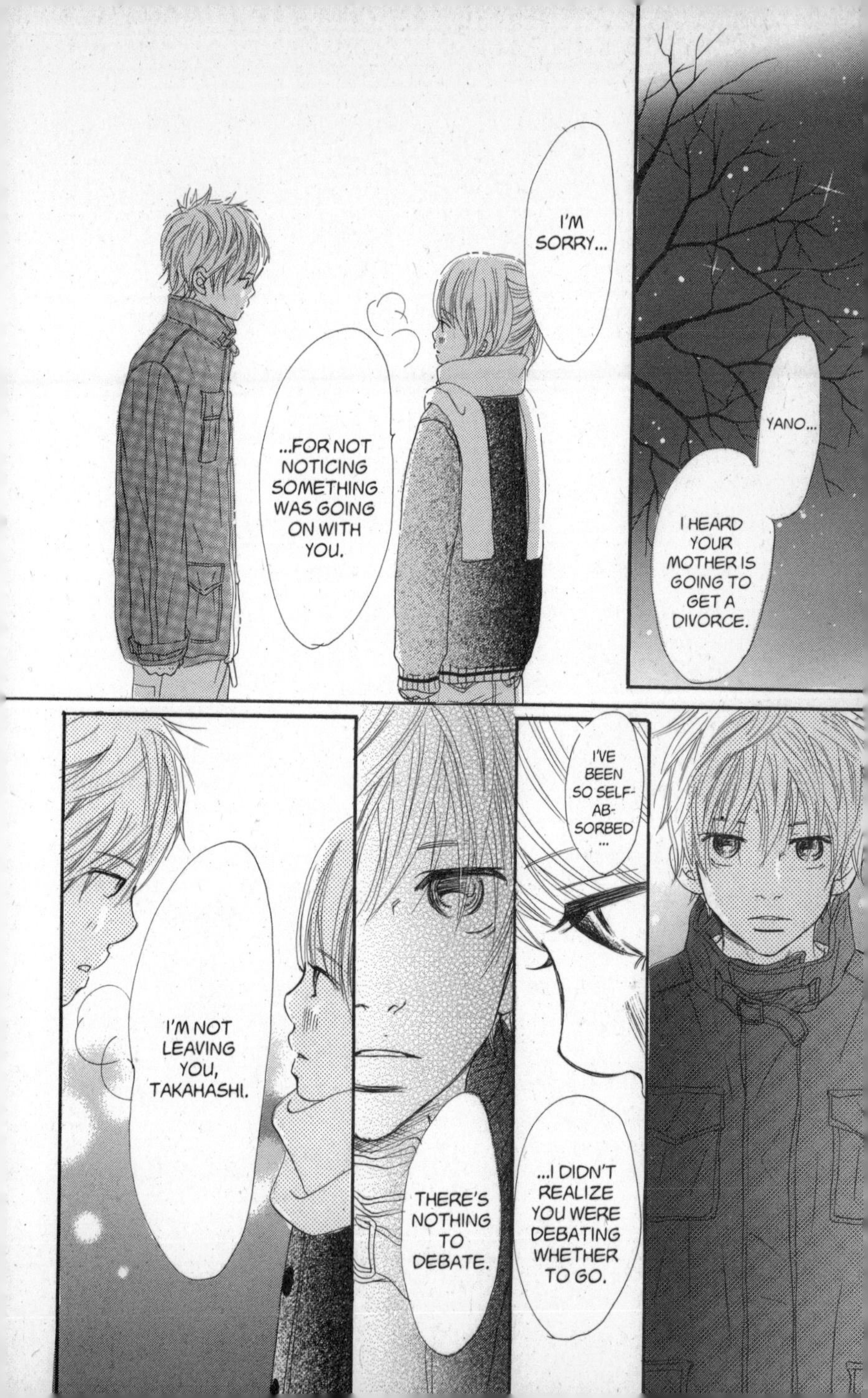
YANO...
I HEARD YOUR MOTHER IS GOING TO GET A DIVORCE.
I'M SORRY...
...FOR NOT NOTICING SOMETHING WAS GOING ON WITH YOU.
I'VE BEEN SO SELF-ABSORBED...
...I DIDN'T REALIZE YOU WERE DEBATING WHETHER TO GO.
THERE'S NOTHING TO DEBATE.
I'M NOT LEAVING YOU, TAKAHASHI.

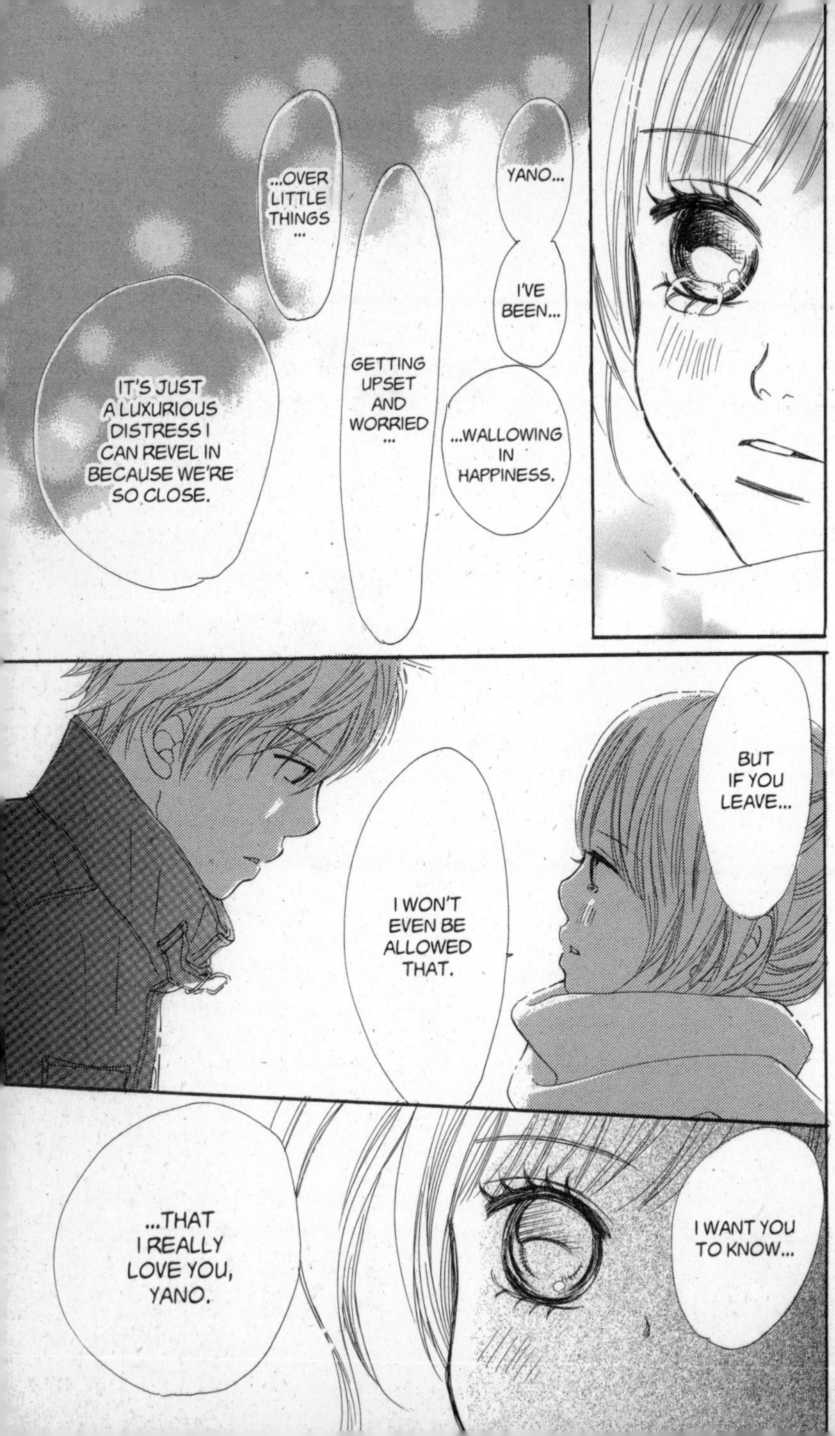
YANO...
I'VE BEEN...
...WALLOWING IN HAPPINESS.
GETTING UPSET AND WORRIED...
...OVER LITTLE THINGS...
IT'S JUST A LUXURIOUS DISTRESS I CAN REVEL IN BECAUSE WE'RE SO CLOSE.
BUT IF YOU LEAVE...
I WON'T EVEN BE ALLOWED THAT.
I WANT YOU TO KNOW...
...THAT I REALLY LOVE YOU, YANO.

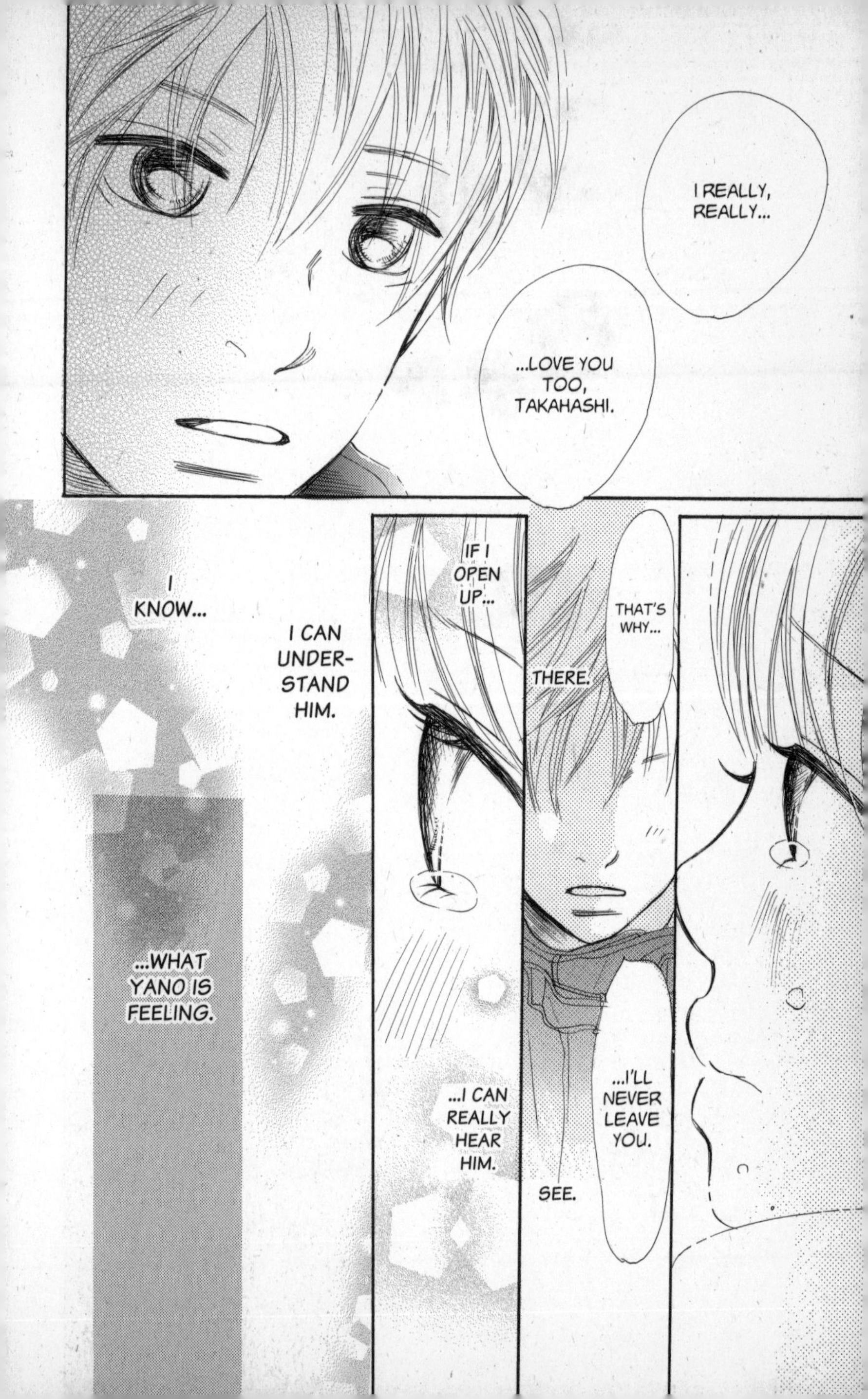
I REALLY, REALLY...
...LOVE YOU TOO, TAKAHASHI.
THAT'S WHY...
...I'LL NEVER LEAVE YOU.
THERE.
SEE.
IF I OPEN UP...
...I CAN REALLY HEAR HIM.
I CAN UNDER-STAND HIM.
I KNOW...
...WHAT YANO IS FEELING.

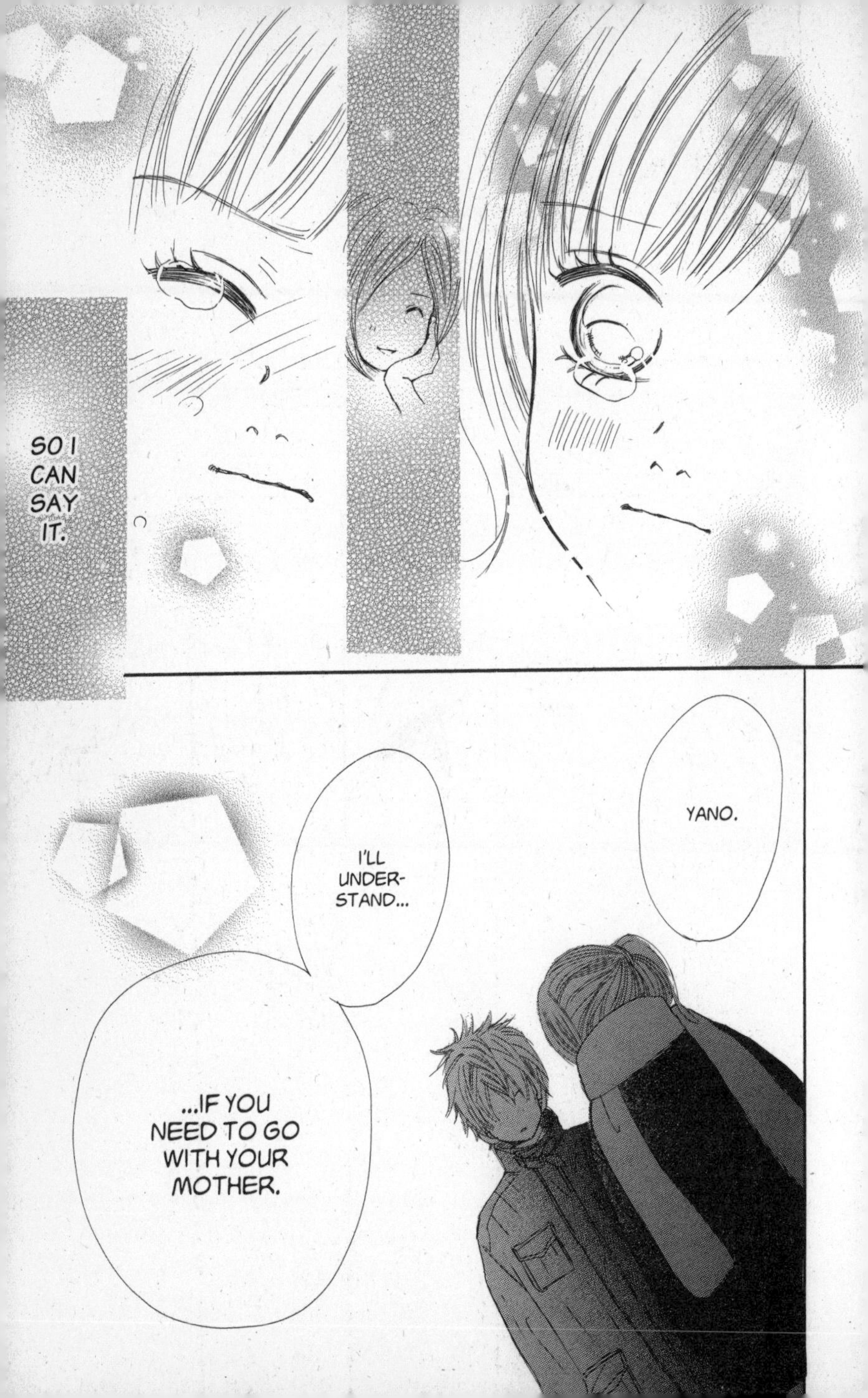
SO I CAN SAY IT.
YANO.
I'LL UNDER-STAND...
...IF YOU NEED TO GO WITH YOUR MOTHER.

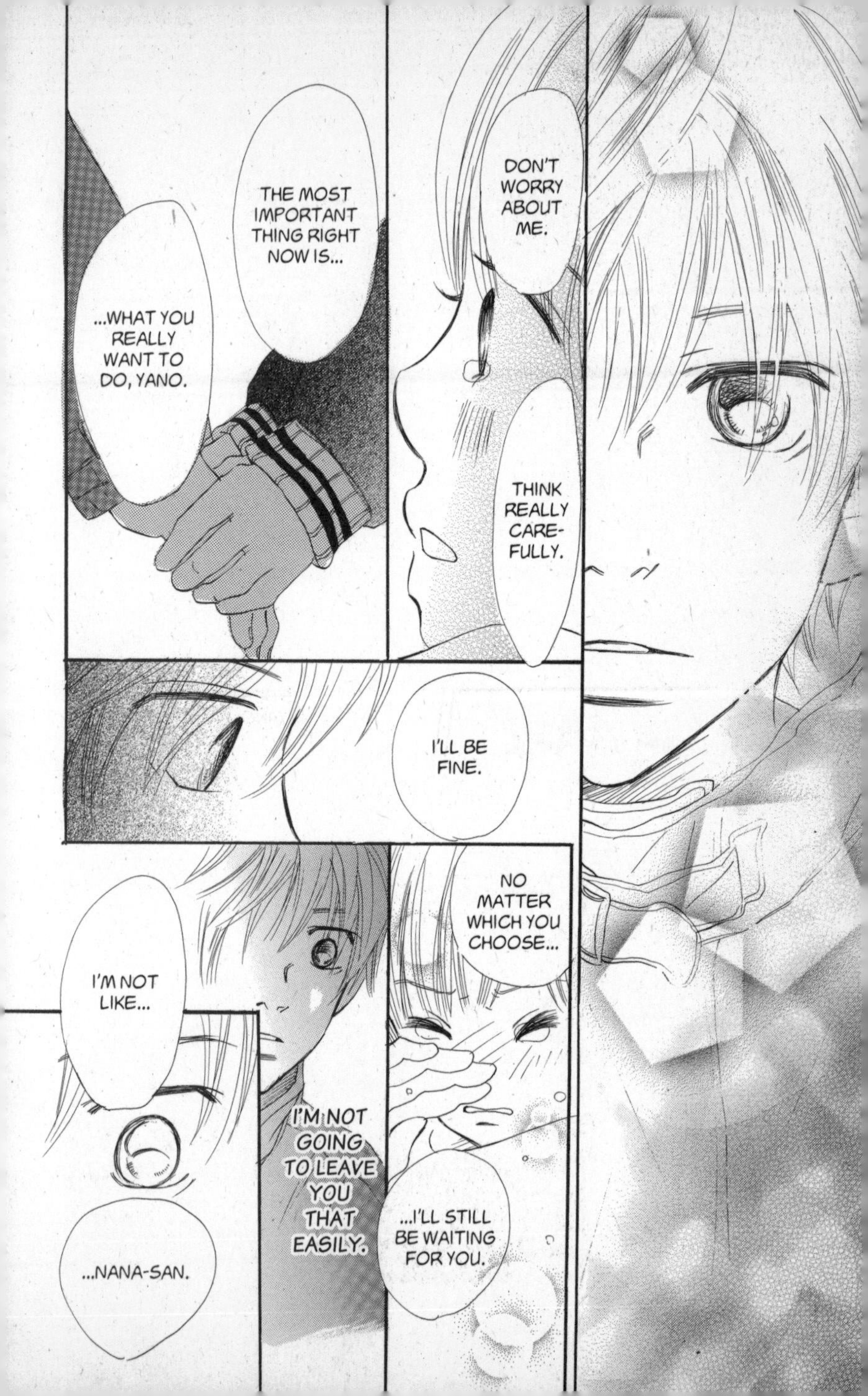
DON'T WORRY ABOUT ME.
THINK REALLY CARE-FULLY.
THE MOST IMPORTANT THING RIGHT NOW IS...
...WHAT YOU REALLY WANT TO DO, YANO.
I'LL BE FINE.
NO MATTER WHICH YOU CHOOSE...
...I'LL STILL BE WAITING FOR YOU.
I'M NOT GOING TO LEAVE YOU THAT EASILY.
I'M NOT LIKE...
...NANA-SAN.

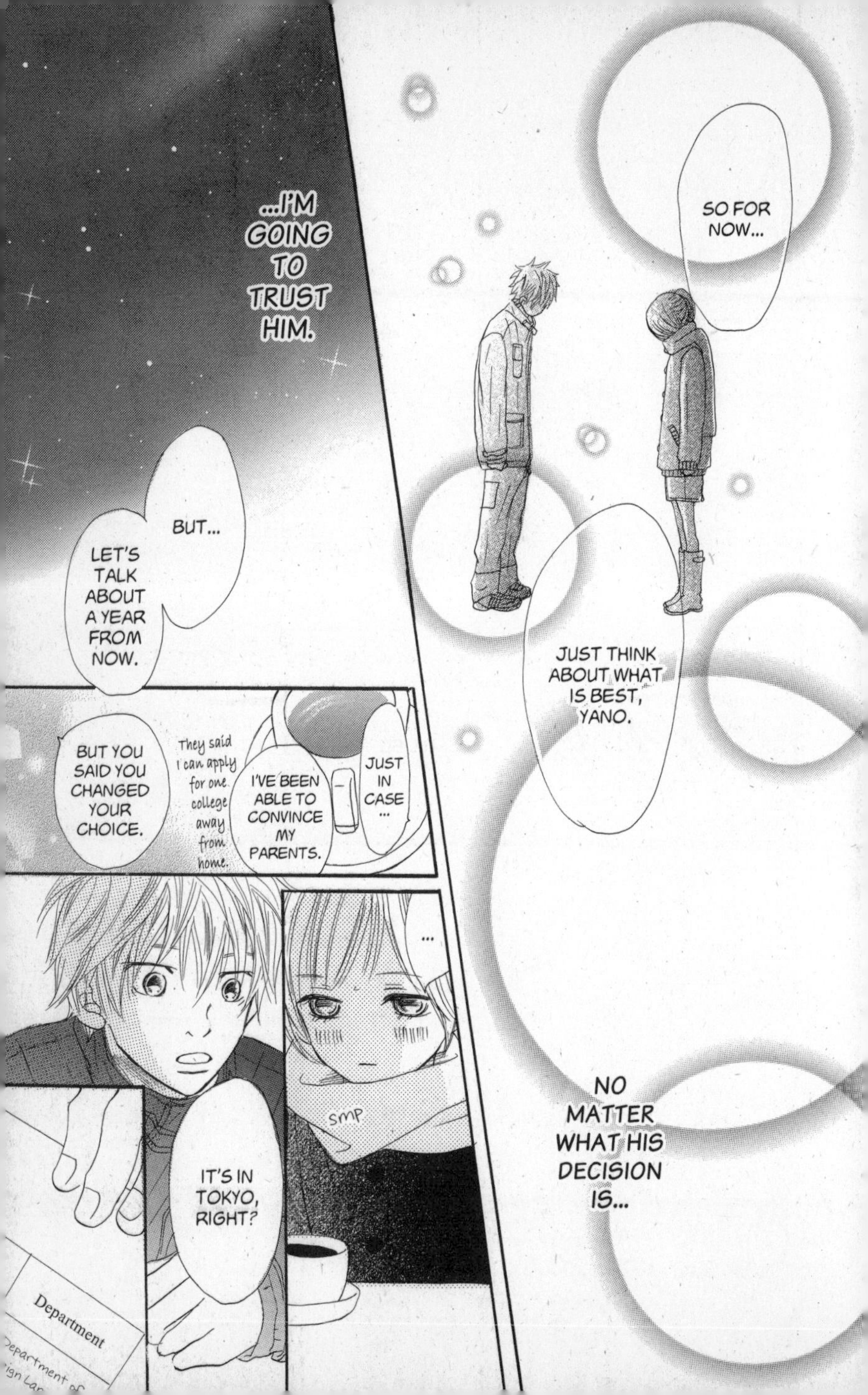
SO FOR NOW...
JUST THINK ABOUT WHAT IS BEST, YANO.
NO MATTER WHAT HIS DECISION IS...
...I'M GOING TO TRUST HIM.
BUT... LET'S TALK ABOUT A YEAR FROM NOW.
JUST IN CASE...
I'VE BEEN ABLE TO CONVINCE MY PARENTS.
They said I can apply for one college away from home.
BUT YOU SAID YOU CHANGED YOUR CHOICE.
...
SMP
IT'S IN TOKYO, RIGHT?
Department

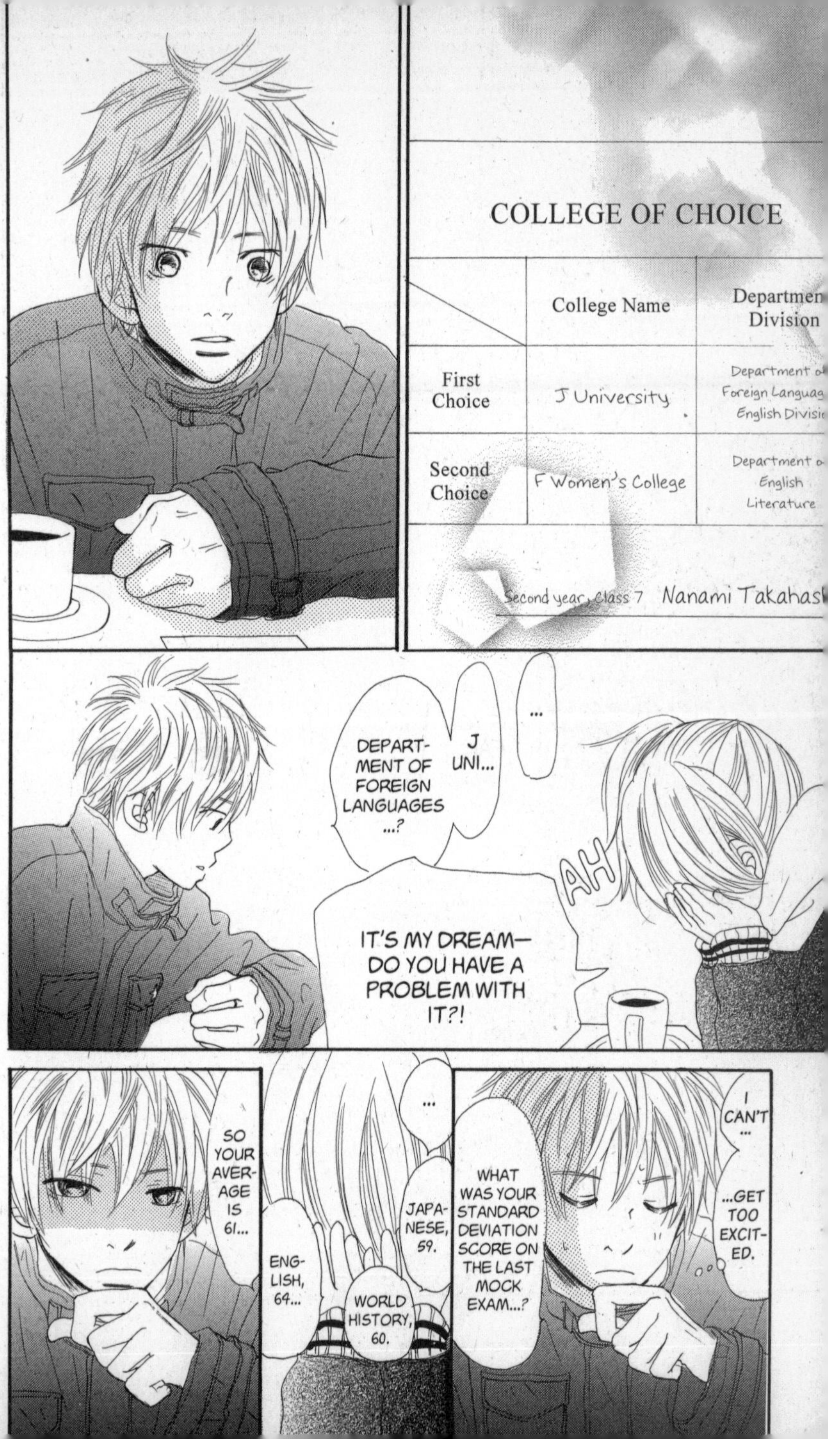
COLLEGE OF CHOICE
College Name
Departmen Division
First Choice
J University
Department o Foreign Languag English Divisi
Second Choice
F Women's College
Department o English Literature
Second year, Class 7
Nanami Takahas
...
J UNI...
DEPARTMENT OF FOREIGN LANGUAGES ...?
AH
IT'S MY DREAM—DO YOU HAVE A PROBLEM WITH IT?!
I CAN'T ...
...GET TOO EXCITED.
WHAT WAS YOUR STANDARD DEVIATION SCORE ON THE LAST MOCK EXAM...?
...
JAPANESE, 59.
ENGLISH, 64...
WORLD HISTORY, 60.
SO YOUR AVERAGE IS 61...

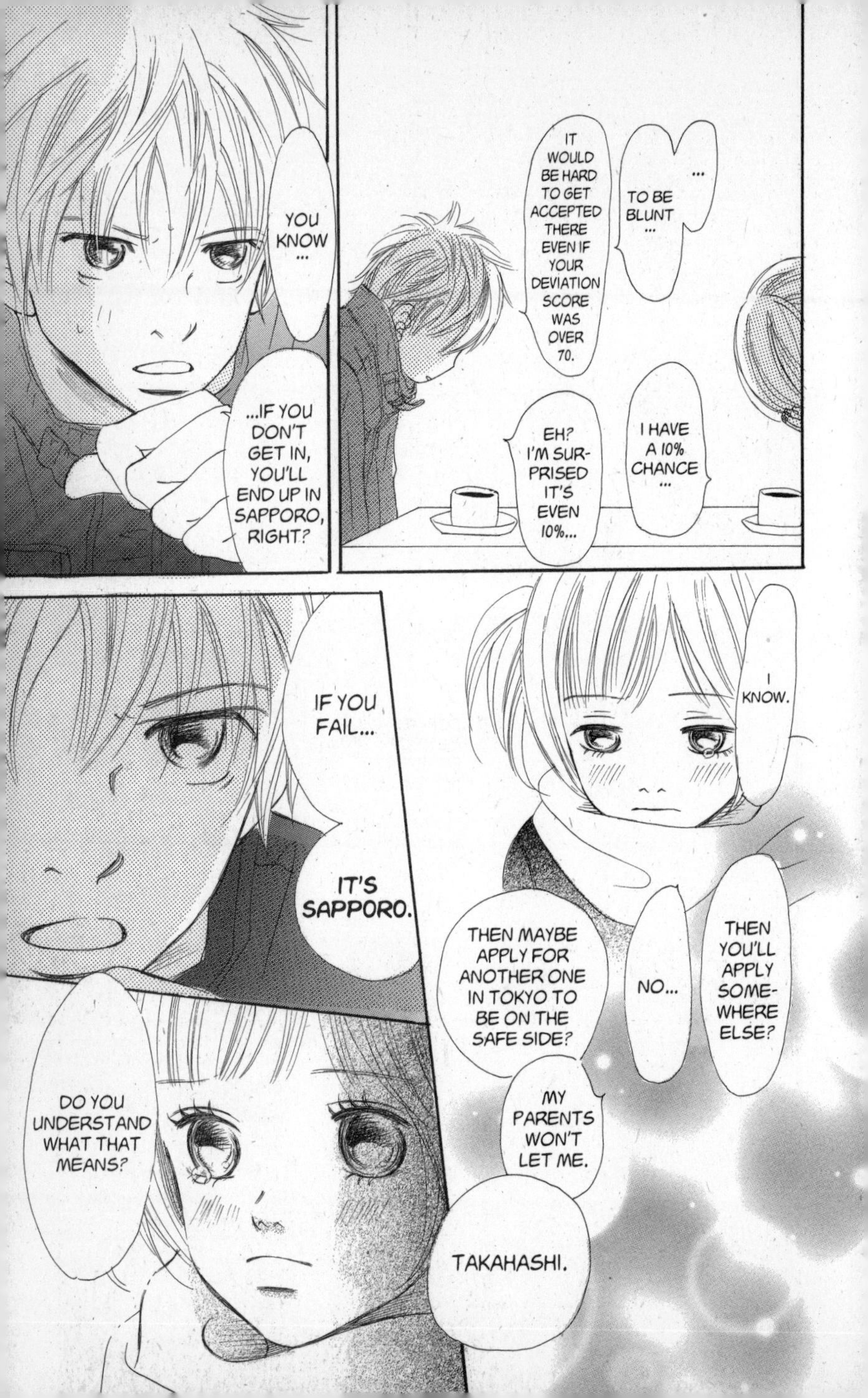
...
TO BE BLUNT ...
IT WOULD BE HARD TO GET ACCEPTED THERE EVEN IF YOUR DEVIATION SCORE WAS OVER 70.
I HAVE A 10% CHANCE ...
EH? I'M SURPRISED IT'S EVEN 10%...
YOU KNOW ...
...IF YOU DON'T GET IN, YOU'LL END UP IN SAPPORO, RIGHT?
I KNOW.
THEN YOU'LL APPLY SOMEWHERE ELSE?
NO...
THEN MAYBE APPLY FOR ANOTHER ONE IN TOKYO TO BE ON THE SAFE SIDE?
MY PARENTS WON'T LET ME.
TAKAHASHI.
IF YOU FAIL...
IT'S SAPPORO.
DO YOU UNDERSTAND WHAT THAT MEANS?

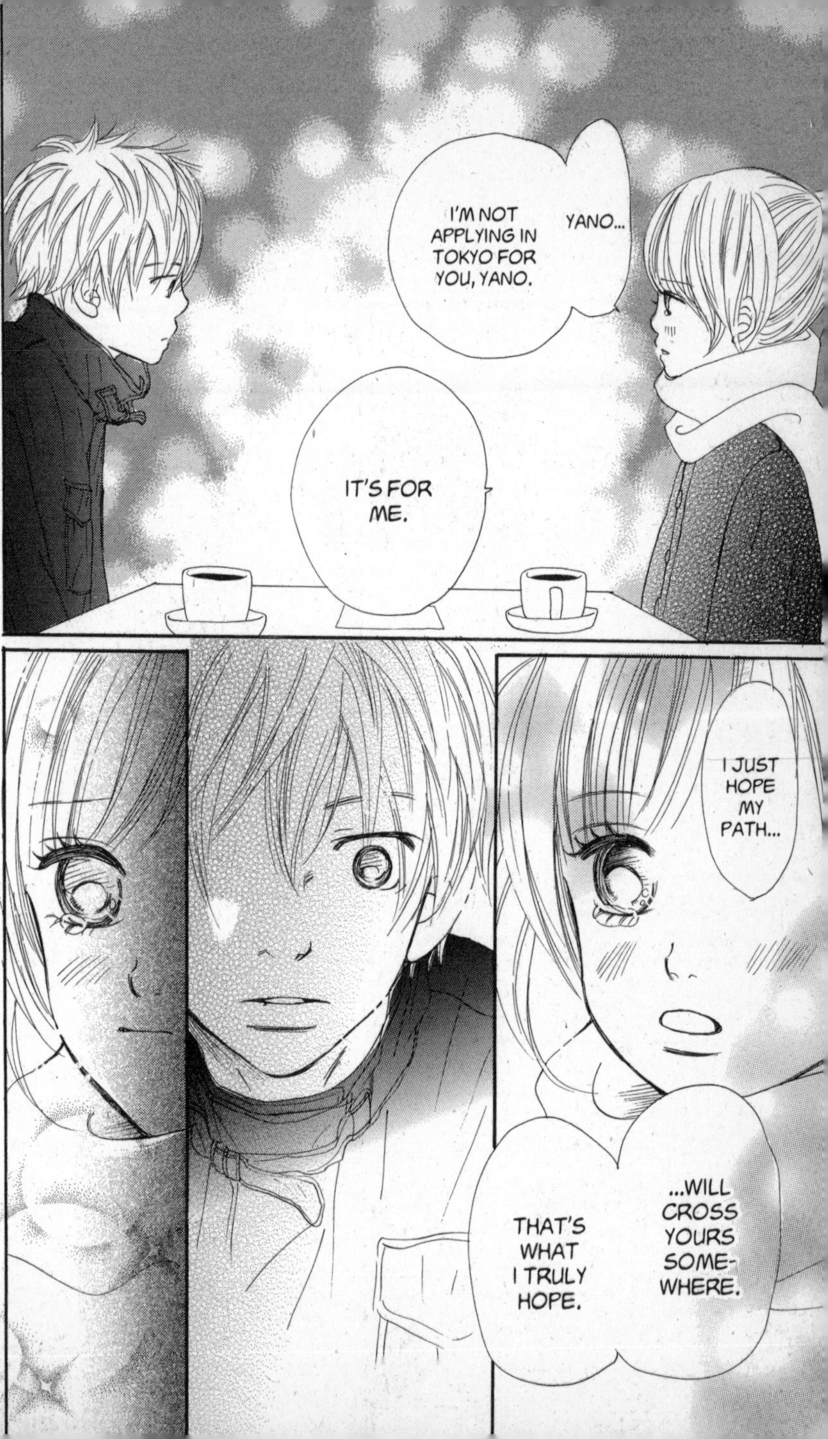
YANO...
I'M NOT APPLYING IN TOKYO FOR YOU, YANO.
IT'S FOR ME.
I JUST HOPE MY PATH...
...WILL CROSS YOURS SOMEWHERE.
THAT'S WHAT I TRULY HOPE.

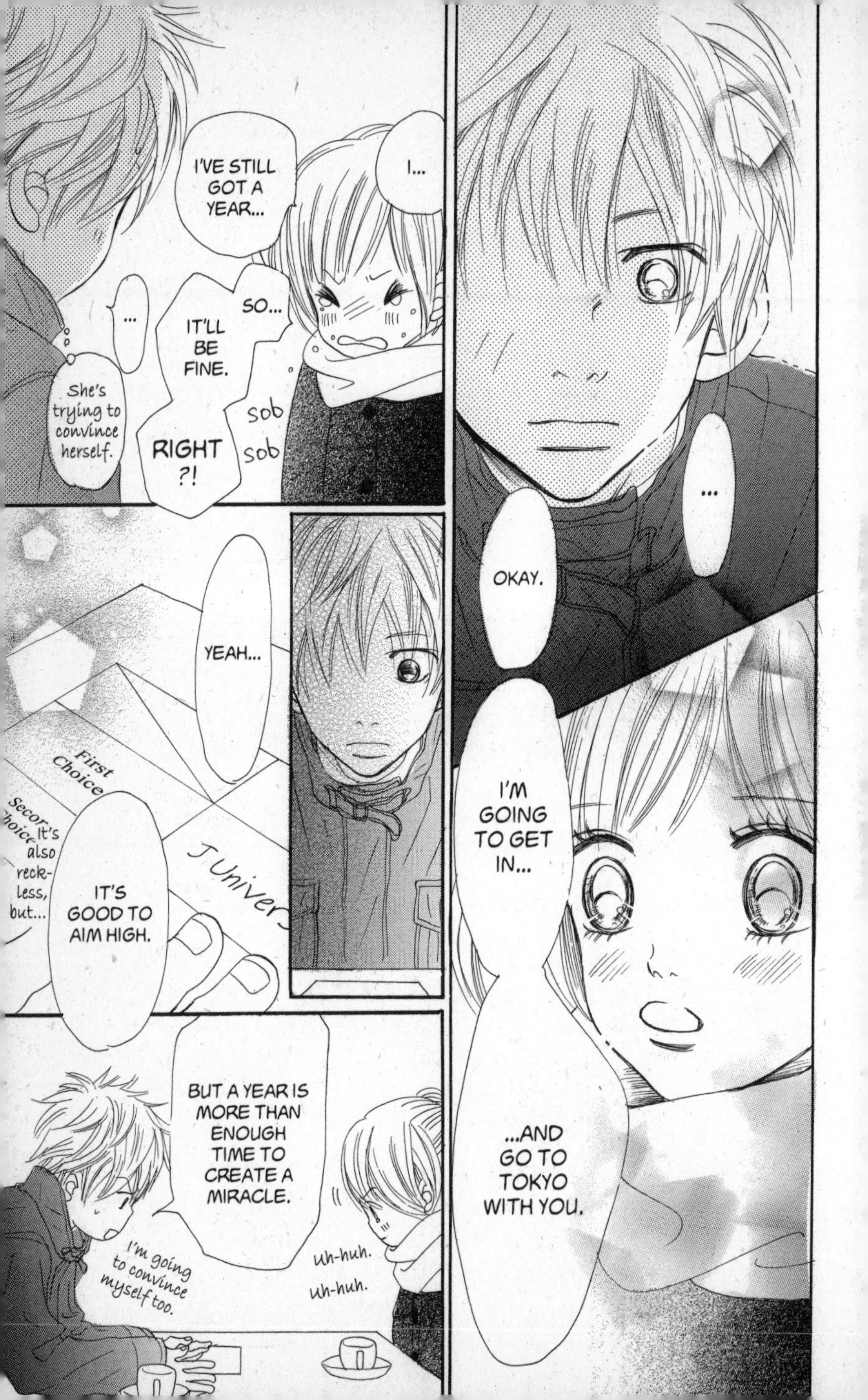
...
OKAY.
I'M GOING TO GET IN...
...AND GO TO TOKYO WITH YOU.
I...
I'VE STILL GOT A YEAR...
SO... IT'LL BE FINE. RIGHT?!
sob sob
...
She's trying to convince herself.
YEAH...
First Choice
IT'S GOOD TO AIM HIGH.
It's also reckless, but...
BUT A YEAR IS MORE THAN ENOUGH TIME TO CREATE A MIRACLE.
Uh-huh. Uh-huh.
I'm going to convince myself too.

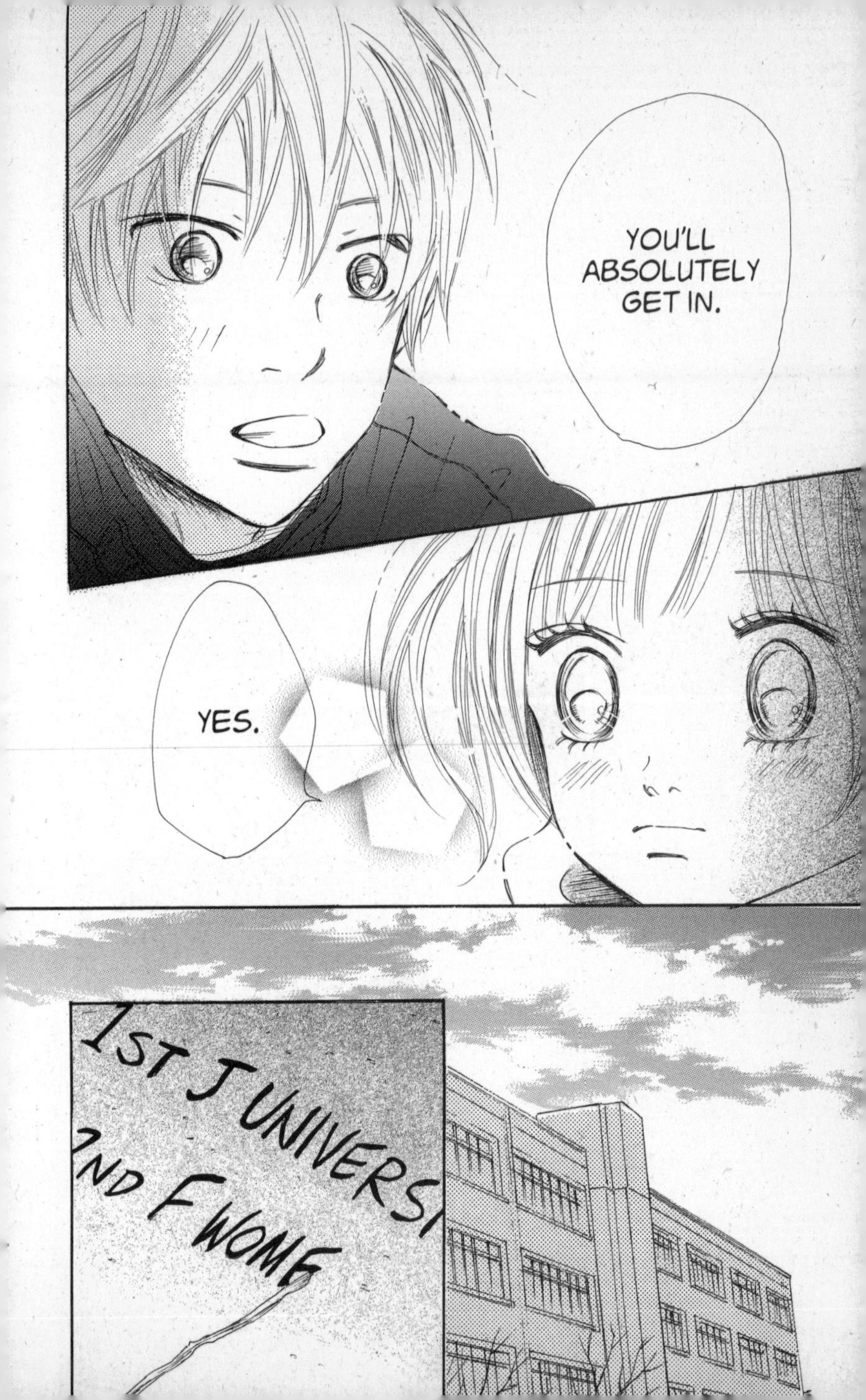
YOU'LL ABSOLUTELY GET IN.
YES.
1ST J UNIVERSI
2ND F WOME

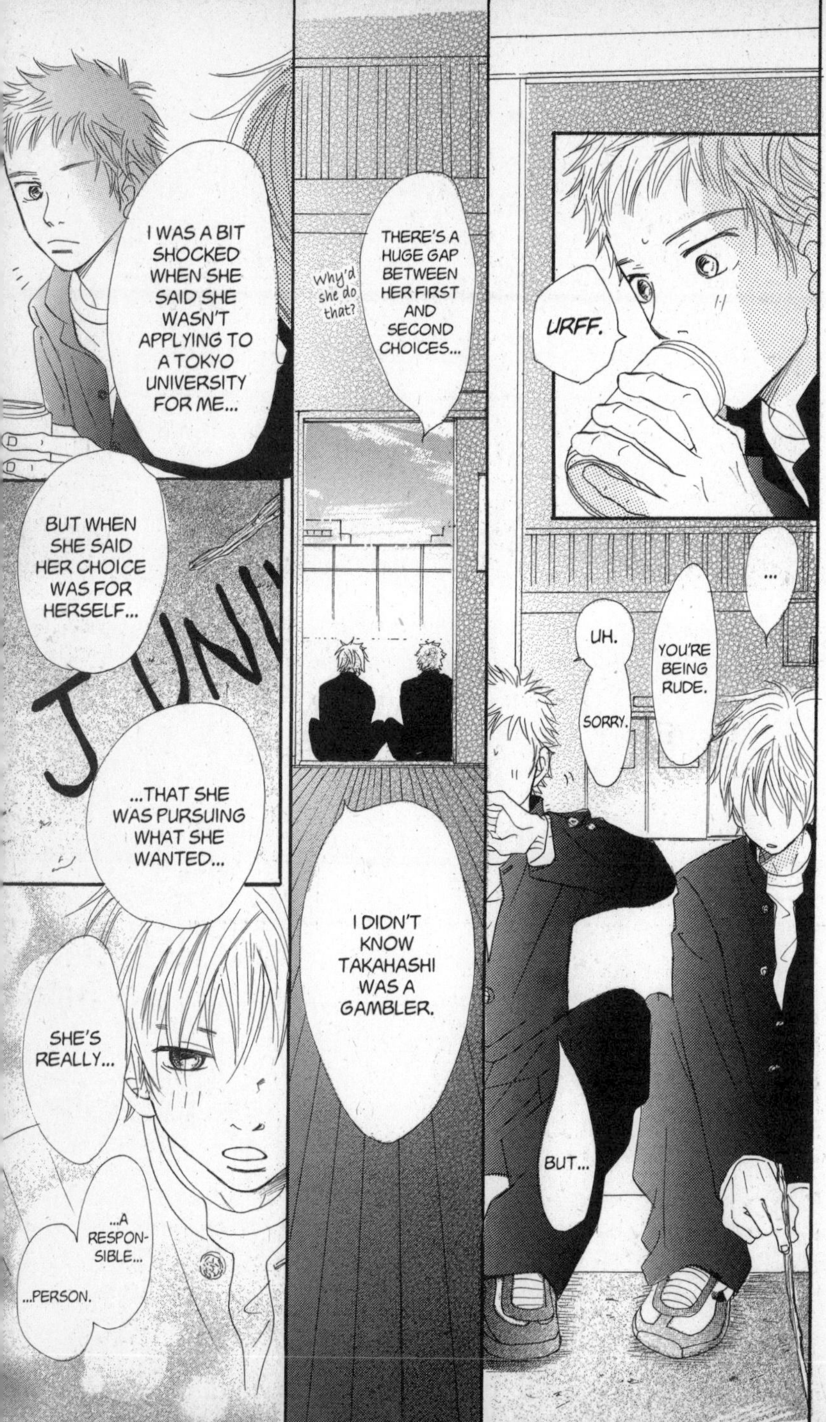
URFF.
...
YOU'RE BEING RUDE.
UH.
SORRY.
BUT...
THERE'S A HUGE GAP BETWEEN HER FIRST AND SECOND CHOICES...
Why'd she do that?
I DIDN'T KNOW TAKAHASHI WAS A GAMBLER.
I WAS A BIT SHOCKED WHEN SHE SAID SHE WASN'T APPLYING TO A TOKYO UNIVERSITY FOR ME...
BUT WHEN SHE SAID HER CHOICE WAS FOR HERSELF...
...THAT SHE WAS PURSUING WHAT SHE WANTED...
SHE'S REALLY...
...A RESPON-SIBLE...
...PERSON.

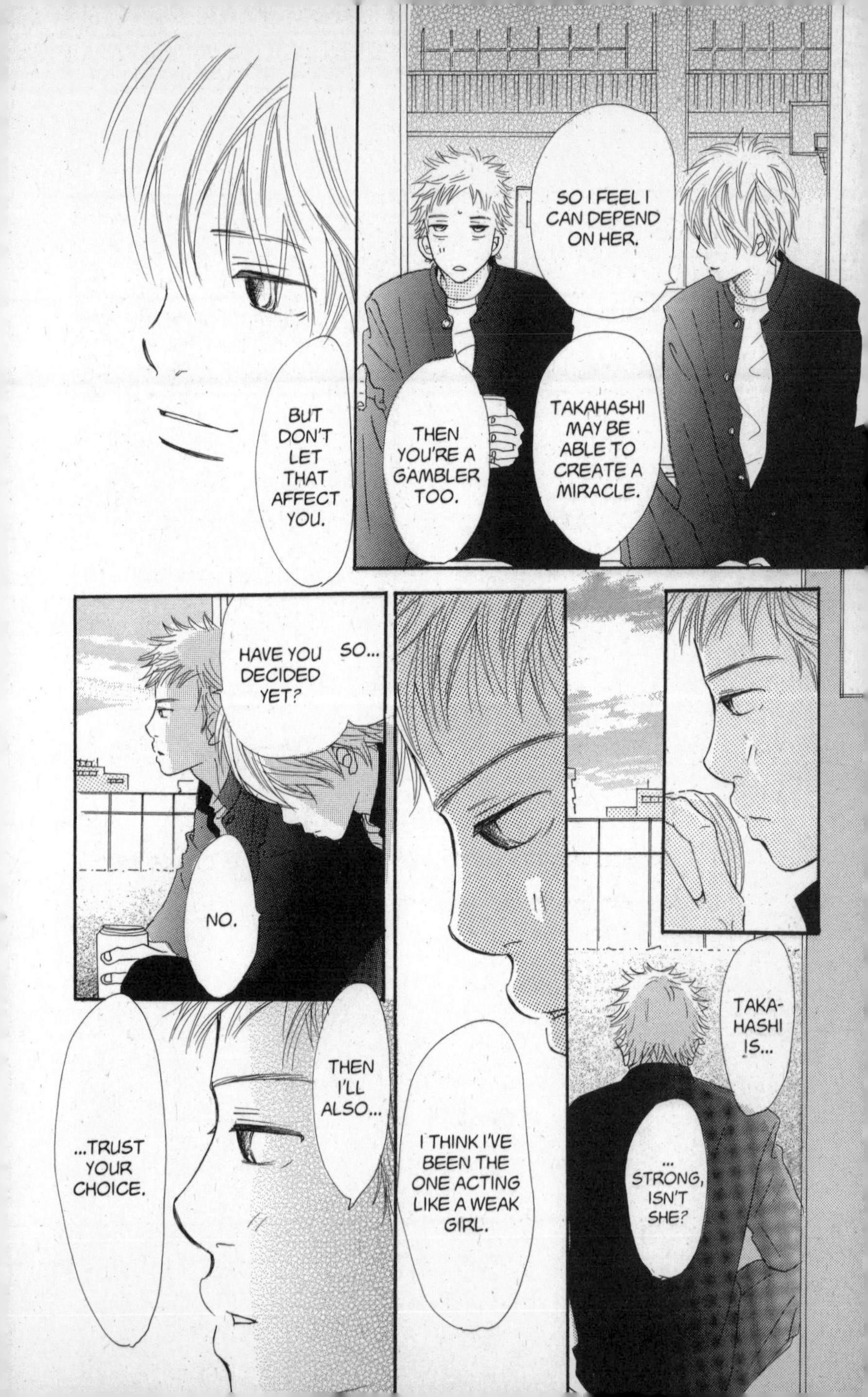
SO I FEEL I CAN DEPEND ON HER.
TAKAHASHI MAY BE ABLE TO CREATE A MIRACLE.
THEN YOU'RE A GAMBLER TOO.
BUT DON'T LET THAT AFFECT YOU.
TAKA-HASHI IS...
...STRONG, ISN'T SHE?
I THINK I'VE BEEN THE ONE ACTING LIKE A WEAK GIRL.
SO...
HAVE YOU DECIDED YET?
NO.
THEN I'LL ALSO...
...TRUST YOUR CHOICE.

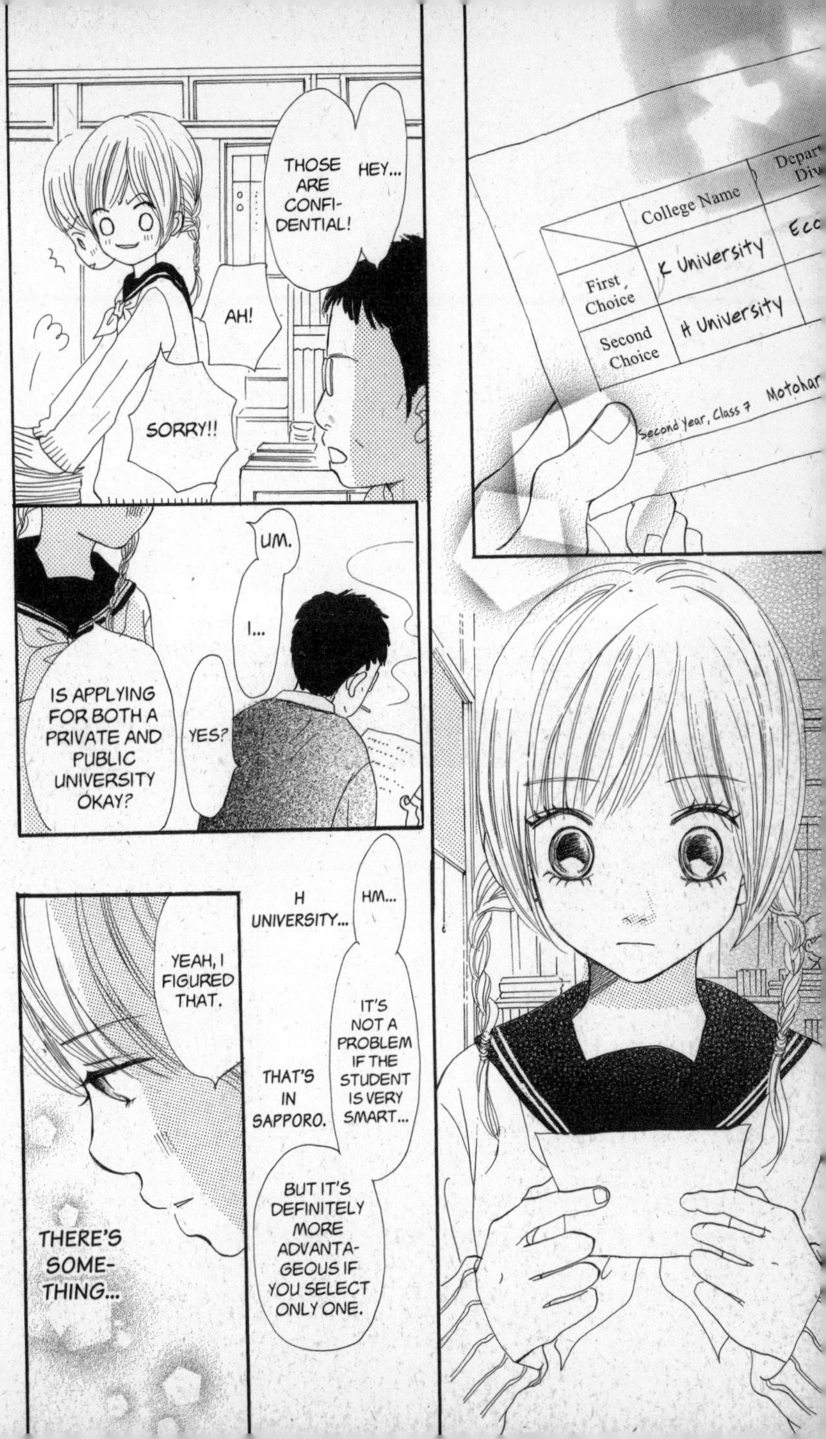
College Name
First Choice
K University
Second Choice
H University
Second Year, Class 7
HEY...
THOSE ARE CONFIDENTIAL!
AH!
SORRY!!
UM.
I...
YES?
IS APPLYING FOR BOTH A PRIVATE AND PUBLIC UNIVERSITY OKAY?
HM...
H UNIVERSITY...
THAT'S IN SAPPORO.
YEAH, I FIGURED THAT.
IT'S NOT A PROBLEM IF THE STUDENT IS VERY SMART...
BUT IT'S DEFINITELY MORE ADVANTAGEOUS IF YOU SELECT ONLY ONE.
THERE'S SOMETHING...

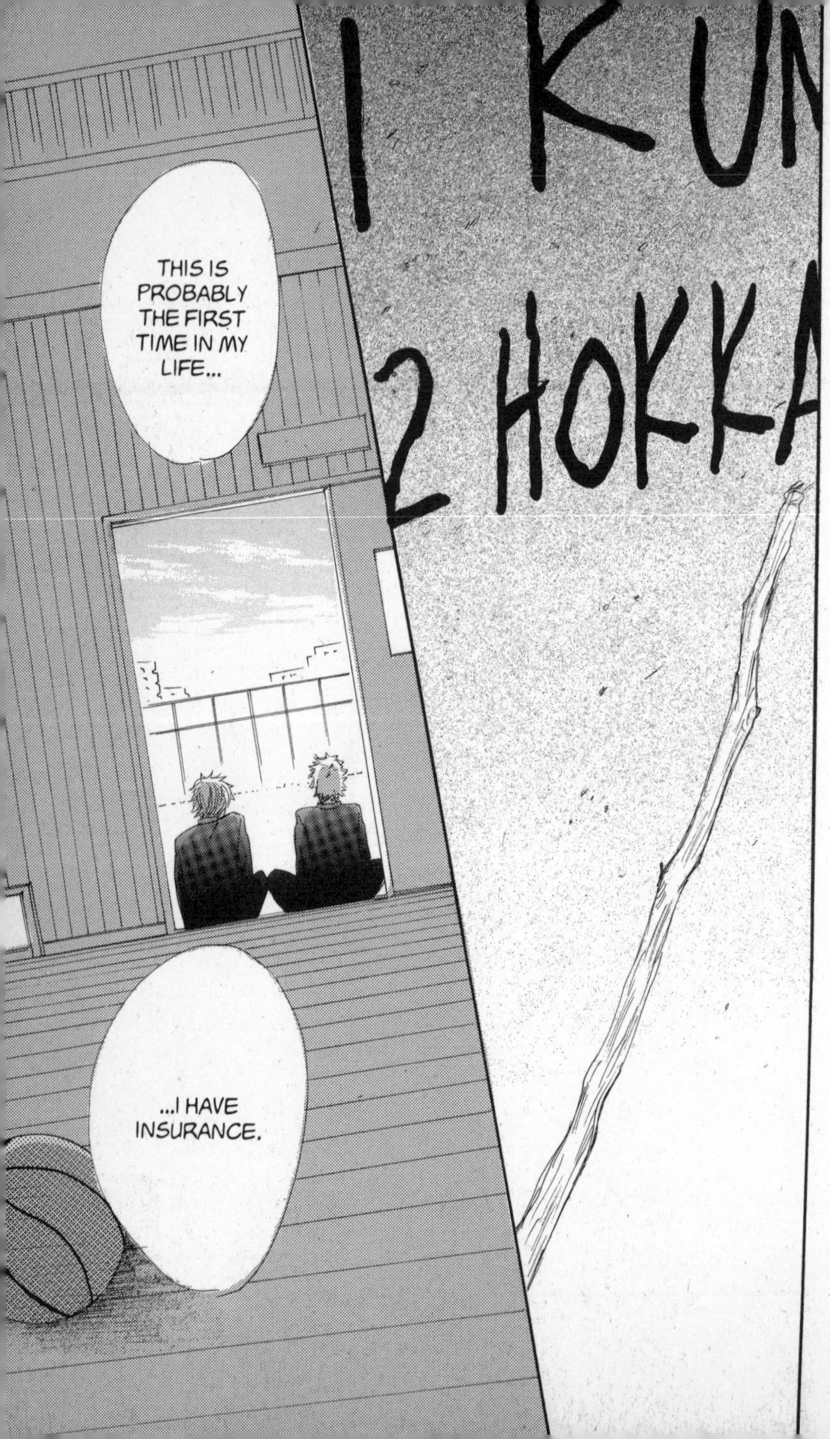
I KUN
2 HOKKA
THIS IS PROBABLY THE FIRST TIME IN MY LIFE...
...I HAVE INSURANCE.

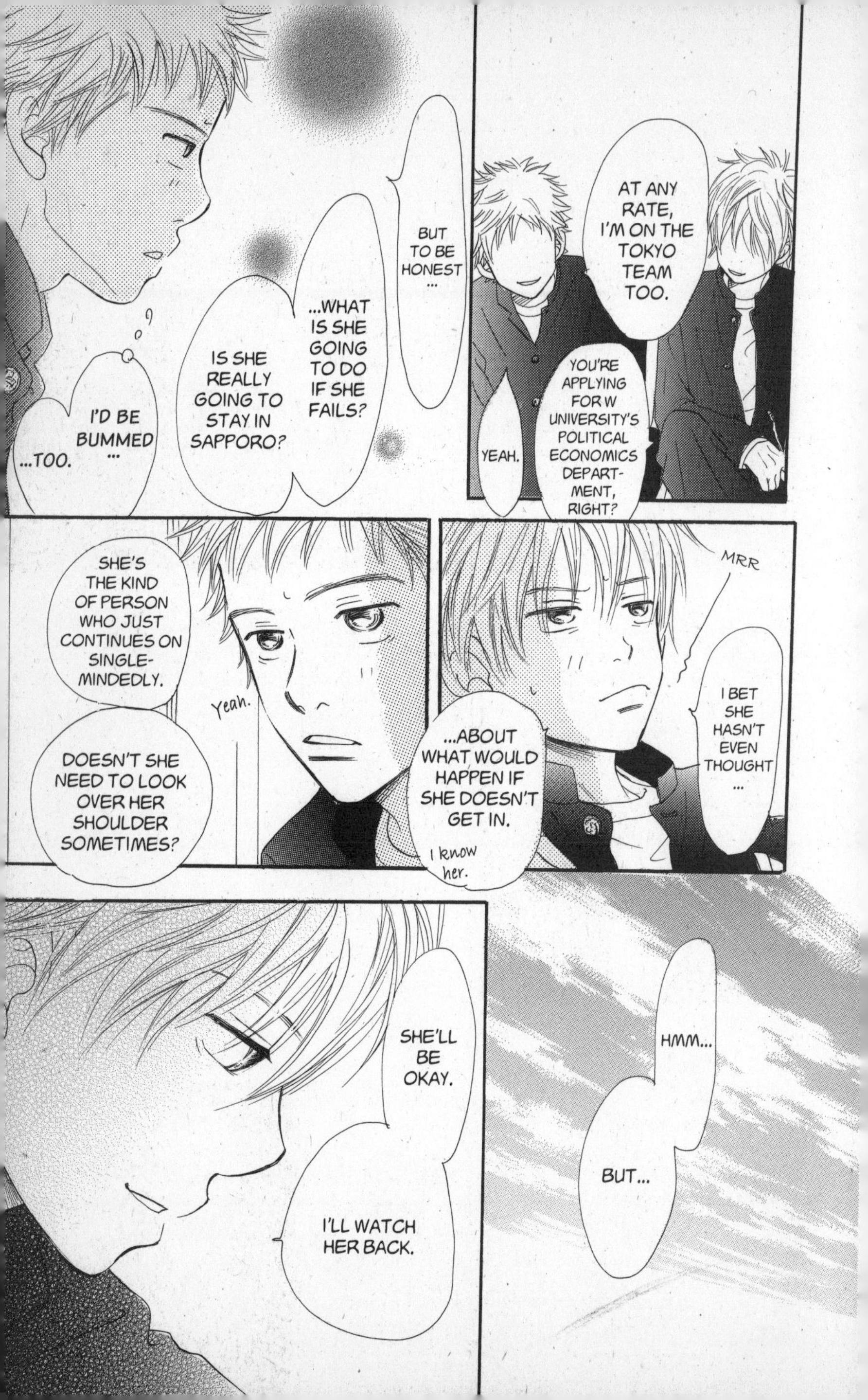
AT ANY RATE, I'M ON THE TOKYO TEAM TOO.
YOU'RE APPLYING FOR W UNIVERSITY'S POLITICAL ECONOMICS DEPARTMENT, RIGHT?
YEAH.
BUT TO BE HONEST...
...WHAT IS SHE GOING TO DO IF SHE FAILS?
IS SHE REALLY GOING TO STAY IN SAPPORO?
I'D BE BUMMED...
...TOO.
MRR
I BET SHE HASN'T EVEN THOUGHT...
...ABOUT WHAT WOULD HAPPEN IF SHE DOESN'T GET IN.
I know her.
Yeah.
SHE'S THE KIND OF PERSON WHO JUST CONTINUES ON SINGLE-MINDEDLY.
DOESN'T SHE NEED TO LOOK OVER HER SHOULDER SOMETIMES?
HMM...
BUT...
SHE'LL BE OKAY.
I'LL WATCH HER BACK.

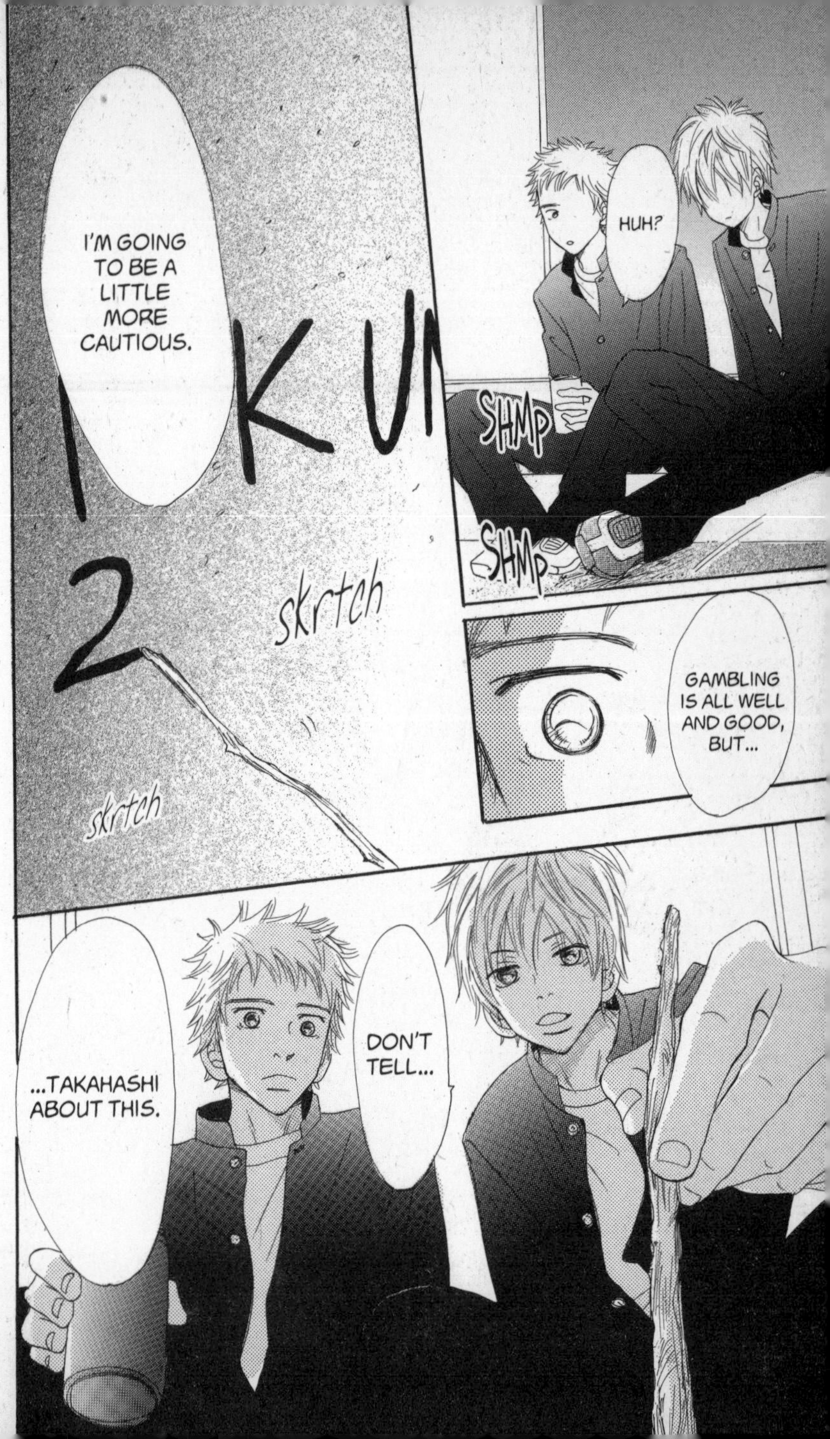
HUH?
SHMP
SHMP
GAMBLING IS ALL WELL AND GOOD, BUT...
I'M GOING TO BE A LITTLE MORE CAUTIOUS.
skrtch
skrtch
DON'T TELL...
...TAKAHASHI ABOUT THIS.

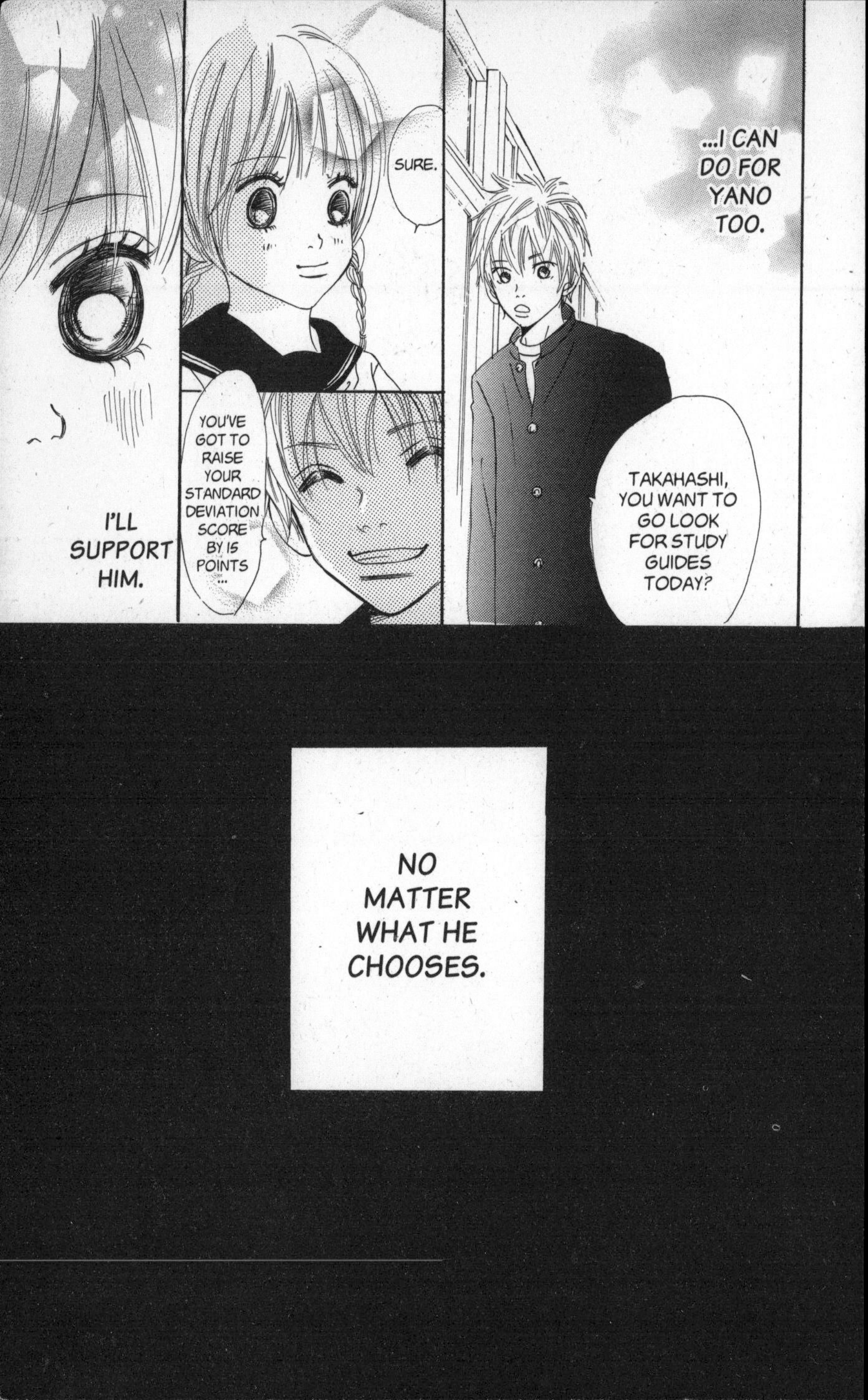
...I CAN DO FOR YANO TOO.
TAKAHASHI, YOU WANT TO GO LOOK FOR STUDY GUIDES TODAY?
SURE.
YOU'VE GOT TO RAISE YOUR STANDARD DEVIATION SCORE BY 15 POINTS...
I'LL SUPPORT HIM.
NO MATTER WHAT HE CHOOSES.

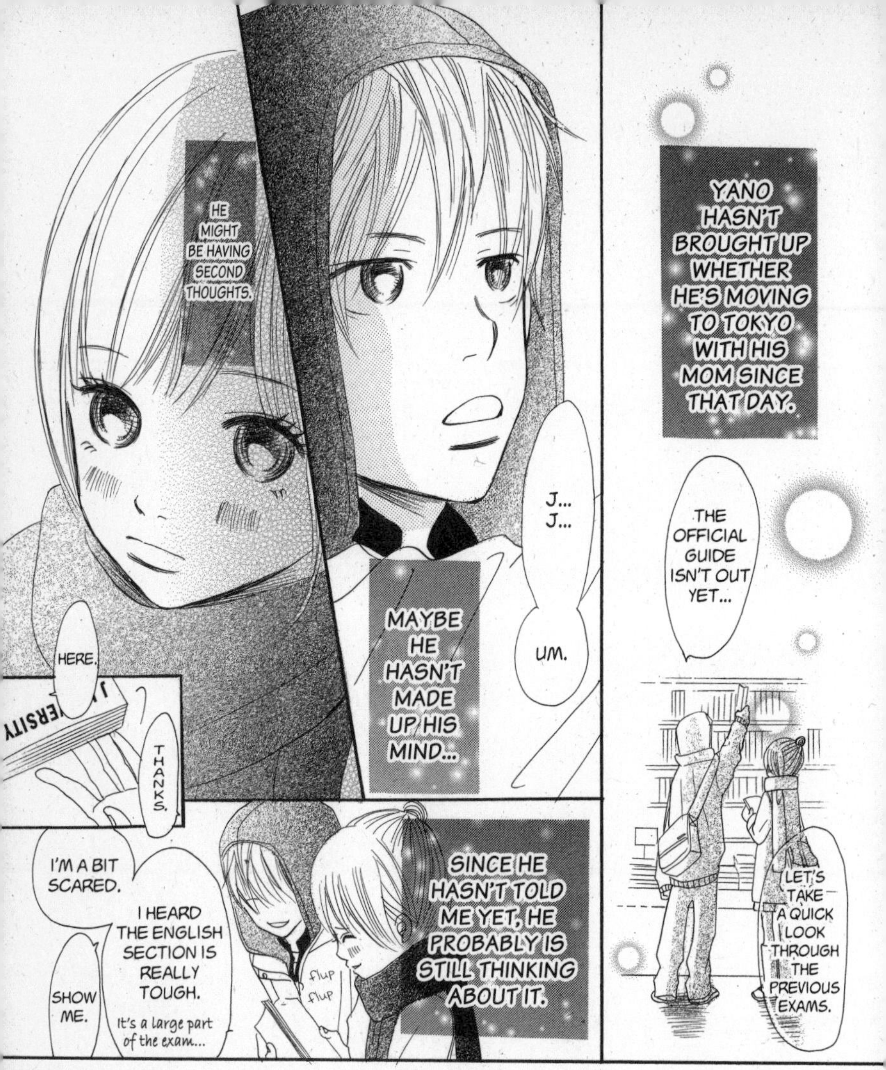
YANO HASN'T BROUGHT UP WHETHER HE'S MOVING TO TOKYO WITH HIS MOM SINCE THAT DAY.
THE OFFICIAL GUIDE ISN'T OUT YET...
LET'S TAKE A QUICK LOOK THROUGH THE PREVIOUS EXAMS.
J... J...
UM.
MAYBE HE HASN'T MADE UP HIS MIND...
HE MIGHT BE HAVING SECOND THOUGHTS.
HERE.
THANKS.
SINCE HE HASN'T TOLD ME YET, HE PROBABLY IS STILL THINKING ABOUT IT.
flup flup
I'M A BIT SCARED.
I HEARD THE ENGLISH SECTION IS REALLY TOUGH.
It's a large part of the exam...
SHOW ME.

Chapter 29

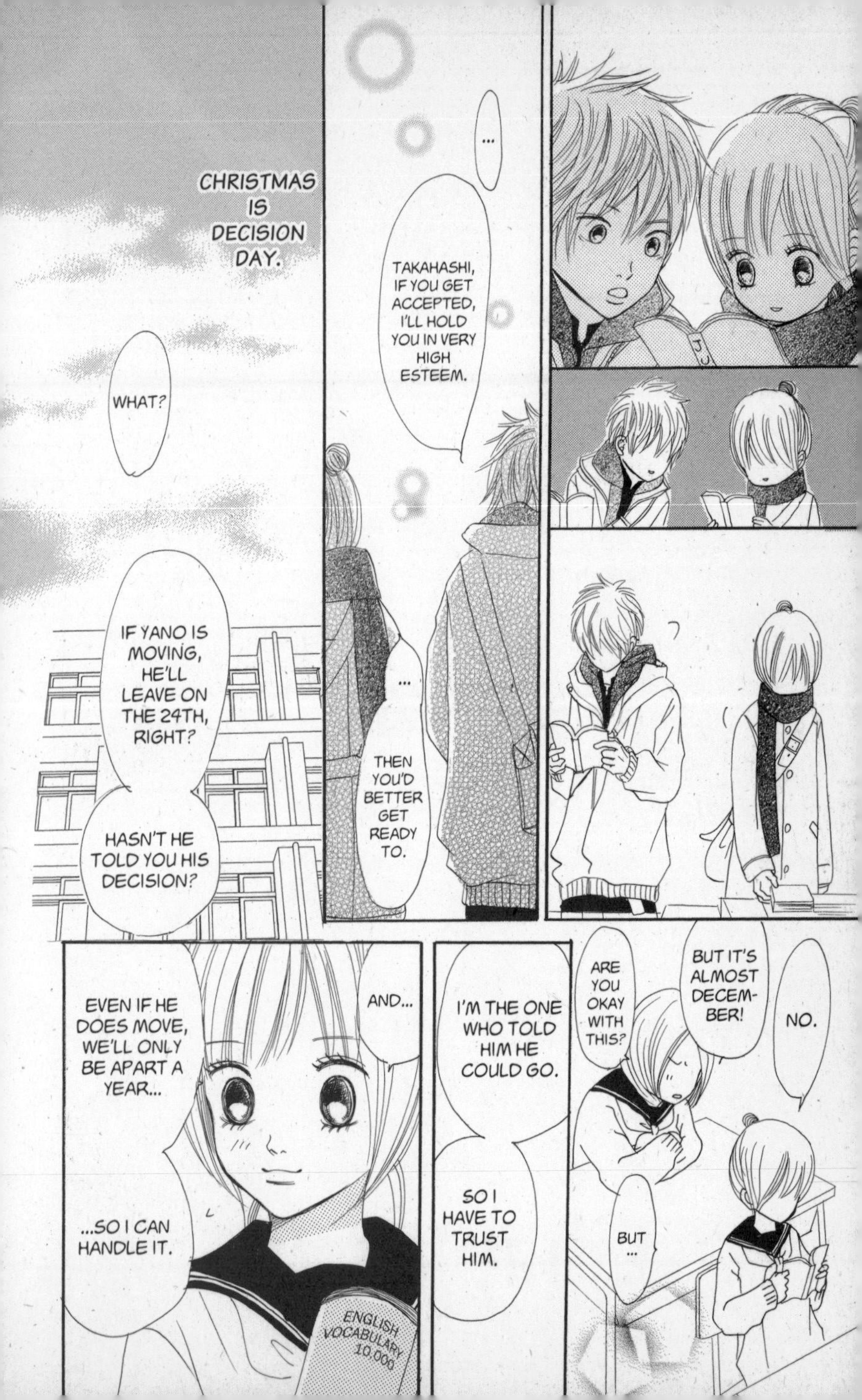
...
TAKAHASHI, IF YOU GET ACCEPTED, I'LL HOLD YOU IN VERY HIGH ESTEEM.
...
THEN YOU'D BETTER GET READY TO.
CHRISTMAS IS DECISION DAY.
WHAT?
IF YANO IS MOVING, HE'LL LEAVE ON THE 24TH, RIGHT?
HASN'T HE TOLD YOU HIS DECISION?
NO.
BUT IT'S ALMOST DECEMBER!
ARE YOU OKAY WITH THIS?
BUT ...
I'M THE ONE WHO TOLD HIM HE COULD GO.
SO I HAVE TO TRUST HIM.
AND...
EVEN IF HE DOES MOVE, WE'LL ONLY BE APART A YEAR...
...SO I CAN HANDLE IT.
ENGLISH VOCABULARY 10,000

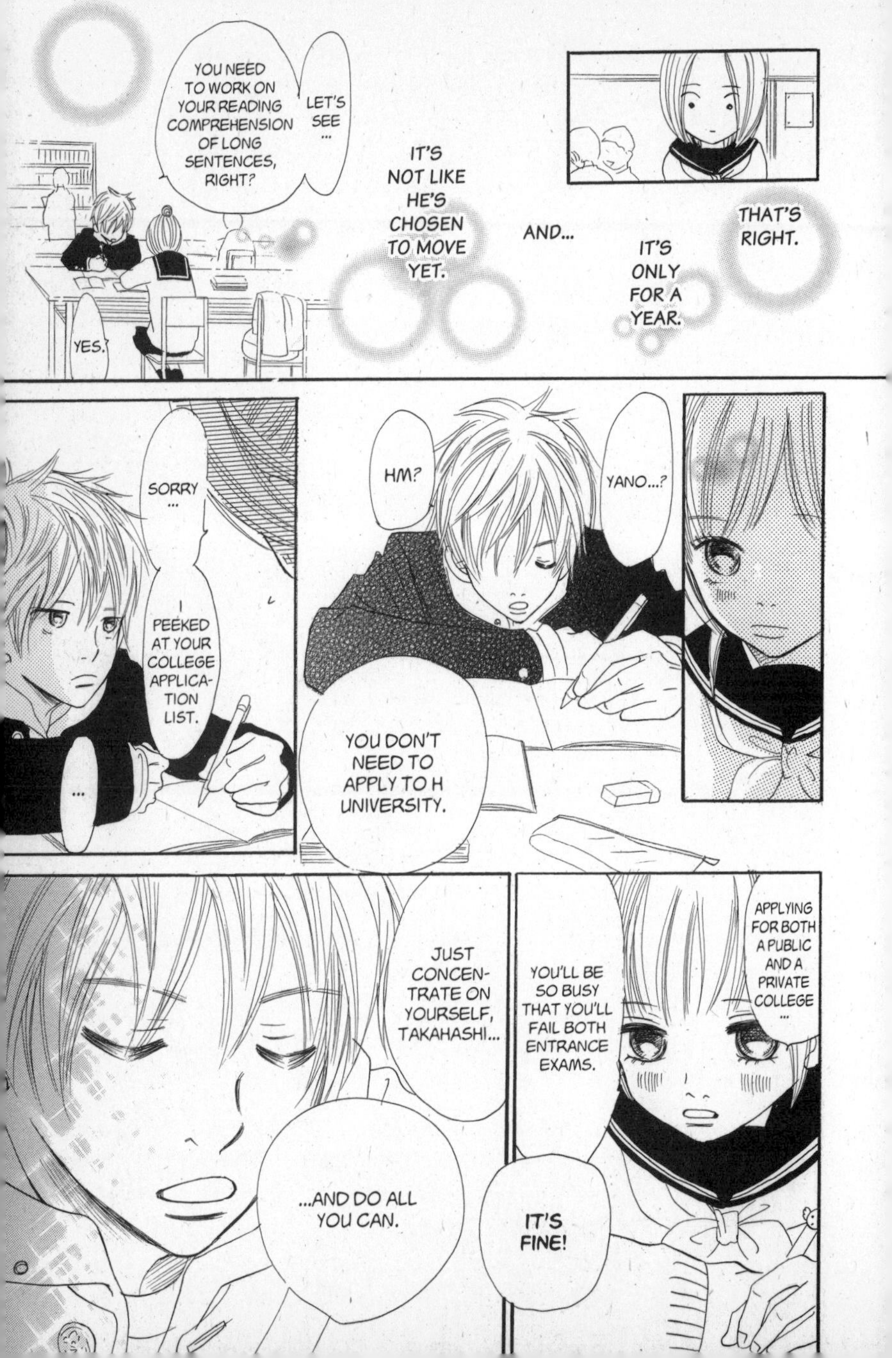
THAT'S RIGHT.
IT'S ONLY FOR A YEAR.
AND...
IT'S NOT LIKE HE'S CHOSEN TO MOVE YET.
LET'S SEE ...
YOU NEED TO WORK ON YOUR READING COMPREHENSION OF LONG SENTENCES, RIGHT?
YES.
YANO...?
HM?
SORRY ...
I PEEKED AT YOUR COLLEGE APPLICA-TION LIST.
...
YOU DON'T NEED TO APPLY TO H UNIVERSITY.
APPLYING FOR BOTH A PUBLIC AND A PRIVATE COLLEGE ...
YOU'LL BE SO BUSY THAT YOU'LL FAIL BOTH ENTRANCE EXAMS.
IT'S FINE!
JUST CONCEN-TRATE ON YOURSELF, TAKAHASHI...
...AND DO ALL YOU CAN.

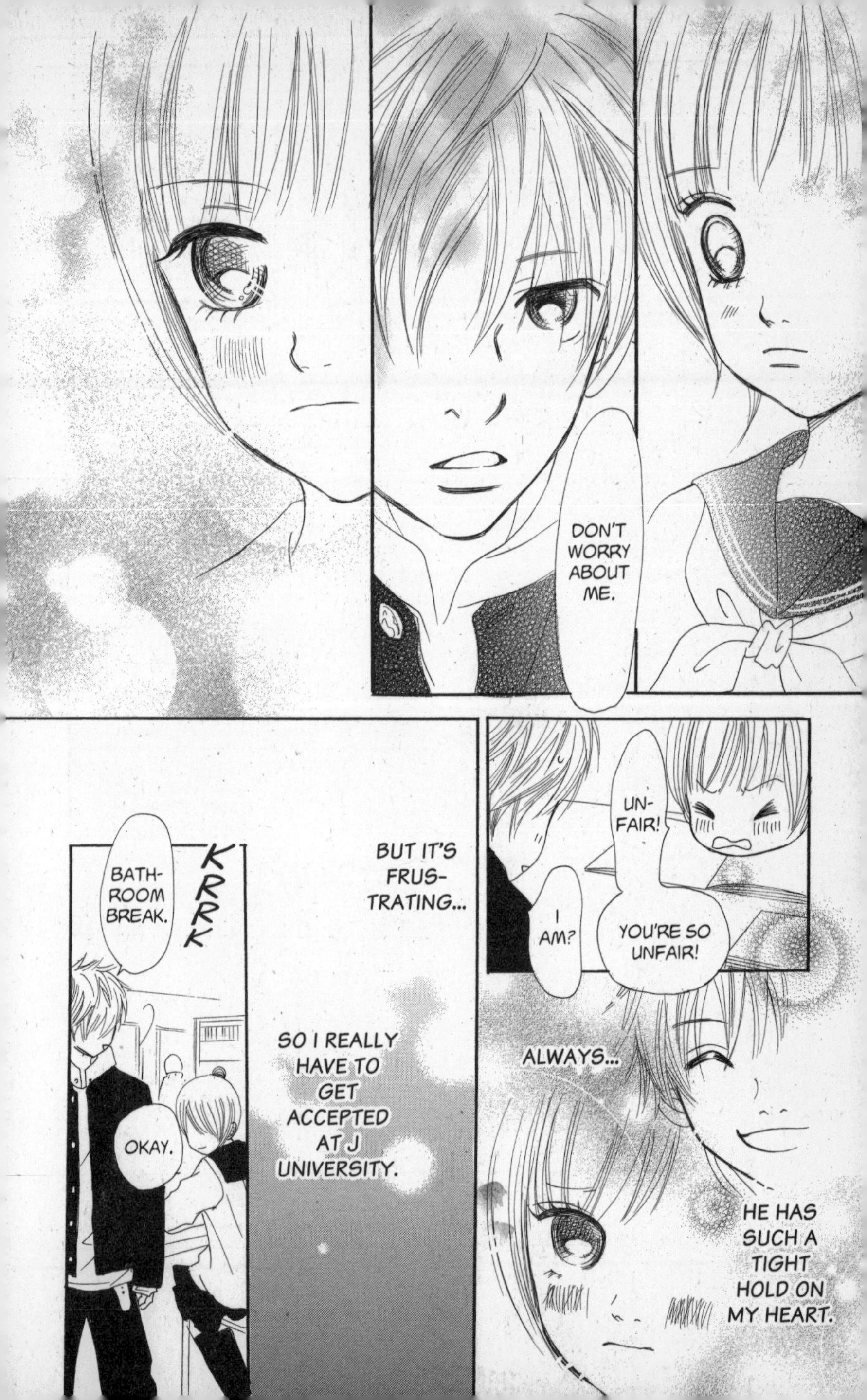

DON'T WORRY ABOUT ME.
UN-FAIR!
I AM?
YOU'RE SO UNFAIR!
ALWAYS...
HE HAS SUCH A TIGHT HOLD ON MY HEART.
BUT IT'S FRUS-TRATING...
SO I REALLY HAVE TO GET ACCEPTED AT J UNIVERSITY.
BATH-ROOM BREAK.
KRRK
OKAY.

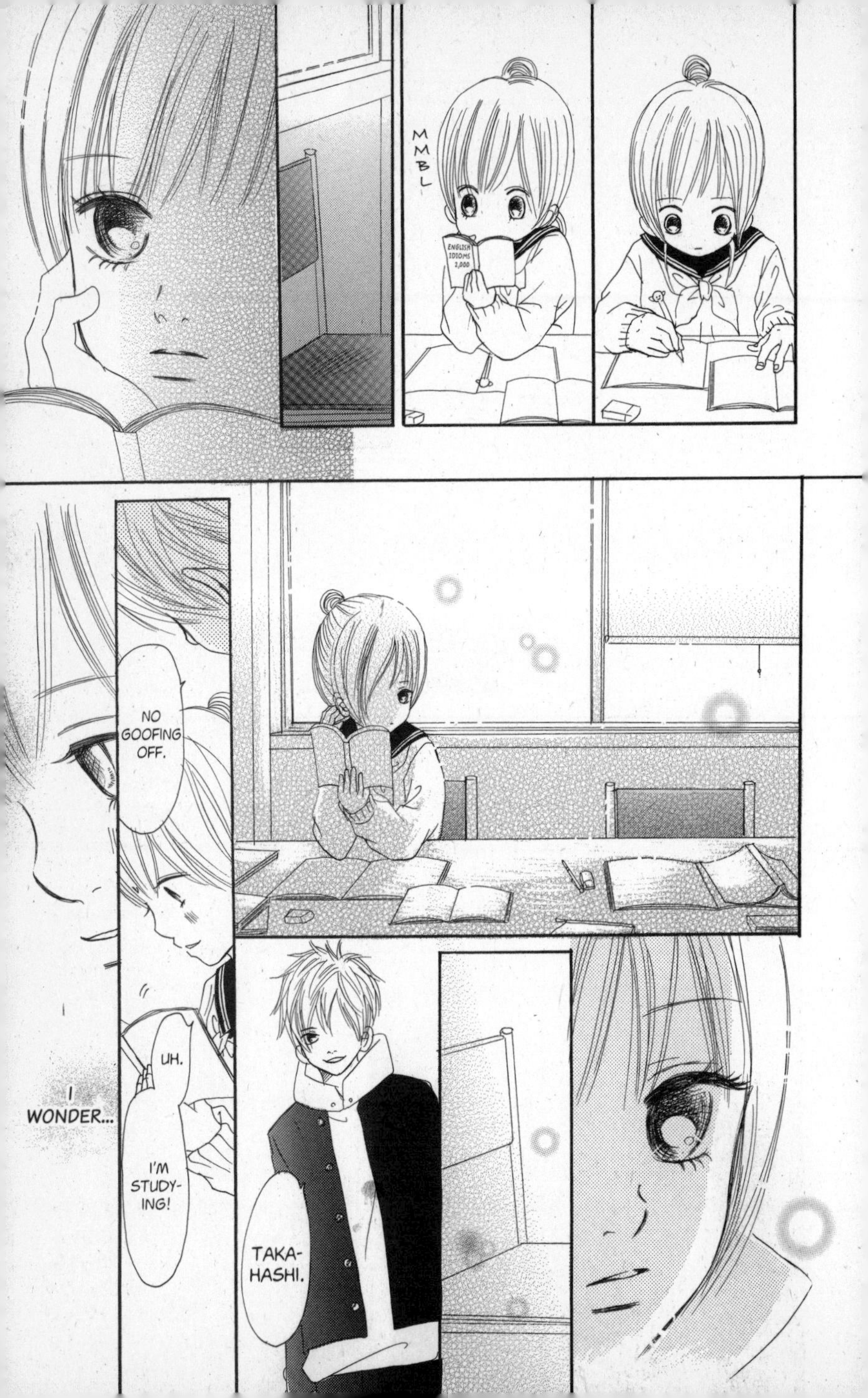
ENGLISH IDIOMS 2,000
MMBL
TAKA-HASHI.
NO GOOFING OFF.
UH.
I'M STUDY-ING!
I WONDER...

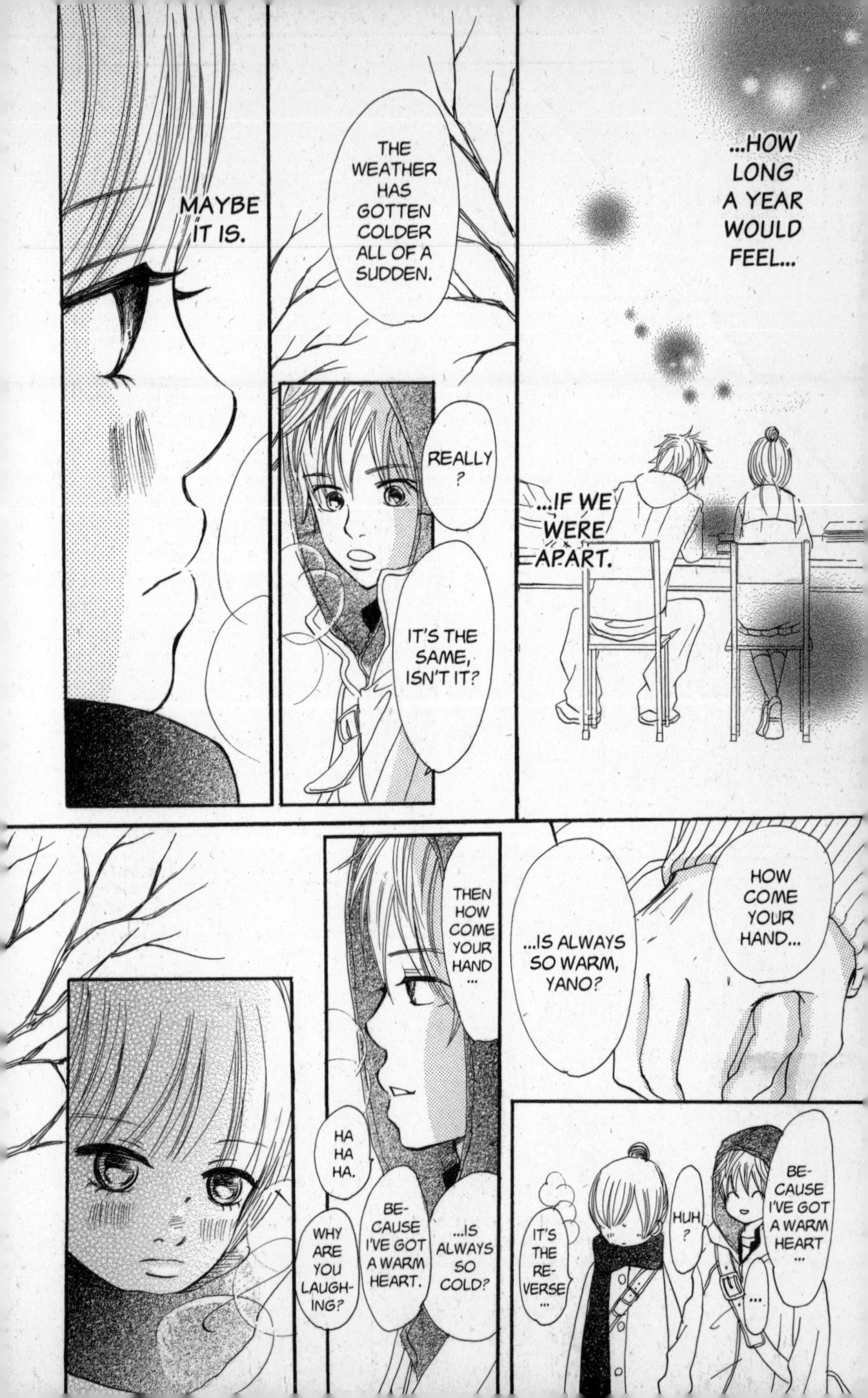

...HOW LONG A YEAR WOULD FEEL...
...IF WE WERE APART.
THE WEATHER HAS GOTTEN COLDER ALL OF A SUDDEN.
REALLY?
IT'S THE SAME, ISN'T IT?
MAYBE IT IS.
HOW COME YOUR HAND...
...IS ALWAYS SO WARM, YANO?
BE-CAUSE I'VE GOT A WARM HEART...
HUH?
...
IT'S THE RE-VERSE...
THEN HOW COME YOUR HAND...
...IS ALWAYS SO COLD?
BE-CAUSE I'VE GOT A WARM HEART.
HA HA HA.
WHY ARE YOU LAUGH-ING?

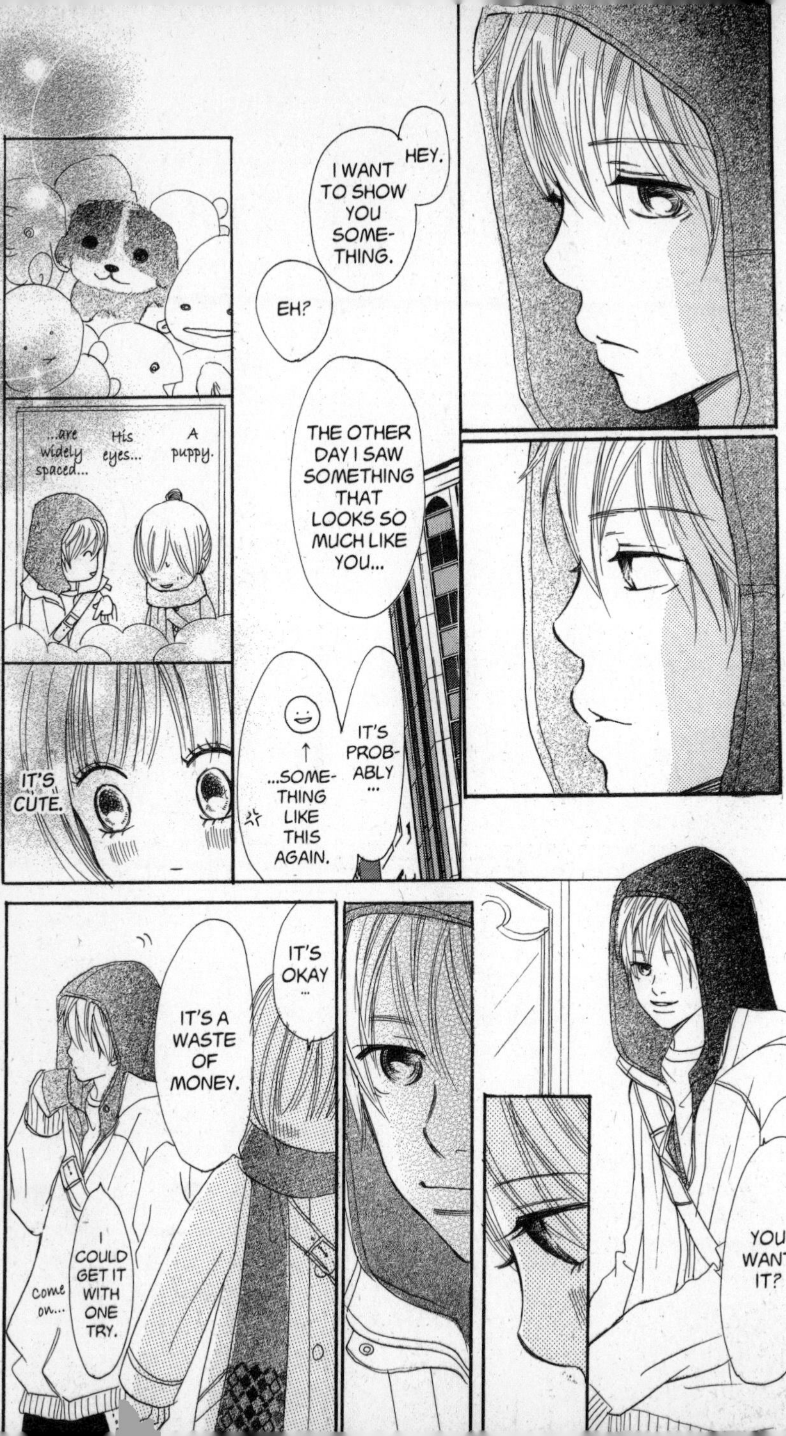
HEY.
I WANT TO SHOW YOU SOME-THING.
EH?
THE OTHER DAY I SAW SOMETHING THAT LOOKS SO MUCH LIKE YOU...
IT'S PROB-ABLY...
...SOME-THING LIKE THIS AGAIN.
A puppy.
His eyes...
...are widely spaced...
IT'S CUTE.
YOU WANT IT?
IT'S OKAY...
IT'S A WASTE OF MONEY.
I COULD GET IT WITH ONE TRY.
come on...

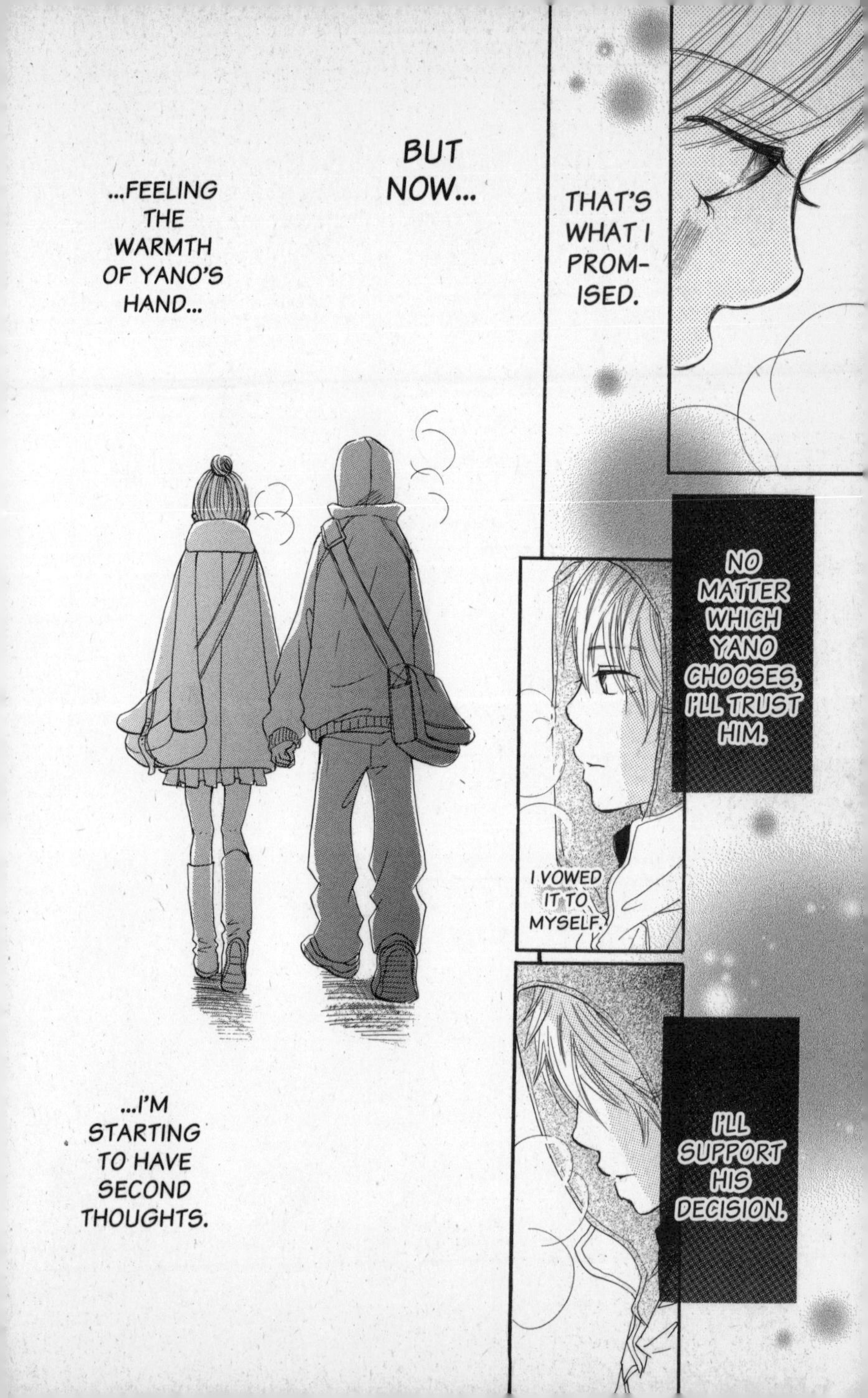
THAT'S WHAT I PROMISED.
NO MATTER WHICH YANO CHOOSES, I'LL TRUST HIM.
I VOWED IT TO MYSELF.
I'LL SUPPORT HIS DECISION.
BUT NOW...
...FEELING THE WARMTH OF YANO'S HAND...
...I'M STARTING TO HAVE SECOND THOUGHTS.

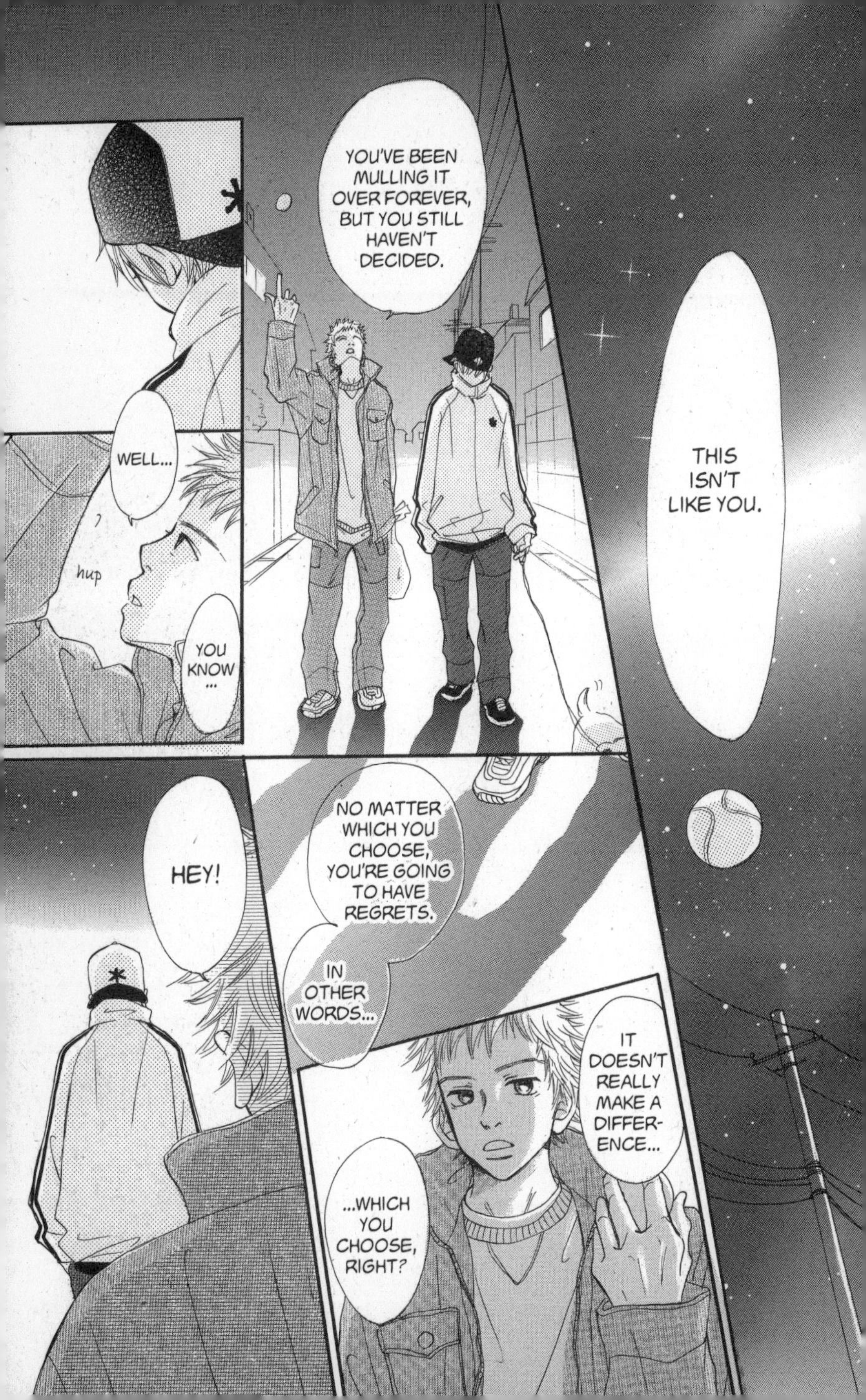
YOU'VE BEEN MULLING IT OVER FOREVER, BUT YOU STILL HAVEN'T DECIDED.
THIS ISN'T LIKE YOU.
WELL...
hup
YOU KNOW ...
NO MATTER WHICH YOU CHOOSE, YOU'RE GOING TO HAVE REGRETS.
IN OTHER WORDS...
IT DOESN'T REALLY MAKE A DIFFER-ENCE...
...WHICH YOU CHOOSE, RIGHT?
HEY!

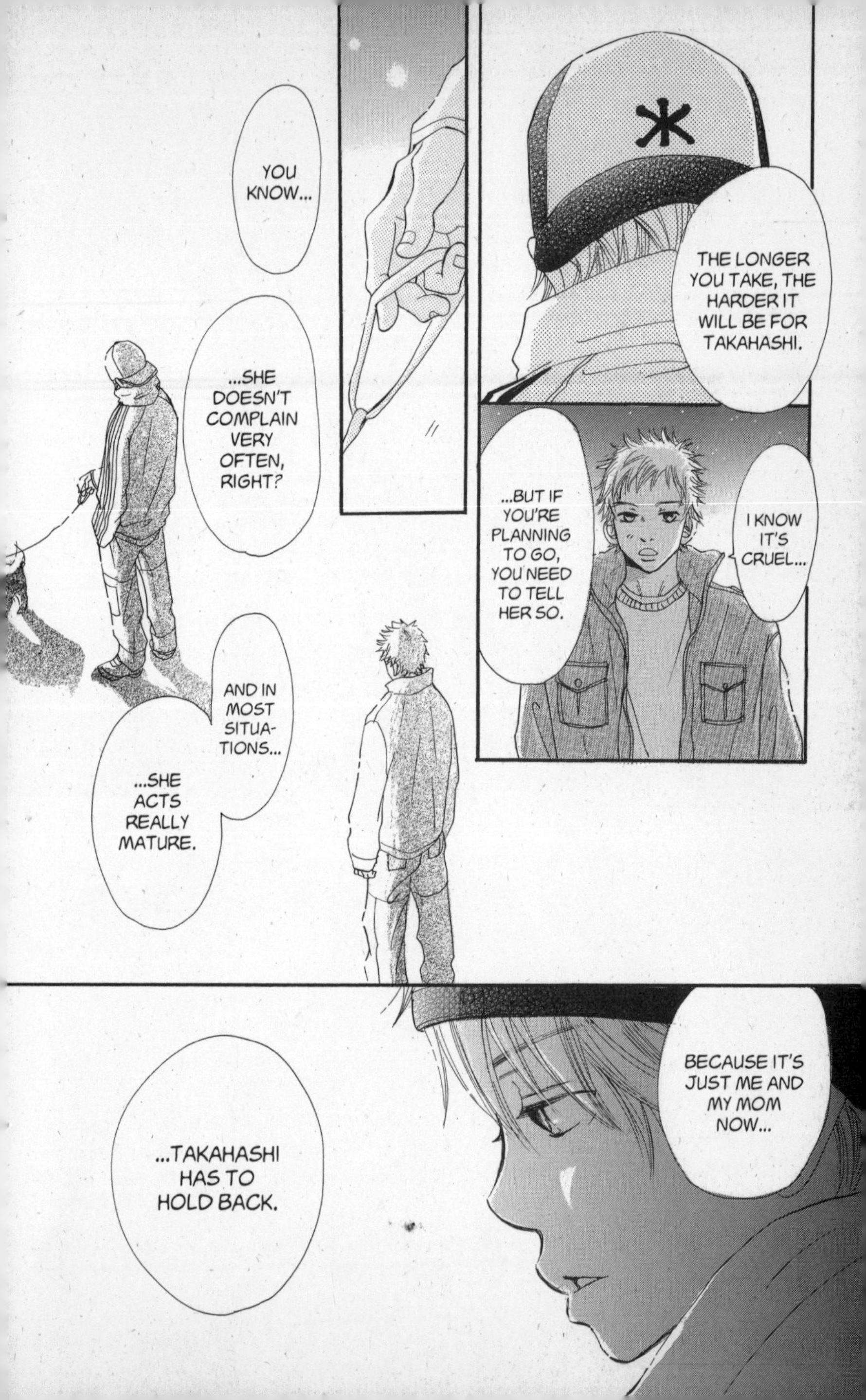
THE LONGER YOU TAKE, THE HARDER IT WILL BE FOR TAKAHASHI.
I KNOW IT'S CRUEL...
...BUT IF YOU'RE PLANNING TO GO, YOU NEED TO TELL HER SO.
YOU KNOW...
...SHE DOESN'T COMPLAIN VERY OFTEN, RIGHT?
AND IN MOST SITUATIONS...
...SHE ACTS REALLY MATURE.
BECAUSE IT'S JUST ME AND MY MOM NOW...
...TAKAHASHI HAS TO HOLD BACK.

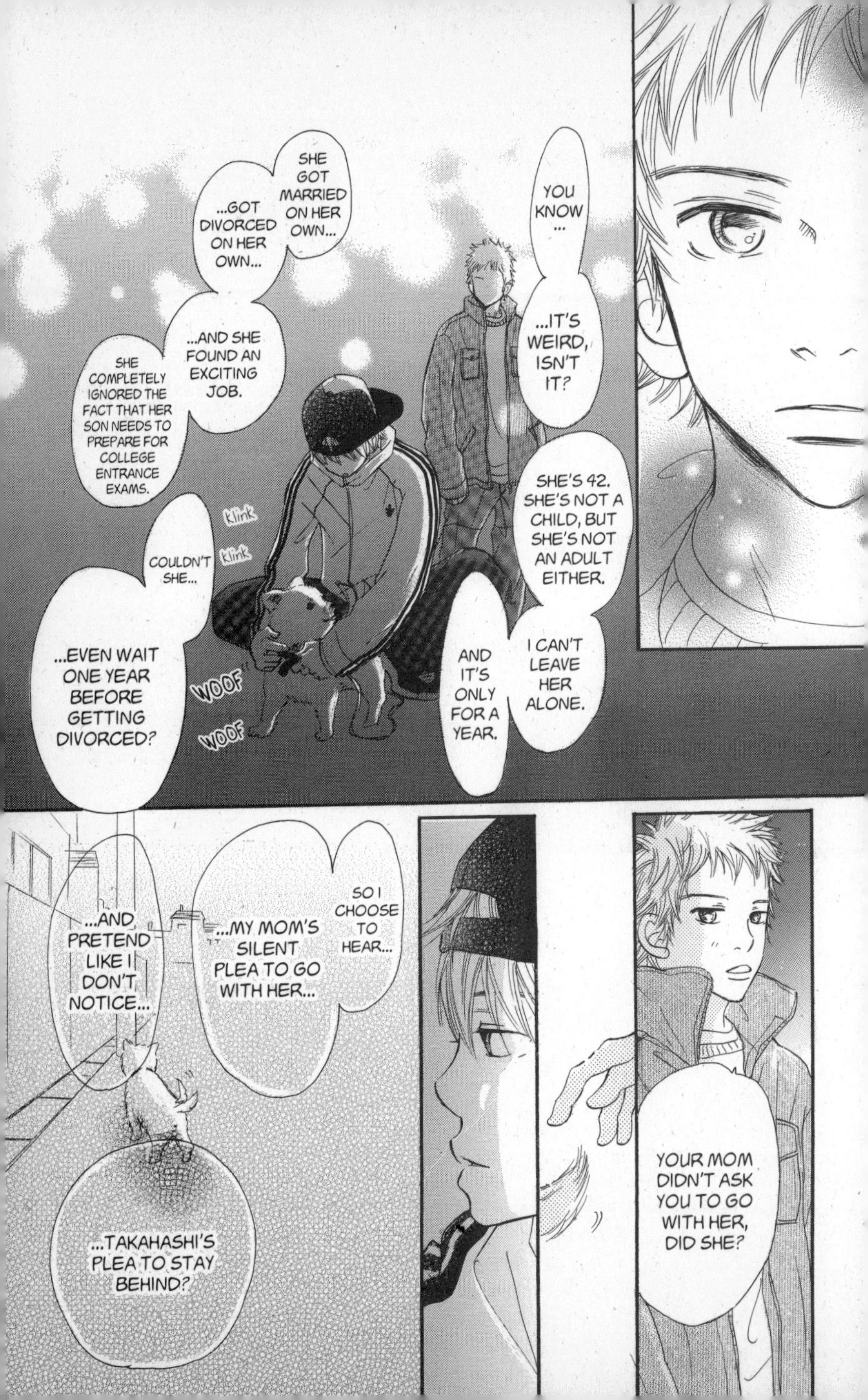
YOU KNOW ...
...IT'S WEIRD, ISN'T IT?
SHE'S 42. SHE'S NOT A CHILD, BUT SHE'S NOT AN ADULT EITHER.
I CAN'T LEAVE HER ALONE.
AND IT'S ONLY FOR A YEAR.
SHE GOT MARRIED ON HER OWN...
...GOT DIVORCED ON HER OWN...
...AND SHE FOUND AN EXCITING JOB.
SHE COMPLETELY IGNORED THE FACT THAT HER SON NEEDS TO PREPARE FOR COLLEGE ENTRANCE EXAMS.
klink
klink
COULDN'T SHE...
...EVEN WAIT ONE YEAR BEFORE GETTING DIVORCED?
WOOF
WOOF
YOUR MOM DIDN'T ASK YOU TO GO WITH HER, DID SHE?
SO I CHOOSE TO HEAR...
...MY MOM'S SILENT PLEA TO GO WITH HER...
...AND PRETEND LIKE I DON'T NOTICE...
...TAKAHASHI'S PLEA TO STAY BEHIND?

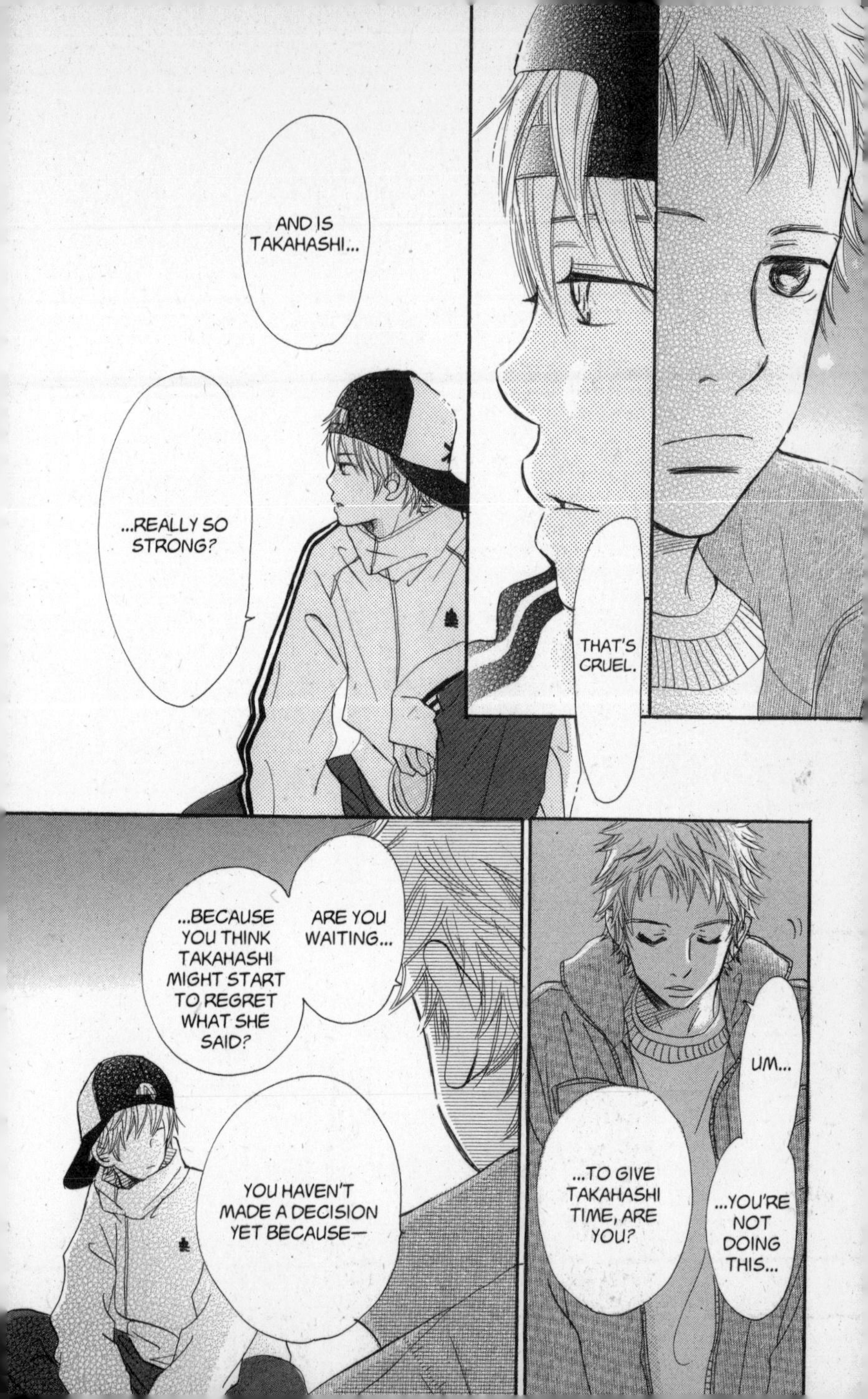
THAT'S CRUEL.
AND IS TAKAHASHI...
...REALLY SO STRONG?
UM...
...YOU'RE NOT DOING THIS...
...TO GIVE TAKAHASHI TIME, ARE YOU?
ARE YOU WAITING...
...BECAUSE YOU THINK TAKAHASHI MIGHT START TO REGRET WHAT SHE SAID?
YOU HAVEN'T MADE A DECISION YET BECAUSE—

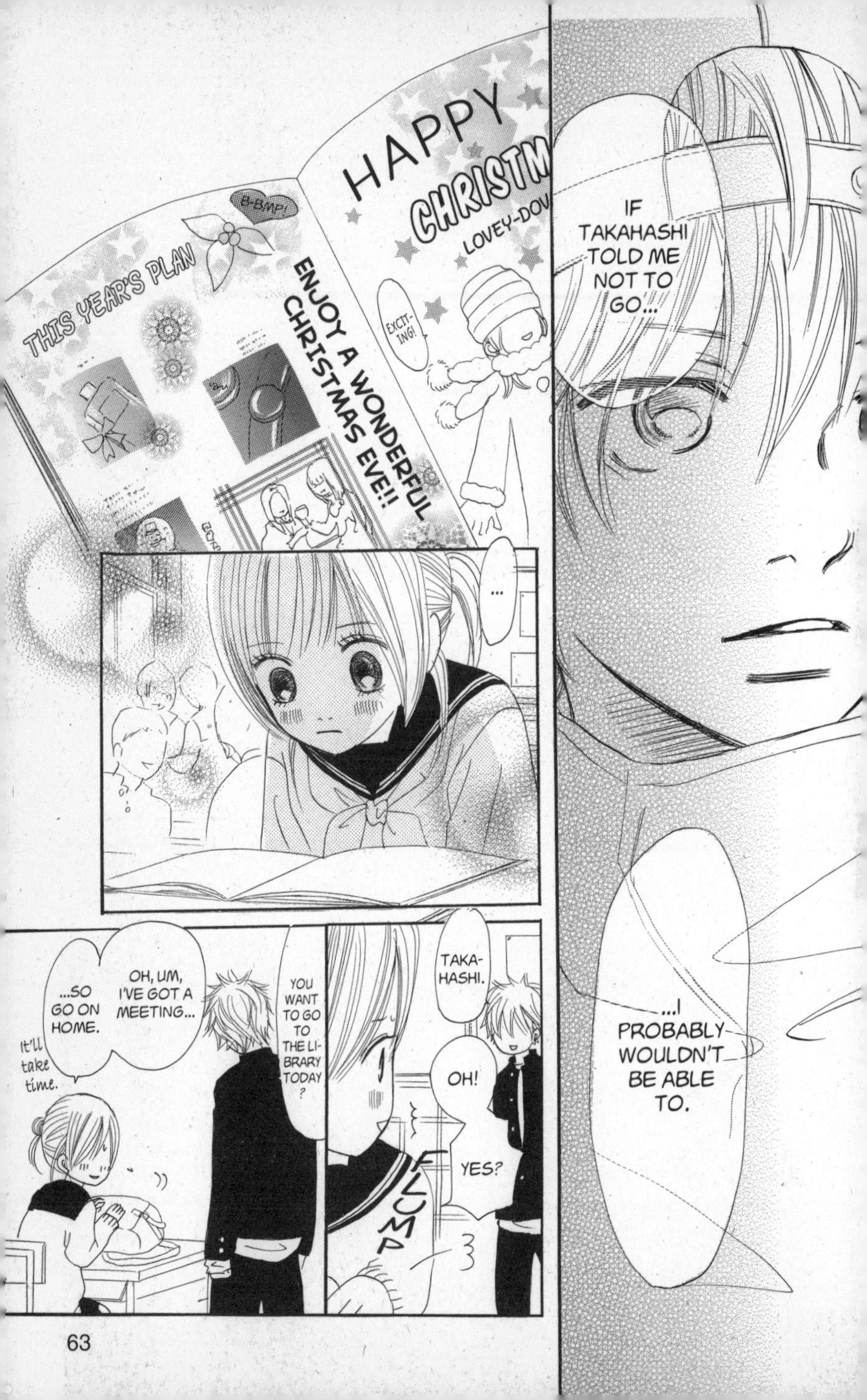

IF TAKAHASHI TOLD ME NOT TO GO...
...I PROBABLY WOULDN'T BE ABLE TO.
HAPPY
CHRISTM
LOVEY-DOV
EXCIT-ING!
ENJOY A WONDERFUL CHRISTMAS EVE!!
B-BMP!
THIS YEAR'S PLAN
...
TAKA-HASHI.
OH!
YES?
FLUMP
YOU WANT TO GO TO THE LIBRARY TODAY?
OH, UM, I'VE GOT A MEETING...
...SO GO ON HOME.
It'll take time.

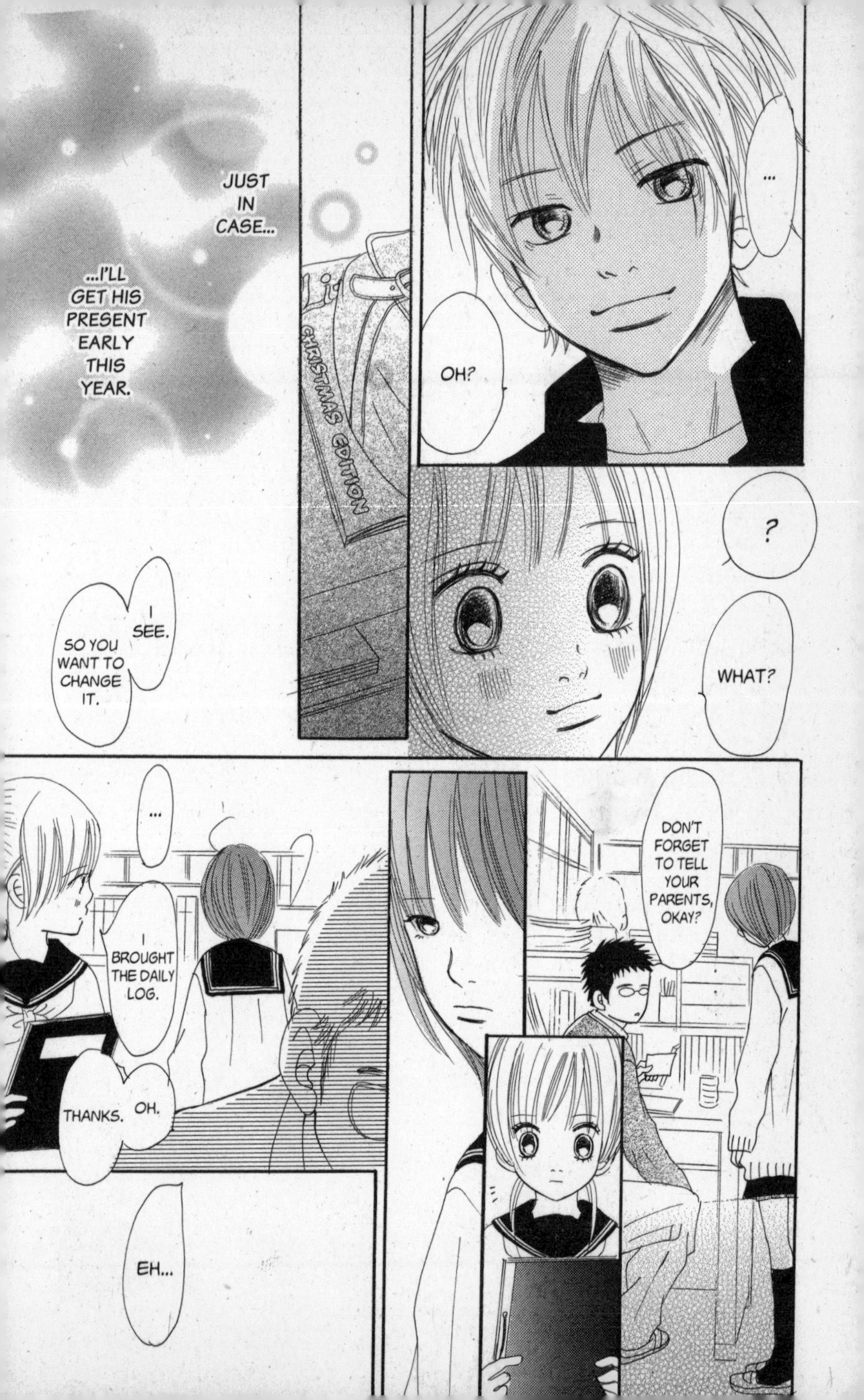
...
OH?
?
WHAT?
CHRISTMAS EDITION
JUST IN CASE...
...I'LL GET HIS PRESENT EARLY THIS YEAR.
I SEE.
SO YOU WANT TO CHANGE IT.
DON'T FORGET TO TELL YOUR PARENTS, OKAY?
...
I BROUGHT THE DAILY LOG.
OH.
THANKS.
EH...

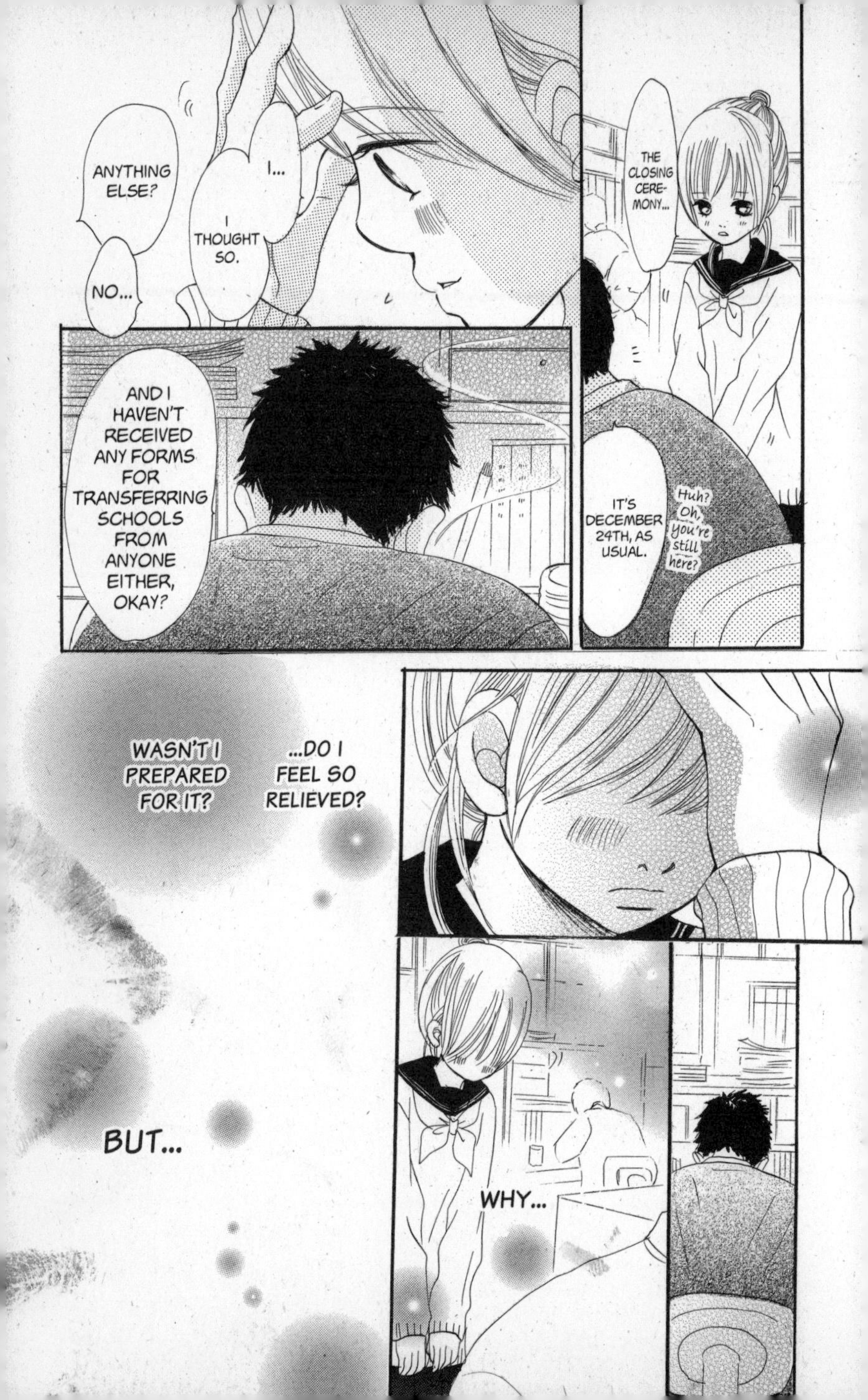
THE CLOSING CEREMONY...
Huh? Oh, you're still here?
IT'S DECEMBER 24TH, AS USUAL.
I...
I THOUGHT SO.
ANYTHING ELSE?
NO...
AND I HAVEN'T RECEIVED ANY FORMS FOR TRANSFERRING SCHOOLS FROM ANYONE EITHER, OKAY?
WHY...
...DO I FEEL SO RELIEVED?
WASN'T I PREPARED FOR IT?
BUT...

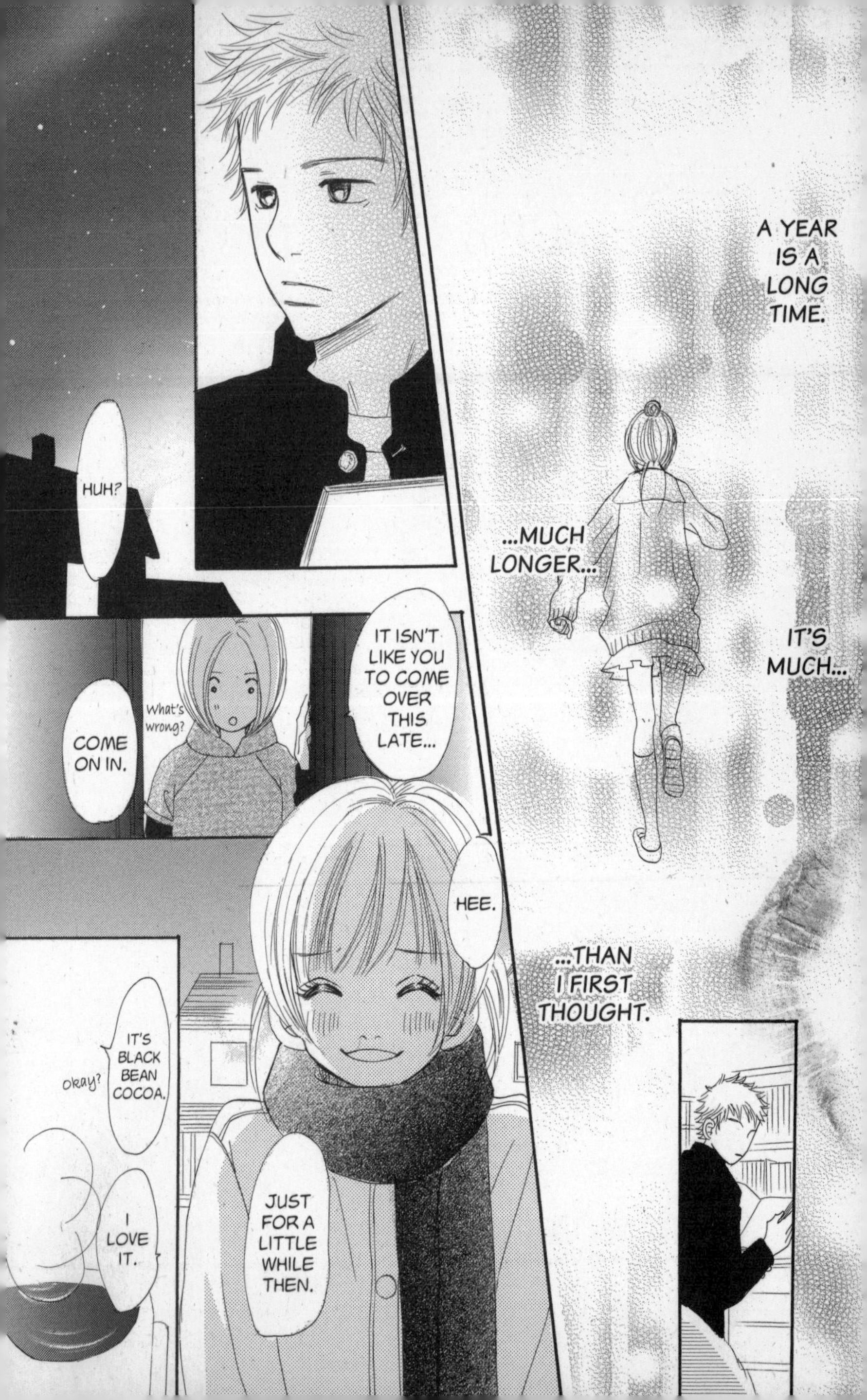
A YEAR IS A LONG TIME.
IT'S MUCH...
...MUCH LONGER...
...THAN I FIRST THOUGHT.
HUH?
IT ISN'T LIKE YOU TO COME OVER THIS LATE...
What's wrong?
COME ON IN.
HEE.
JUST FOR A LITTLE WHILE THEN.
IT'S BLACK BEAN COCOA.
okay?
I LOVE IT.

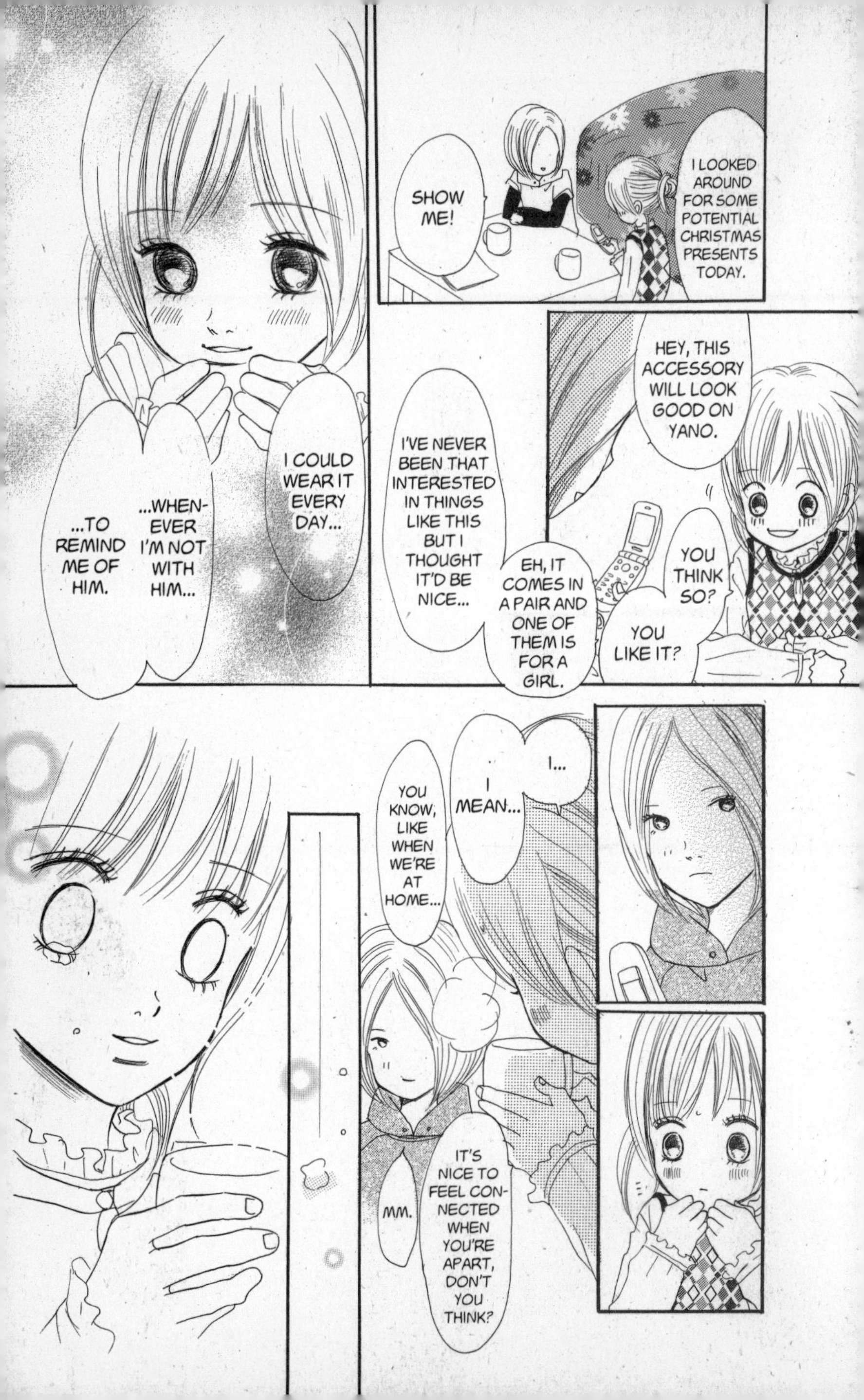
I LOOKED AROUND FOR SOME POTENTIAL CHRISTMAS PRESENTS TODAY.
SHOW ME!
HEY, THIS ACCESSORY WILL LOOK GOOD ON YANO.
YOU THINK SO?
YOU LIKE IT?
EH, IT COMES IN A PAIR AND ONE OF THEM IS FOR A GIRL.
I'VE NEVER BEEN THAT INTERESTED IN THINGS LIKE THIS BUT I THOUGHT IT'D BE NICE...
I COULD WEAR IT EVERY DAY...
...WHEN-EVER I'M NOT WITH HIM...
...TO REMIND ME OF HIM.
I...
I MEAN...
YOU KNOW, LIKE WHEN WE'RE AT HOME...
IT'S NICE TO FEEL CON-NECTED WHEN YOU'RE APART, DON'T YOU THINK?
MM.

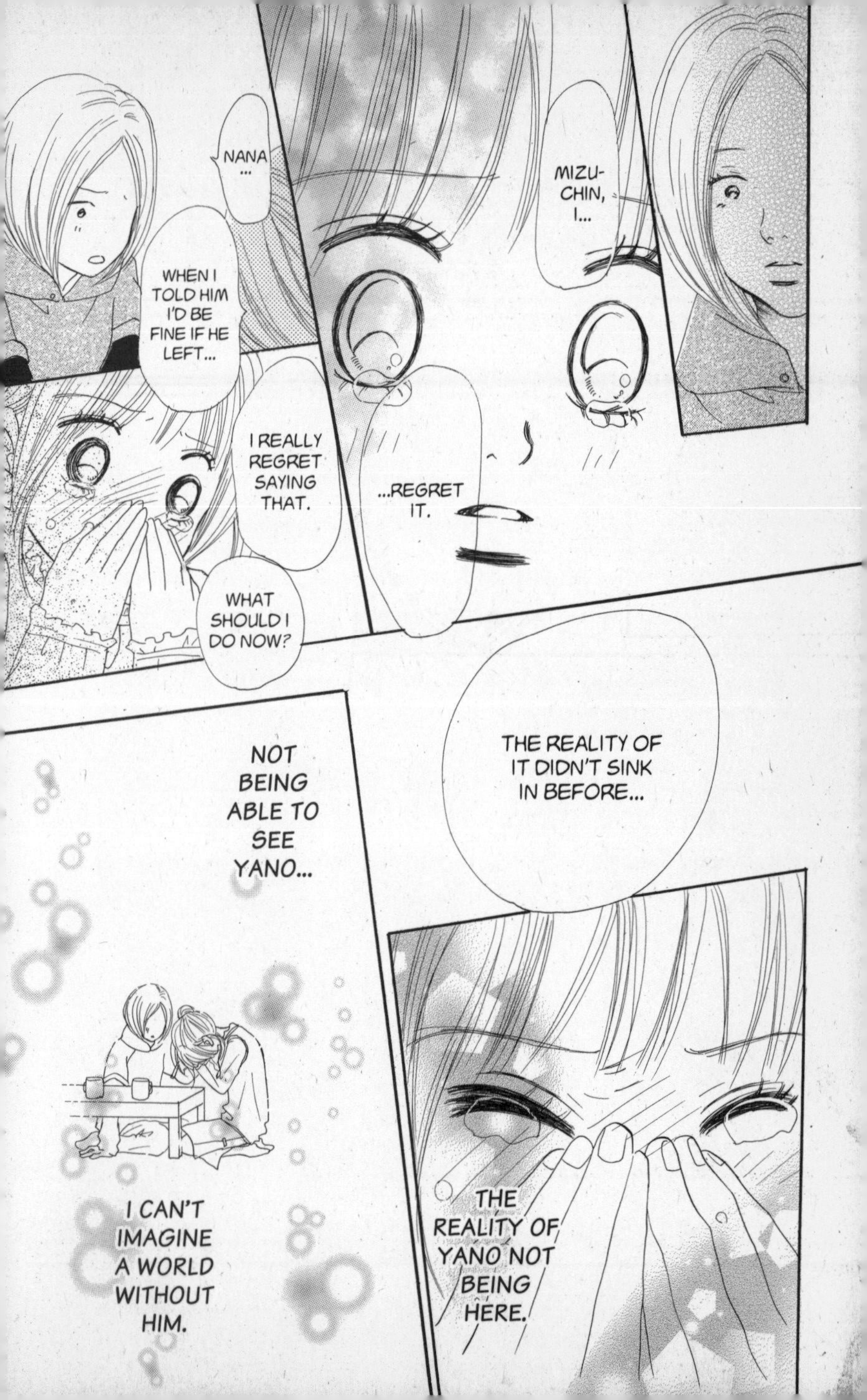
MIZU-CHIN, I...
...REGRET IT.
NANA...
WHEN I TOLD HIM I'D BE FINE IF HE LEFT...
I REALLY REGRET SAYING THAT.
WHAT SHOULD I DO NOW?
THE REALITY OF IT DIDN'T SINK IN BEFORE...
THE REALITY OF YANO NOT BEING HERE.
NOT BEING ABLE TO SEE YANO...
I CAN'T IMAGINE A WORLD WITHOUT HIM.

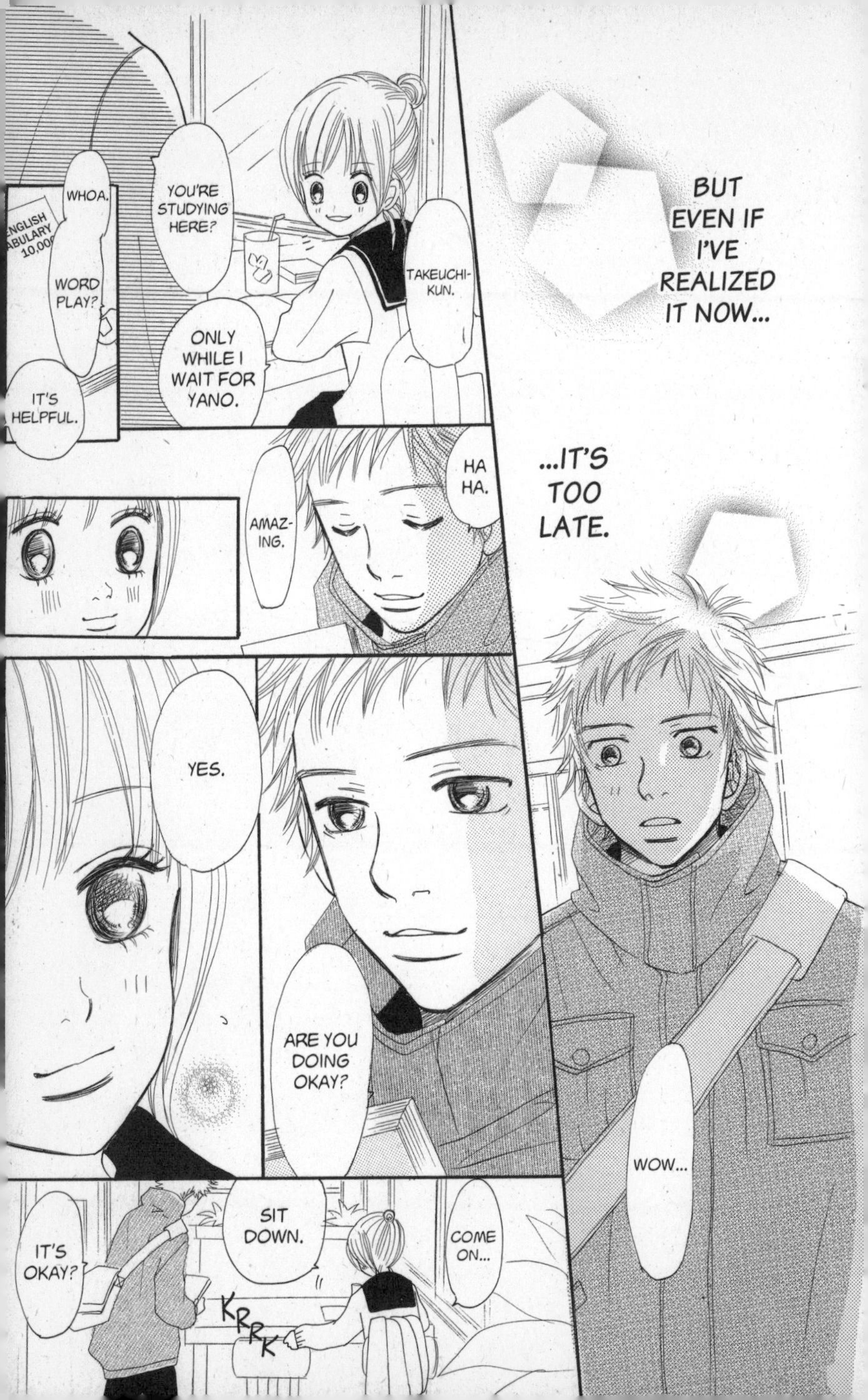
BUT EVEN IF I'VE REALIZED IT NOW...
...IT'S TOO LATE.
WOW...
TAKEUCHI-KUN.
YOU'RE STUDYING HERE?
ONLY WHILE I WAIT FOR YANO.
WHOA.
WORD PLAY?
IT'S HELPFUL.
HA HA.
AMAZ-ING.
YES.
ARE YOU DOING OKAY?
COME ON...
SIT DOWN.
KRRK
IT'S OKAY?

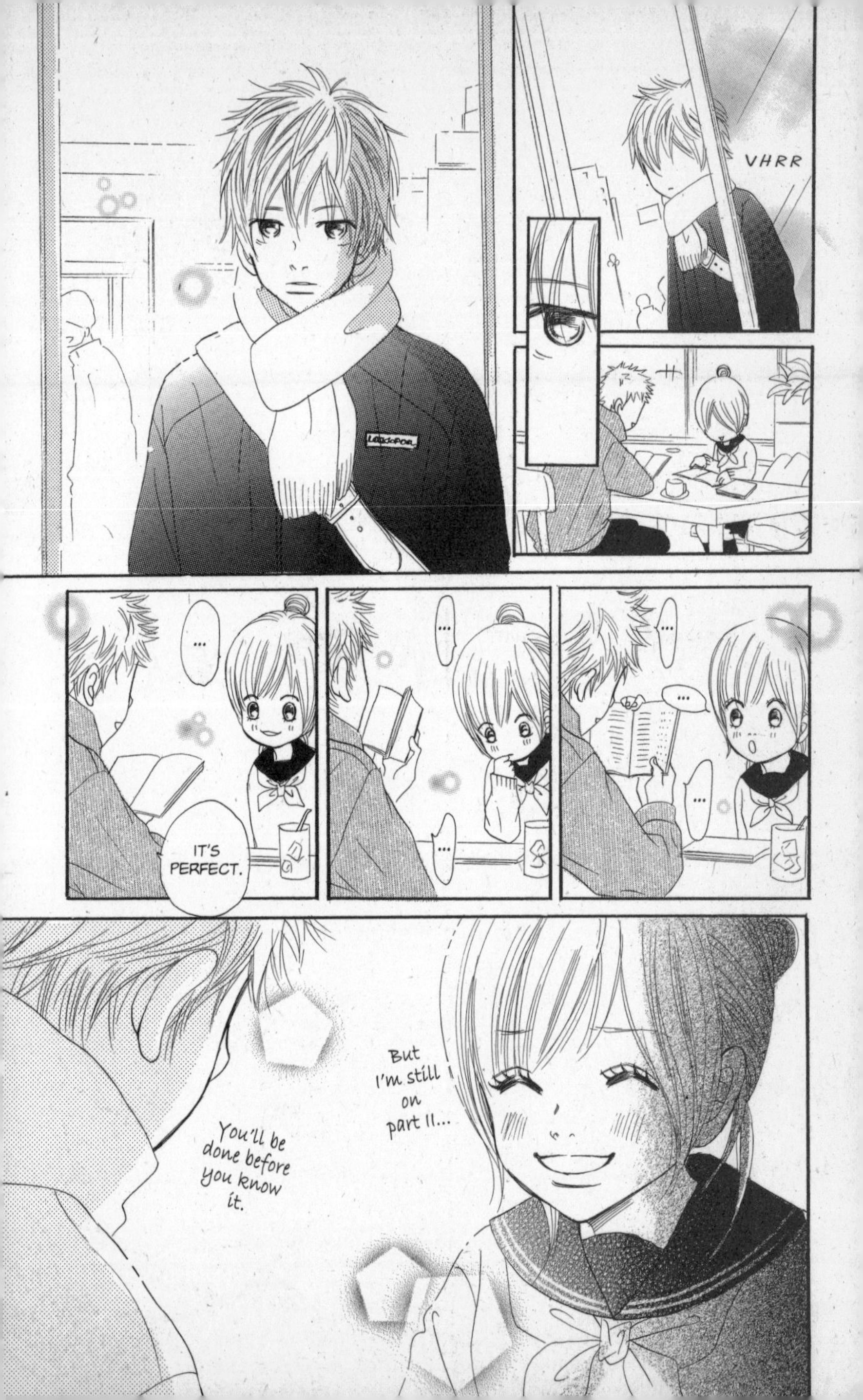

VHRR
...
...
...
...
...
...
IT'S PERFECT.
But I'm still on part 11...
You'll be done before you know it.

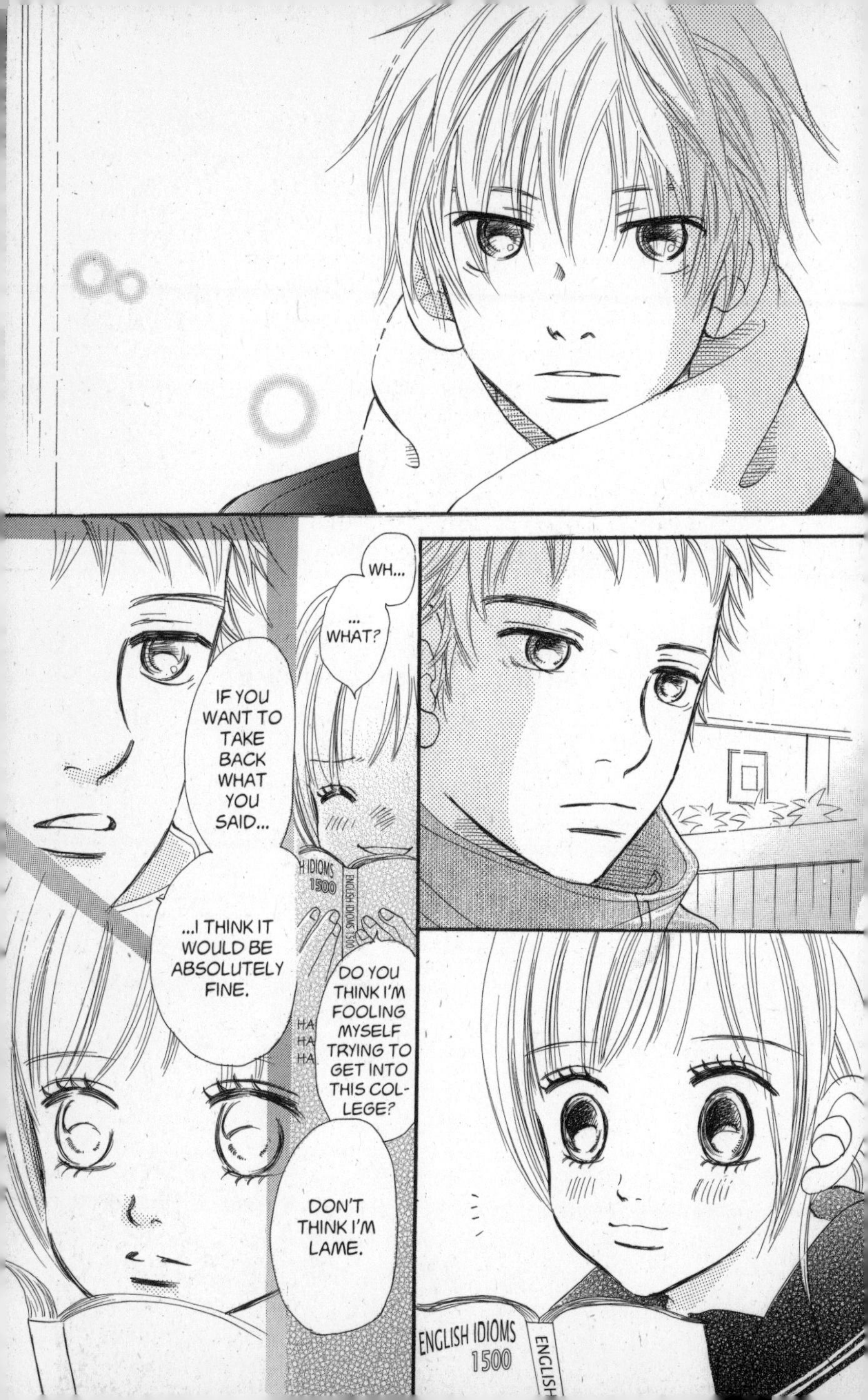
WH...
...WHAT?
ENGLISH IDIOMS 1500
H IDIOMS 1500
HA HA HA
DO YOU THINK I'M FOOLING MYSELF TRYING TO GET INTO THIS COL-LEGE?
DON'T THINK I'M LAME.
IF YOU WANT TO TAKE BACK WHAT YOU SAID...
...I THINK IT WOULD BE ABSOLUTELY FINE.

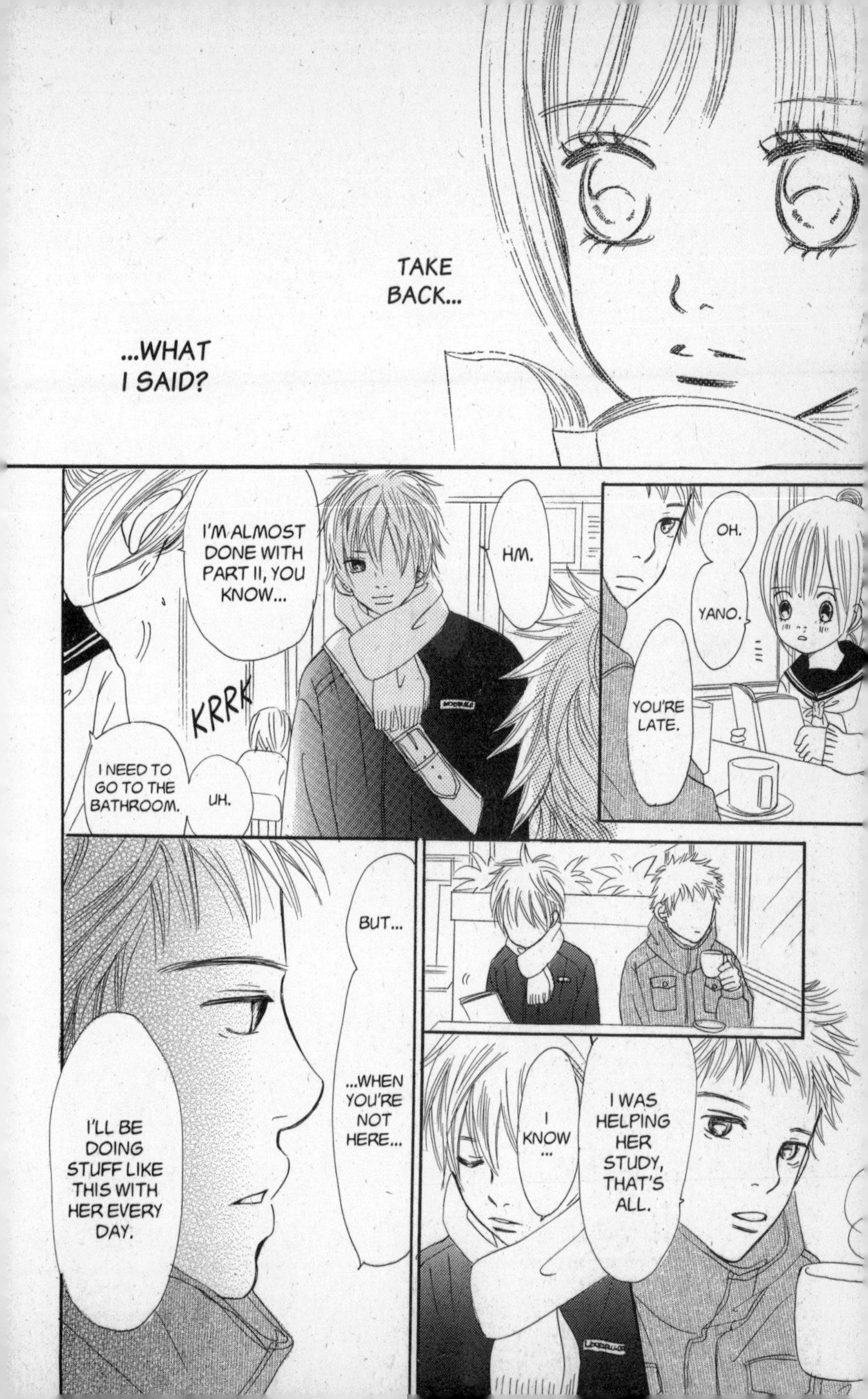

TAKE BACK...
...WHAT I SAID?
OH.
YANO.
YOU'RE LATE.
HM.
I'M ALMOST DONE WITH PART II, YOU KNOW...
KRRK
UH.
I NEED TO GO TO THE BATHROOM.
I WAS HELPING HER STUDY, THAT'S ALL.
I KNOW...
BUT...
...WHEN YOU'RE NOT HERE...
I'LL BE DOING STUFF LIKE THIS WITH HER EVERY DAY.

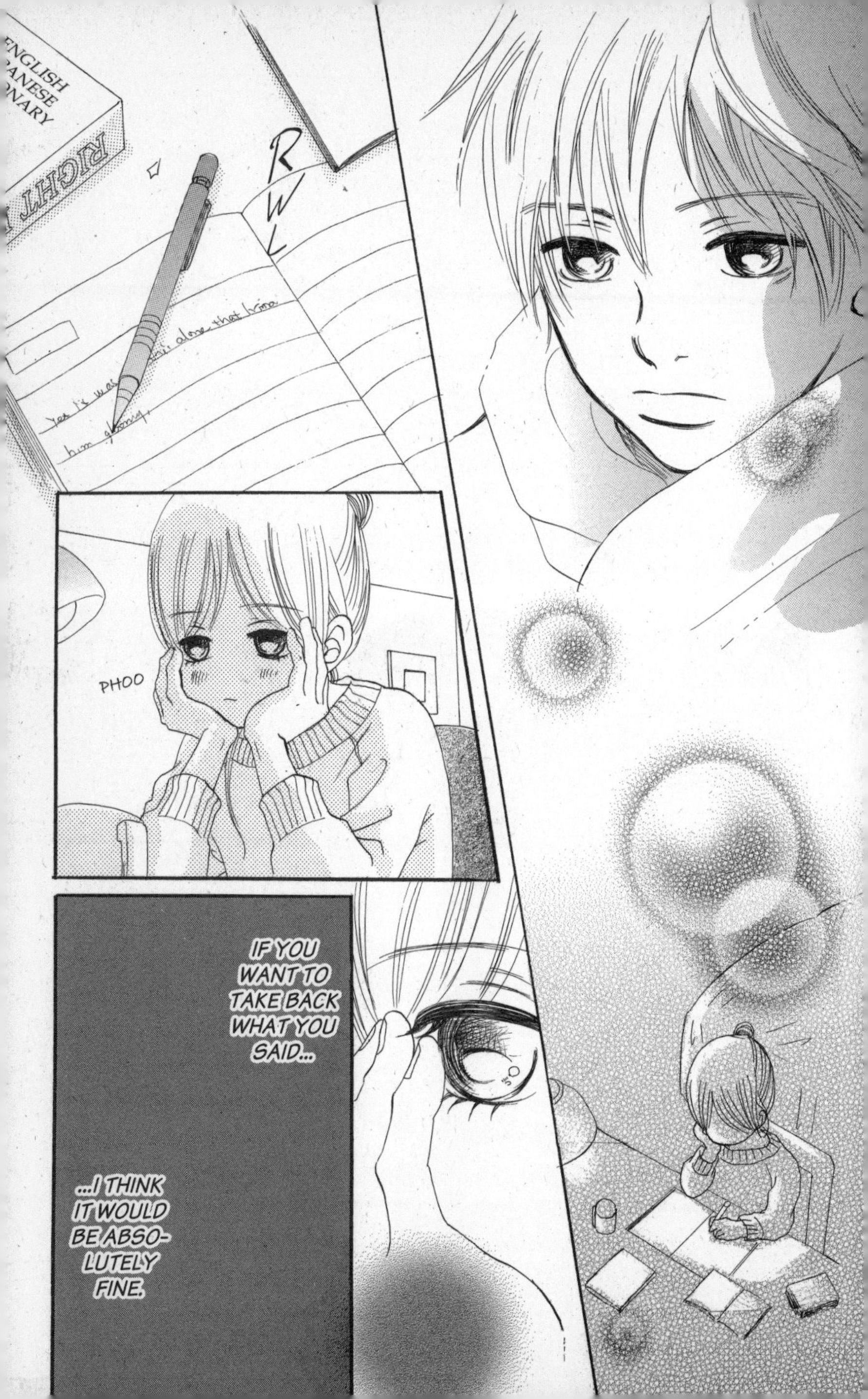
RIGHT
RWL
PHOO
IF YOU WANT TO TAKE BACK WHAT YOU SAID...
...I THINK IT WOULD BE ABSO-LUTELY FINE.

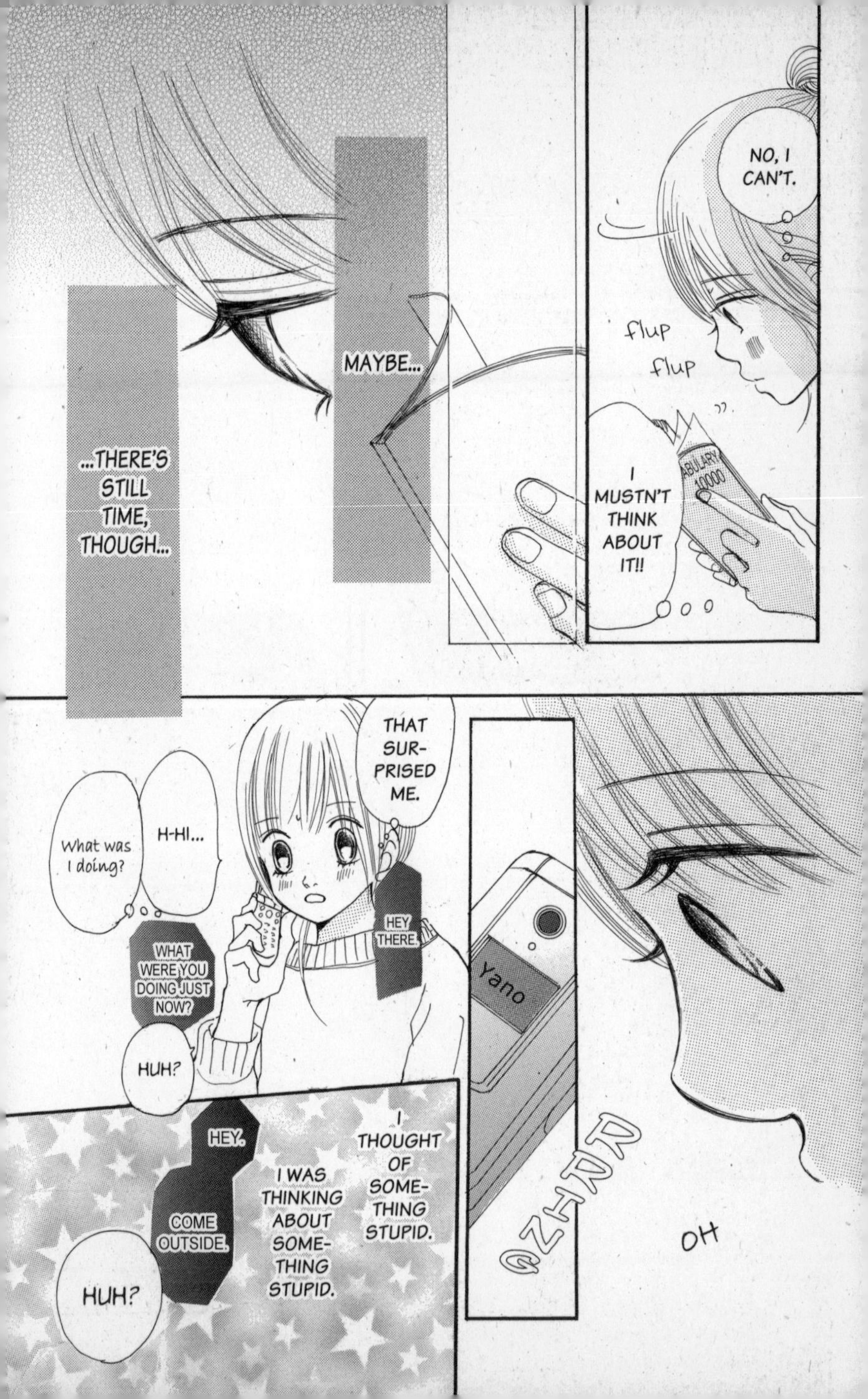
NO, I CAN'T.
flup
flup
I MUSTN'T THINK ABOUT IT!!
ABULARY 10000
MAYBE...
...THERE'S STILL TIME, THOUGH...
OH
Yano
GZHRR
THAT SURPRISED ME.
H-HI...
What was I doing?
HEY THERE.
WHAT WERE YOU DOING JUST NOW?
HUH?
I THOUGHT OF SOMETHING STUPID.
I WAS THINKING ABOUT SOMETHING STUPID.
HEY.
COME OUTSIDE.
HUH?

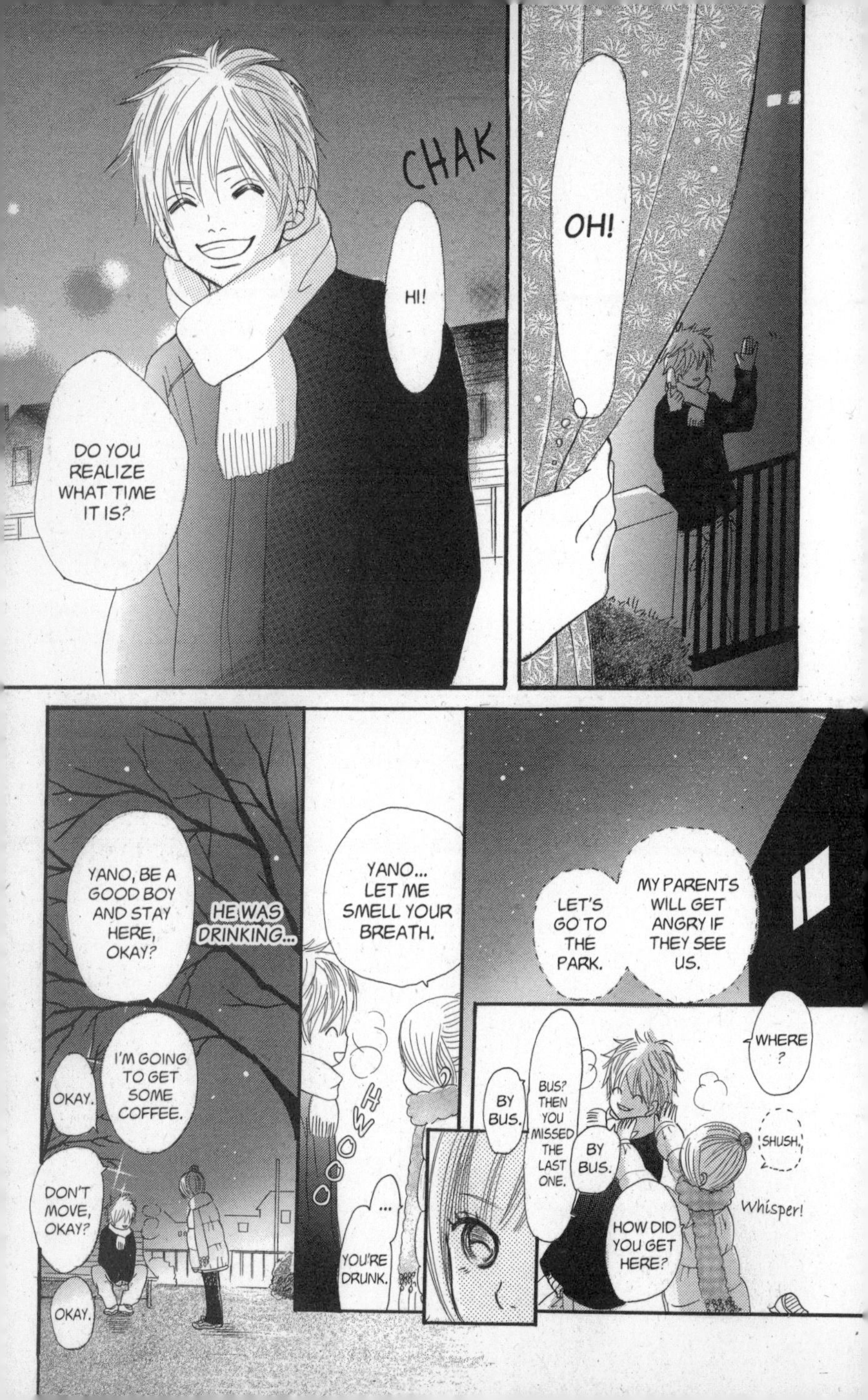
OH!
CHAK
HI!
DO YOU REALIZE WHAT TIME IT IS?
MY PARENTS WILL GET ANGRY IF THEY SEE US.
LET'S GO TO THE PARK.
WHERE?
SHUSH.
Whisper!
HOW DID YOU GET HERE?
BY BUS.
BUS? THEN YOU MISSED THE LAST ONE.
BY BUS.
YANO... LET ME SMELL YOUR BREATH.
...
YOU'RE DRUNK.
HE WAS DRINKING...
YANO, BE A GOOD BOY AND STAY HERE, OKAY?
I'M GOING TO GET SOME COFFEE.
OKAY.
DON'T MOVE, OKAY?
OKAY.

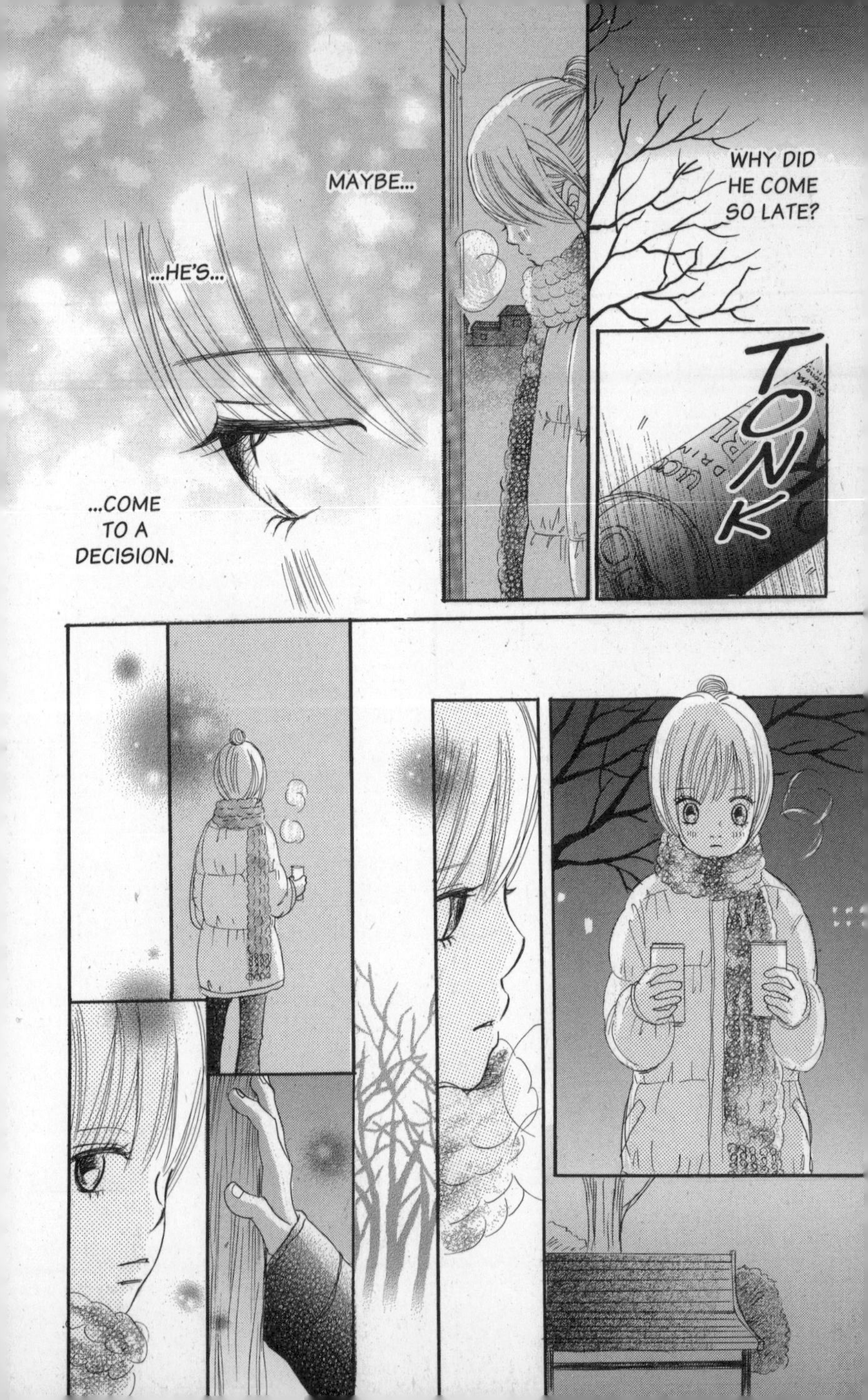
WHY DID HE COME SO LATE?
TONK
MAYBE...
...HE'S...
...COME TO A DECISION.

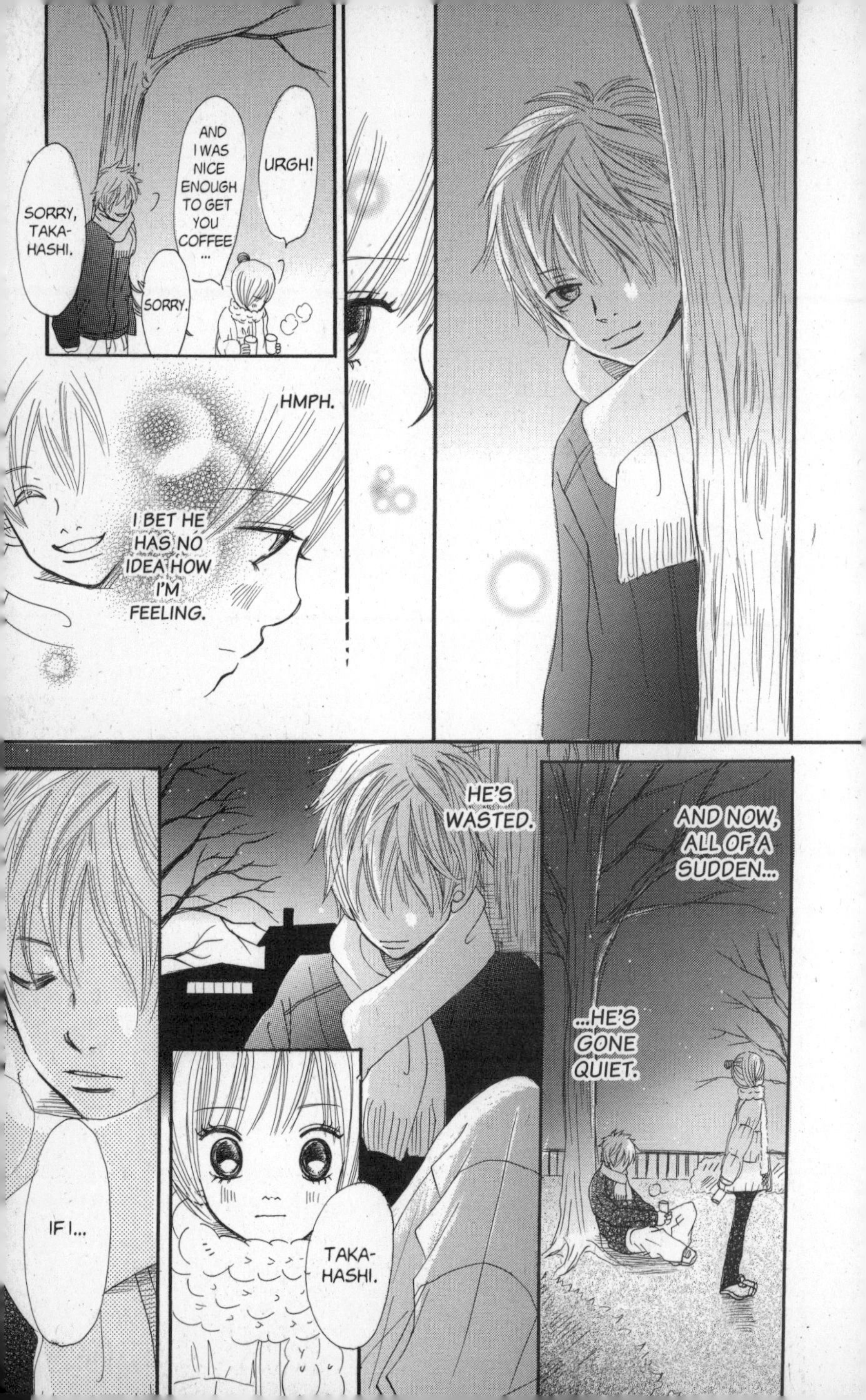
URGH!
AND I WAS NICE ENOUGH TO GET YOU COFFEE...
SORRY, TAKA-HASHI.
SORRY.
HMPH.
I BET HE HAS NO IDEA HOW I'M FEELING.
AND NOW, ALL OF A SUDDEN...
...HE'S GONE QUIET.
HE'S WASTED.
TAKA-HASHI.
IF I...

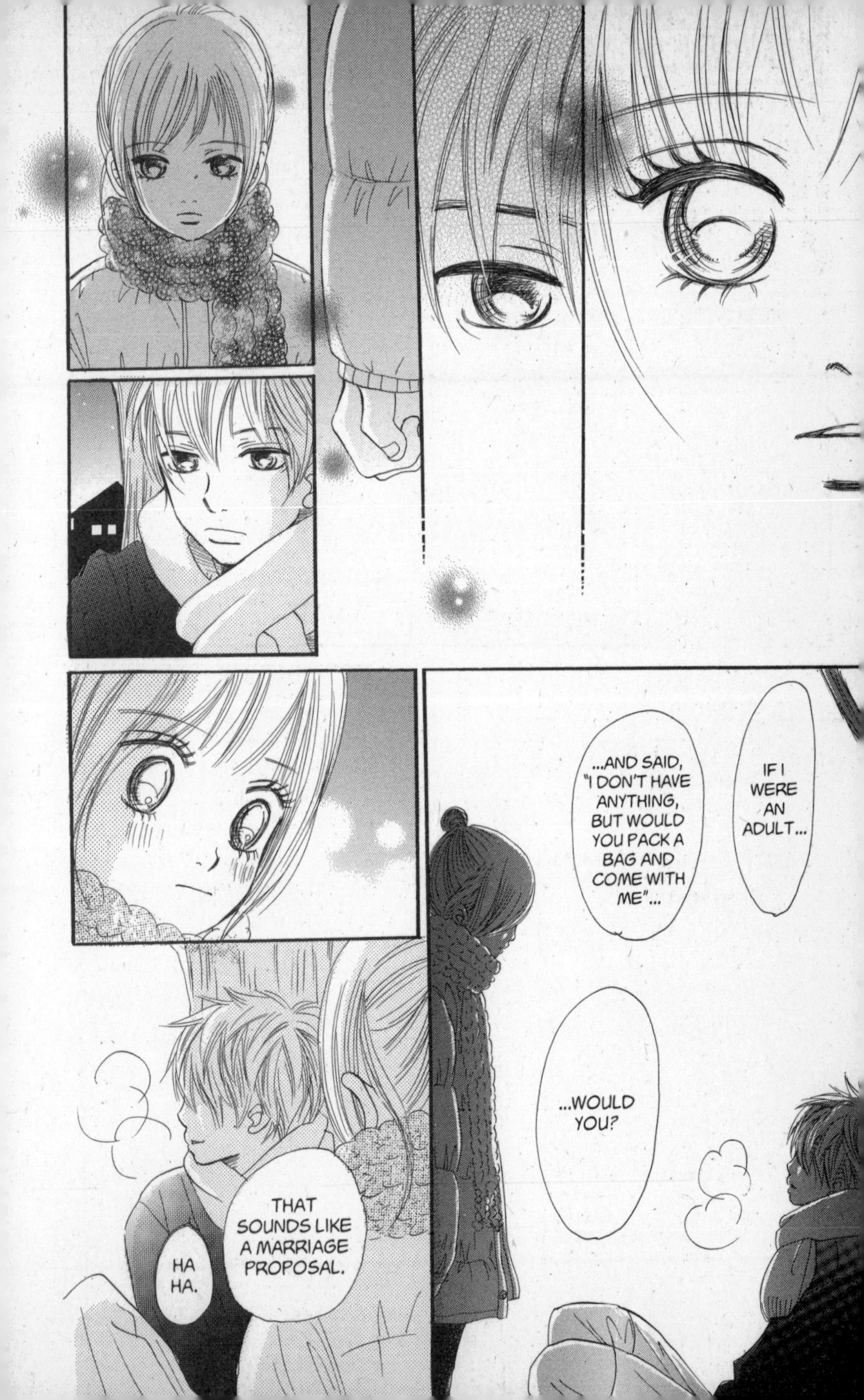
IF I WERE AN ADULT...
...AND SAID, "I DON'T HAVE ANYTHING, BUT WOULD YOU PACK A BAG AND COME WITH ME"...
...WOULD YOU?
THAT SOUNDS LIKE A MARRIAGE PROPOSAL.
HA HA.

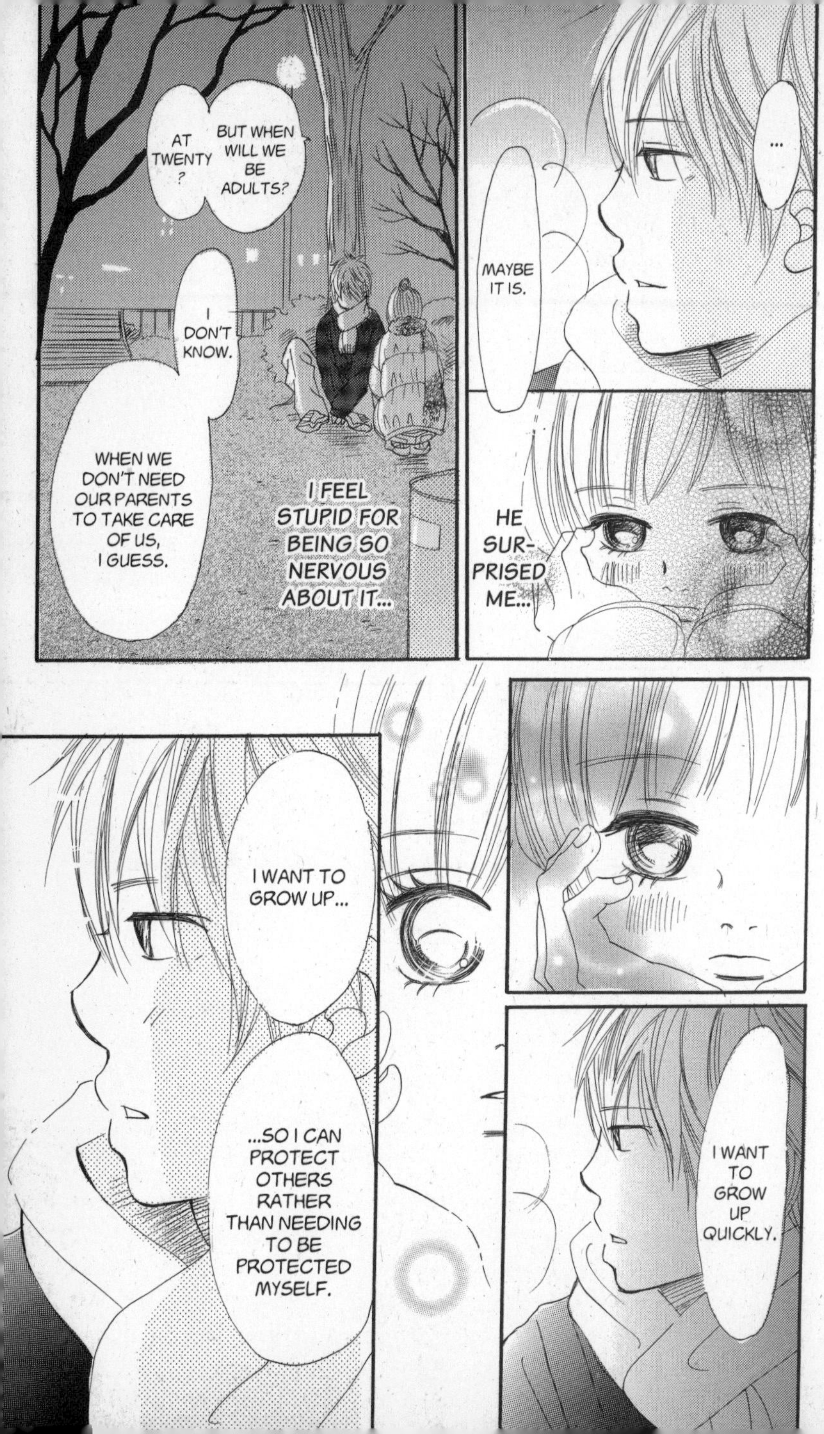
...
MAYBE IT IS.
HE SURPRISED ME...
BUT WHEN WILL WE BE ADULTS?
AT TWENTY?
I DON'T KNOW.
WHEN WE DON'T NEED OUR PARENTS TO TAKE CARE OF US, I GUESS.
I FEEL STUPID FOR BEING SO NERVOUS ABOUT IT...
I WANT TO GROW UP QUICKLY.
I WANT TO GROW UP...
...SO I CAN PROTECT OTHERS RATHER THAN NEEDING TO BE PROTECTED MYSELF.

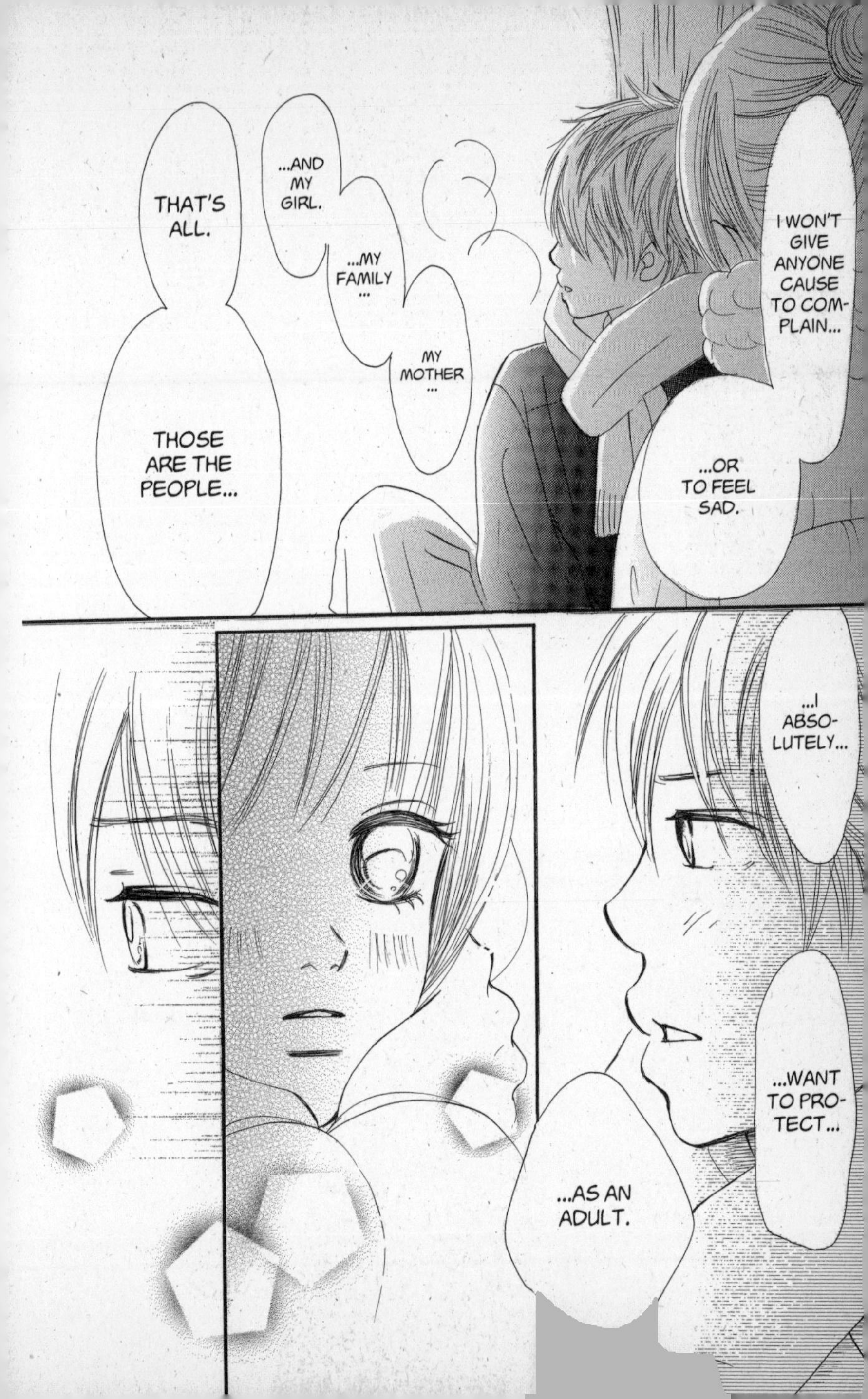
I WON'T GIVE ANYONE CAUSE TO COM-PLAIN...
...OR TO FEEL SAD.
MY MOTHER...
...MY FAMILY...
...AND MY GIRL.
THAT'S ALL.
THOSE ARE THE PEOPLE...
...I ABSO-LUTELY...
...WANT TO PRO-TECT...
...AS AN ADULT.

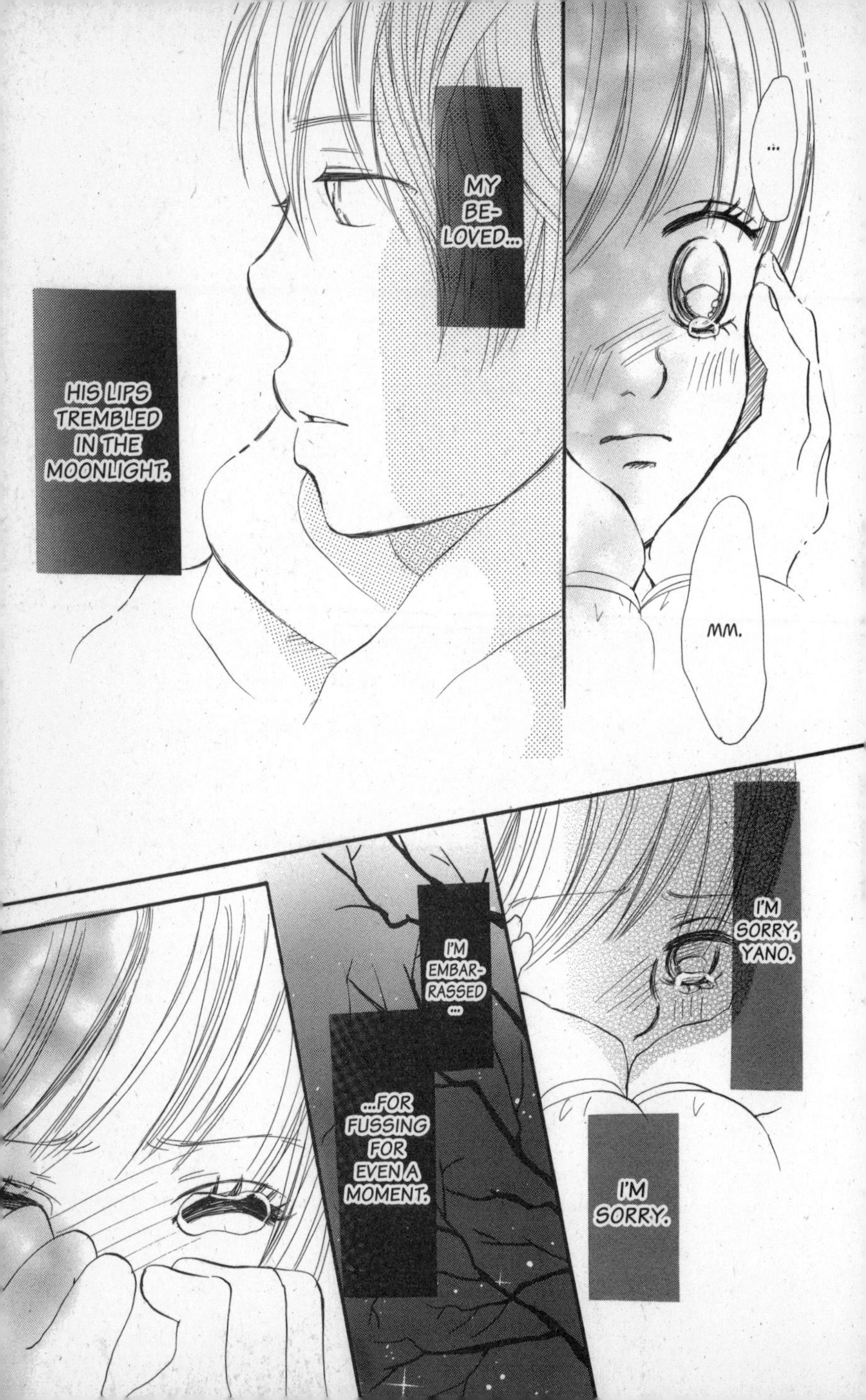
...
MM.
MY BE-LOVED...
HIS LIPS TREMBLED IN THE MOONLIGHT.
I'M SORRY, YANO.
I'M SORRY.
I'M EMBAR-RASSED...
...FOR FUSSING FOR EVEN A MOMENT.

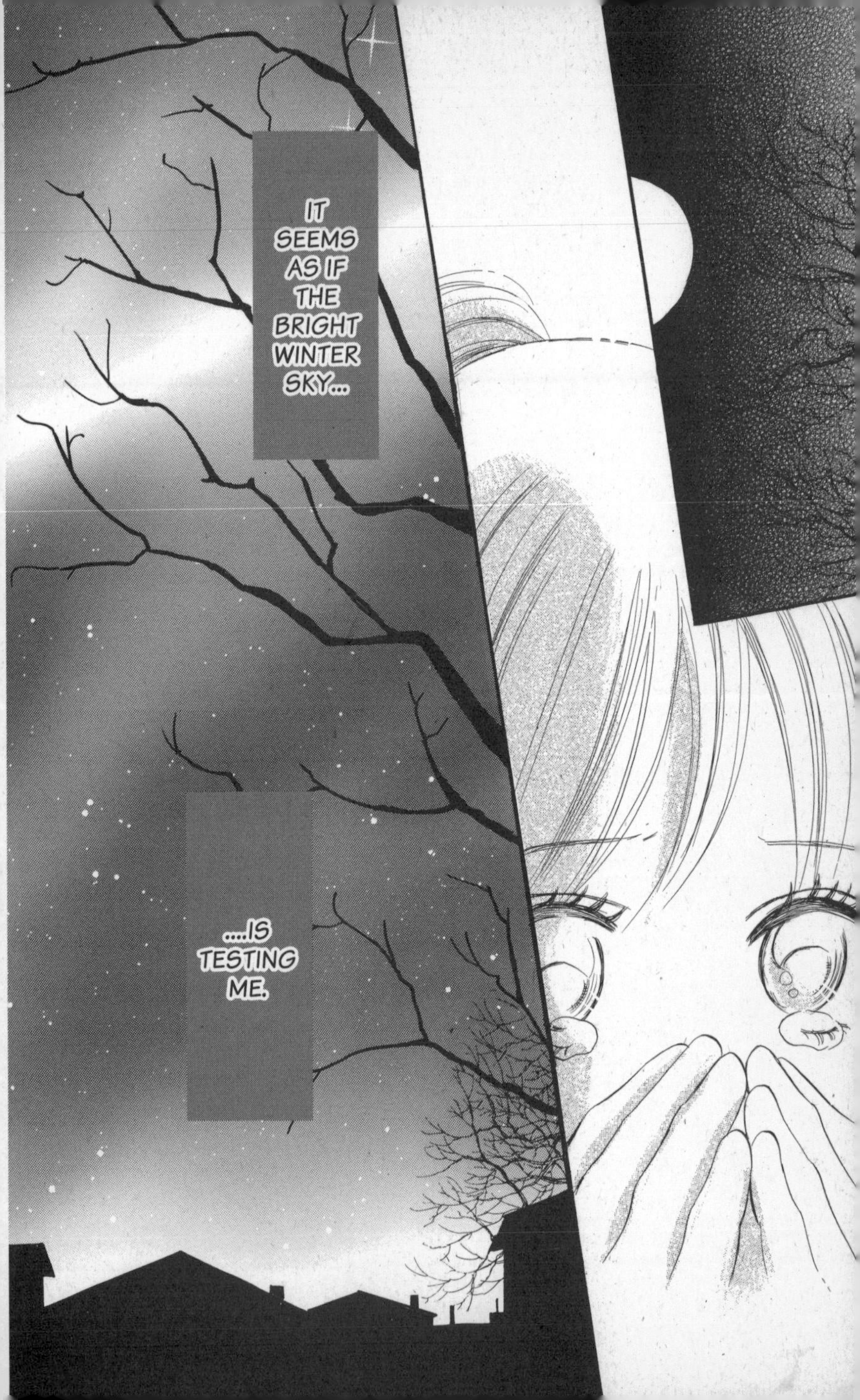
IT SEEMS AS IF THE BRIGHT WINTER SKY...
....IS TESTING ME.

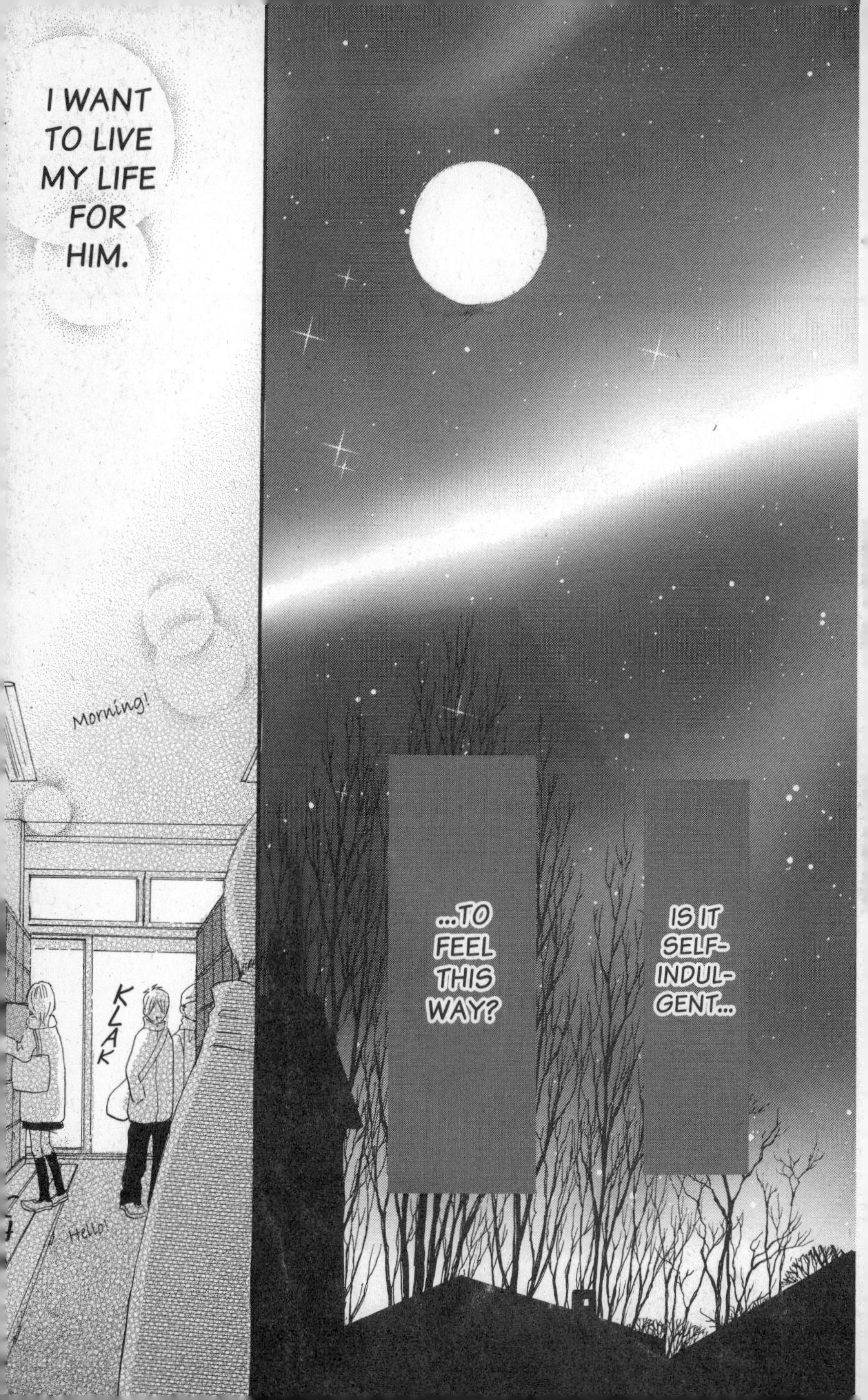
IS IT SELF-INDULGENT...
...TO FEEL THIS WAY?
I WANT TO LIVE MY LIFE FOR HIM.
Morning!
KLAK
Hello!

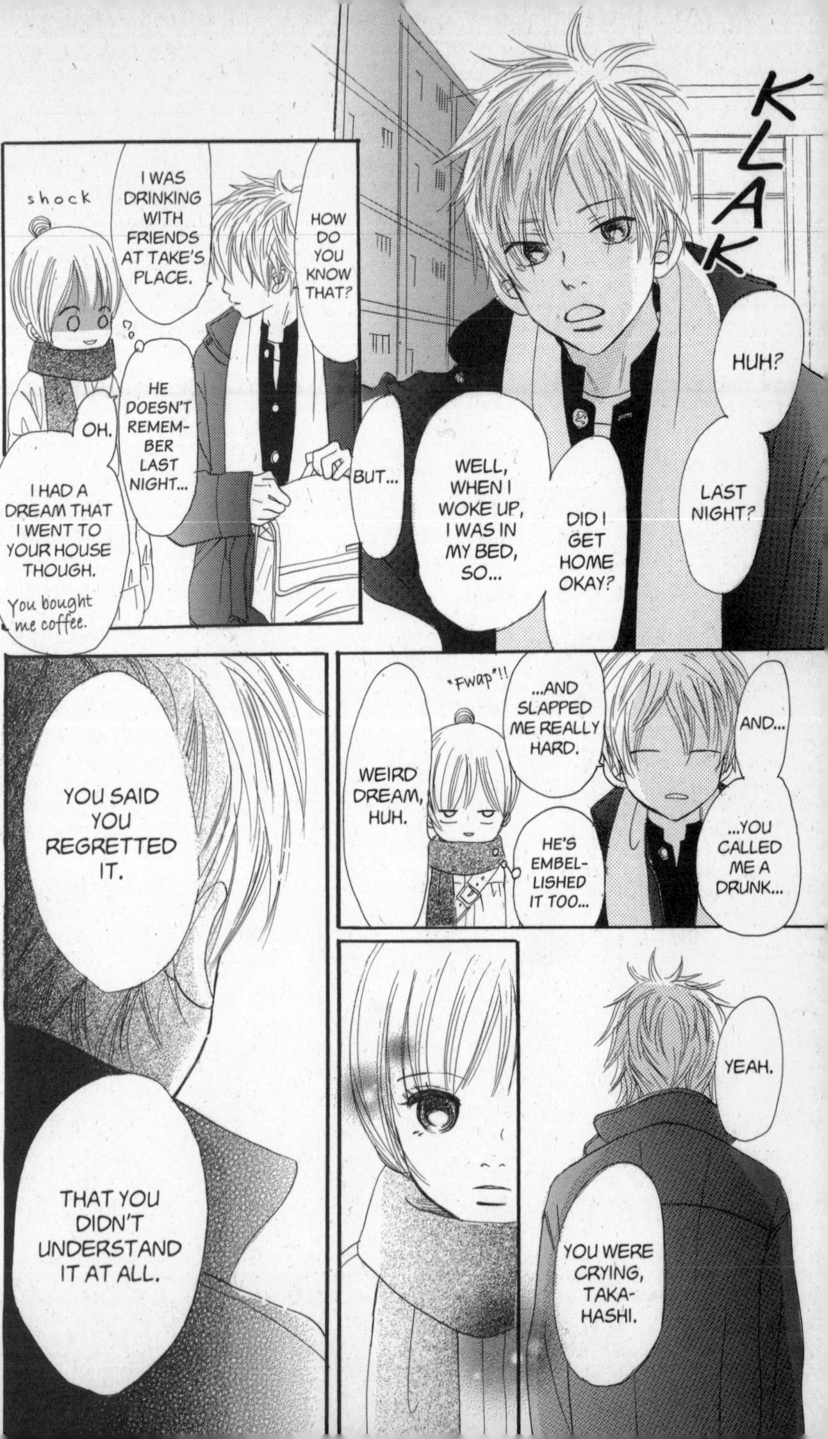
KLAK
HUH?
LAST NIGHT?
DID I GET HOME OKAY?
WELL, WHEN I WOKE UP, I WAS IN MY BED, SO...
BUT...
HOW DO YOU KNOW THAT?
I WAS DRINKING WITH FRIENDS AT TAKE'S PLACE.
shock
HE DOESN'T REMEMBER LAST NIGHT...
OH.
I HAD A DREAM THAT I WENT TO YOUR HOUSE THOUGH.
You bought me coffee.
AND...
...YOU CALLED ME A DRUNK...
...AND SLAPPED ME REALLY HARD.
"Fwap"!!
HE'S EMBELLISHED IT TOO...
WEIRD DREAM, HUH.
YEAH.
YOU WERE CRYING, TAKAHASHI.
YOU SAID YOU REGRETTED IT.
THAT YOU DIDN'T UNDERSTAND IT AT ALL.

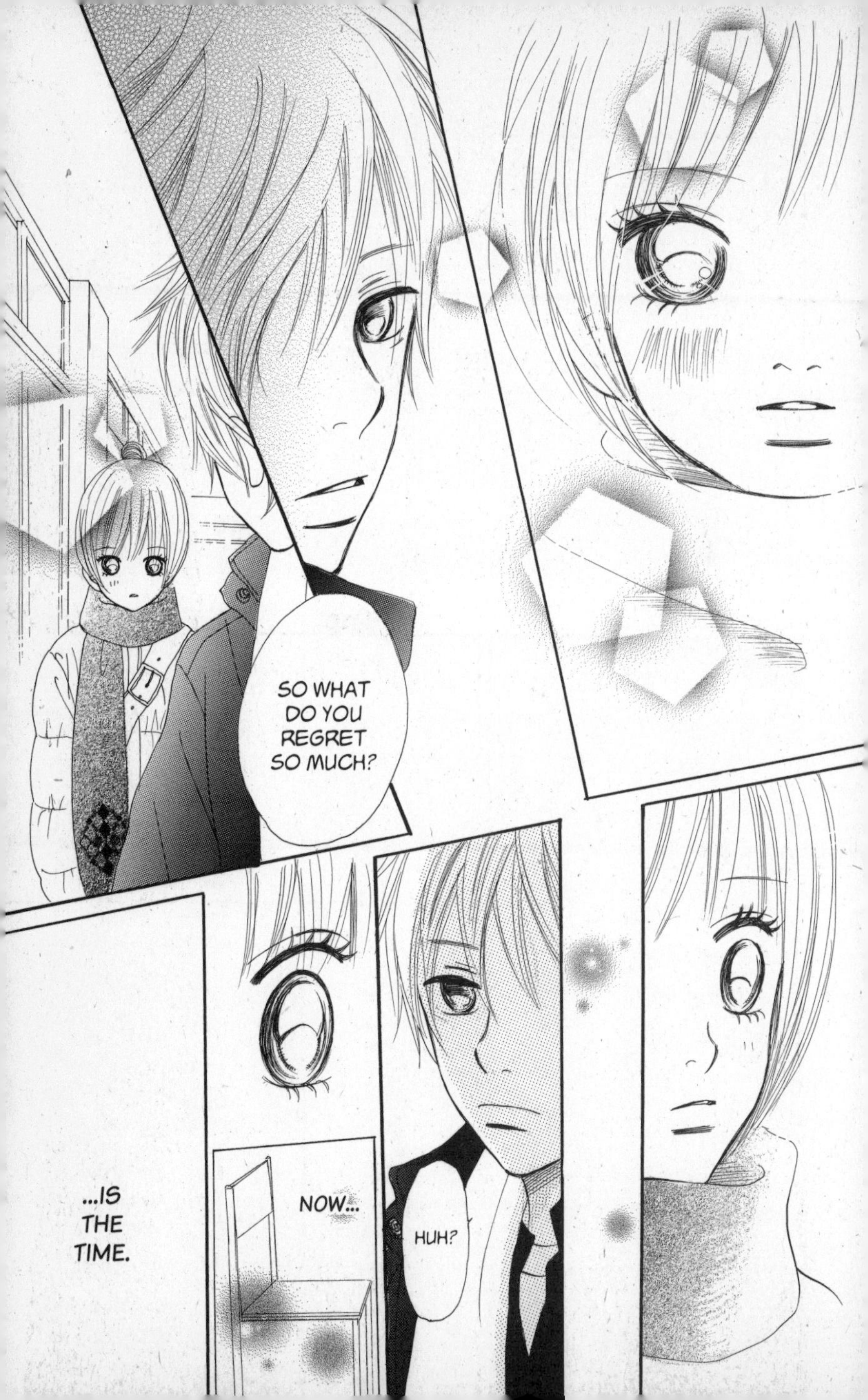
SO WHAT DO YOU REGRET SO MUCH?
HUH?
NOW...
...IS THE TIME.

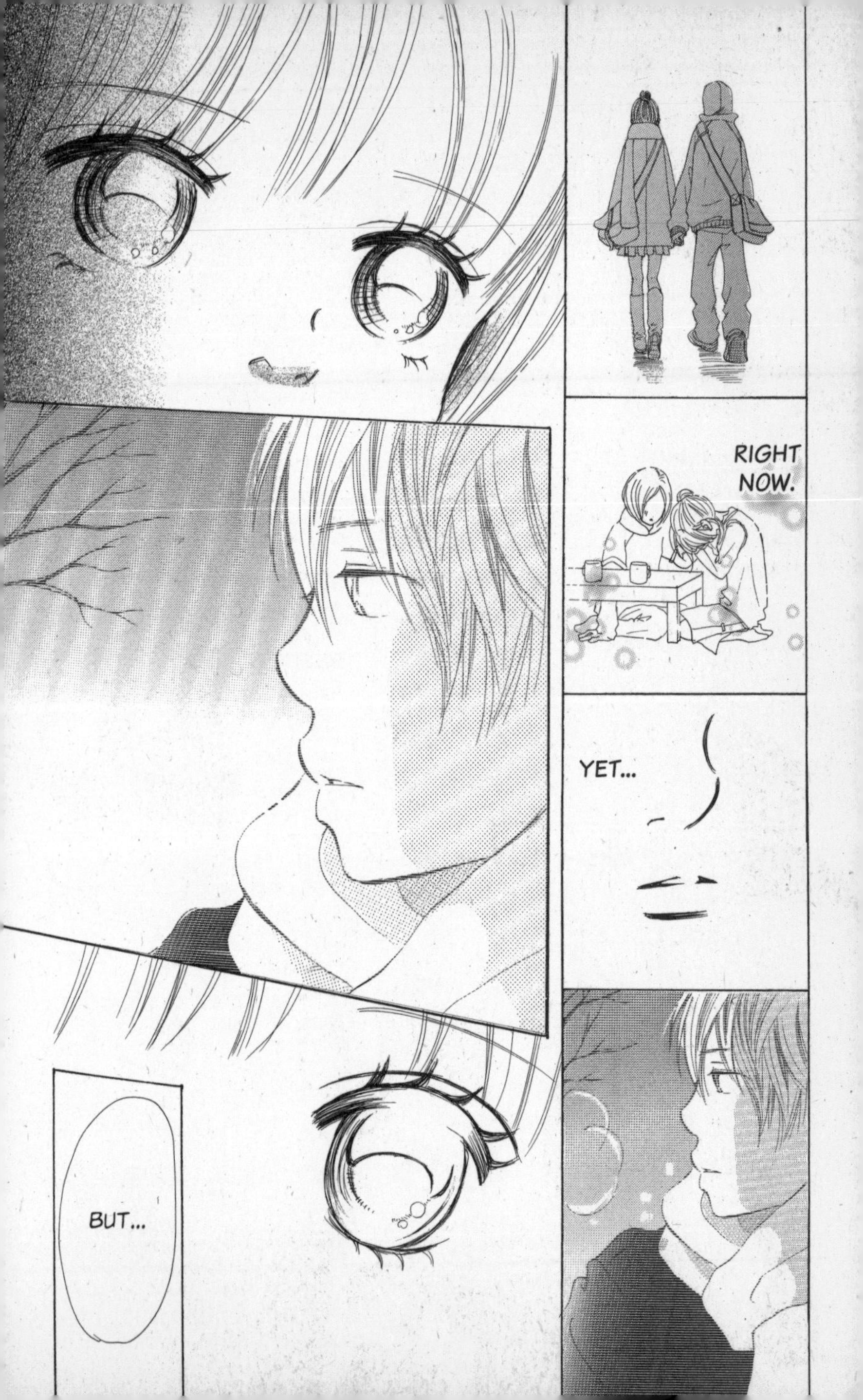
RIGHT NOW.
YET...
BUT...

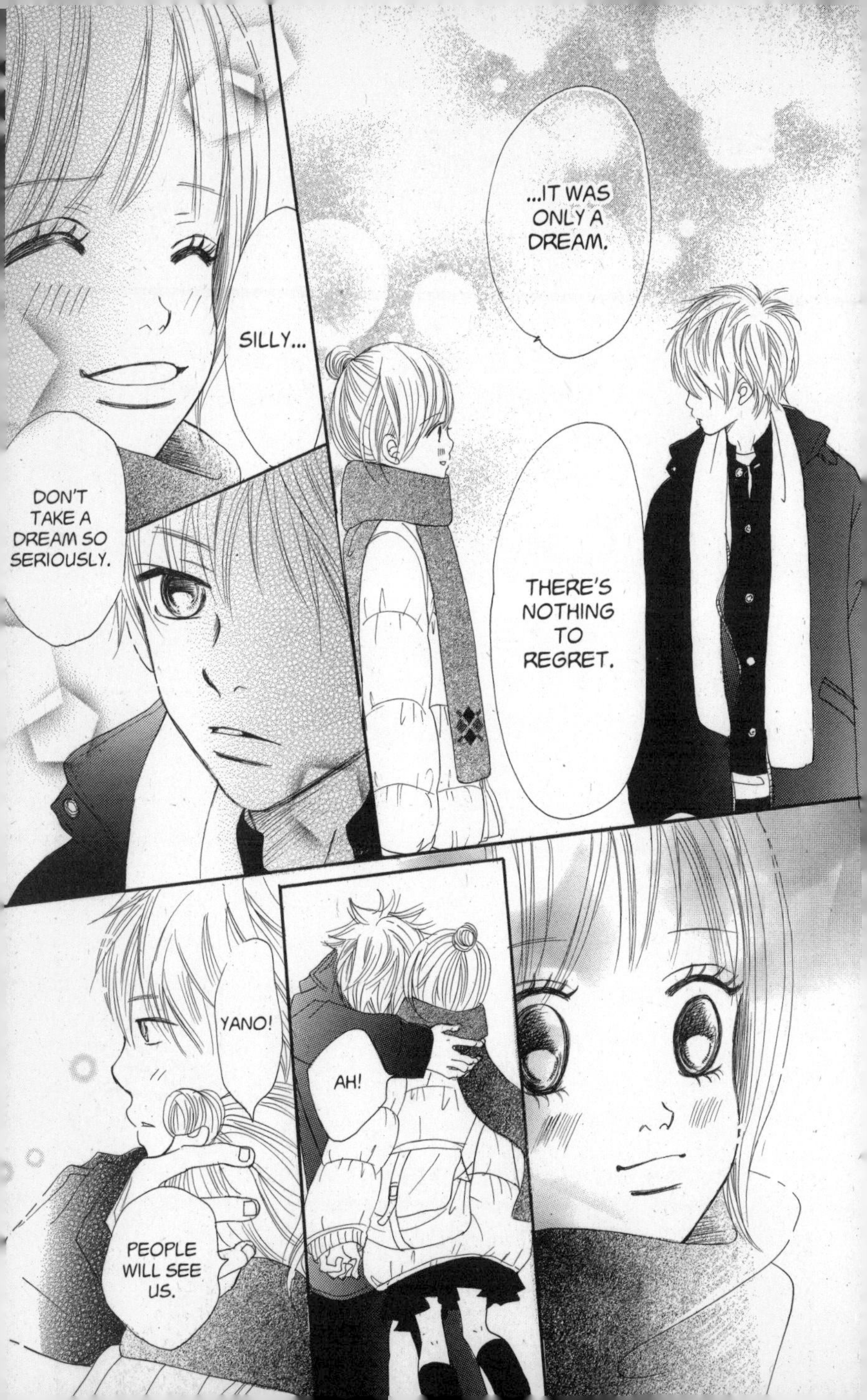
...IT WAS ONLY A DREAM.
THERE'S NOTHING TO REGRET.
SILLY...
DON'T TAKE A DREAM SO SERIOUSLY.
AH!
YANO!
PEOPLE WILL SEE US.

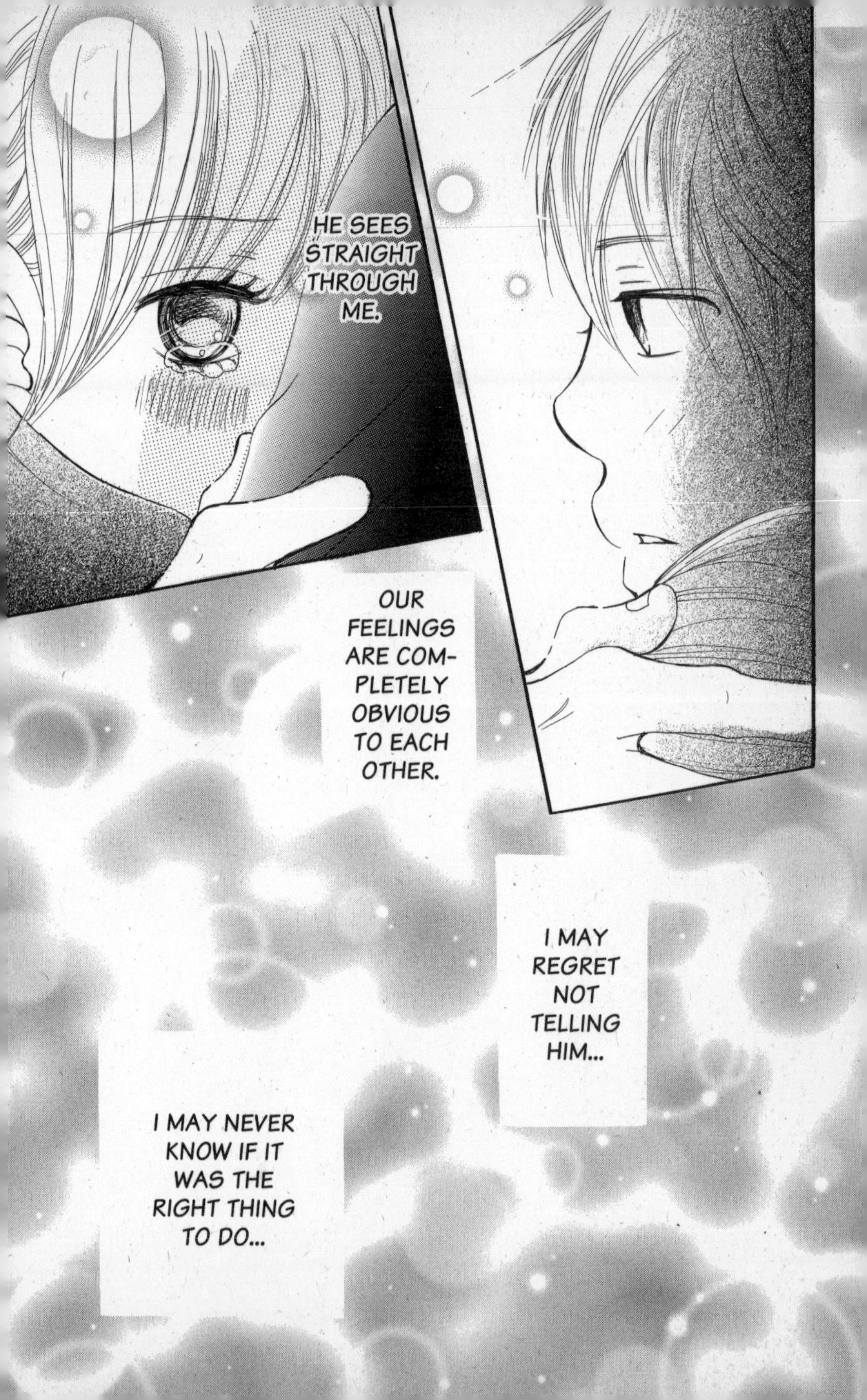
HE SEES STRAIGHT THROUGH ME.
OUR FEELINGS ARE COM-PLETELY OBVIOUS TO EACH OTHER.
I MAY REGRET NOT TELLING HIM...
I MAY NEVER KNOW IF IT WAS THE RIGHT THING TO DO...

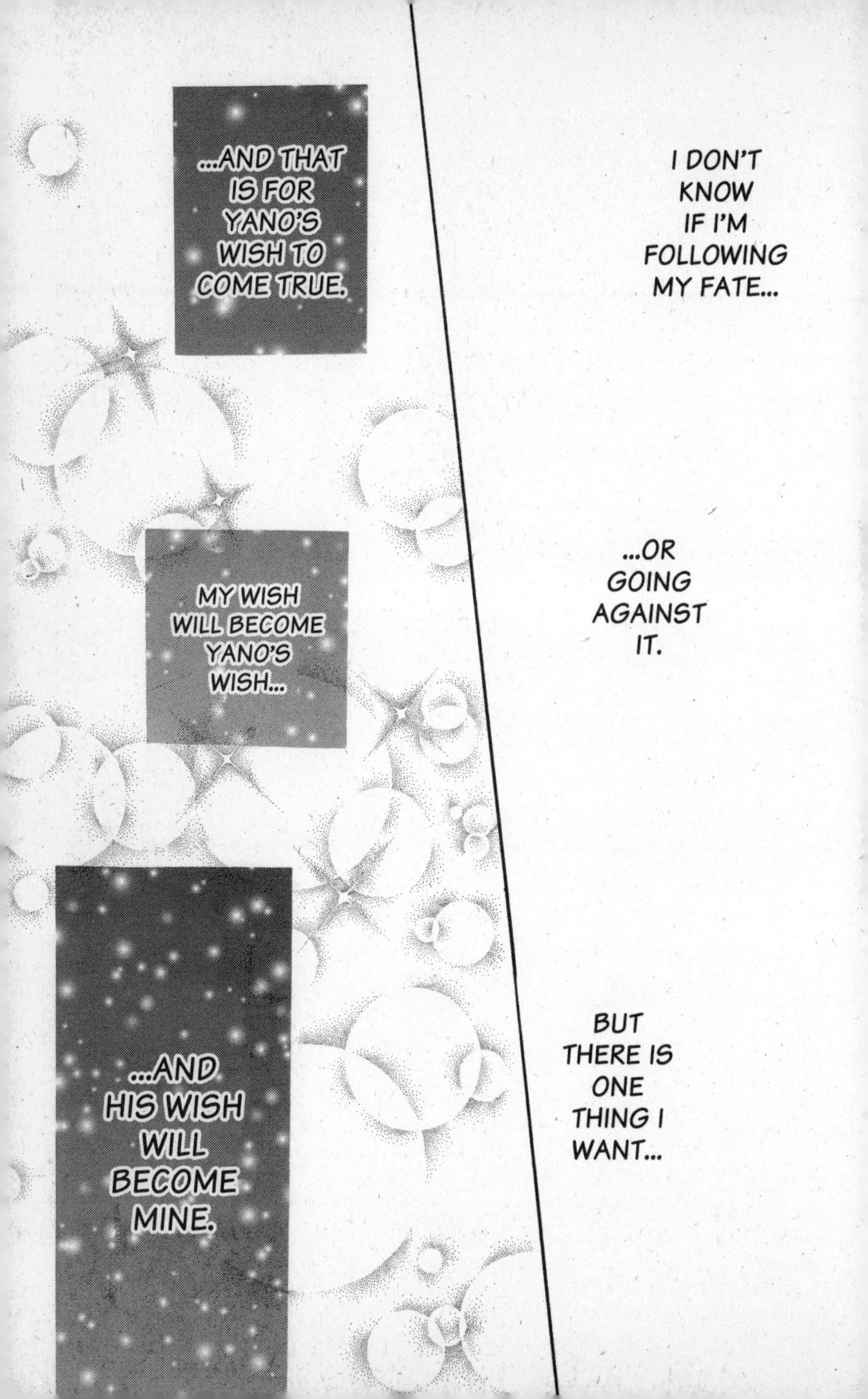
I DON'T KNOW IF I'M FOLLOWING MY FATE...
...OR GOING AGAINST IT.
BUT THERE IS ONE THING I WANT...
...AND THAT IS FOR YANO'S WISH TO COME TRUE.
MY WISH WILL BECOME YANO'S WISH...
...AND HIS WISH WILL BECOME MINE.

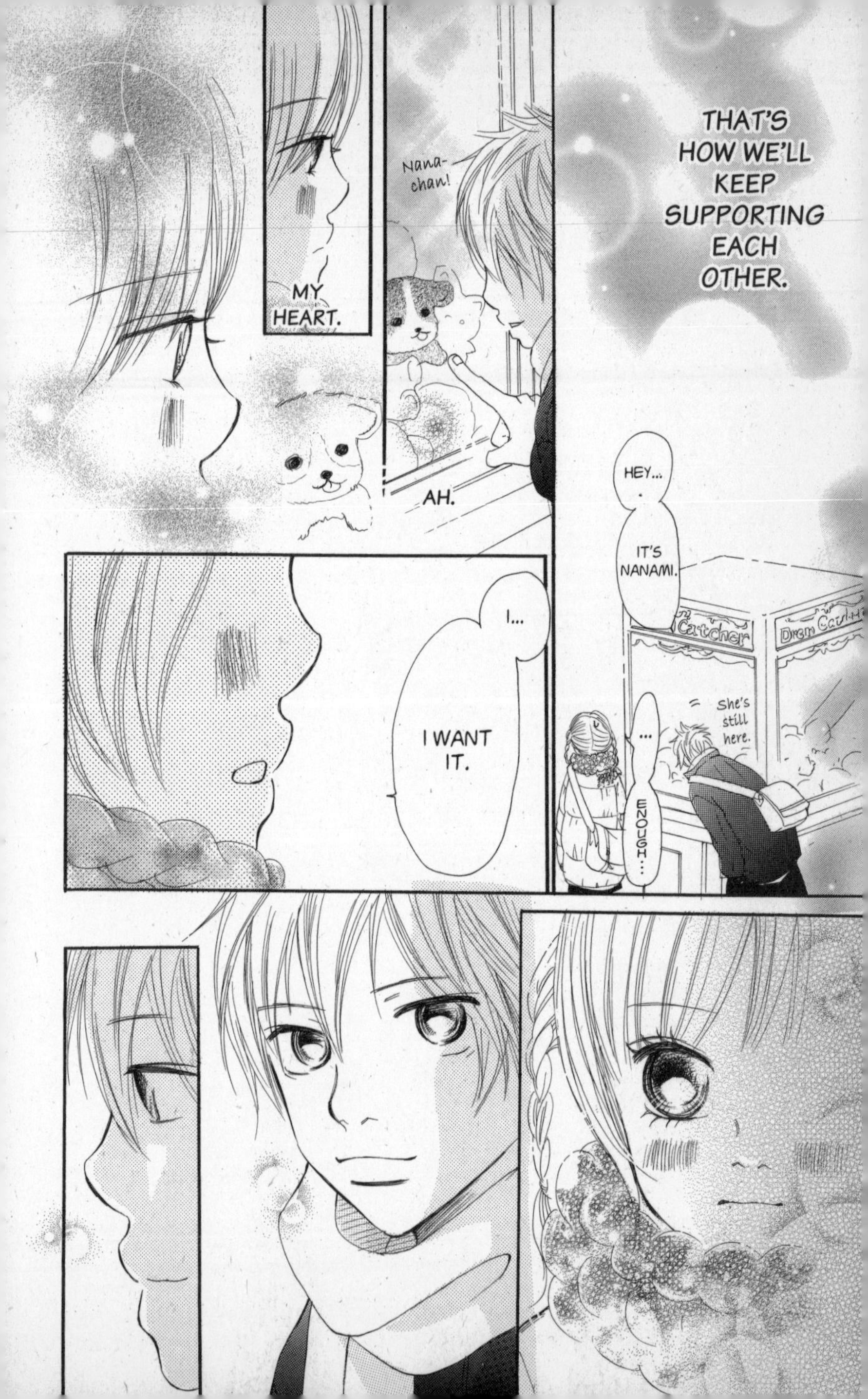
THAT'S HOW WE'LL KEEP SUPPORTING EACH OTHER.
Nana-chan!
AH.
MY HEART.
HEY...
IT'S NANAMI.
She's still here.
...
ENOUGH...
I...
I WANT IT.

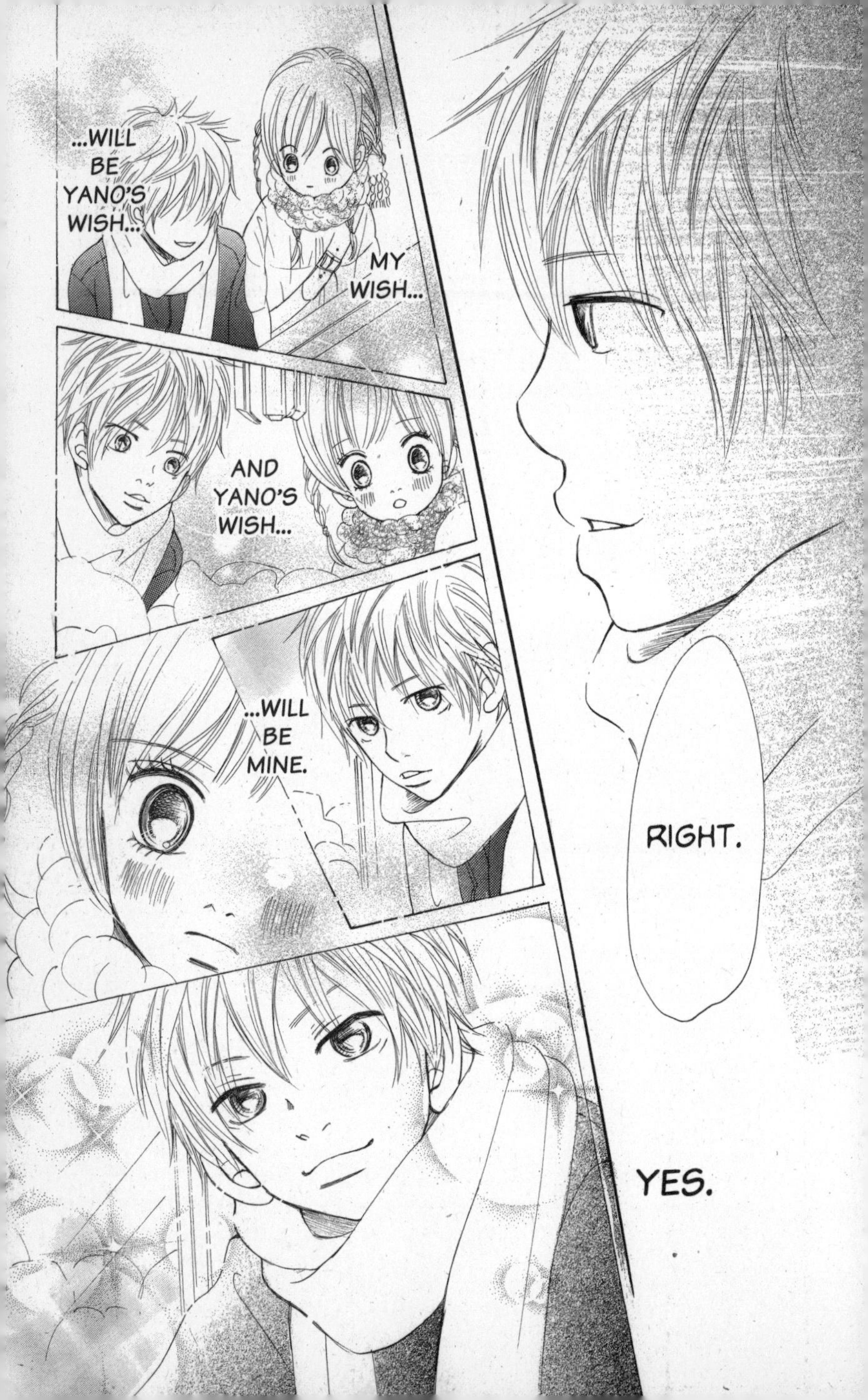
RIGHT.
YES.
MY WISH...
...WILL BE YANO'S WISH...
AND YANO'S WISH...
...WILL BE MINE.

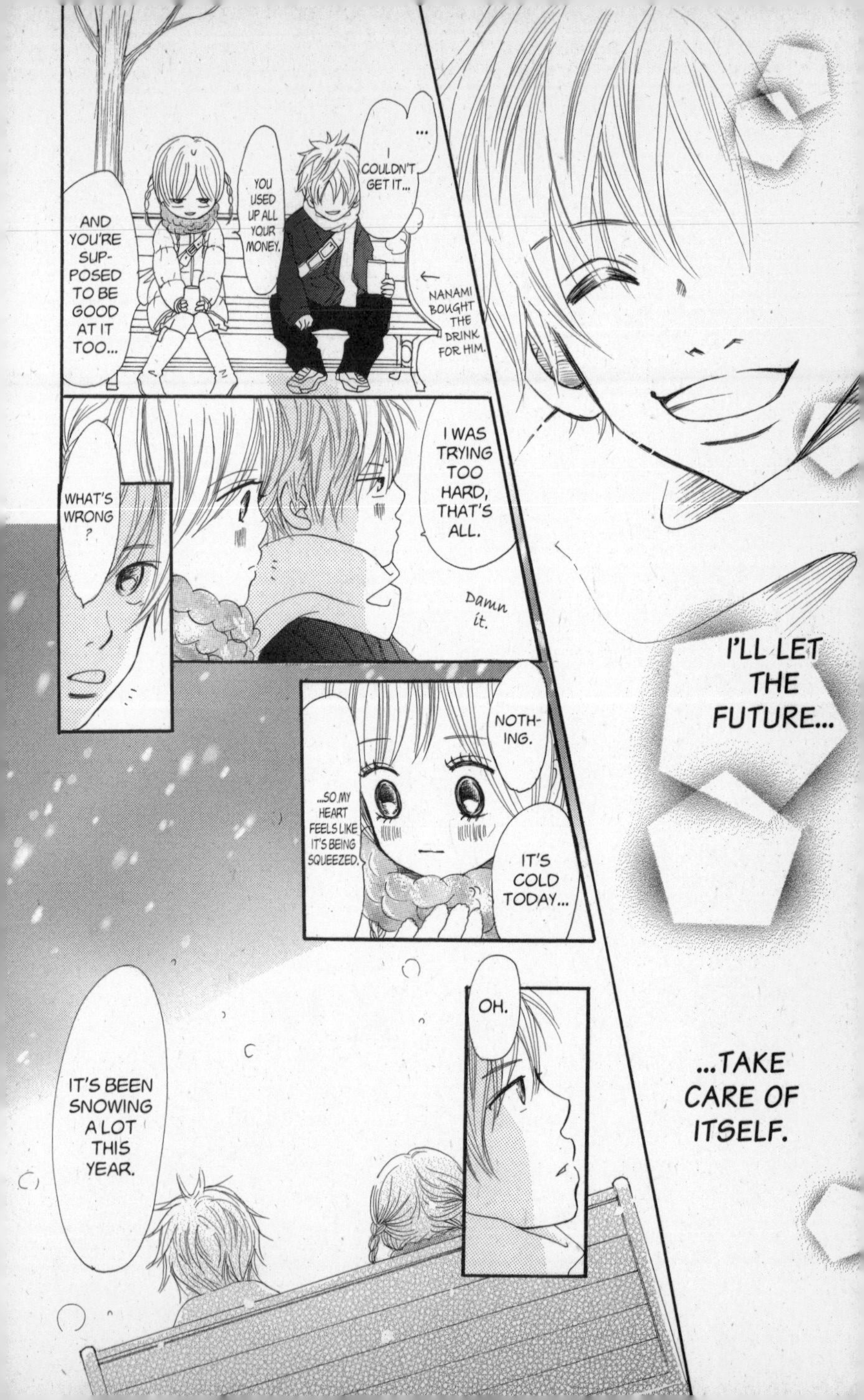
I'LL LET THE FUTURE...
...TAKE CARE OF ITSELF.
...
I COULDN'T GET IT...
YOU USED UP ALL YOUR MONEY.
AND YOU'RE SUP-POSED TO BE GOOD AT IT TOO...
← NANAMI BOUGHT THE DRINK FOR HIM.
I WAS TRYING TOO HARD, THAT'S ALL.
Damn it.
WHAT'S WRONG?
NOTH-ING.
IT'S COLD TODAY...
...SO MY HEART FEELS LIKE IT'S BEING SQUEEZED.
OH.
IT'S BEEN SNOWING A LOT THIS YEAR.

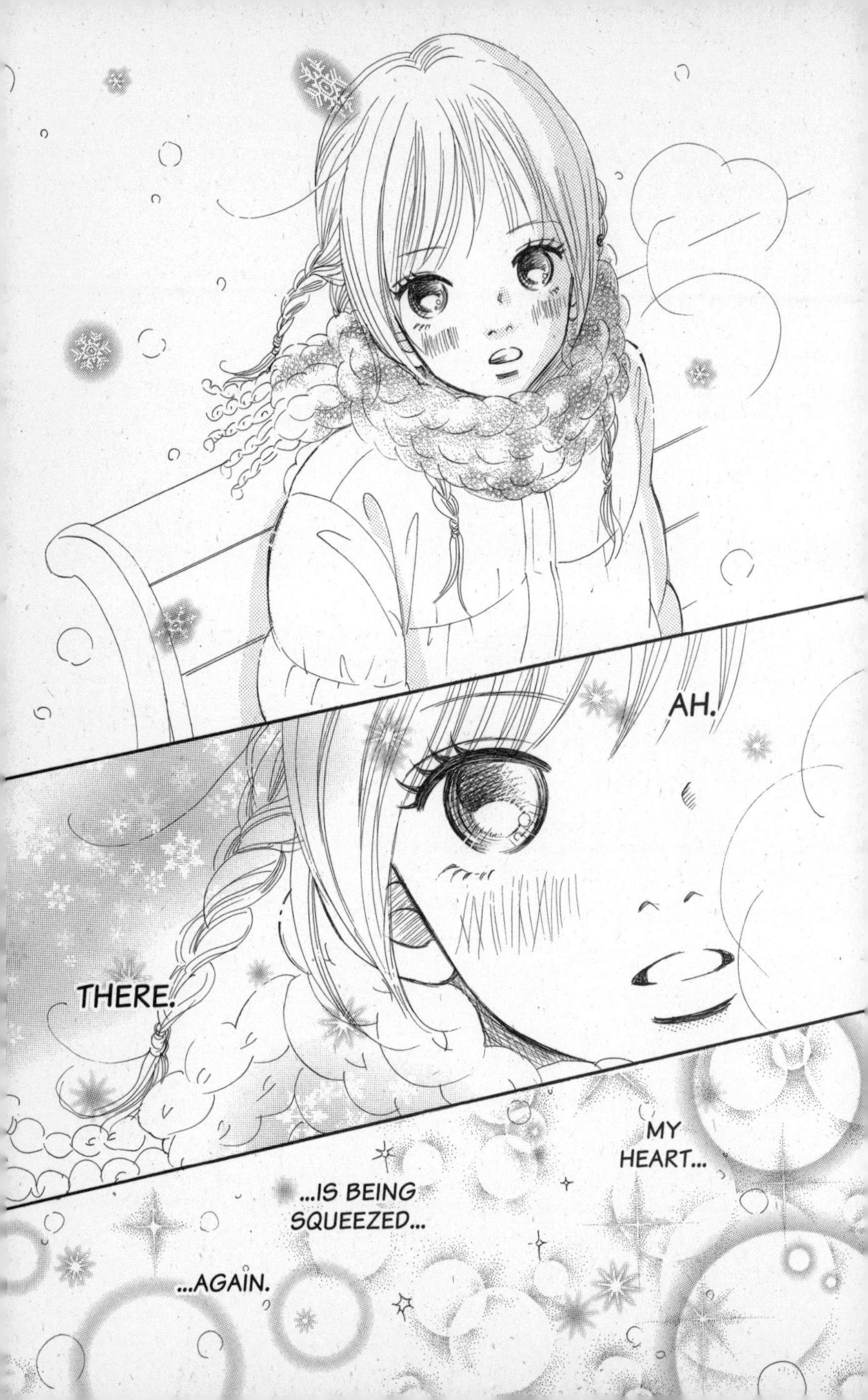
AH.
THERE.
MY HEART...
...IS BEING SQUEEZED...
...AGAIN.

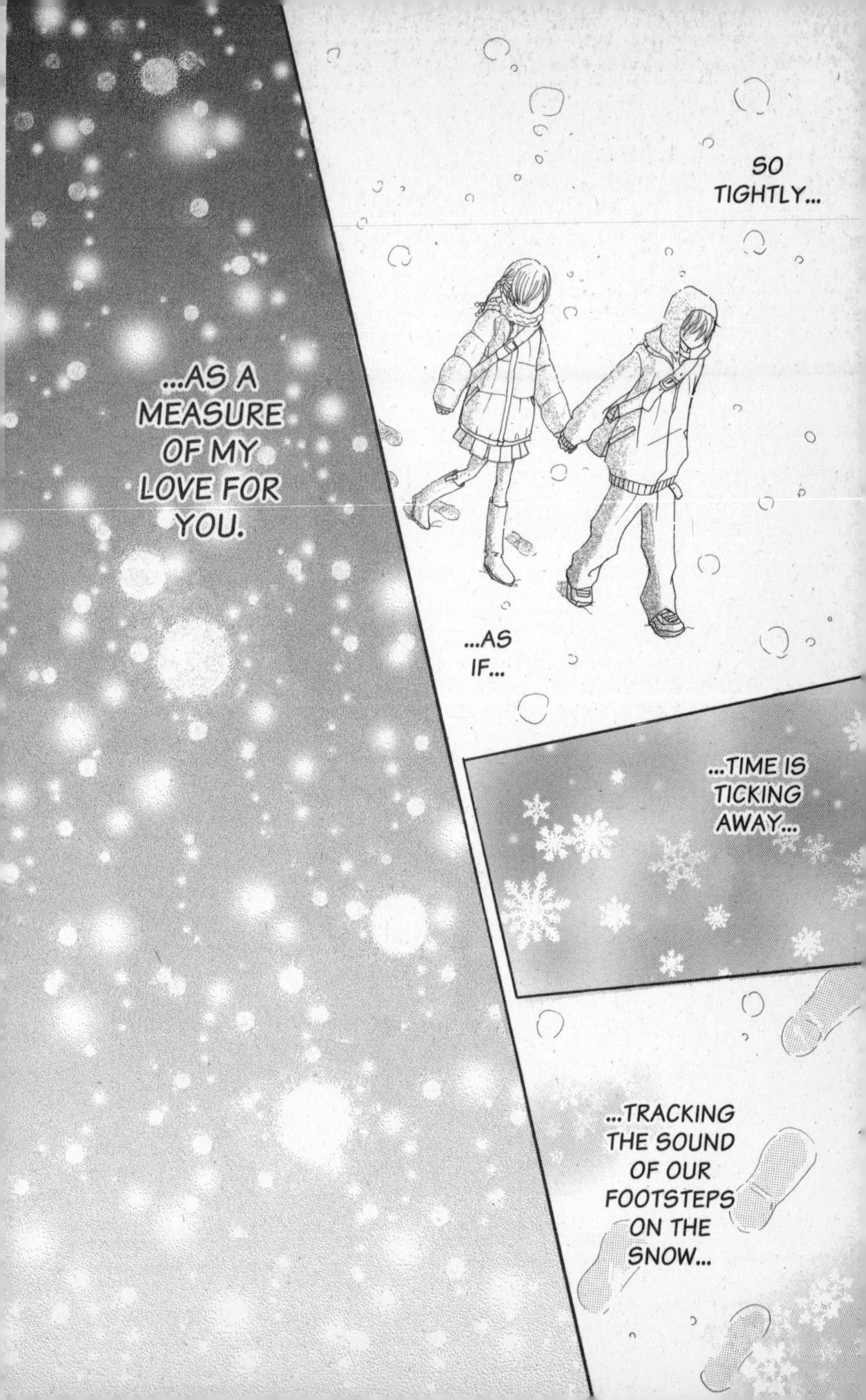
SO TIGHTLY...
...AS IF...
...TIME IS TICKING AWAY...
...TRACKING THE SOUND OF OUR FOOTSTEPS ON THE SNOW...
...AS A MEASURE OF MY LOVE FOR YOU.

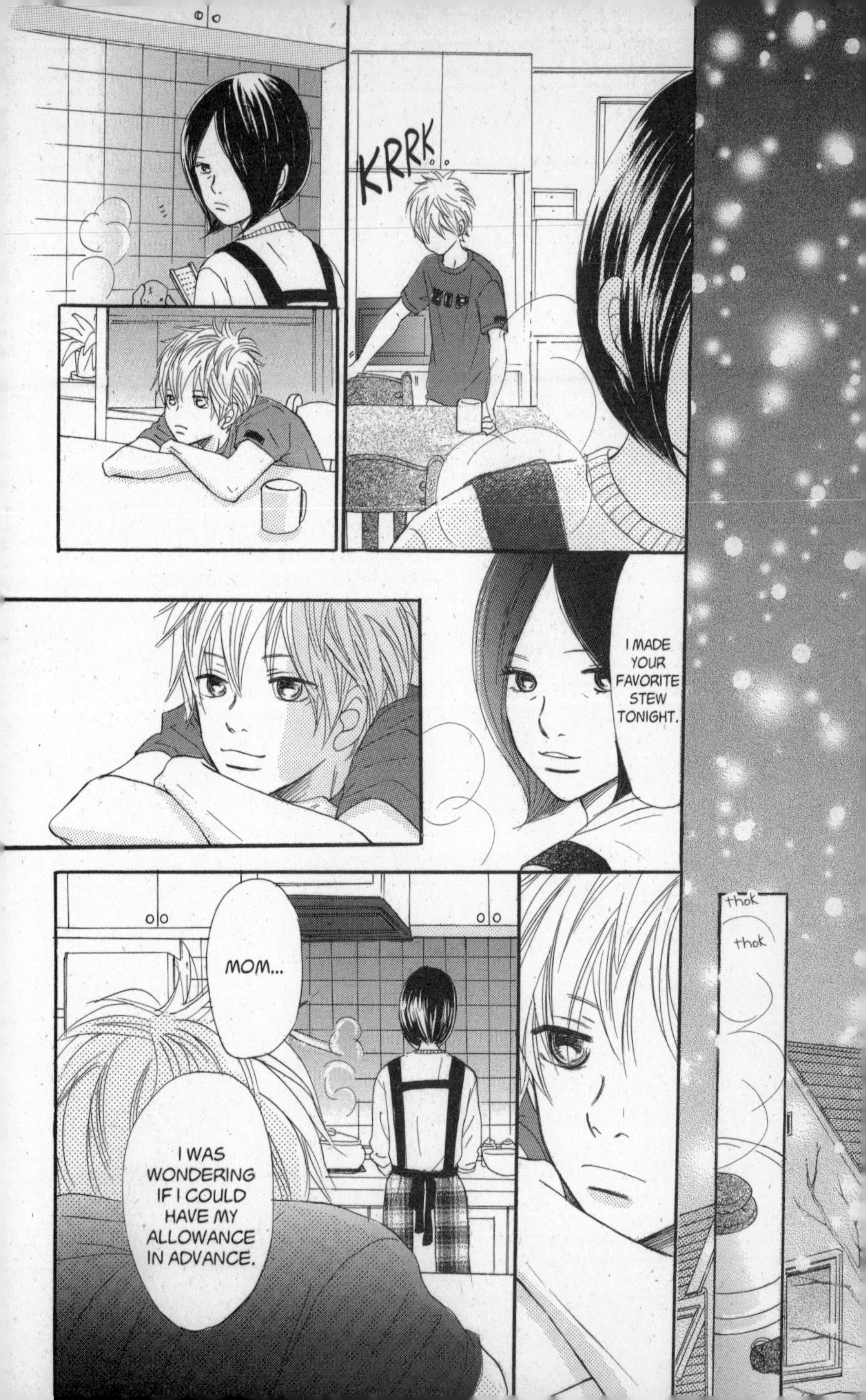
KRRK
I MADE YOUR FAVORITE STEW TONIGHT.
thok
thok
MOM...
I WAS WONDERING IF I COULD HAVE MY ALLOWANCE IN ADVANCE.

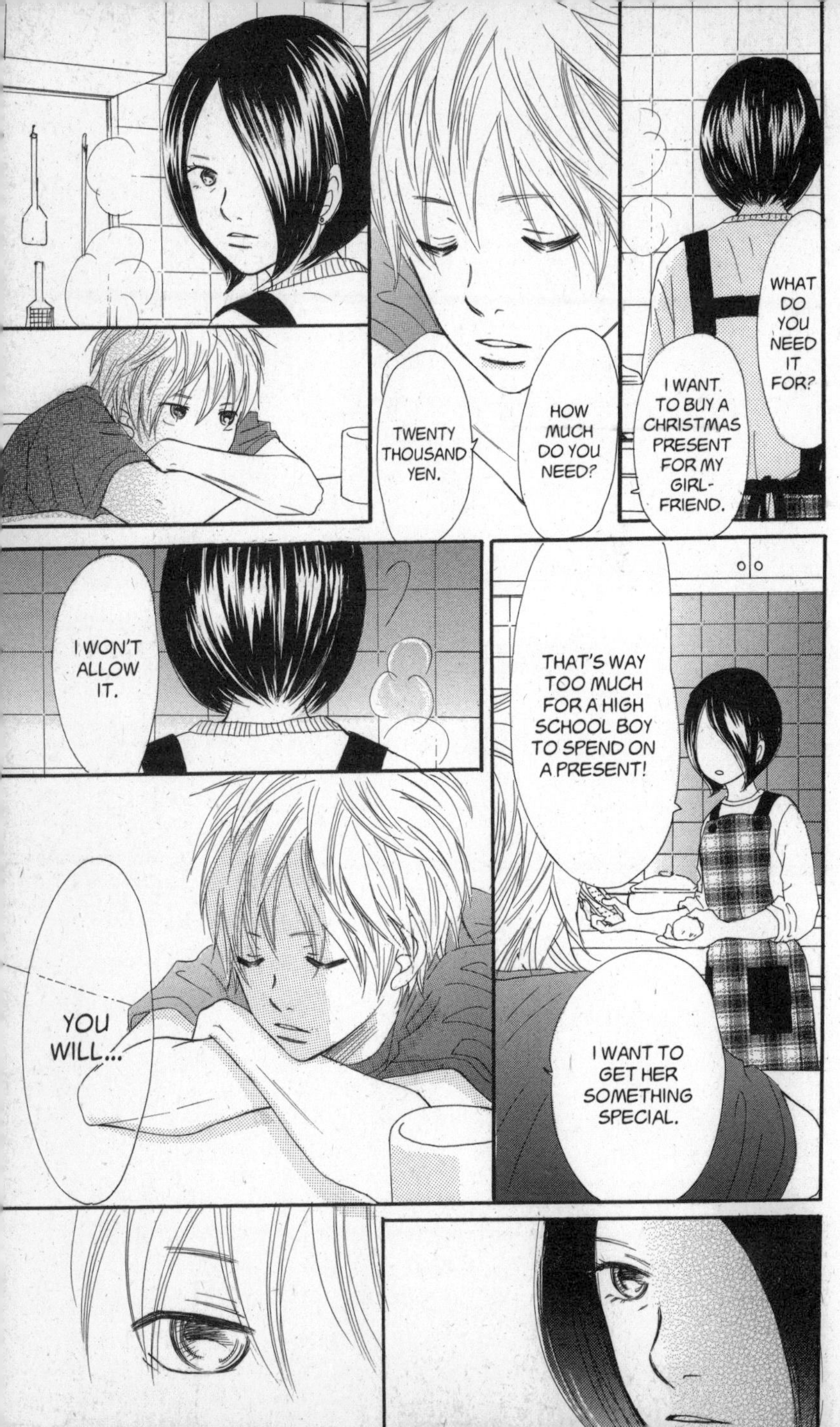
WHAT DO YOU NEED IT FOR?
I WANT TO BUY A CHRISTMAS PRESENT FOR MY GIRLFRIEND.
HOW MUCH DO YOU NEED?
TWENTY THOUSAND YEN.
THAT'S WAY TOO MUCH FOR A HIGH SCHOOL BOY TO SPEND ON A PRESENT!
I WANT TO GET HER SOMETHING SPECIAL.
I WON'T ALLOW IT.
YOU WILL...

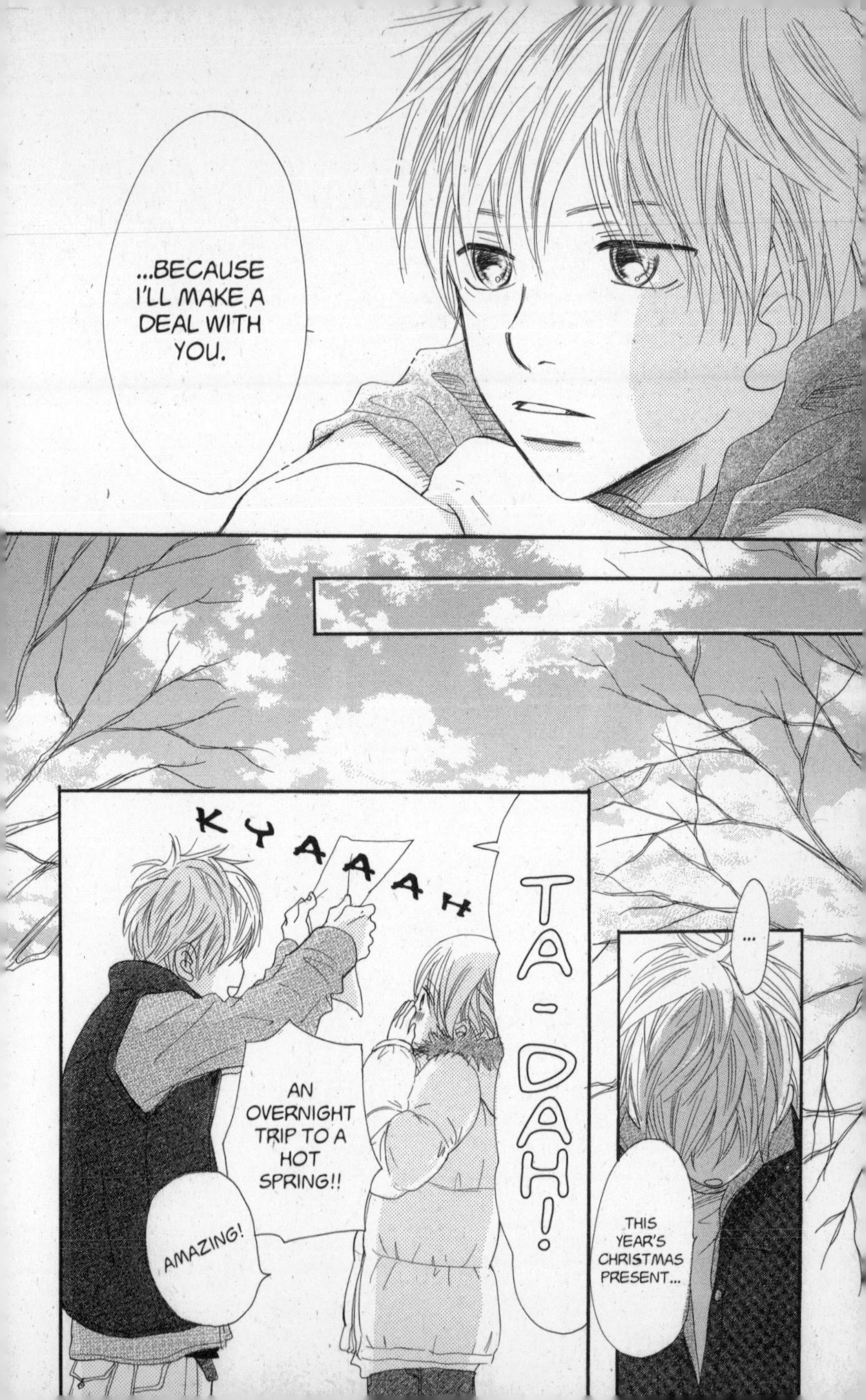
...BECAUSE I'LL MAKE A DEAL WITH YOU.
...
THIS YEAR'S CHRISTMAS PRESENT...
TA-DAH!
KYAAAH
AN OVERNIGHT TRIP TO A HOT SPRING!!
AMAZING!

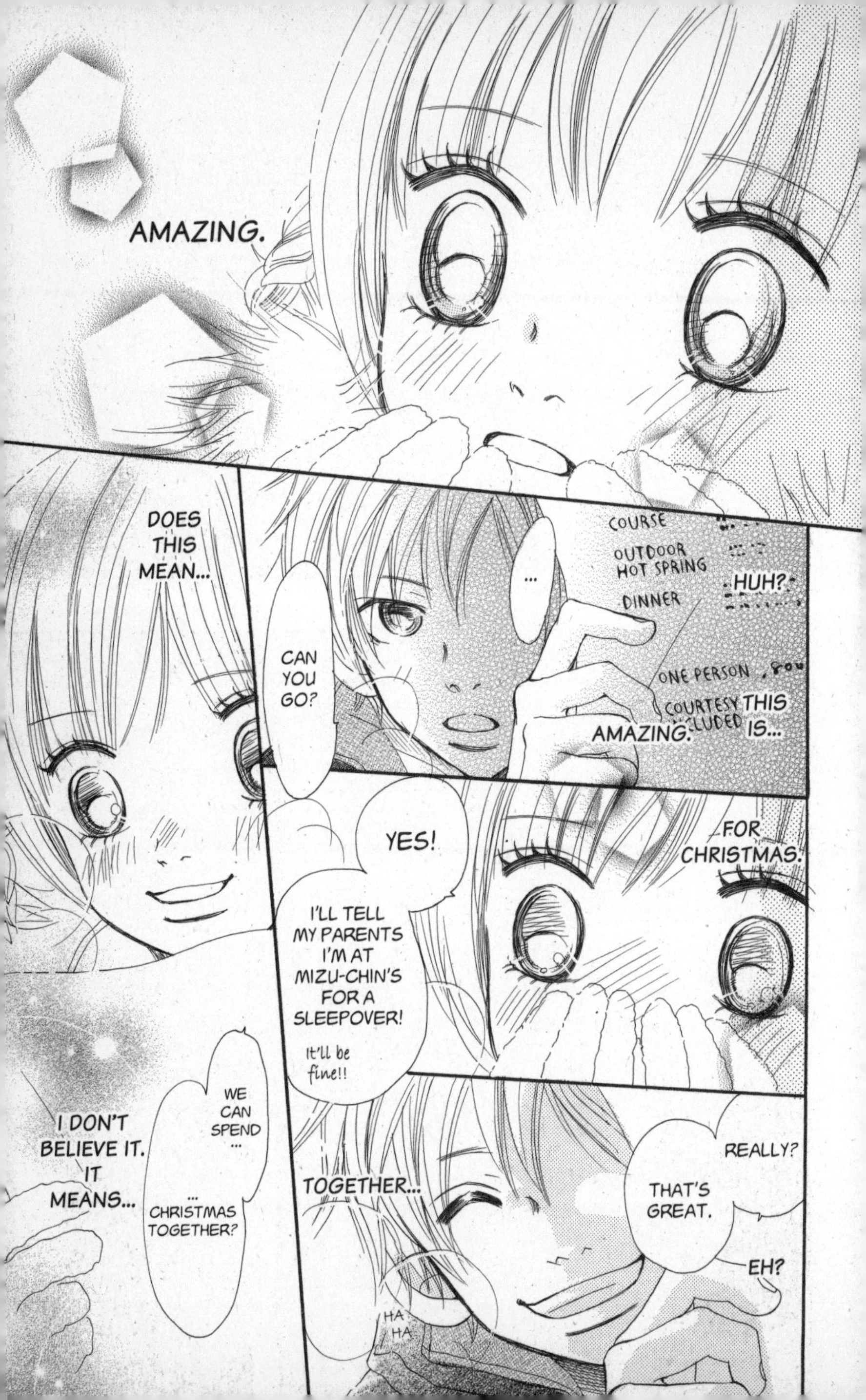
AMAZING.
COURSE
OUTDOOR HOT SPRING
DINNER
ONE PERSON
COURTESY INCLUDED
HUH?
THIS IS...
AMAZING.
...
CAN YOU GO?
FOR CHRISTMAS.
YES!
I'LL TELL MY PARENTS I'M AT MIZU-CHIN'S FOR A SLEEPOVER!
It'll be fine!!
DOES THIS MEAN...
REALLY?
THAT'S GREAT.
EH?
TOGETHER...
HA HA
I DON'T BELIEVE IT. IT MEANS...
WE CAN SPEND ...
... CHRISTMAS TOGETHER?

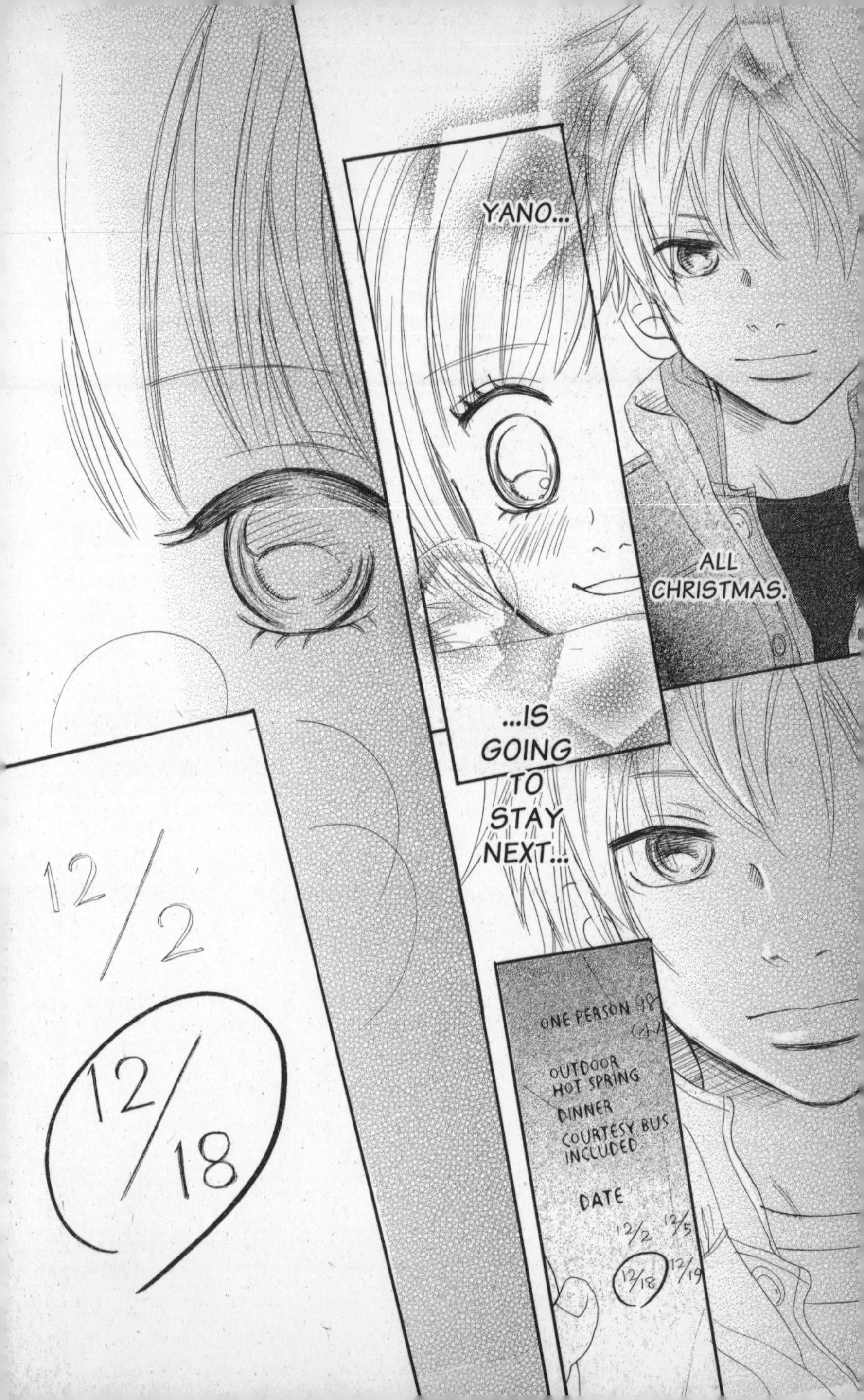
YANO...
...IS GOING TO STAY NEXT...
ALL CHRISTMAS.
ONE PERSON 98
OUTDOOR HOT SPRING
DINNER
COURTESY BUS INCLUDED
DATE
12/2 12/5
12/18 12/19
12/2
12/18

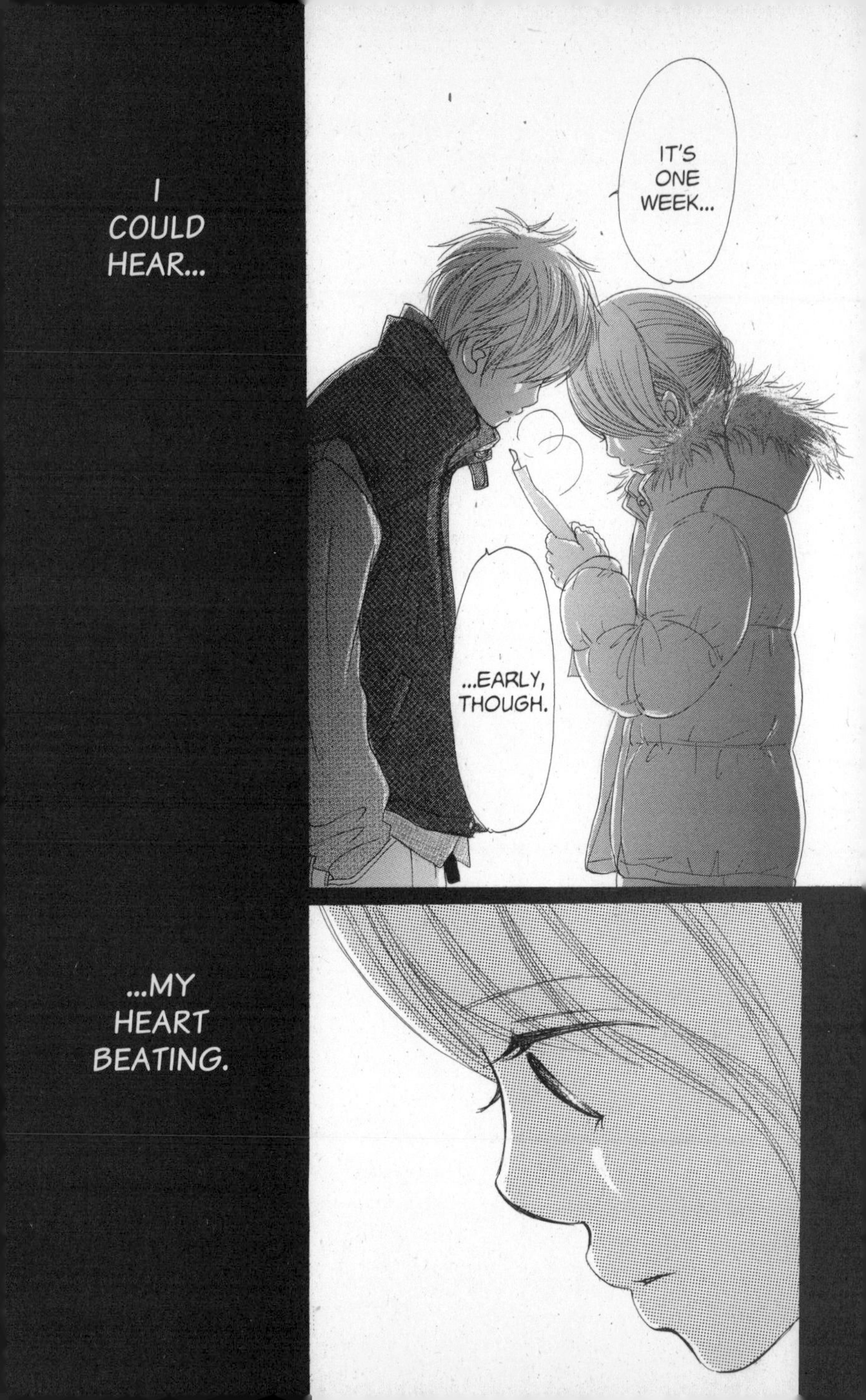
IT'S ONE WEEK...
...EARLY, THOUGH.
I COULD HEAR...
...MY HEART BEATING.

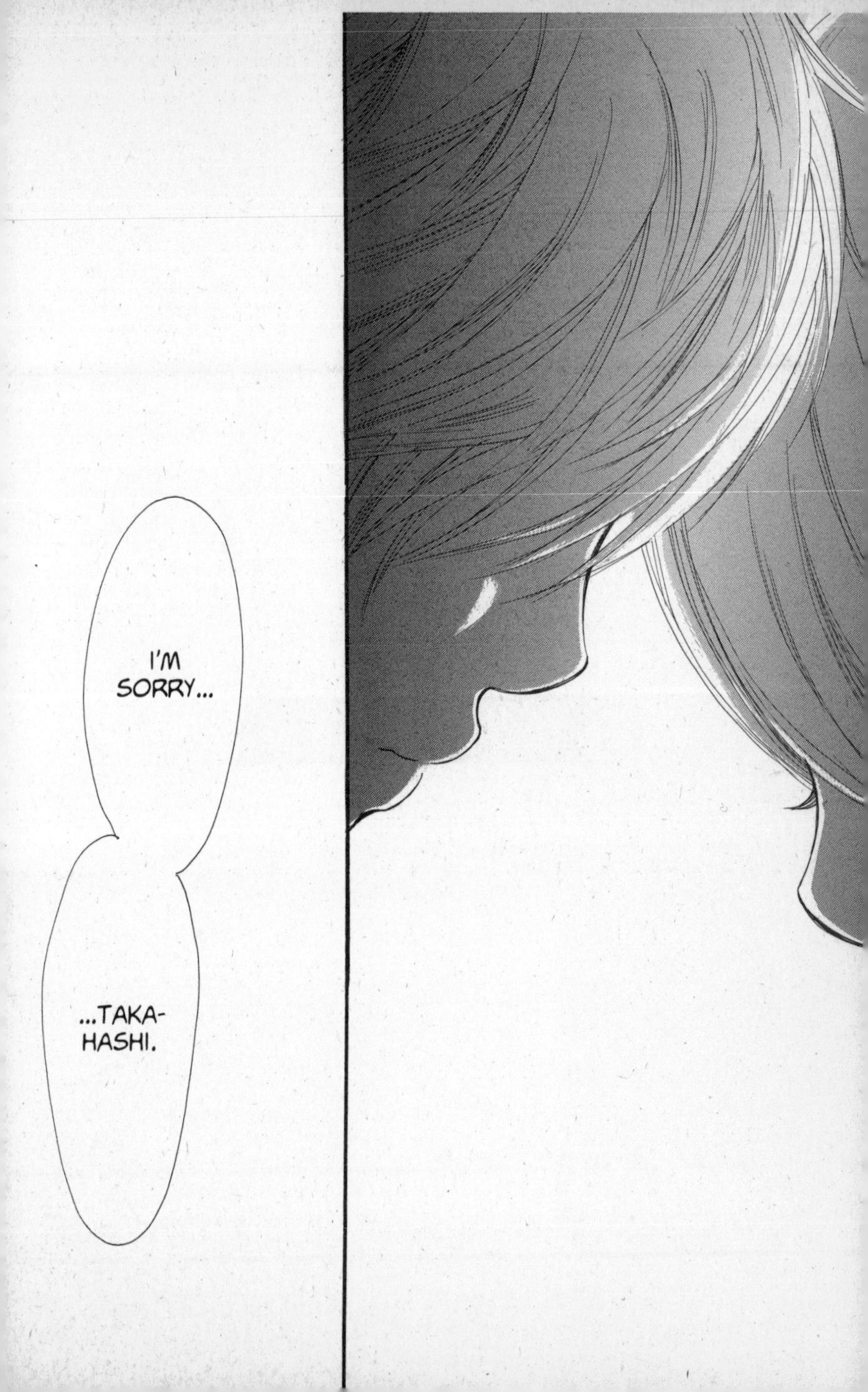
I'M SORRY...
...TAKA-HASHI.

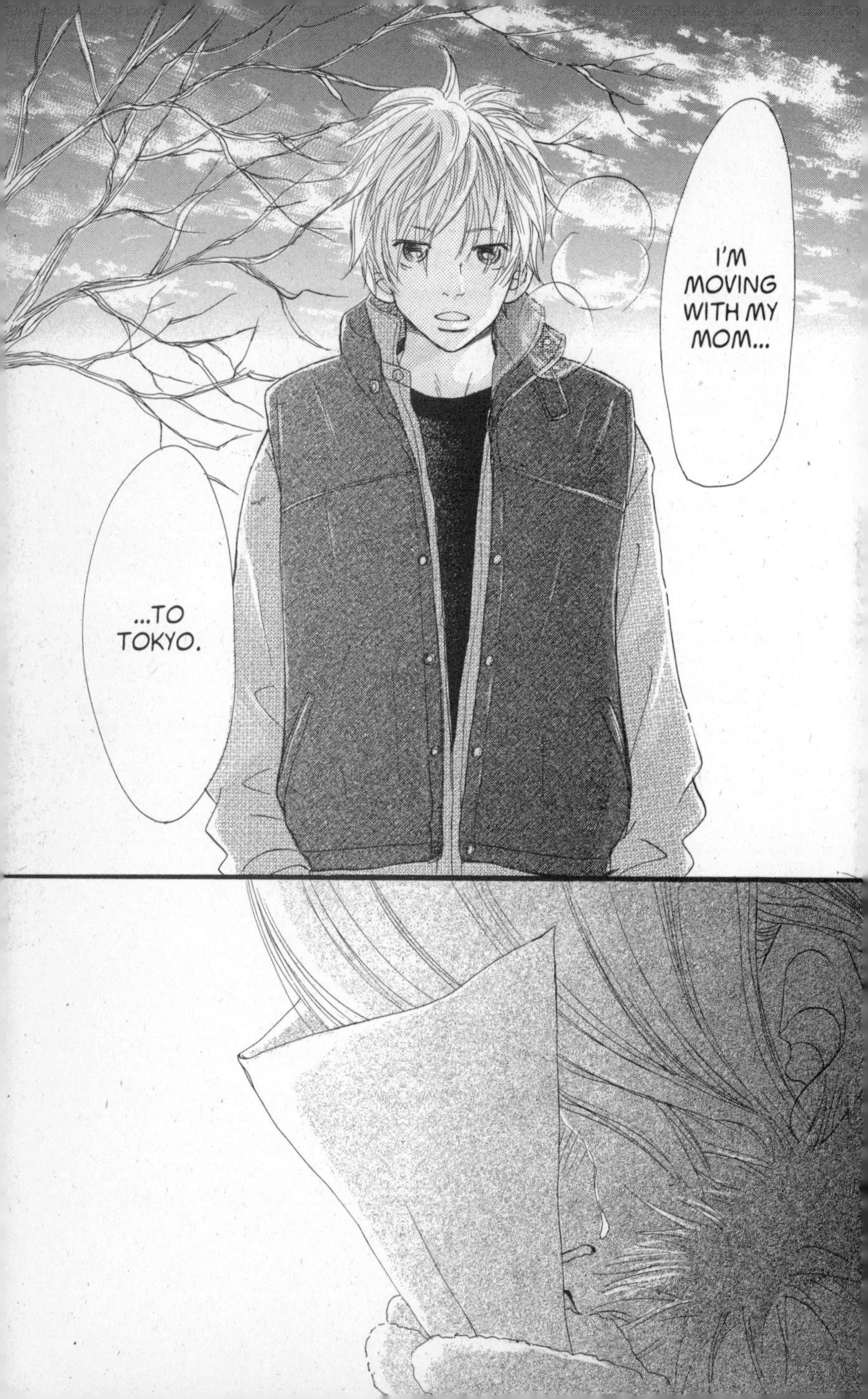
I'M MOVING WITH MY MOM...
...TO TOKYO.

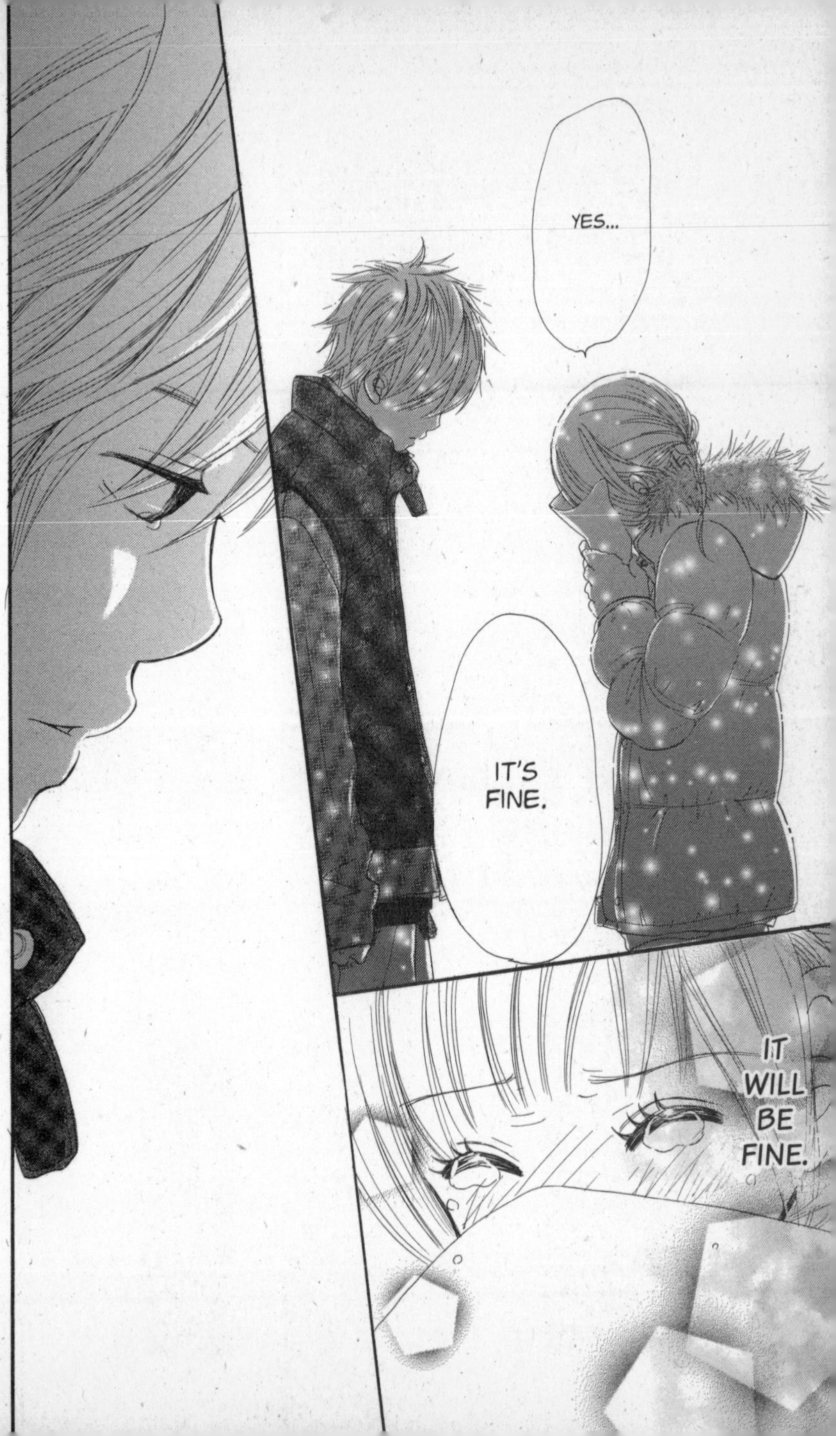
YES...
IT'S FINE.
IT WILL BE FINE.

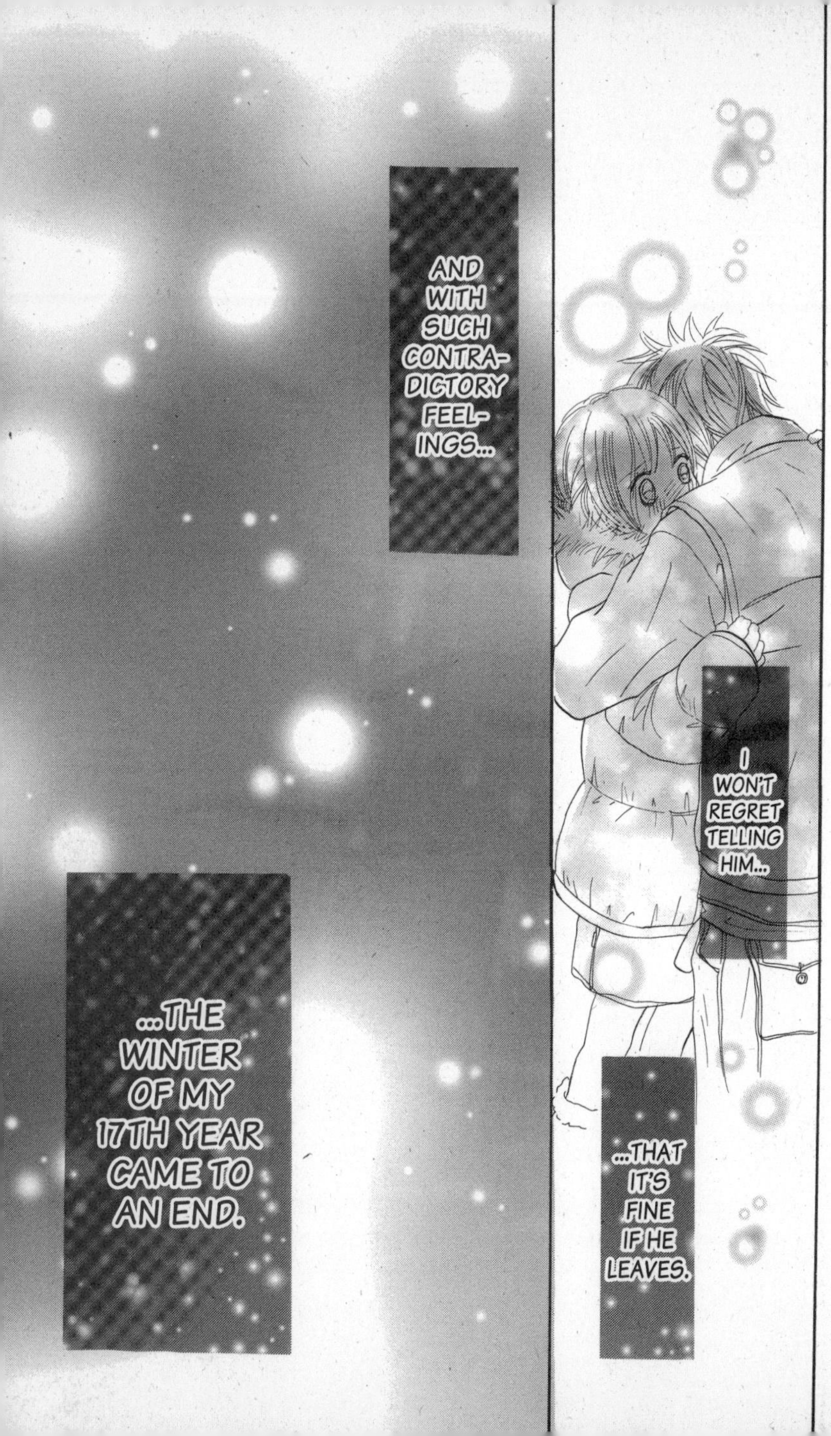
I WON'T REGRET TELLING HIM...
...THAT IT'S FINE IF HE LEAVES.
AND WITH SUCH CONTRA-DICTORY FEEL-INGS...
...THE WINTER OF MY 17TH YEAR CAME TO AN END.

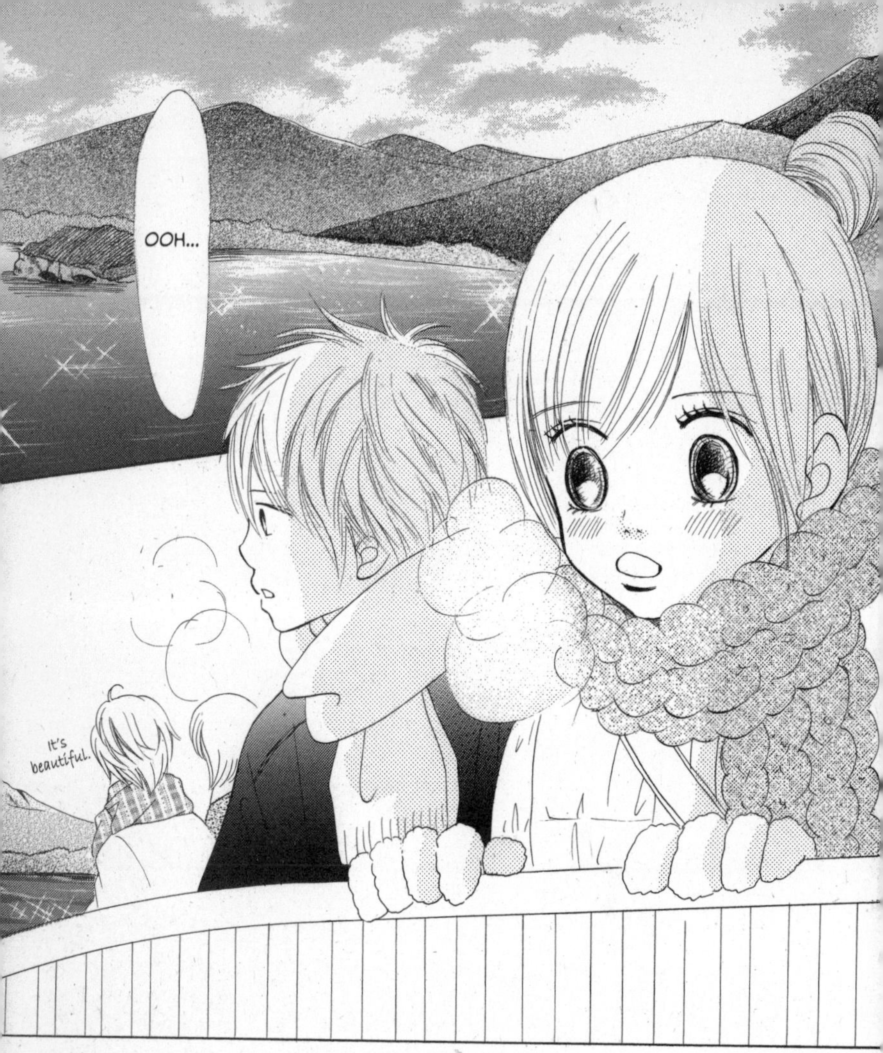
OOH...
It's beautiful.

Chapter 30

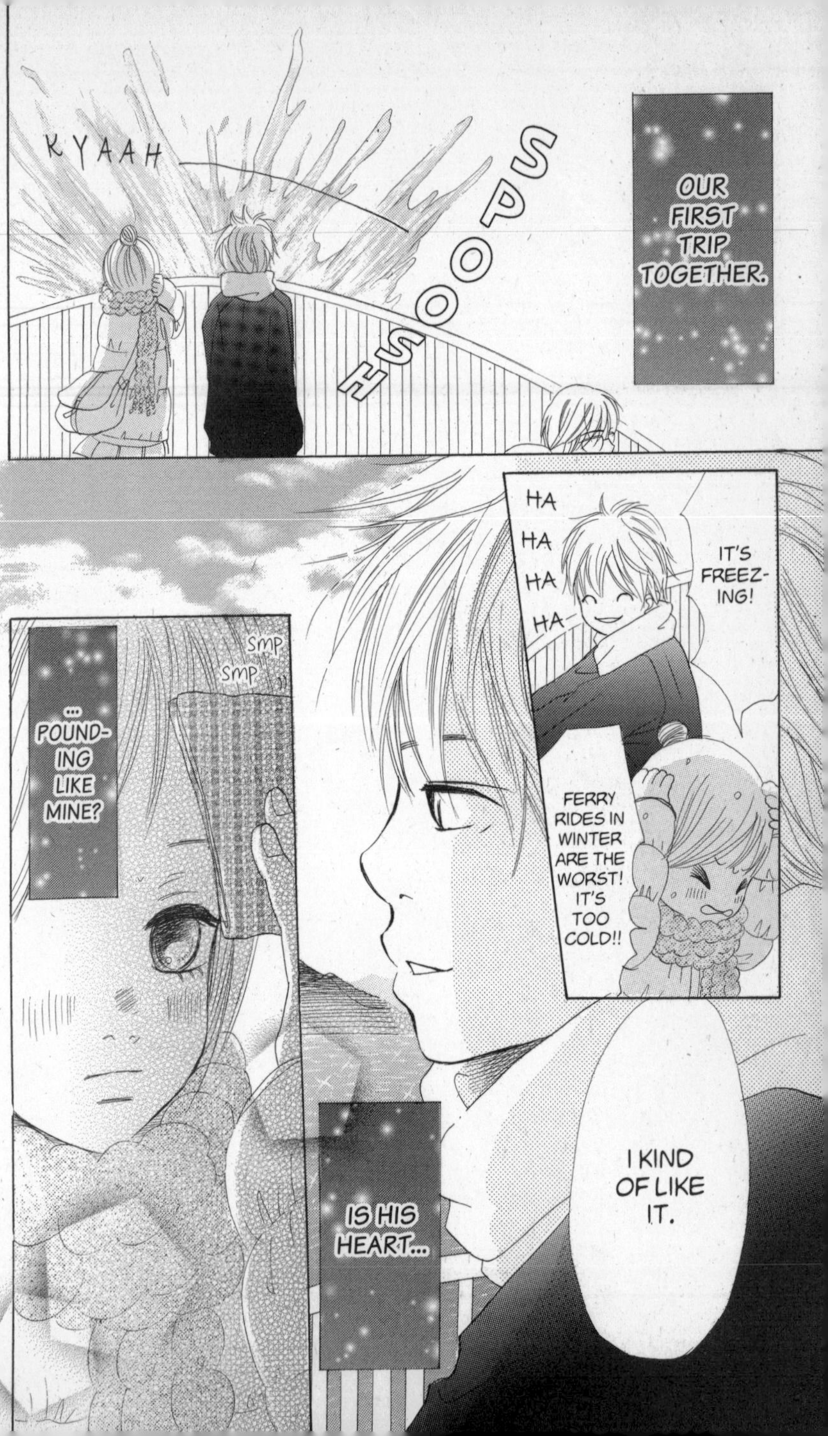
OUR FIRST TRIP TOGETHER.
SPOOSH
KYAAH
IT'S FREEZ-ING!
HA HA HA HA
FERRY RIDES IN WINTER ARE THE WORST! IT'S TOO COLD!!
I KIND OF LIKE IT.
IS HIS HEART...
SMP SMP
...POUND-ING LIKE MINE?

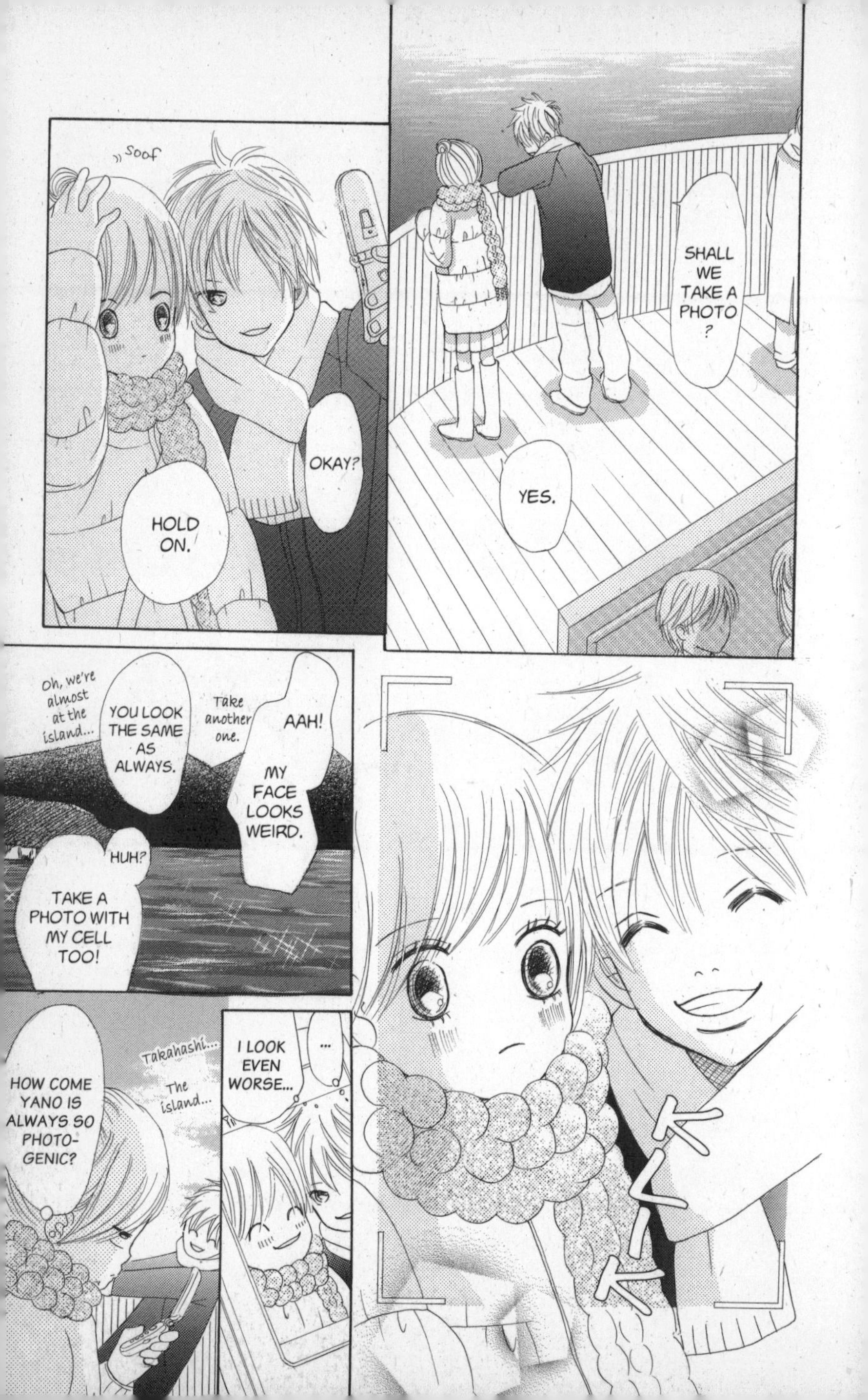
SHALL WE TAKE A PHOTO?
YES.
soof
OKAY?
HOLD ON.
AAH!
MY FACE LOOKS WEIRD.
Take another one.
YOU LOOK THE SAME AS ALWAYS.
Oh, we're almost at the island...
HUH?
TAKE A PHOTO WITH MY CELL TOO!
...
I LOOK EVEN WORSE...
Takahashi...
The island...
HOW COME YANO IS ALWAYS SO PHOTO-GENIC?

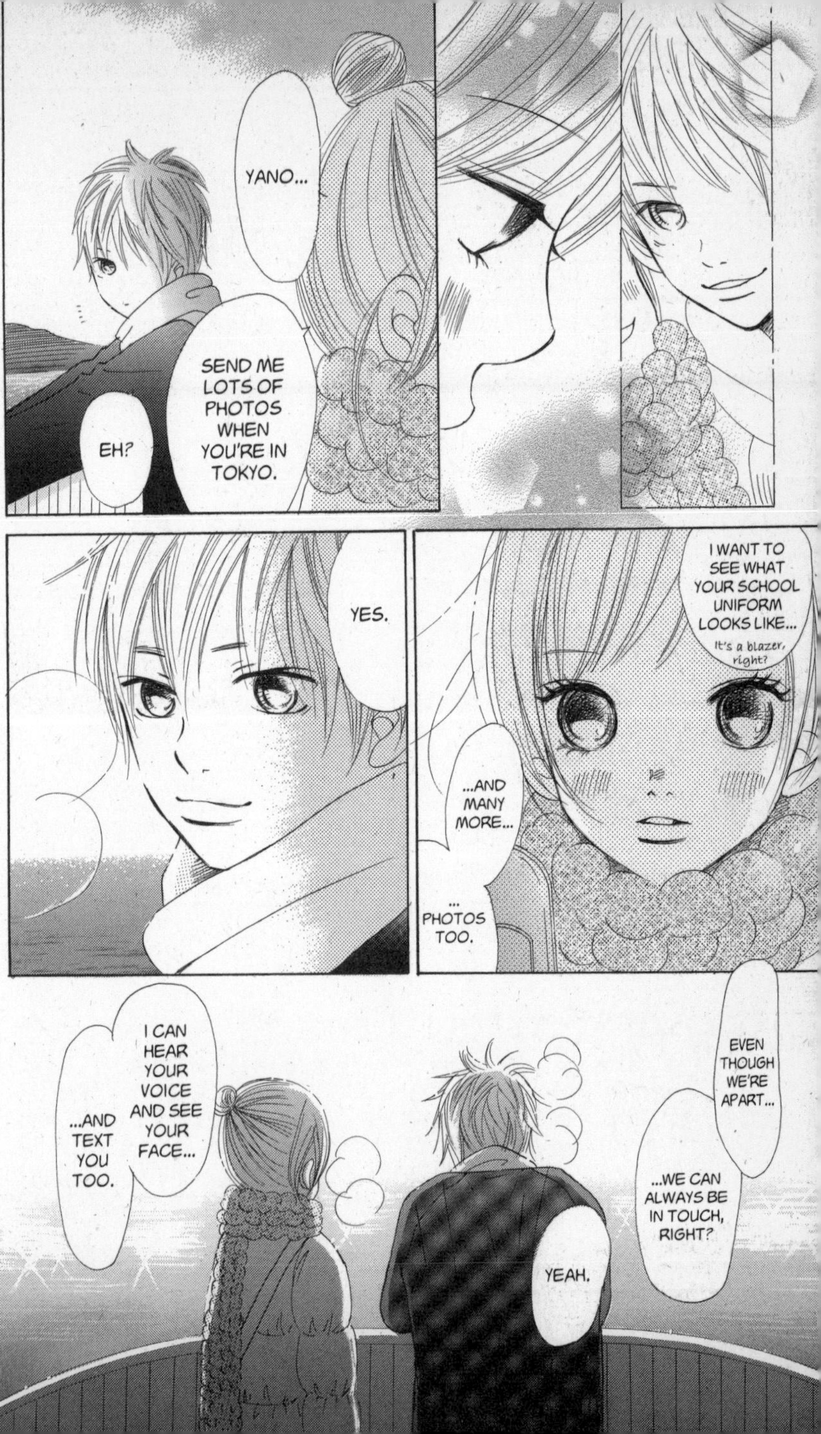
YANO...
SEND ME LOTS OF PHOTOS WHEN YOU'RE IN TOKYO.
EH?
I WANT TO SEE WHAT YOUR SCHOOL UNIFORM LOOKS LIKE...
It's a blazer, right?
...AND MANY MORE...
... PHOTOS TOO.
YES.
EVEN THOUGH WE'RE APART...
...WE CAN ALWAYS BE IN TOUCH, RIGHT?
YEAH.
I CAN HEAR YOUR VOICE AND SEE YOUR FACE...
...AND TEXT YOU TOO.

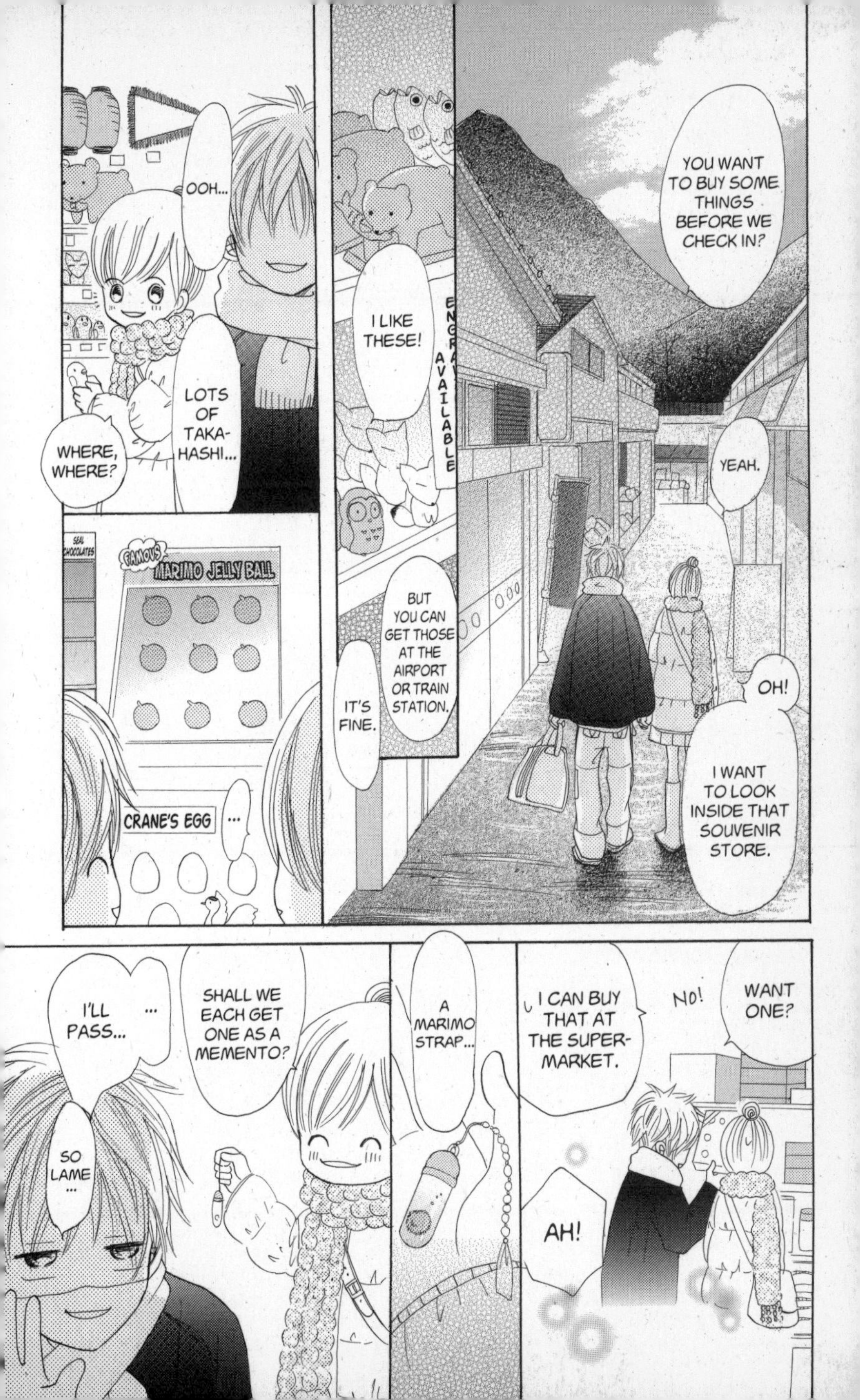
YOU WANT TO BUY SOME THINGS BEFORE WE CHECK IN?
YEAH.
OH!
I WANT TO LOOK INSIDE THAT SOUVENIR STORE.
I LIKE THESE!
ENGRA
AVAILABLE
BUT YOU CAN GET THOSE AT THE AIRPORT OR TRAIN STATION.
IT'S FINE.
OOH...
LOTS OF TAKAHASHI...
WHERE, WHERE?
SEAL CHOCOLATES
FAMOUS
MARIMO JELLY BALL
CRANE'S EGG
...
WANT ONE?
NO!
I CAN BUY THAT AT THE SUPERMARKET.
AH!
A MARIMO STRAP...
SHALL WE EACH GET ONE AS A MEMENTO?
I'LL PASS...
...
SO LAME
...

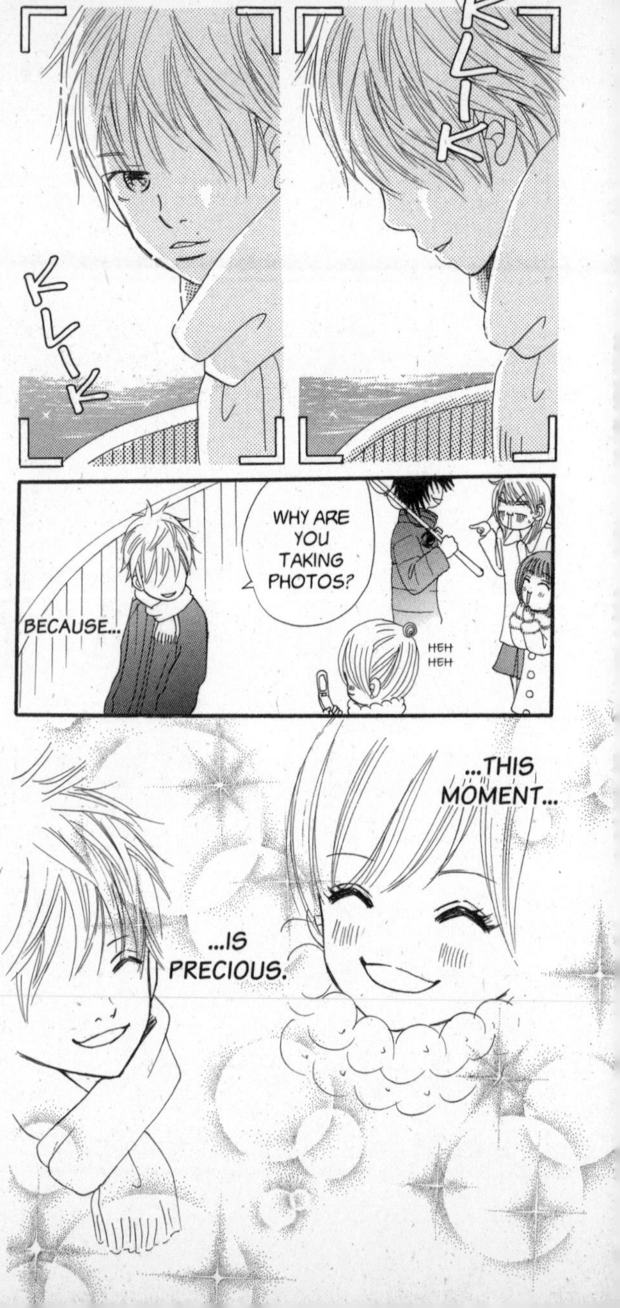
KLIK
KLIK
WHY ARE YOU TAKING PHOTOS?
HEH HEH
BECAUSE...
...THIS MOMENT...
...IS PRECIOUS.

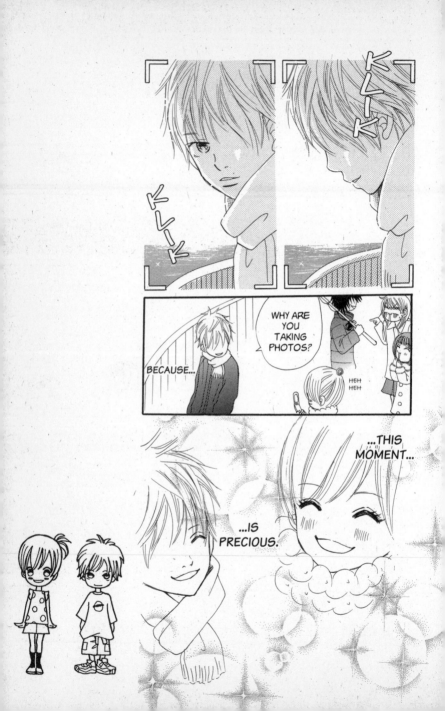

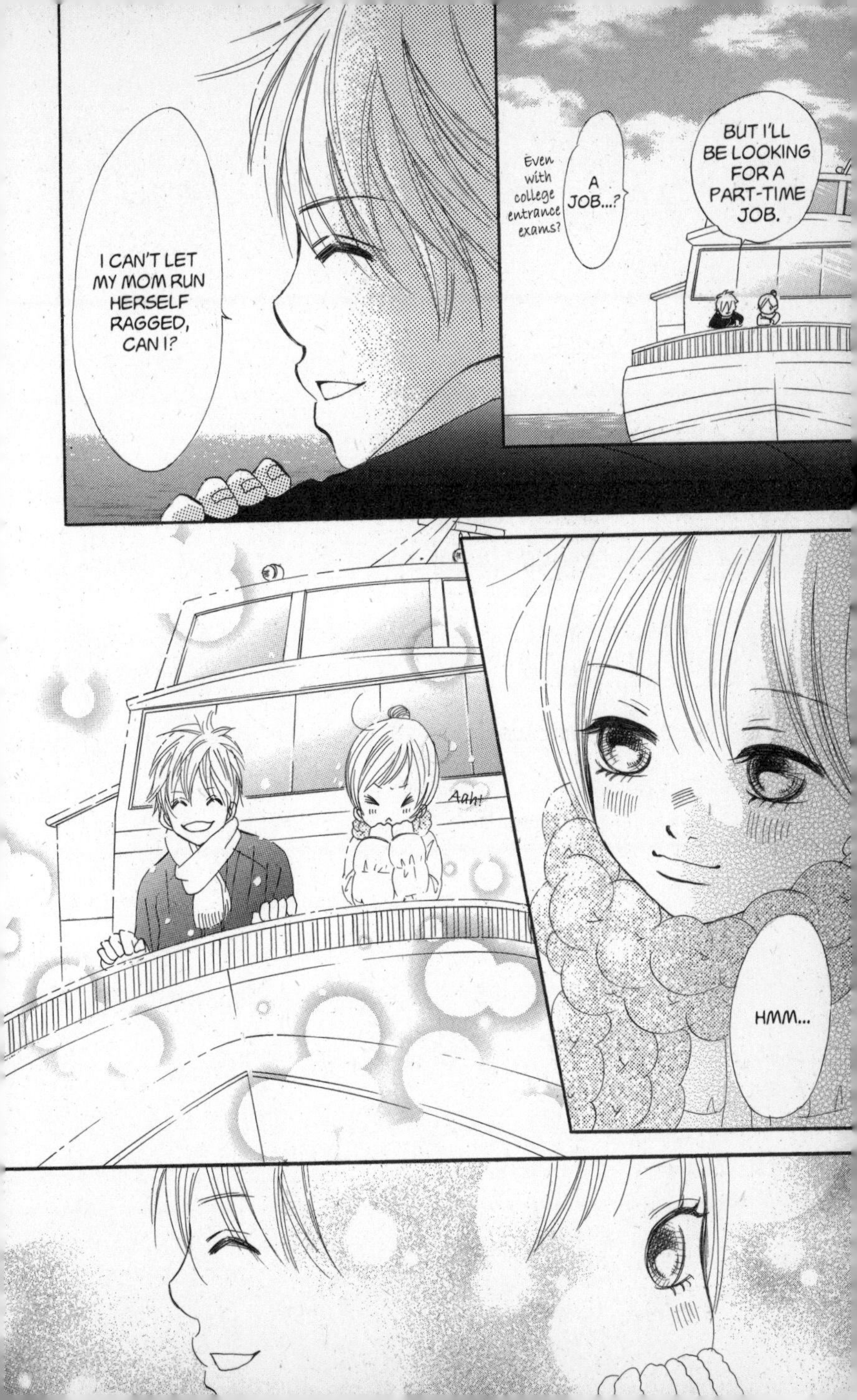
BUT I'LL BE LOOKING FOR A PART-TIME JOB.
A JOB...?
Even with college entrance exams?
I CAN'T LET MY MOM RUN HERSELF RAGGED, CAN I?
HMM...
Aah!

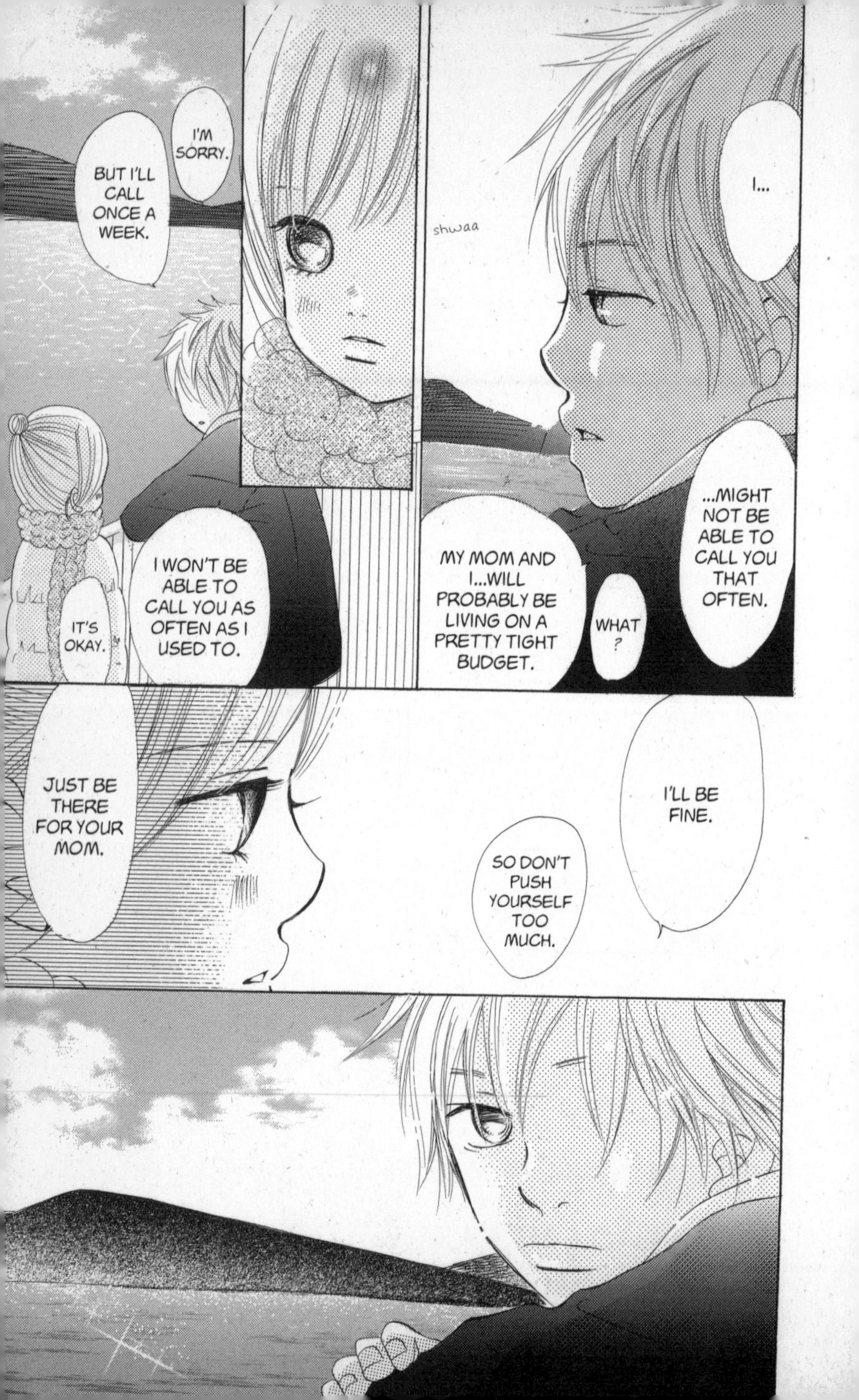
I...
...MIGHT NOT BE ABLE TO CALL YOU THAT OFTEN.
WHAT?
MY MOM AND I...WILL PROBABLY BE LIVING ON A PRETTY TIGHT BUDGET.
shwaa
I'M SORRY.
BUT I'LL CALL ONCE A WEEK.
I WON'T BE ABLE TO CALL YOU AS OFTEN AS I USED TO.
IT'S OKAY.
I'LL BE FINE.
SO DON'T PUSH YOURSELF TOO MUCH.
JUST BE THERE FOR YOUR MOM.

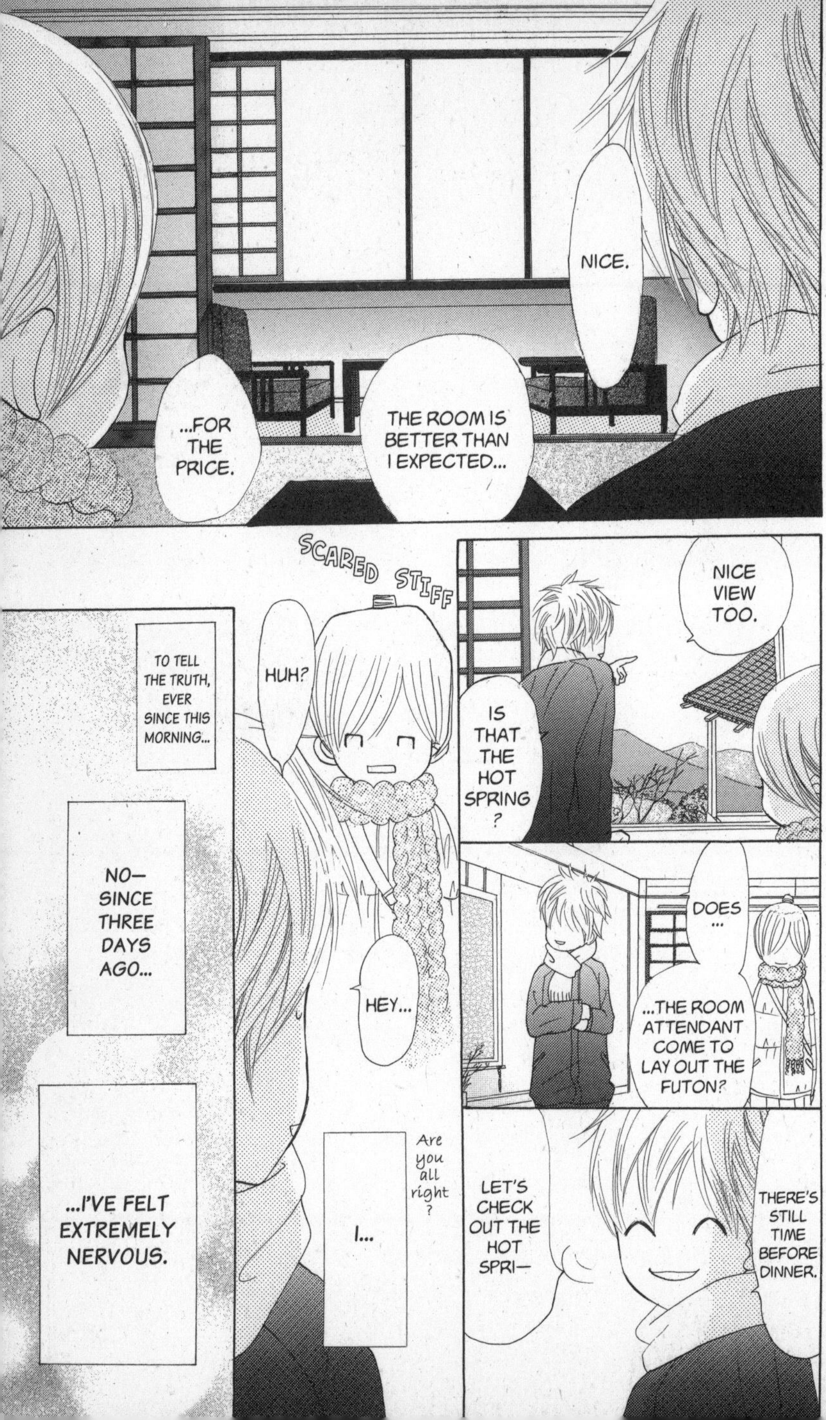
NICE.
THE ROOM IS BETTER THAN I EXPECTED...
...FOR THE PRICE.
NICE VIEW TOO.
IS THAT THE HOT SPRING?
DOES...
...THE ROOM ATTENDANT COME TO LAY OUT THE FUTON?
THERE'S STILL TIME BEFORE DINNER.
LET'S CHECK OUT THE HOT SPRI—
SCARED STIFF
HUH?
HEY...
Are you all right?
I...
TO TELL THE TRUTH, EVER SINCE THIS MORNING...
NO— SINCE THREE DAYS AGO...
...I'VE FELT EXTREMELY NERVOUS.

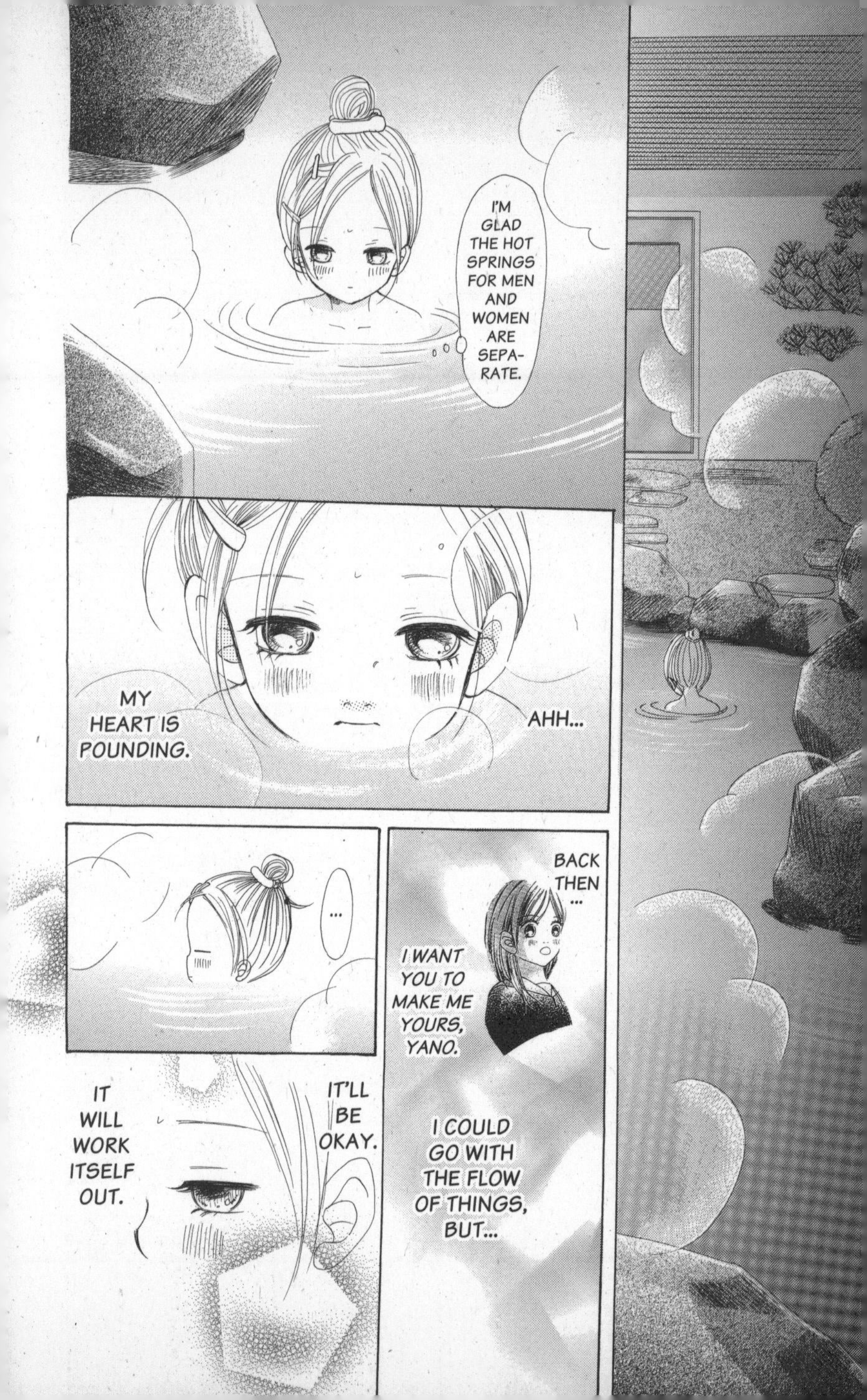
I'M GLAD THE HOT SPRINGS FOR MEN AND WOMEN ARE SEPA-RATE.
AHH...
MY HEART IS POUNDING.
BACK THEN...
I WANT YOU TO MAKE ME YOURS, YANO.
I COULD GO WITH THE FLOW OF THINGS, BUT...
...
IT'LL BE OKAY.
IT WILL WORK ITSELF OUT.

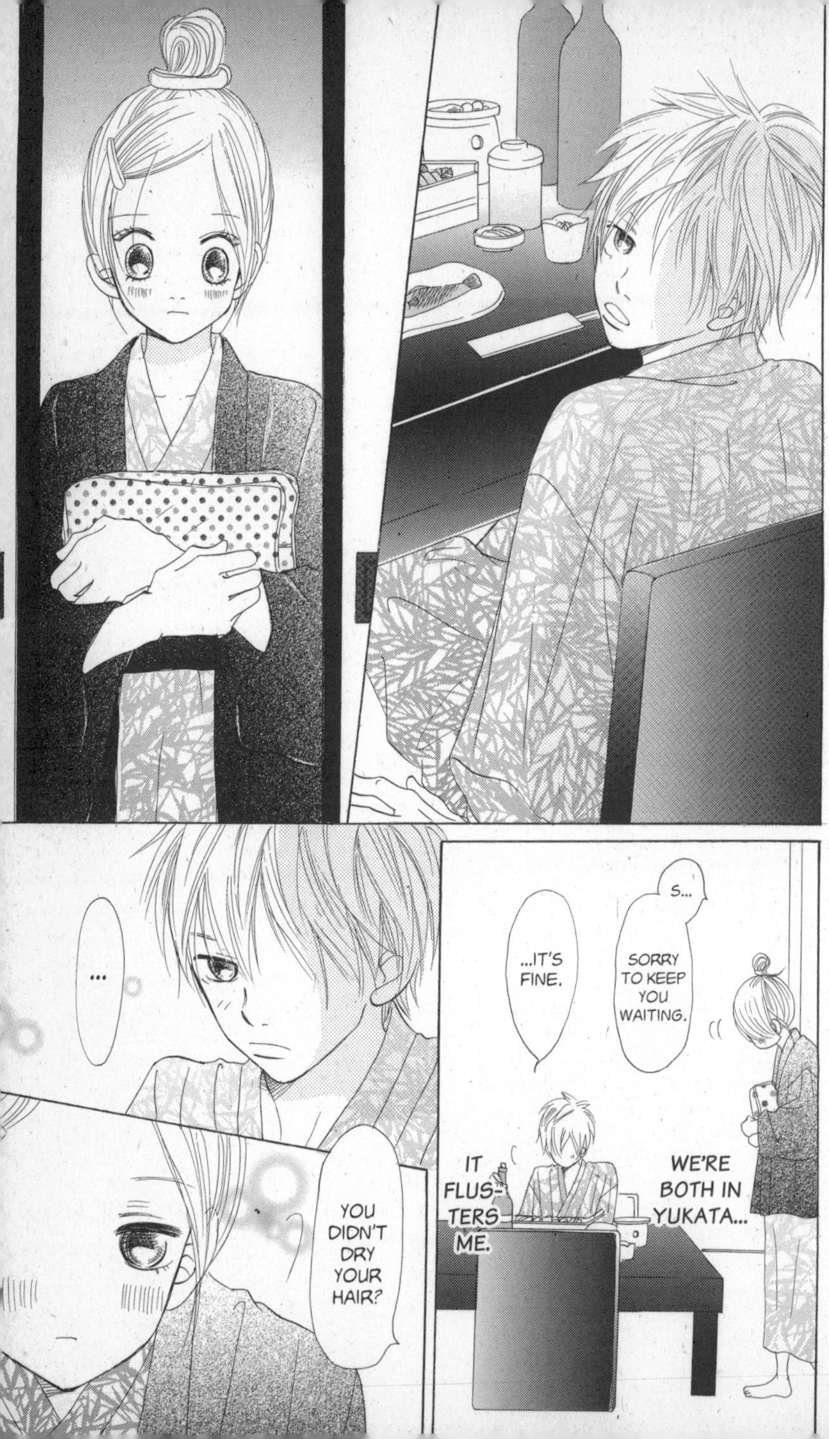
S...
SORRY TO KEEP YOU WAITING.
...IT'S FINE.
WE'RE BOTH IN YUKATA...
IT FLUSTERS ME.
...
YOU DIDN'T DRY YOUR HAIR?

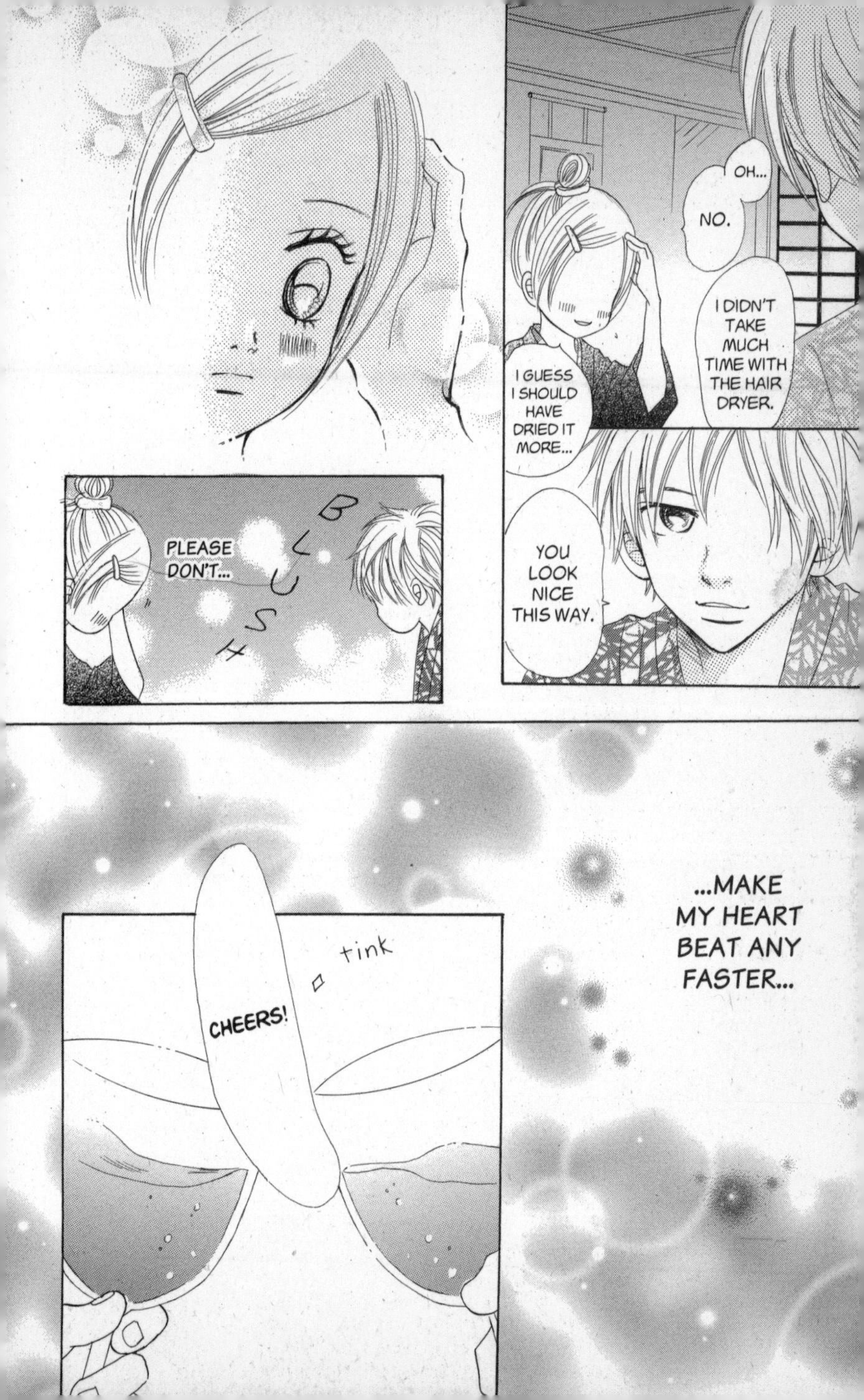
OH...
NO.
I DIDN'T TAKE MUCH TIME WITH THE HAIR DRYER.
I GUESS I SHOULD HAVE DRIED IT MORE...
YOU LOOK NICE THIS WAY.
BLUSH
PLEASE DON'T...
...MAKE MY HEART BEAT ANY FASTER...
tink
CHEERS!

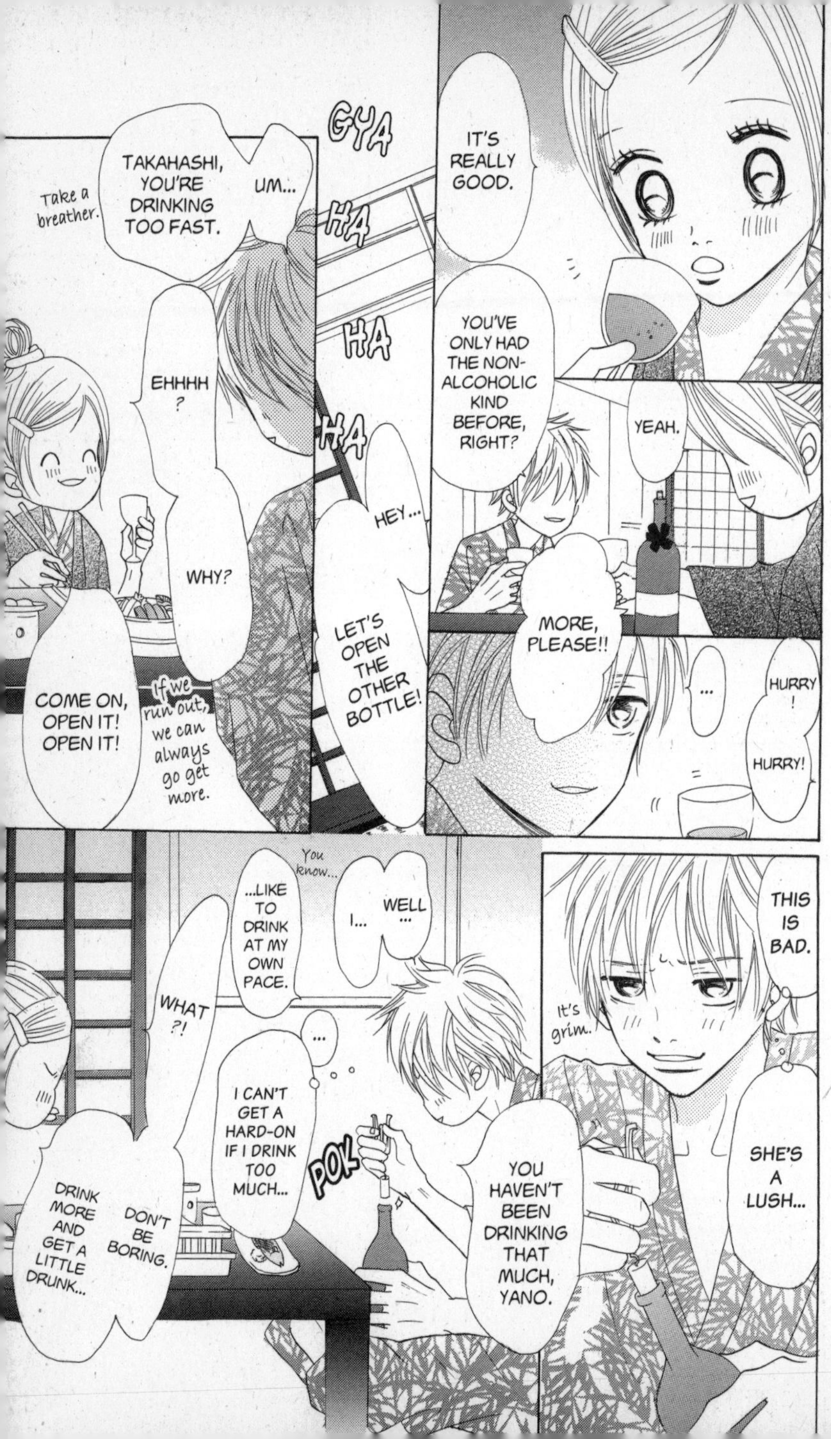
IT'S REALLY GOOD.
YOU'VE ONLY HAD THE NON-ALCOHOLIC KIND BEFORE, RIGHT?
YEAH.
MORE, PLEASE!!
...
HURRY! HURRY!
GYA HA HA HA
HEY...
LET'S OPEN THE OTHER BOTTLE!
UM...
TAKAHASHI, YOU'RE DRINKING TOO FAST.
Take a breather.
EHHHH?
WHY?
COME ON, OPEN IT! OPEN IT!
If we run out, we can always go get more.
THIS IS BAD.
It's grim.
SHE'S A LUSH...
YOU HAVEN'T BEEN DRINKING THAT MUCH, YANO.
WELL...
I...
You know...
...LIKE TO DRINK AT MY OWN PACE.
WHAT?!
...
I CAN'T GET A HARD-ON IF I DRINK TOO MUCH...
POK
DON'T BE BORING.
DRINK MORE AND GET A LITTLE DRUNK...

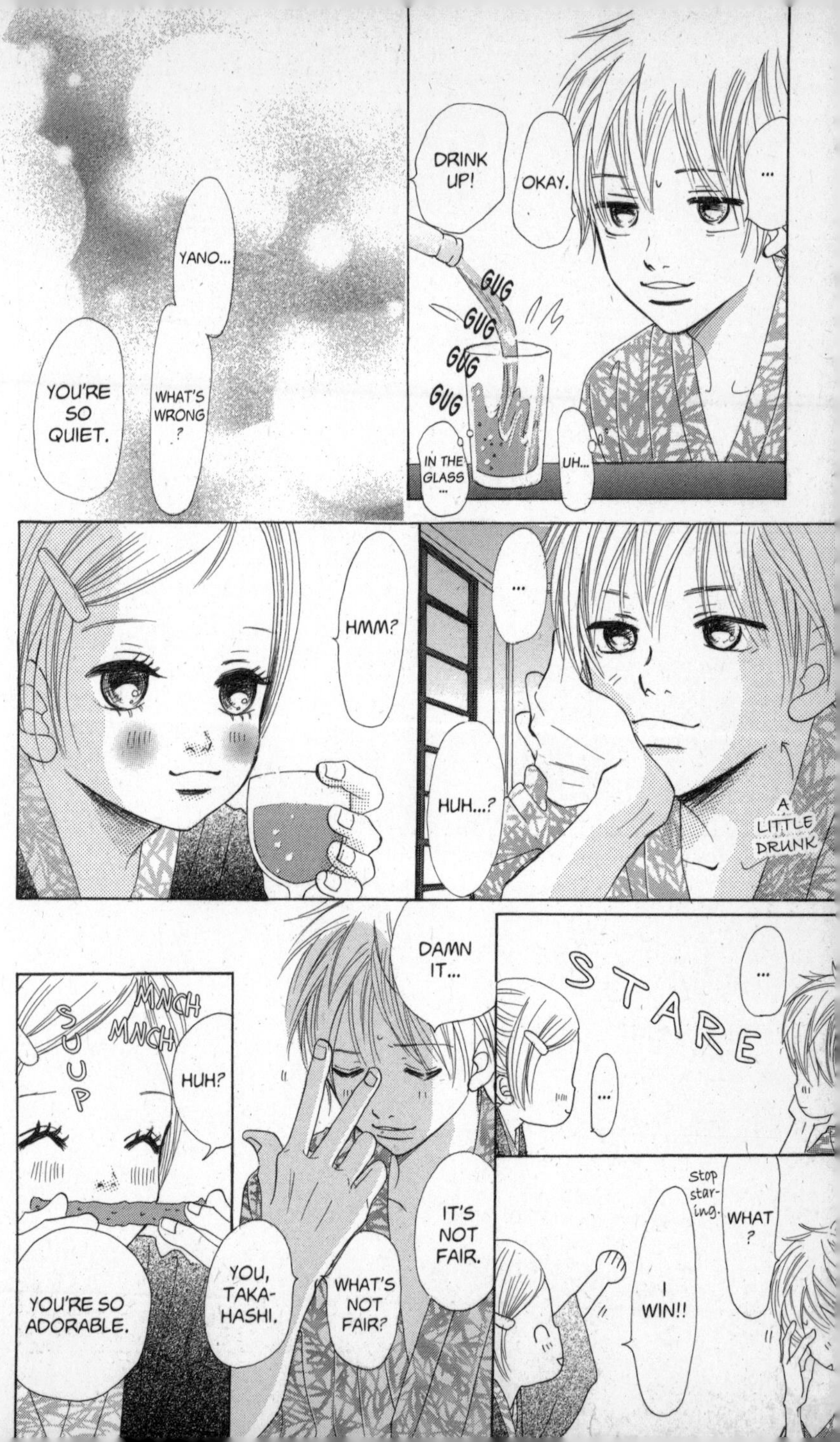
...
OKAY.
DRINK UP!
GUG
GUG
GUG
GUG
UH...
IN THE GLASS ...
YANO...
WHAT'S WRONG ?
YOU'RE SO QUIET.
...
HUH...?
A LITTLE DRUNK
HMM?
...
STARE
...
Stop star-ing.
WHAT ?
I WIN!!
DAMN IT...
IT'S NOT FAIR.
WHAT'S NOT FAIR?
YOU, TAKA-HASHI.
MNCH
MNCH
SUUP
HUH?
YOU'RE SO ADORABLE.

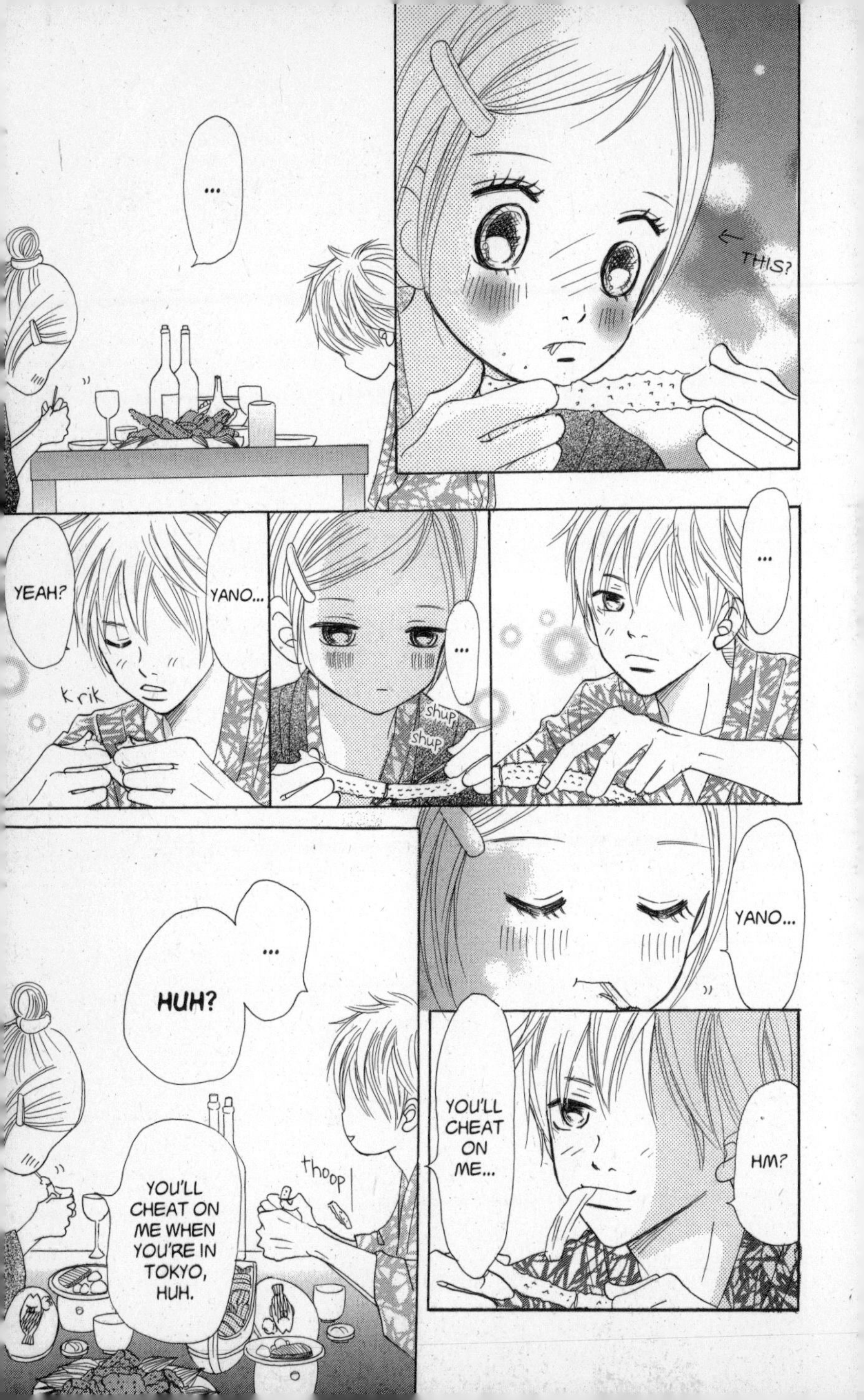
THIS?
...
...
shup
shup
...
YANO...
YEAH?
krik
YANO...
HM?
YOU'LL CHEAT ON ME...
...
HUH?
thoop
YOU'LL CHEAT ON ME WHEN YOU'RE IN TOKYO, HUH.

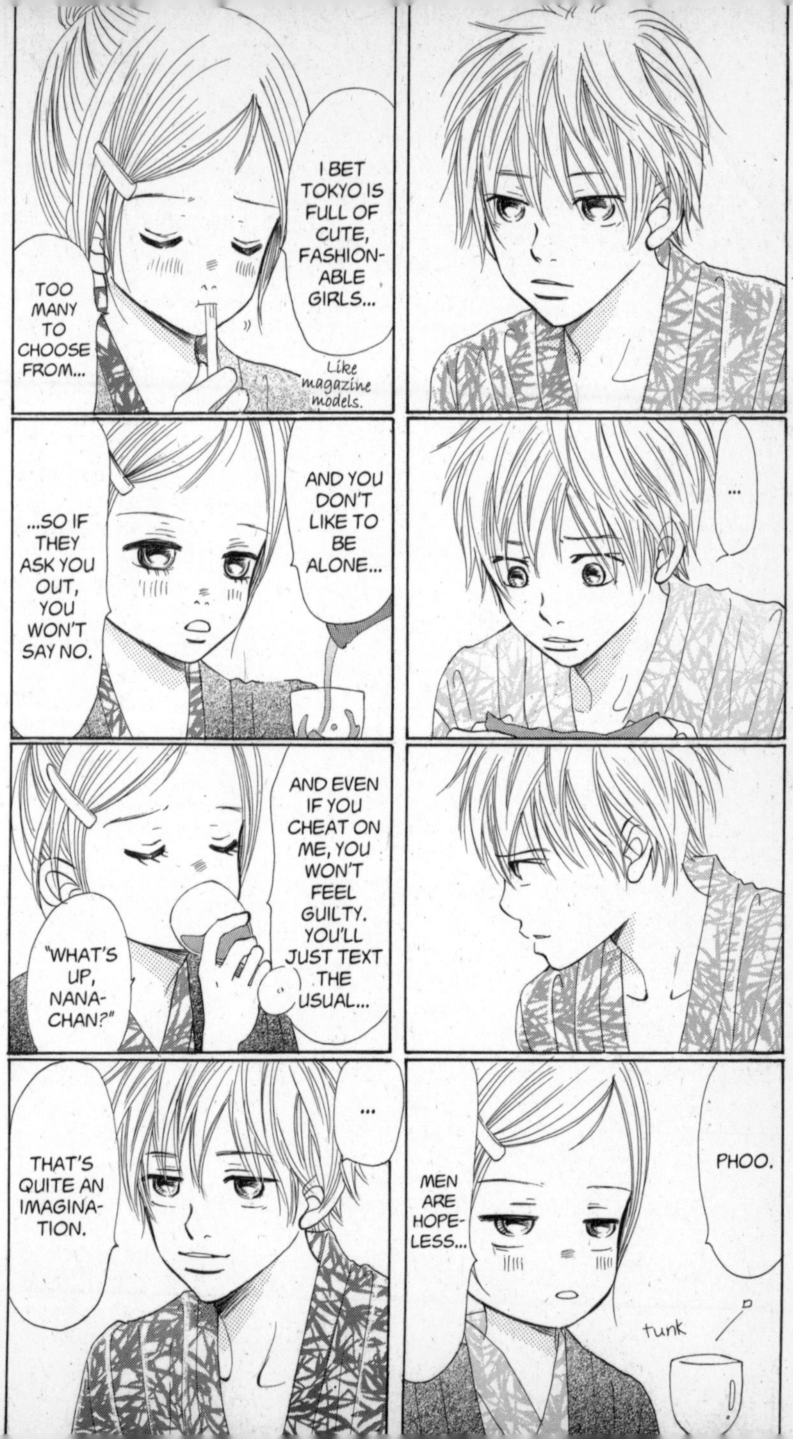
I BET TOKYO IS FULL OF CUTE, FASHIONABLE GIRLS...
Like magazine models.
TOO MANY TO CHOOSE FROM...
...
AND YOU DON'T LIKE TO BE ALONE...
...SO IF THEY ASK YOU OUT, YOU WON'T SAY NO.
AND EVEN IF YOU CHEAT ON ME, YOU WON'T FEEL GUILTY. YOU'LL JUST TEXT THE USUAL...
"WHAT'S UP, NANA-CHAN?"
PHOO.
MEN ARE HOPELESS...
tunk
...
THAT'S QUITE AN IMAGINATION.

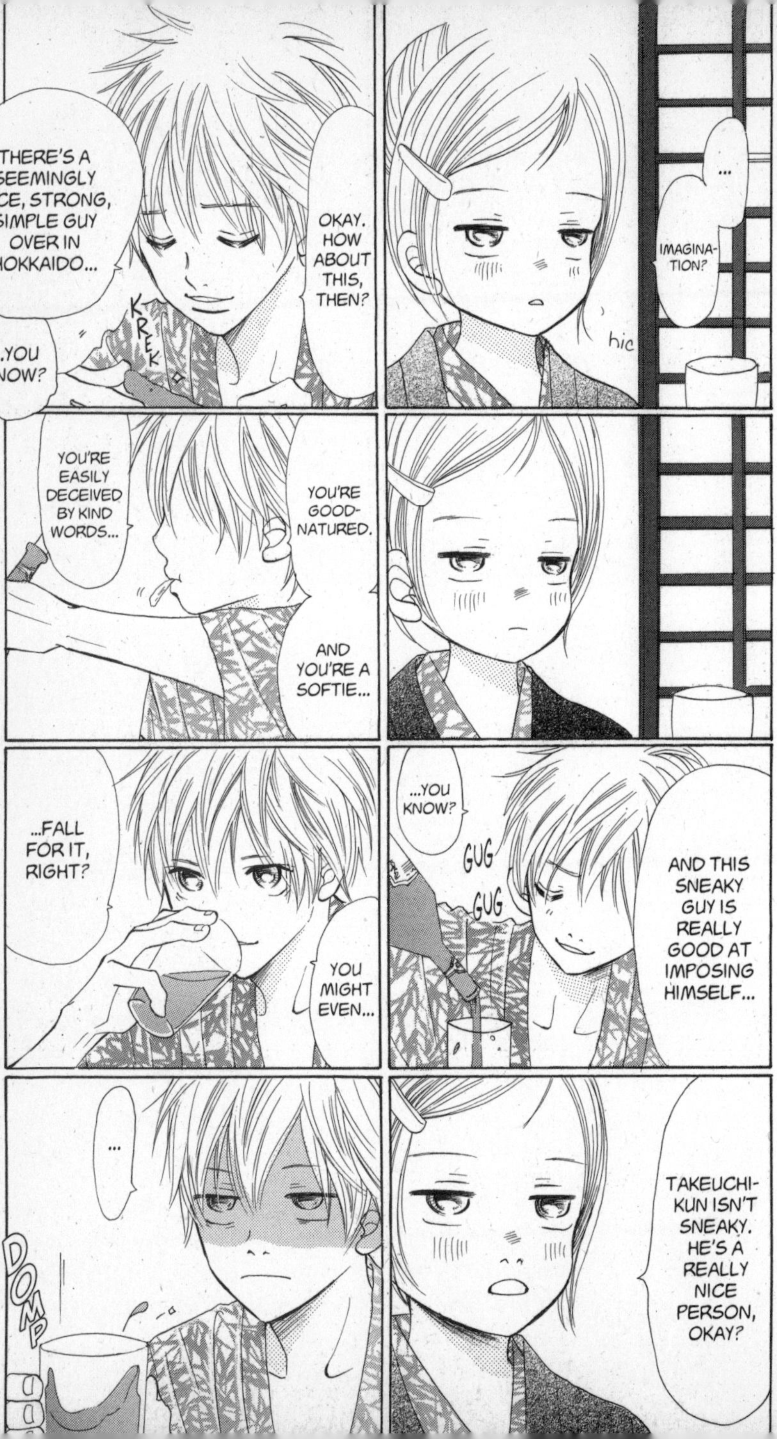
...
IMAGINATION?
hic
OKAY. HOW ABOUT THIS, THEN?
THERE'S A SEEMINGLY NICE, STRONG, SIMPLE GUY OVER IN HOKKAIDO...
KREK
...YOU KNOW?
YOU'RE GOOD-NATURED.
YOU'RE EASILY DECEIVED BY KIND WORDS...
AND YOU'RE A SOFTIE...
...YOU KNOW?
AND THIS SNEAKY GUY IS REALLY GOOD AT IMPOSING HIMSELF...
GUG
GUG
YOU MIGHT EVEN...
...FALL FOR IT, RIGHT?
TAKEUCHI-KUN ISN'T SNEAKY. HE'S A REALLY NICE PERSON, OKAY?
...
DOMP

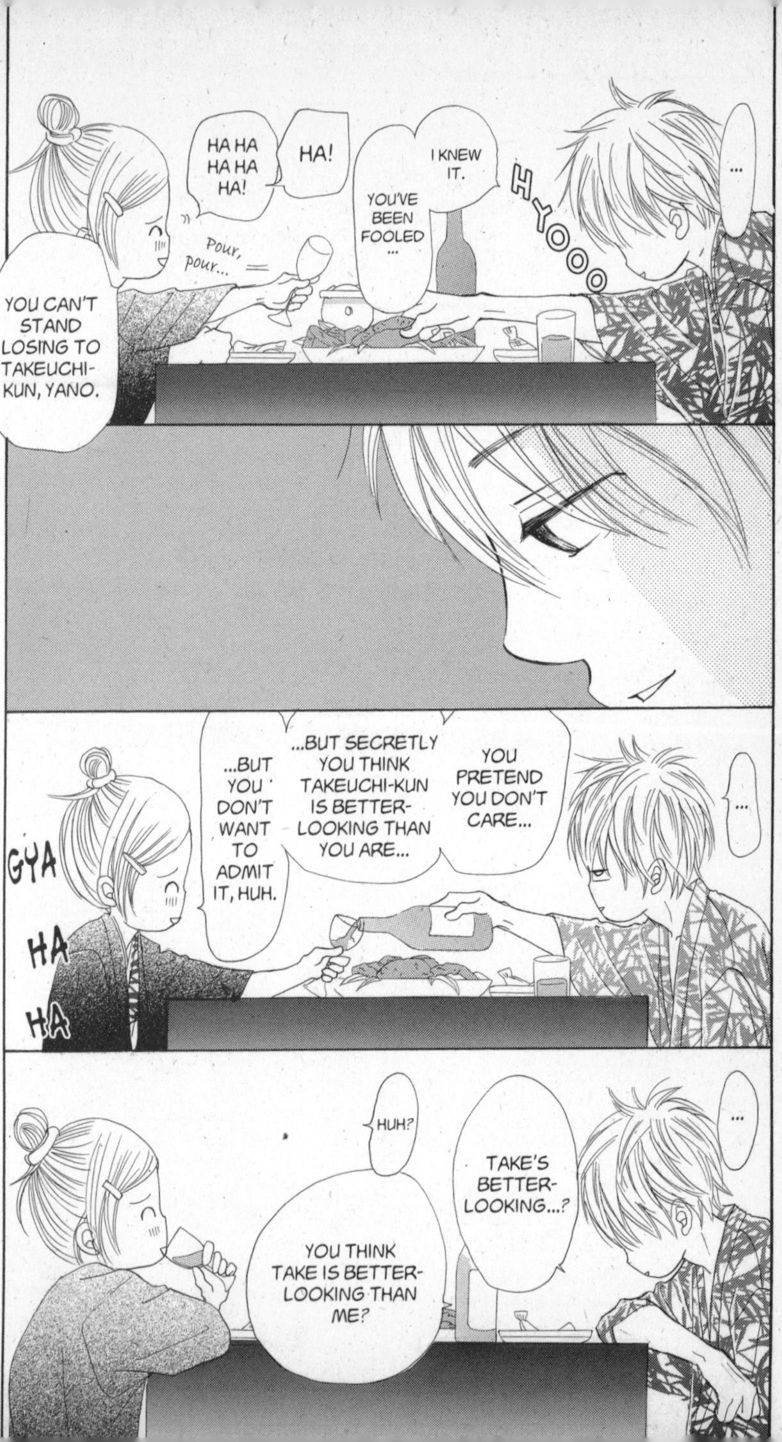
...
HYOOO
I KNEW IT.
YOU'VE BEEN FOOLED ...
HA!
HA HA HA HA HA!
Pour, pour...
YOU CAN'T STAND LOSING TO TAKEUCHI-KUN, YANO.
...
YOU PRETEND YOU DON'T CARE...
...BUT SECRETLY YOU THINK TAKEUCHI-KUN IS BETTER-LOOKING THAN YOU ARE...
...BUT YOU DON'T WANT TO ADMIT IT, HUH.
GYA HA HA
...
TAKE'S BETTER-LOOKING...?
HUH?
YOU THINK TAKE IS BETTER-LOOKING THAN ME?

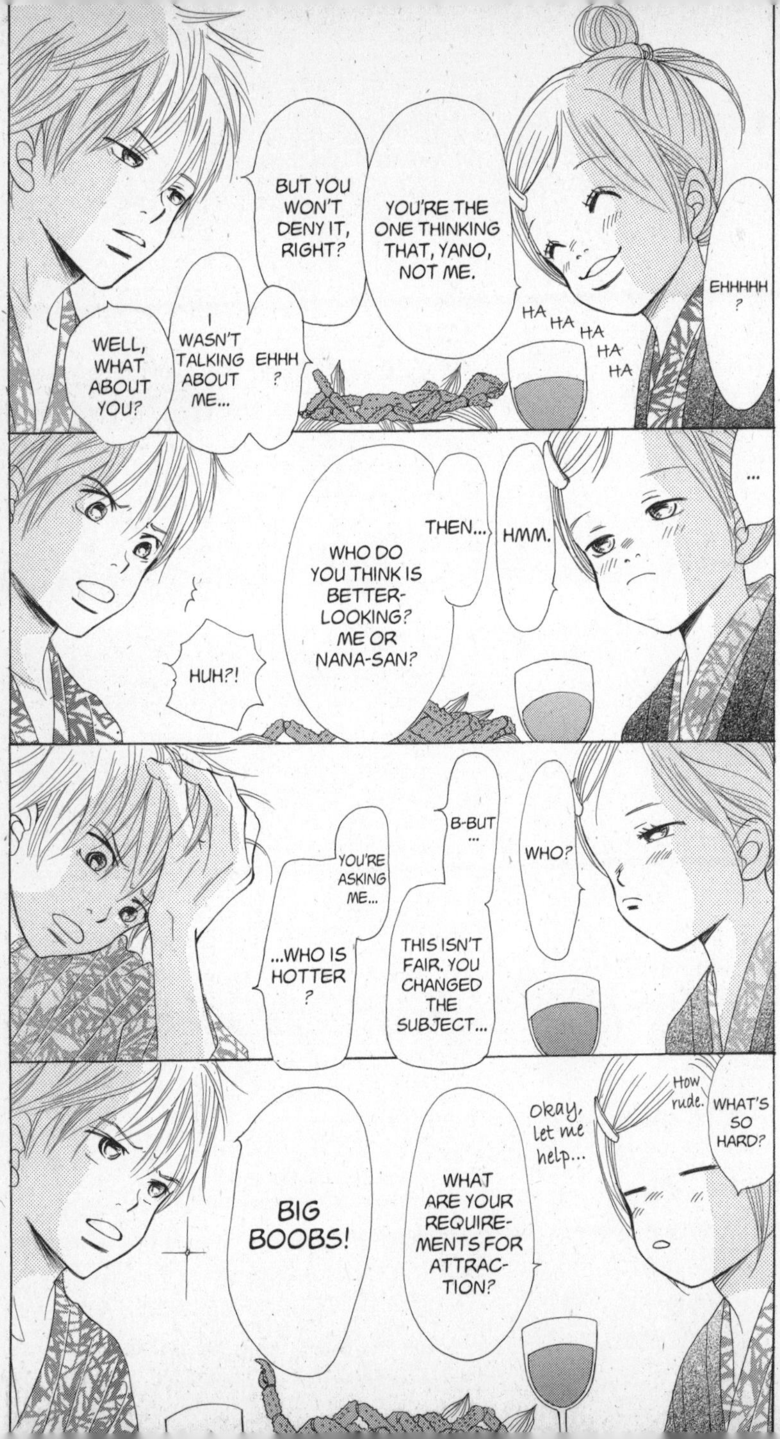
YOU'RE THE ONE THINKING THAT, YANO, NOT ME.
BUT YOU WON'T DENY IT, RIGHT?
EHHHHH?
HA HA HA HA HA
EHHH?
I WASN'T TALKING ABOUT ME...
WELL, WHAT ABOUT YOU?
...
HMM.
THEN...
WHO DO YOU THINK IS BETTER-LOOKING? ME OR NANA-SAN?
HUH?!
WHO?
B-BUT...
THIS ISN'T FAIR. YOU CHANGED THE SUBJECT...
YOU'RE ASKING ME...
...WHO IS HOTTER?
WHAT'S SO HARD?
How rude.
Okay, let me help...
WHAT ARE YOUR REQUIRE-MENTS FOR ATTRAC-TION?
BIG BOOBS!

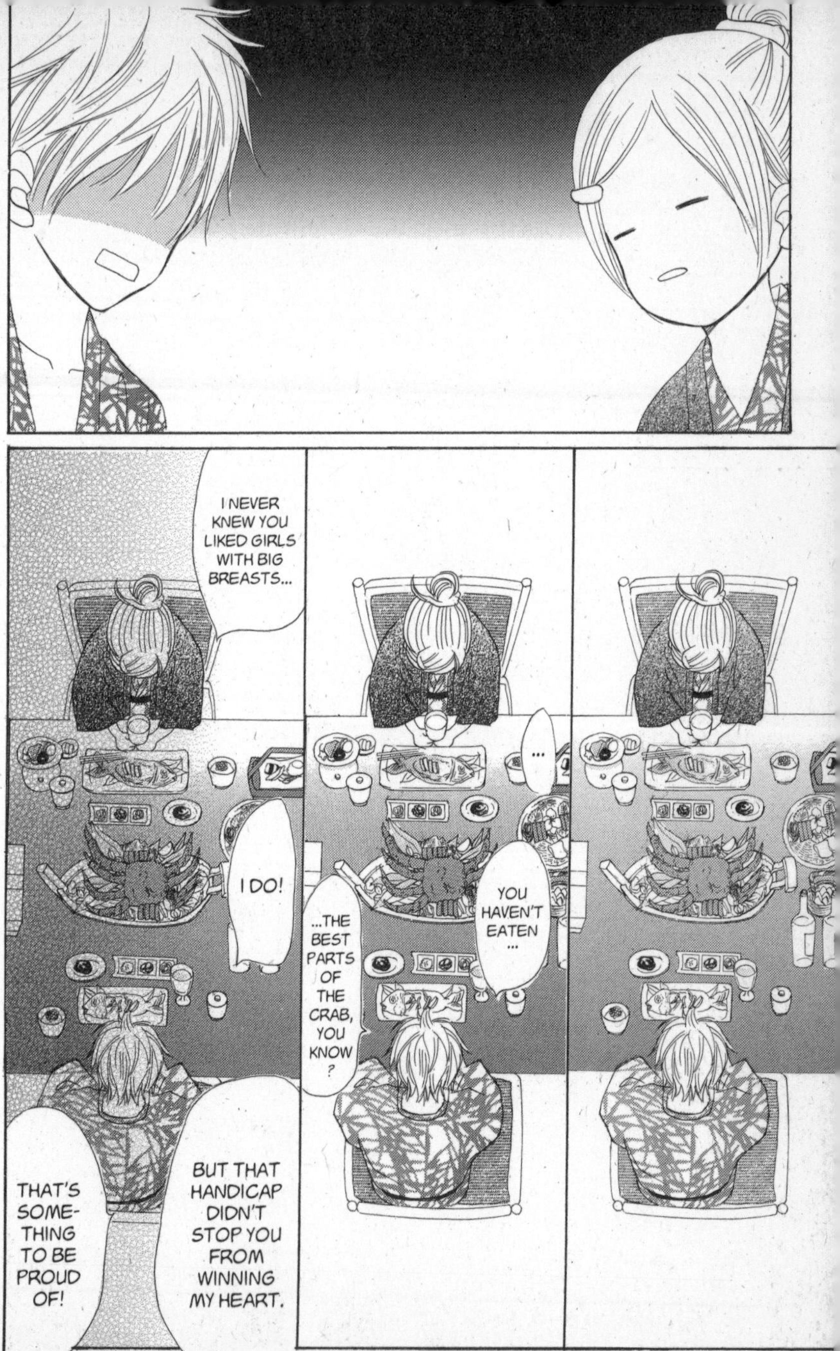
...
YOU HAVEN'T EATEN ...
...THE BEST PARTS OF THE CRAB, YOU KNOW?
I NEVER KNEW YOU LIKED GIRLS WITH BIG BREASTS...
I DO!
BUT THAT HANDICAP DIDN'T STOP YOU FROM WINNING MY HEART.
THAT'S SOME-THING TO BE PROUD OF!

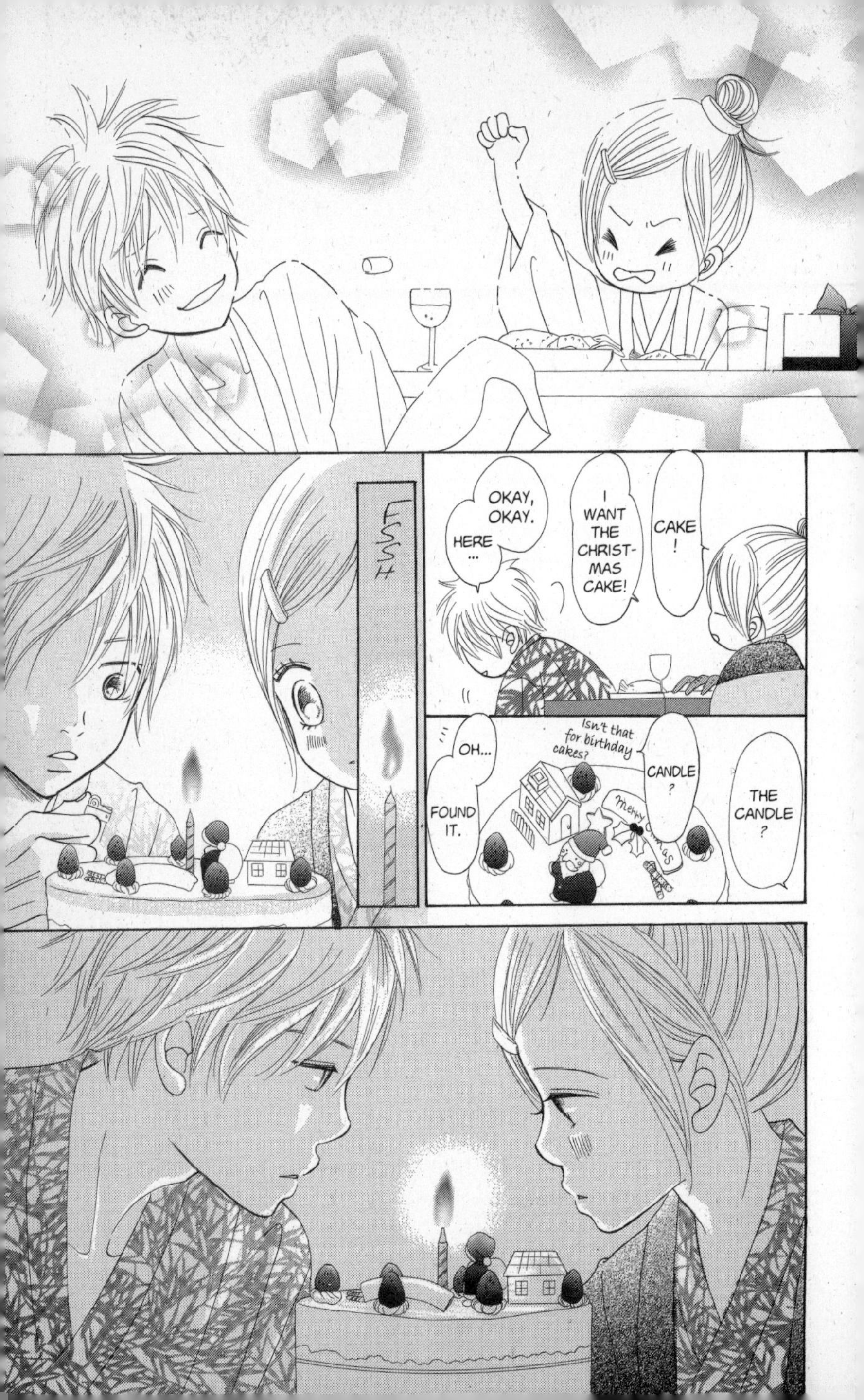
CAKE!
I WANT THE CHRISTMAS CAKE!
OKAY, OKAY. HERE...
THE CANDLE?
CANDLE?
Isn't that for birthday cakes?
OH... FOUND IT.
FSSH
Merry Christmas

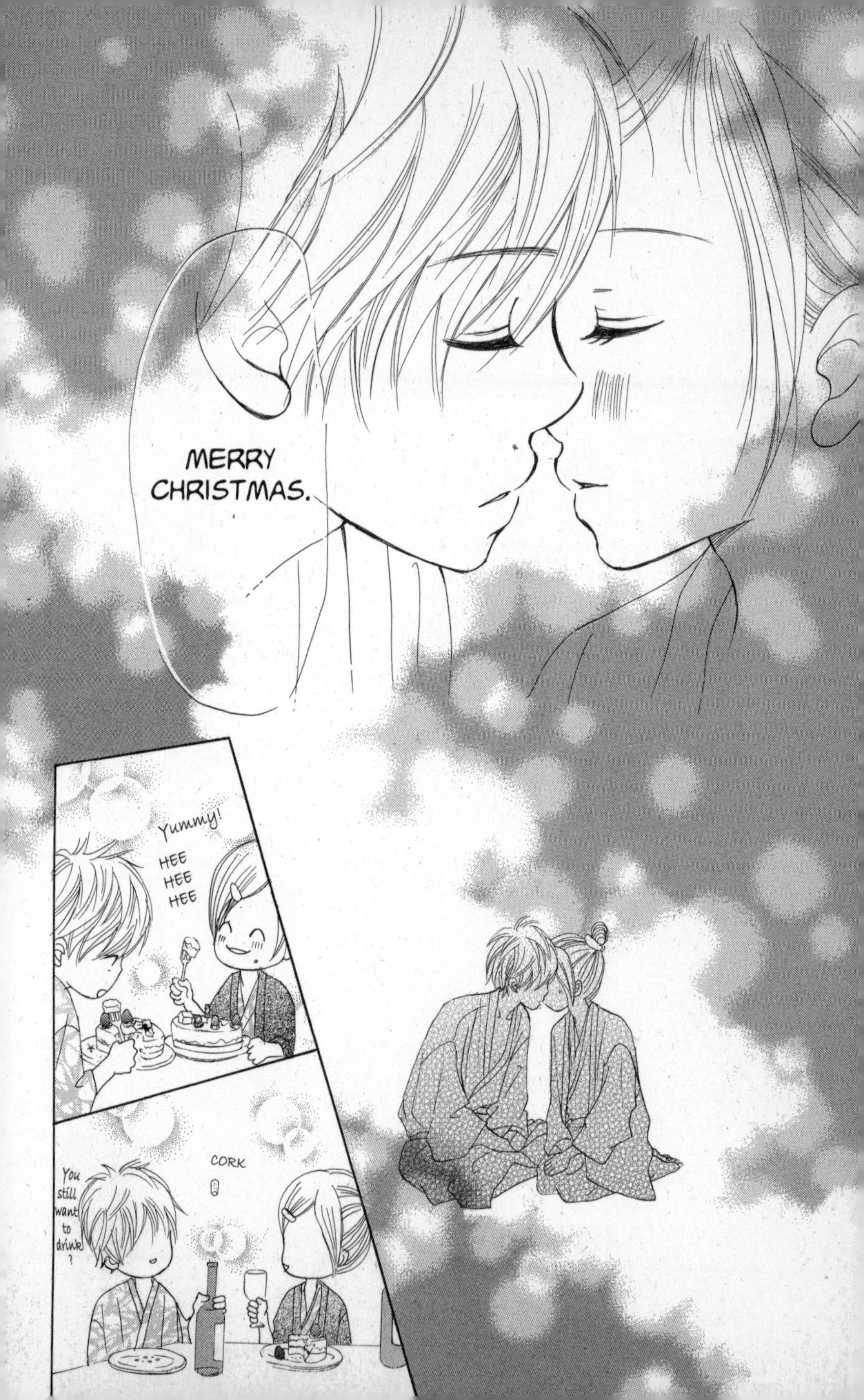
MERRY CHRISTMAS.
Yummy!
HEE HEE HEE
CORK
You still want to drink?

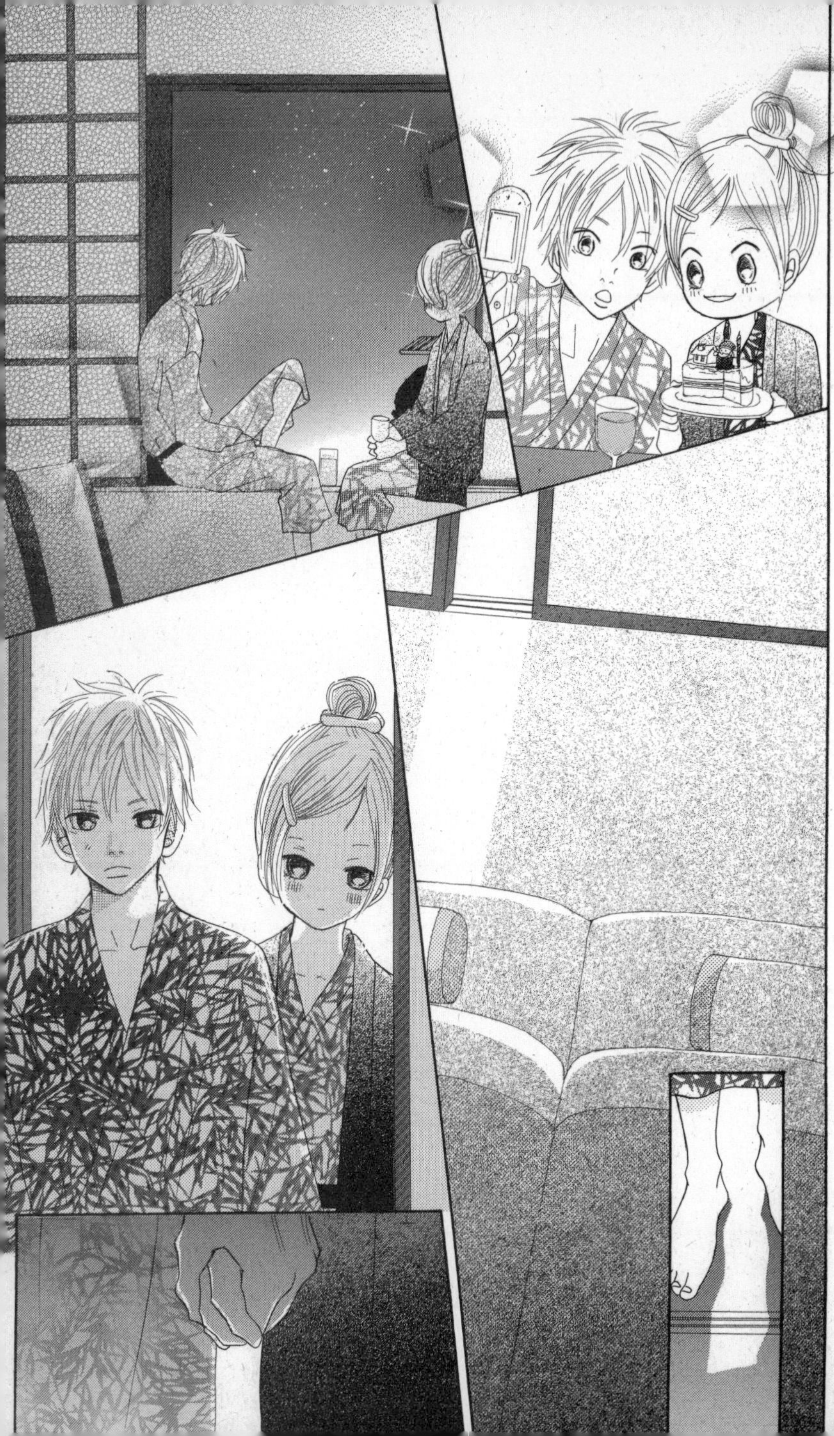

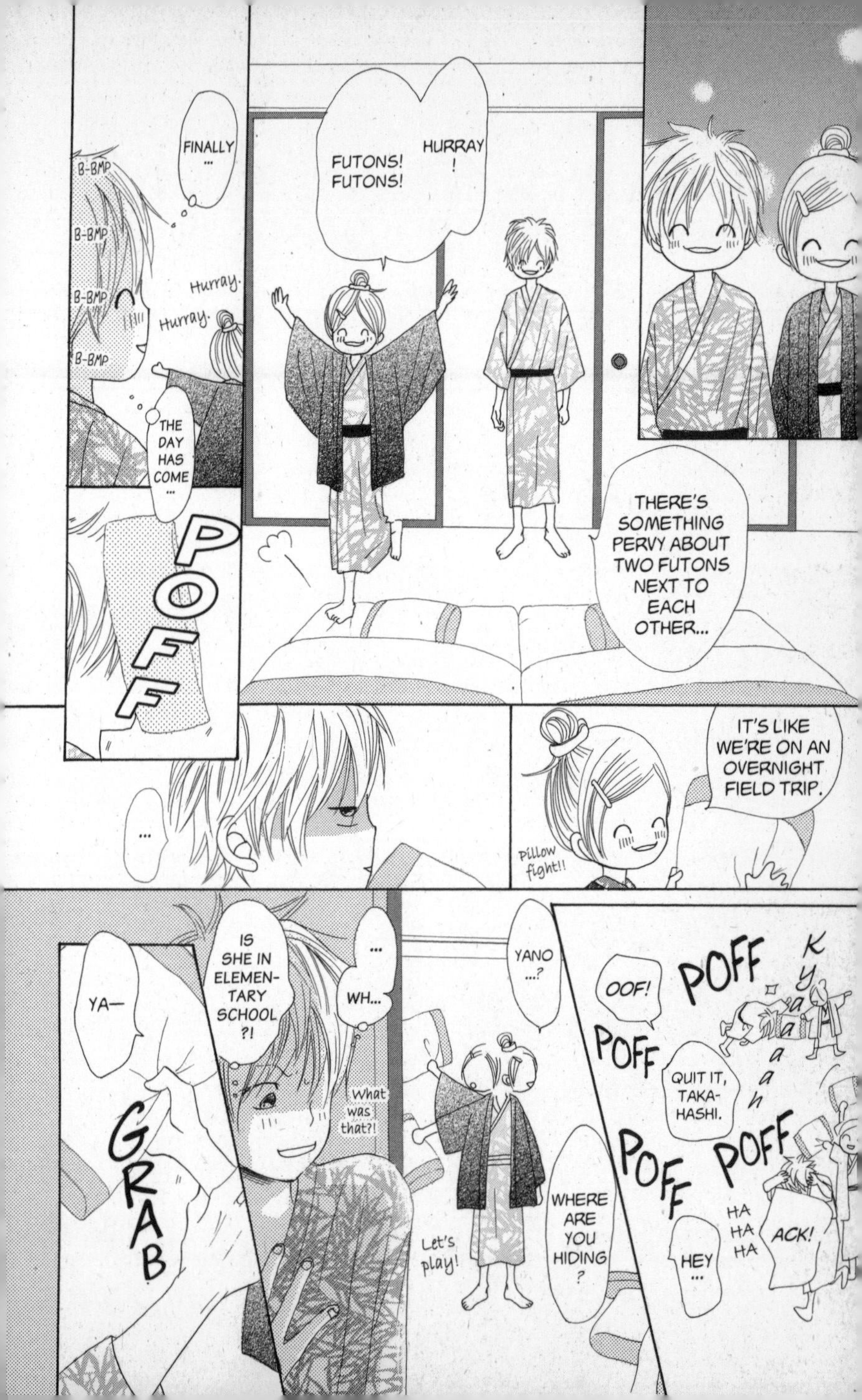
HURRAY!
FUTONS! FUTONS!
THERE'S SOMETHING PERVY ABOUT TWO FUTONS NEXT TO EACH OTHER...
FINALLY...
B-BMP
B-BMP
B-BMP
B-BMP
Hurray.
Hurray.
THE DAY HAS COME...
POFF
IT'S LIKE WE'RE ON AN OVERNIGHT FIELD TRIP.
Pillow fight!!
...
Kyaaaaah
POFF
OOF!
POFF
QUIT IT, TAKAHASHI.
POFF
POFF
HA HA HA
ACK!
HEY...
YANO...?
WHERE ARE YOU HIDING?
Let's play!
...
WH...
IS SHE IN ELEMENTARY SCHOOL?!
What was that?!
YA—
GRAB

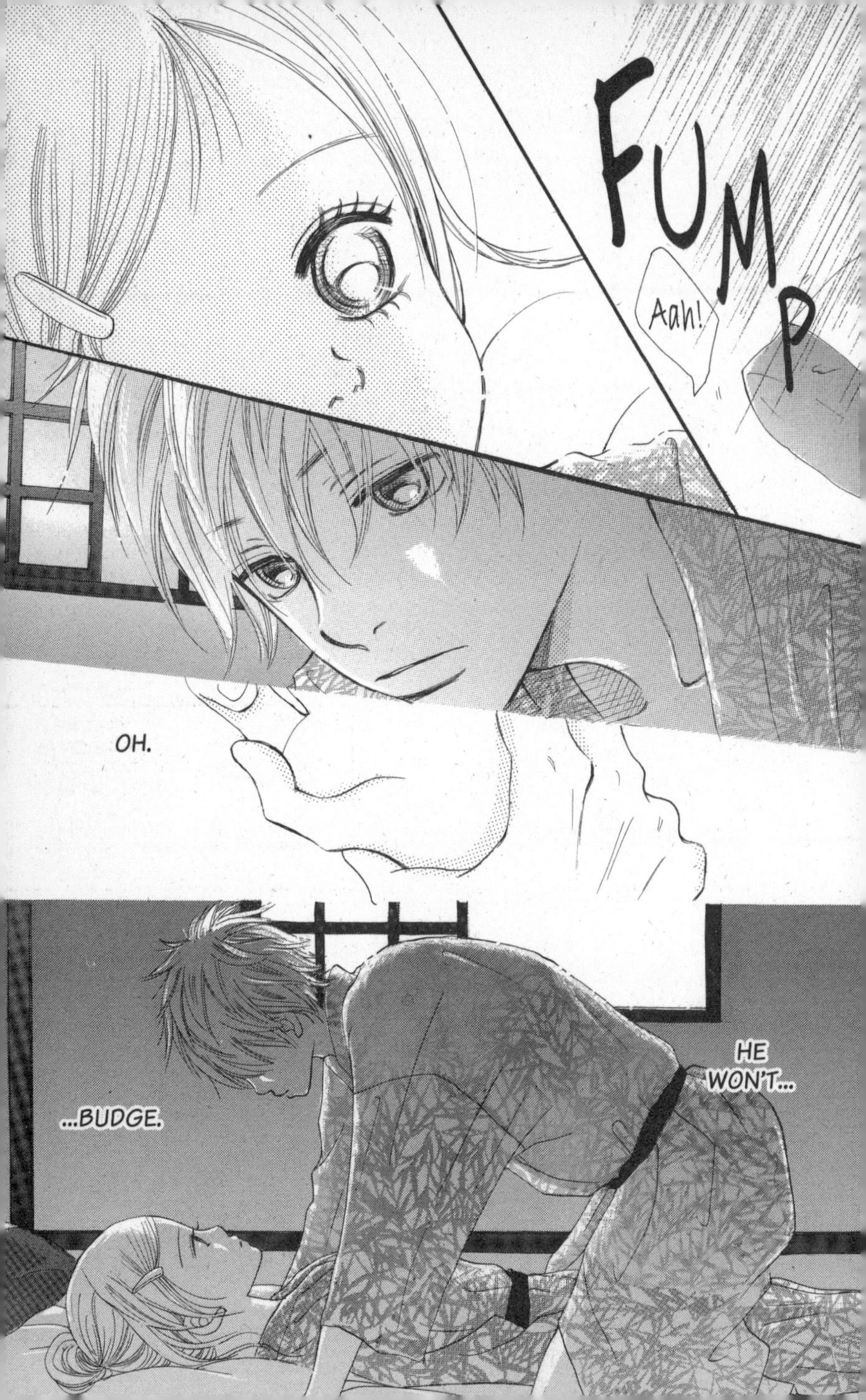
FUMP
Aah!
OH.
HE WON'T...
...BUDGE.

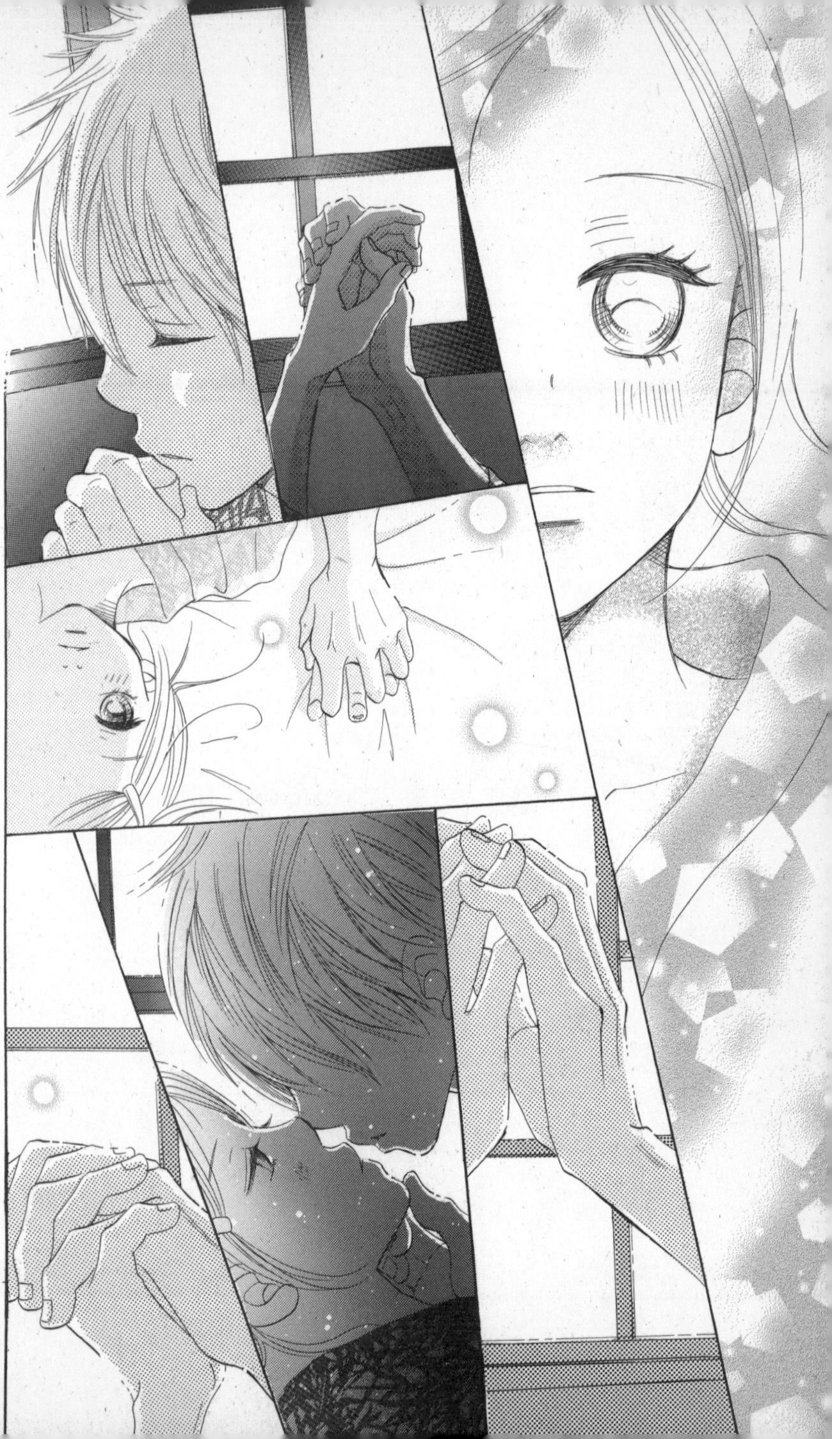

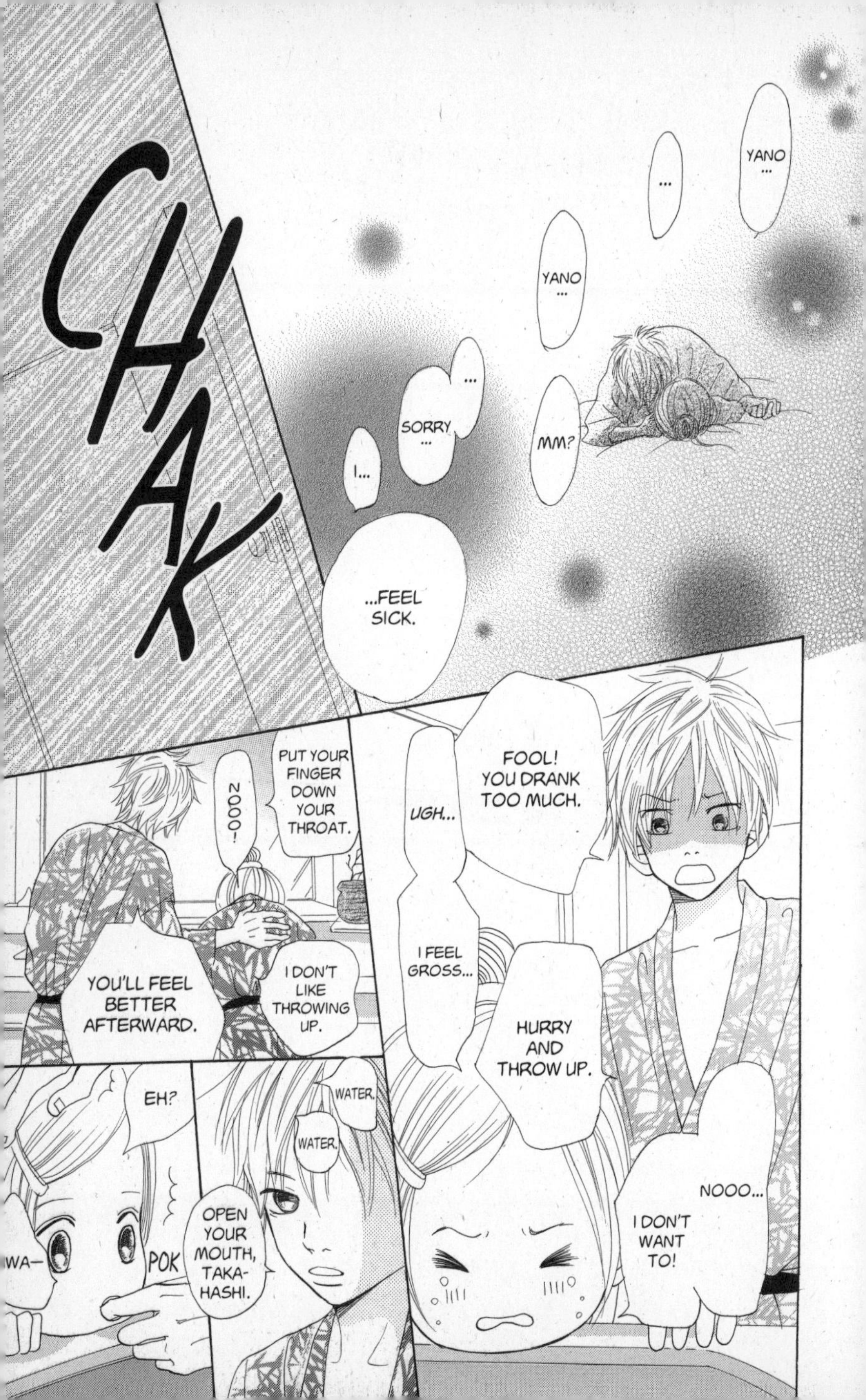
YANO ...
...
YANO ...
MM?
...
SORRY ...
I...
...FEEL SICK.
CHAK
FOOL! YOU DRANK TOO MUCH.
UGH...
I FEEL GROSS...
HURRY AND THROW UP.
NOOO...
I DON'T WANT TO!
PUT YOUR FINGER DOWN YOUR THROAT.
NOOO!
I DON'T LIKE THROWING UP.
YOU'LL FEEL BETTER AFTERWARD.
WATER.
WATER.
OPEN YOUR MOUTH, TAKAHASHI.
EH?
WA—
POK

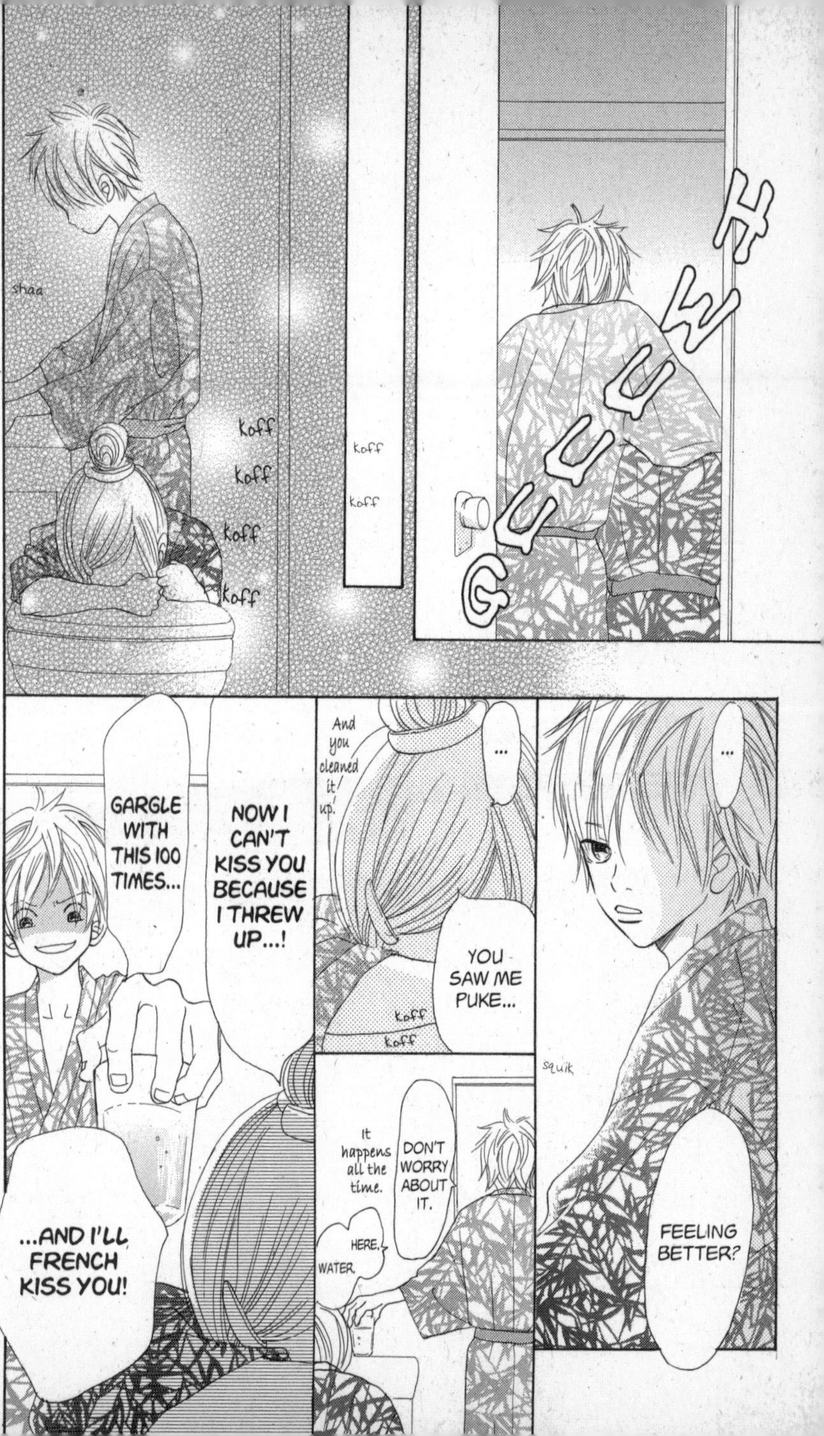
GUUUEH
koff
koff
shaa
koff
koff
koff
koff
...
squik
FEELING BETTER?
...
And you cleaned it up!
YOU SAW ME PUKE...
koff
koff
DON'T WORRY ABOUT IT.
It happens all the time.
HERE, WATER.
NOW I CAN'T KISS YOU BECAUSE I THREW UP...!
GARGLE WITH THIS 100 TIMES...
...AND I'LL FRENCH KISS YOU!

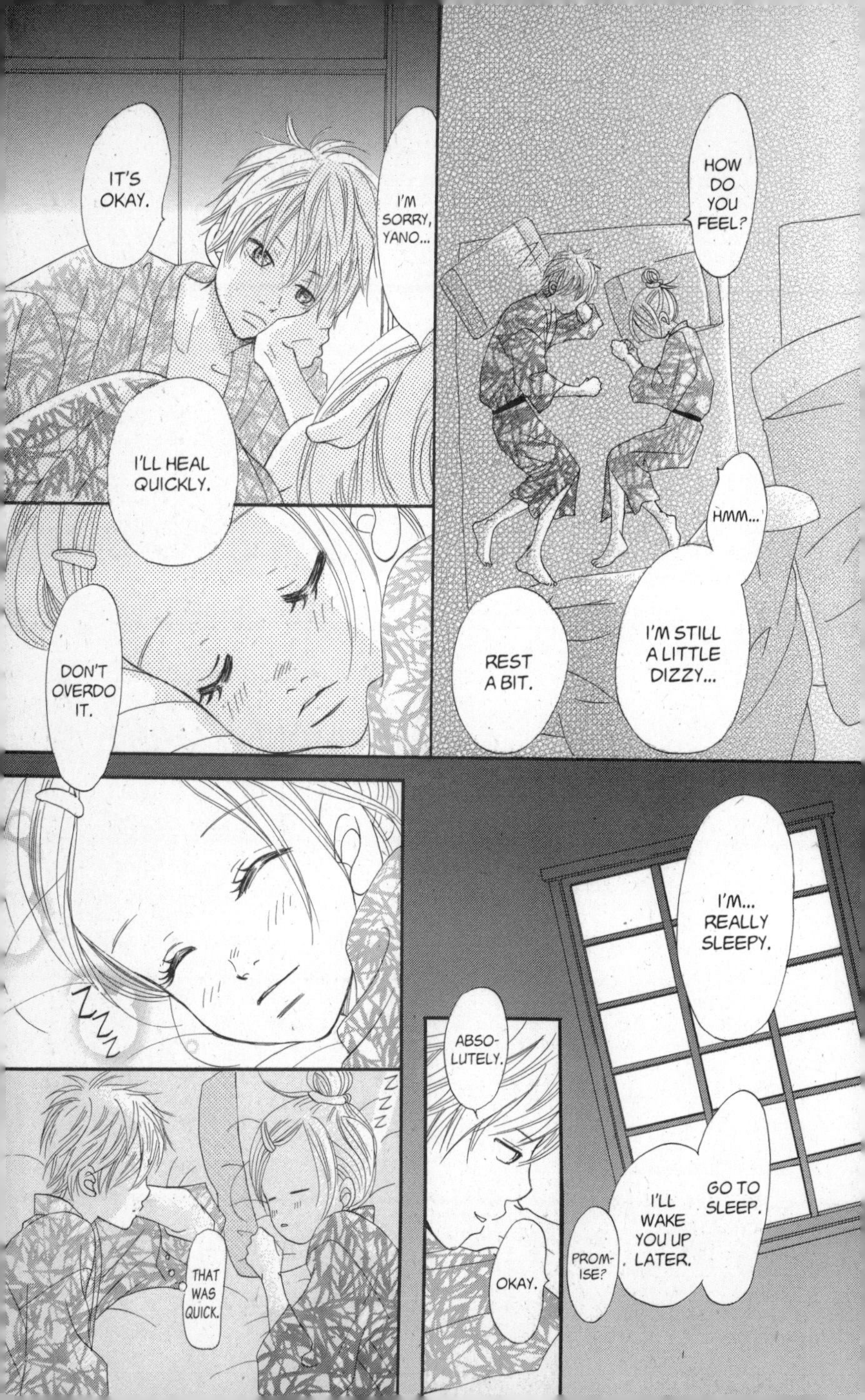
HOW DO YOU FEEL?
HMM...
I'M STILL A LITTLE DIZZY...
REST A BIT.
I'M SORRY, YANO...
IT'S OKAY.
I'LL HEAL QUICKLY.
DON'T OVERDO IT.
I'M... REALLY SLEEPY.
GO TO SLEEP.
I'LL WAKE YOU UP LATER.
PROMISE?
ABSO-LUTELY.
OKAY.
ZZZ
THAT WAS QUICK.

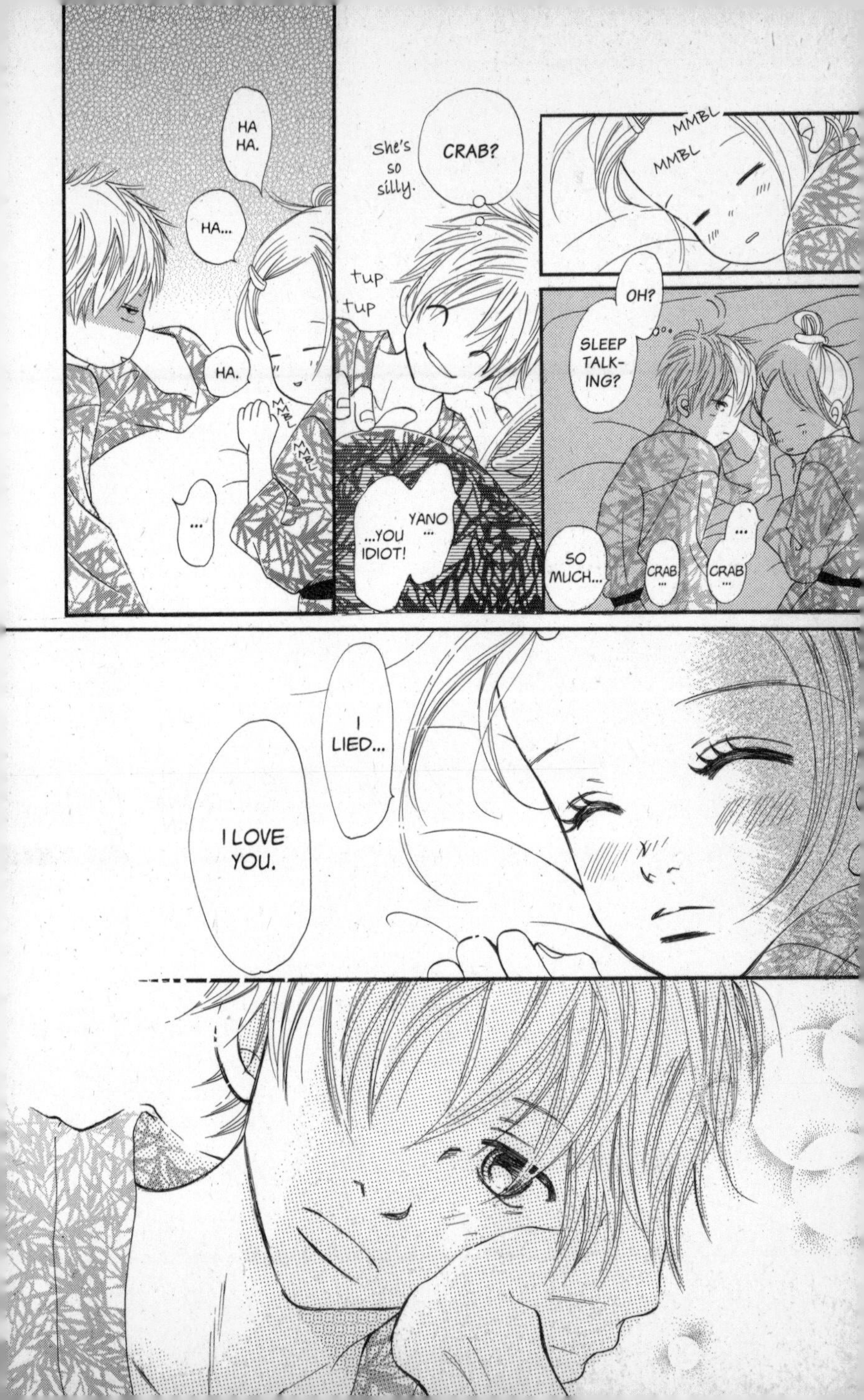
MMBL
MMBL
OH?
SLEEP TALKING?
...
CRAB...
CRAB...
SO MUCH...
CRAB?
She's so silly.
tup
tup
YANO...
...YOU IDIOT!
HA HA.
HA...
HA.
MMBL
MMBL
...
I LIED...
I LOVE YOU.

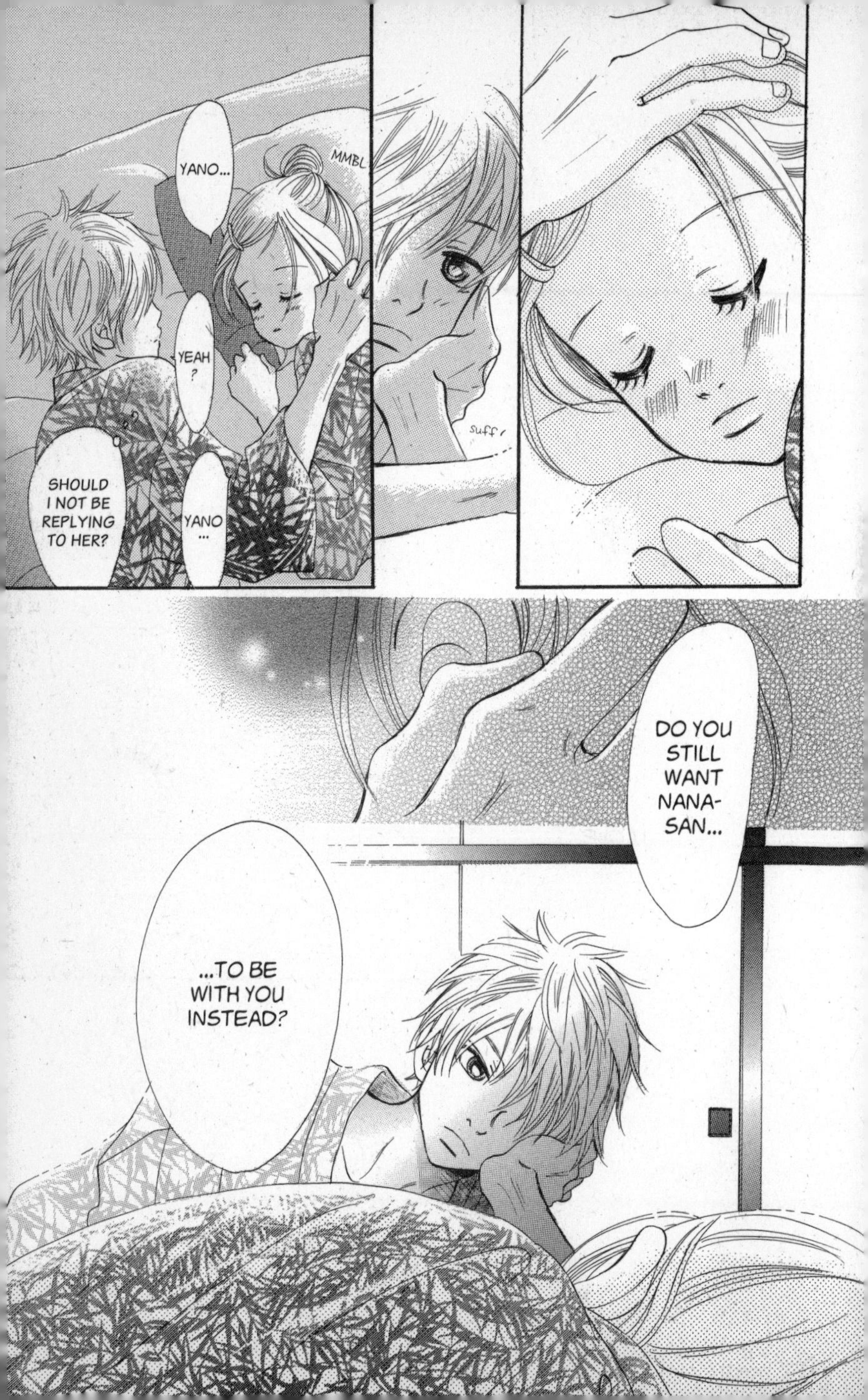
suff
MMBL
YANO...
YEAH ?
YANO ...
SHOULD I NOT BE REPLYING TO HER?
DO YOU STILL WANT NANA-SAN...
...TO BE WITH YOU INSTEAD?

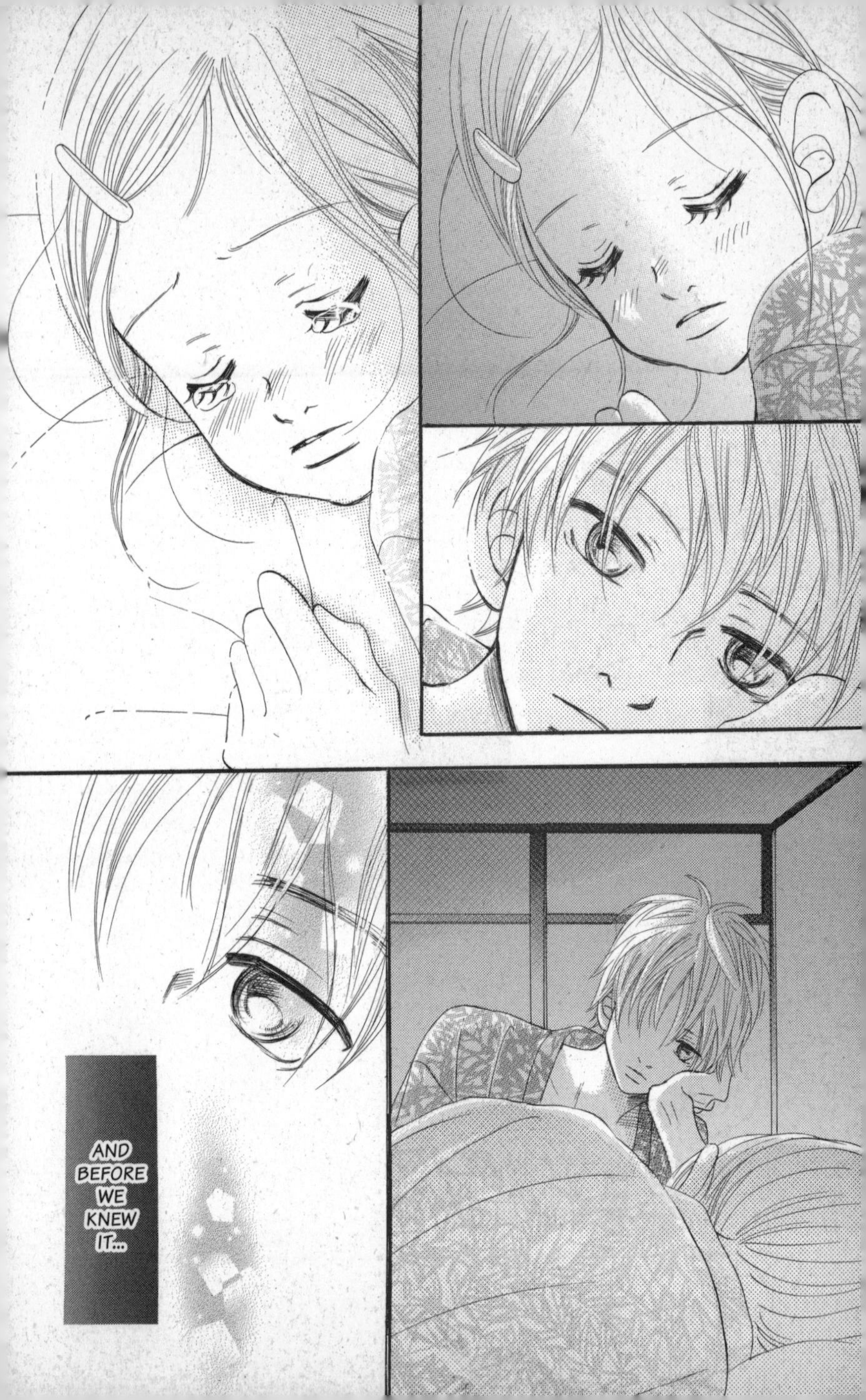
AND BEFORE WE KNEW IT...

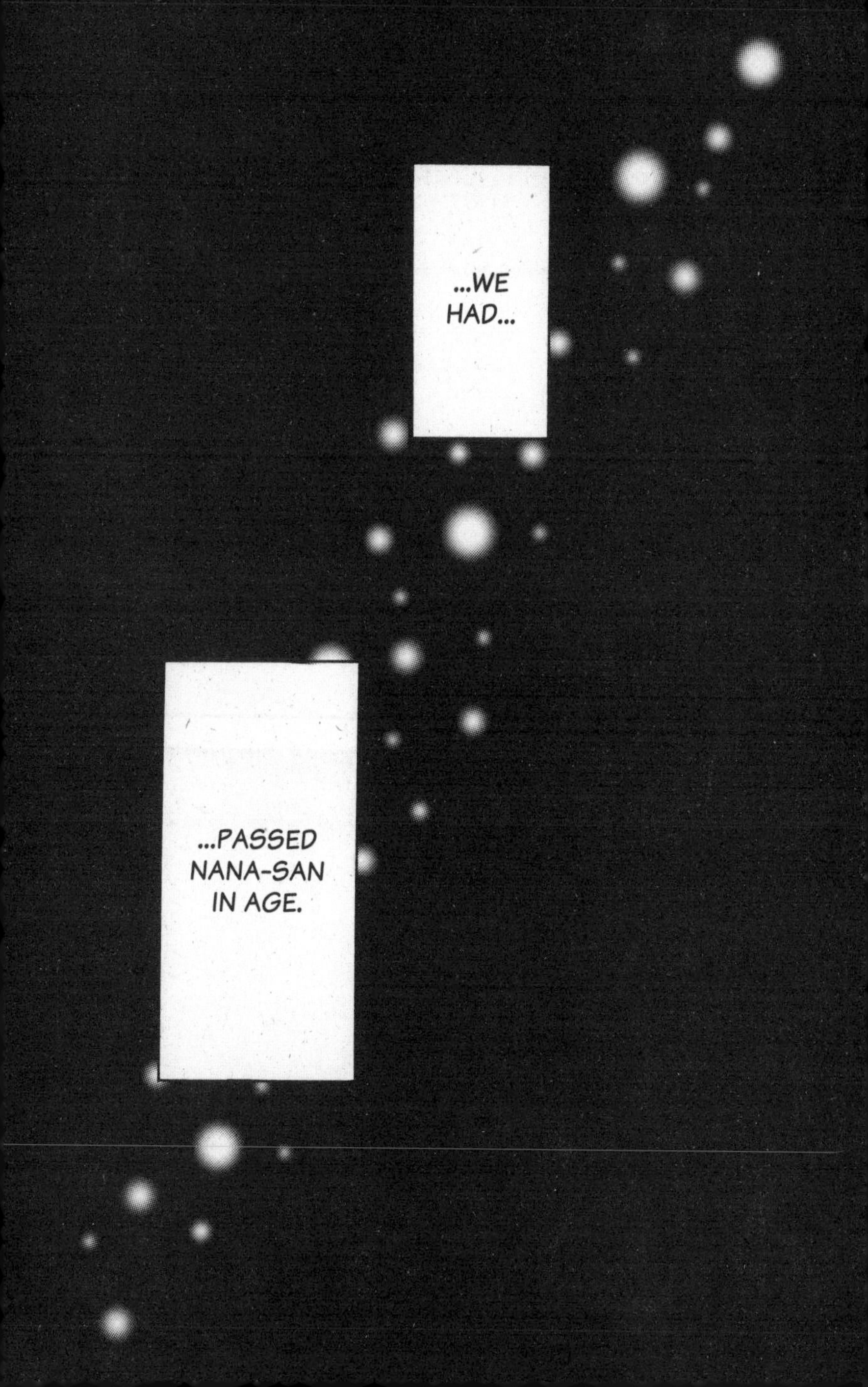
...WE HAD...
...PASSED NANA-SAN IN AGE.

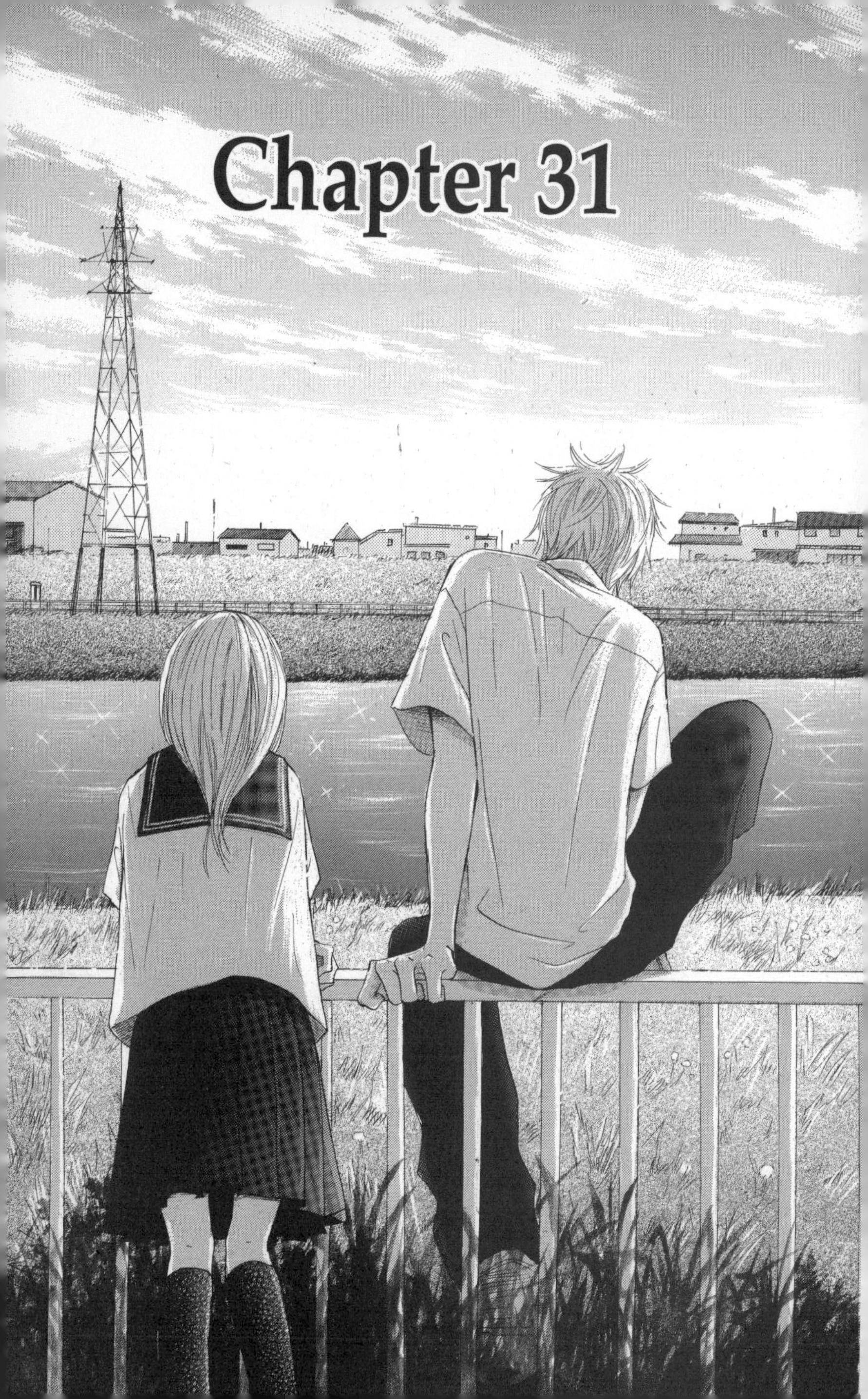
Chapter 31

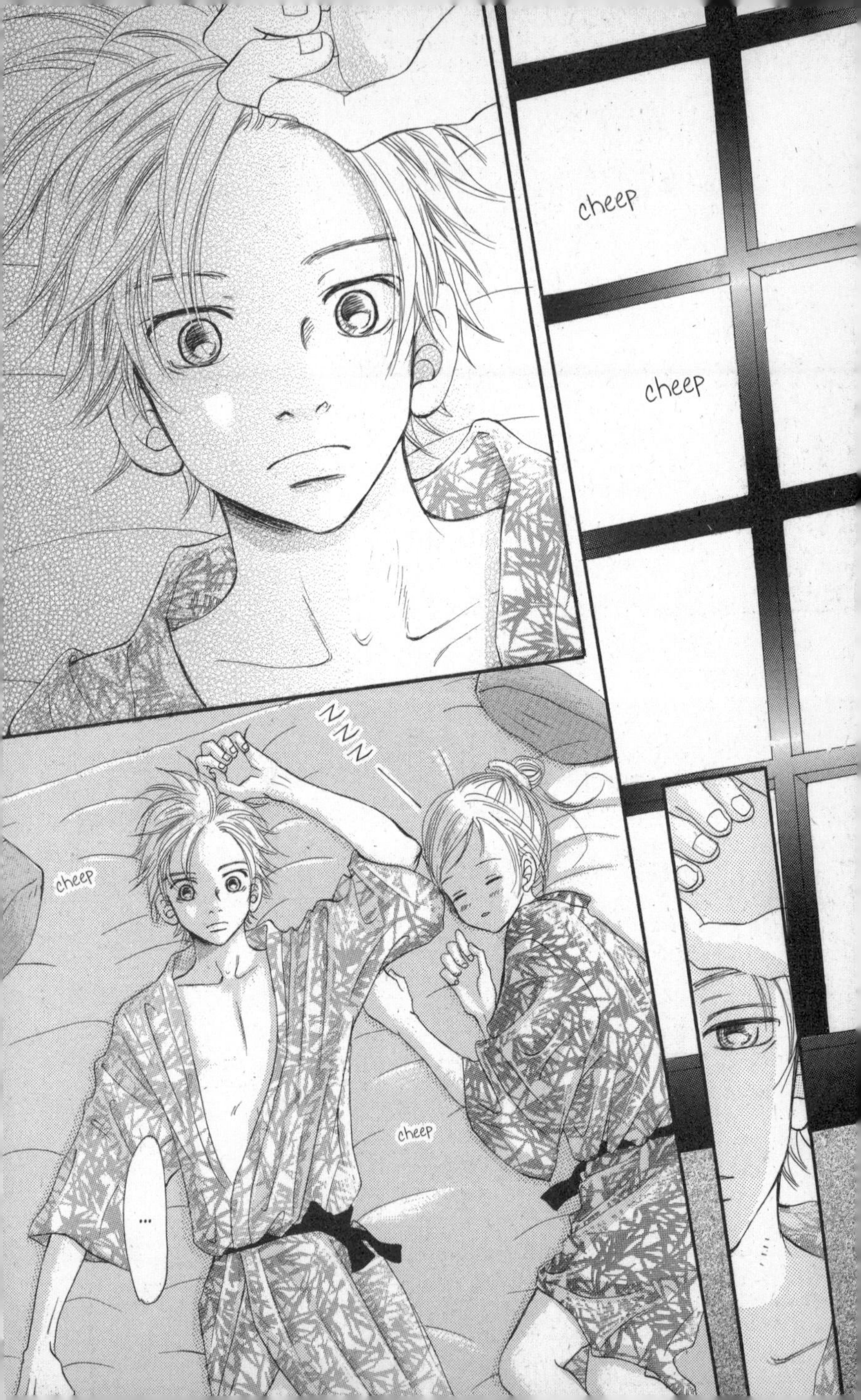
cheep
cheep
NNN—
cheep
cheep
...

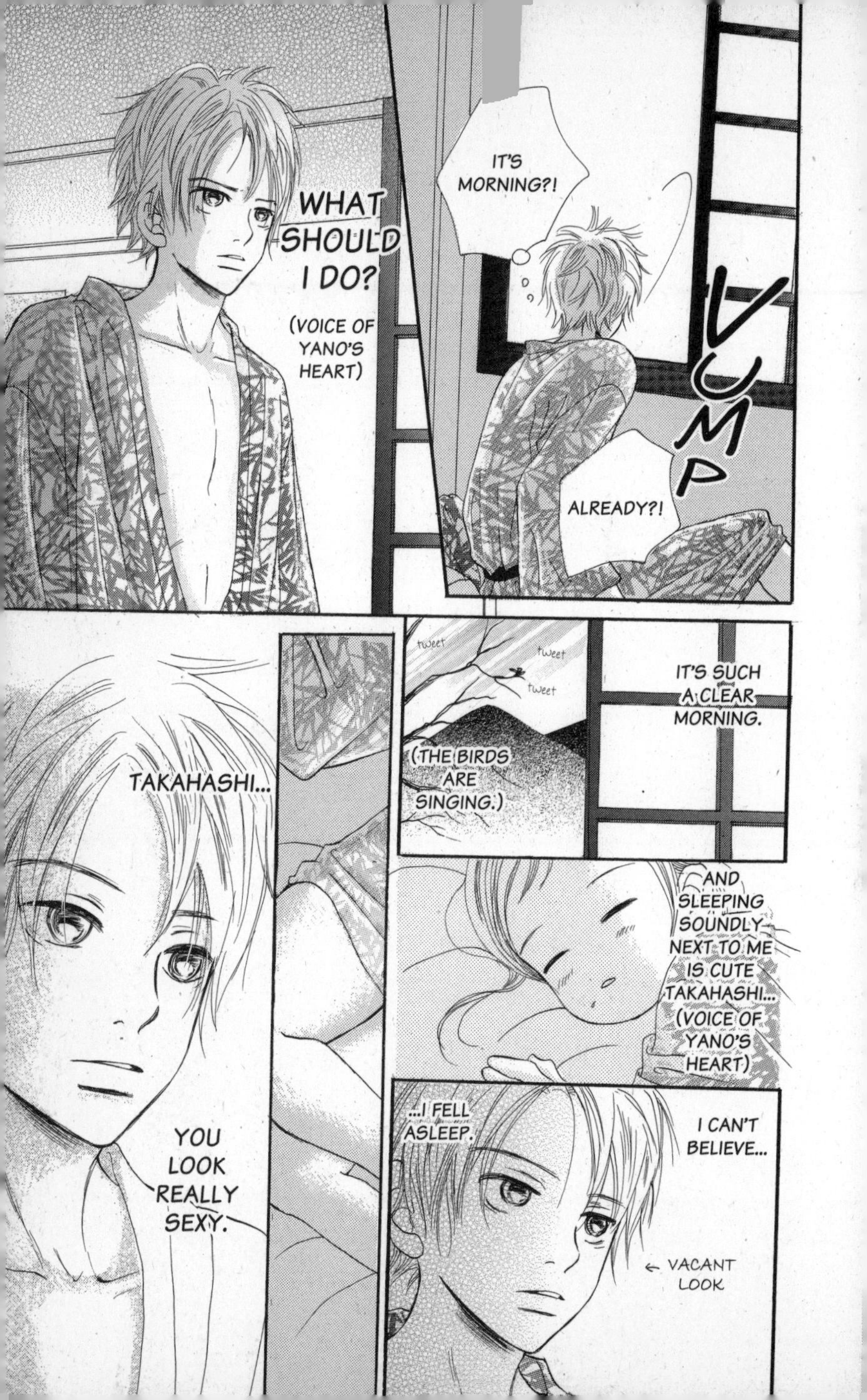
IT'S MORNING?!
ALREADY?!
VUMP
WHAT SHOULD I DO?
(VOICE OF YANO'S HEART)
tweet
tweet
tweet
IT'S SUCH A CLEAR MORNING.
(THE BIRDS ARE SINGING.)
AND SLEEPING SOUNDLY NEXT TO ME IS CUTE TAKAHASHI...
(VOICE OF YANO'S HEART)
I CAN'T BELIEVE...
...I FELL ASLEEP.
← VACANT LOOK
TAKAHASHI...
YOU LOOK REALLY SEXY.

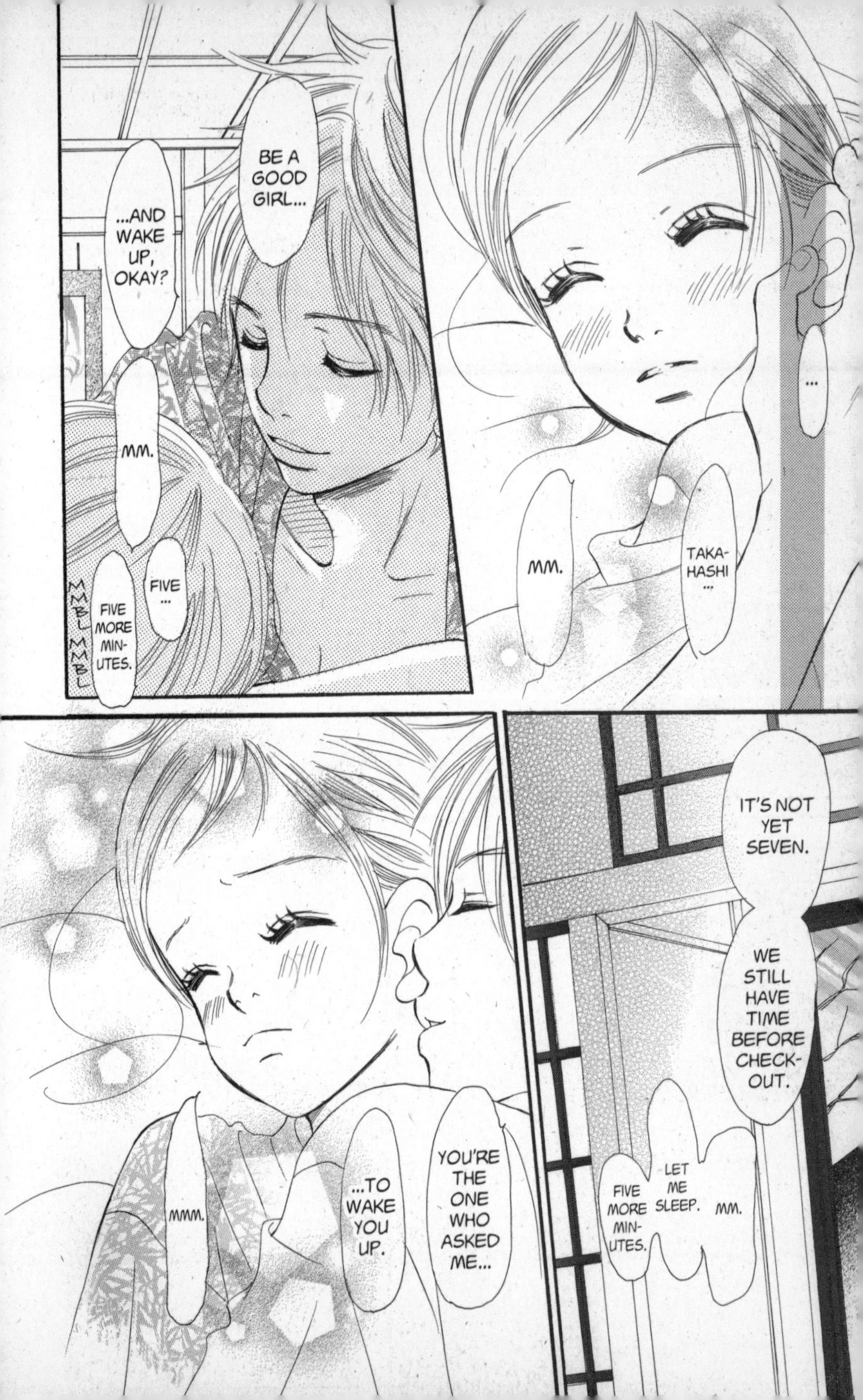
...
TAKAHASHI...
MM.
BE A GOOD GIRL...
...AND WAKE UP, OKAY?
MM.
FIVE...
FIVE MORE MINUTES.
MMBL MMBL
IT'S NOT YET SEVEN.
WE STILL HAVE TIME BEFORE CHECK-OUT.
MM.
LET ME SLEEP.
FIVE MORE MINUTES.
YOU'RE THE ONE WHO ASKED ME...
...TO WAKE YOU UP.
MMM.

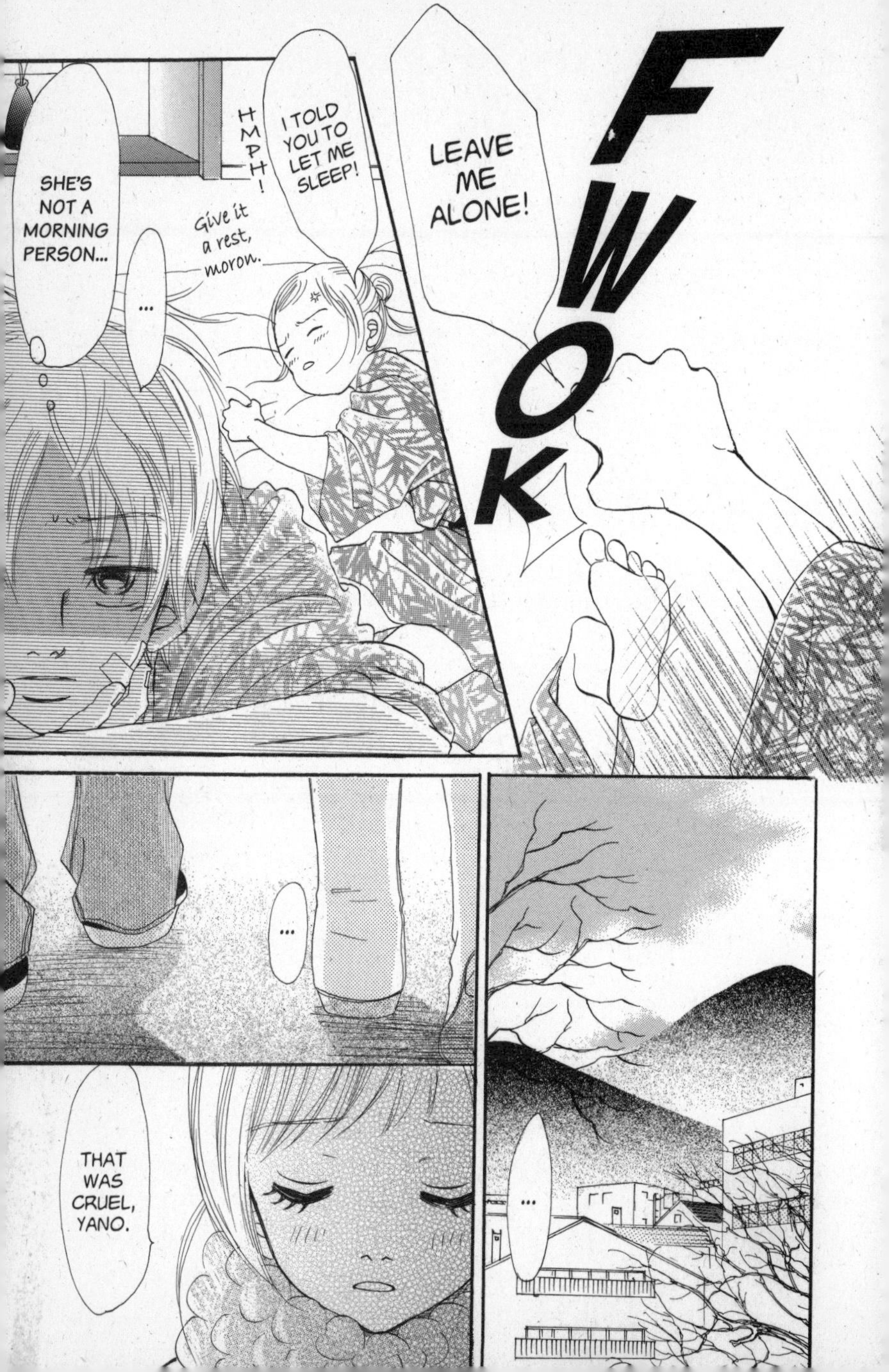
FWOK
LEAVE ME ALONE!
I TOLD YOU TO LET ME SLEEP!
HMPH!
Give it a rest, moron.
SHE'S NOT A MORNING PERSON...
...
...
...
THAT WAS CRUEL, YANO.

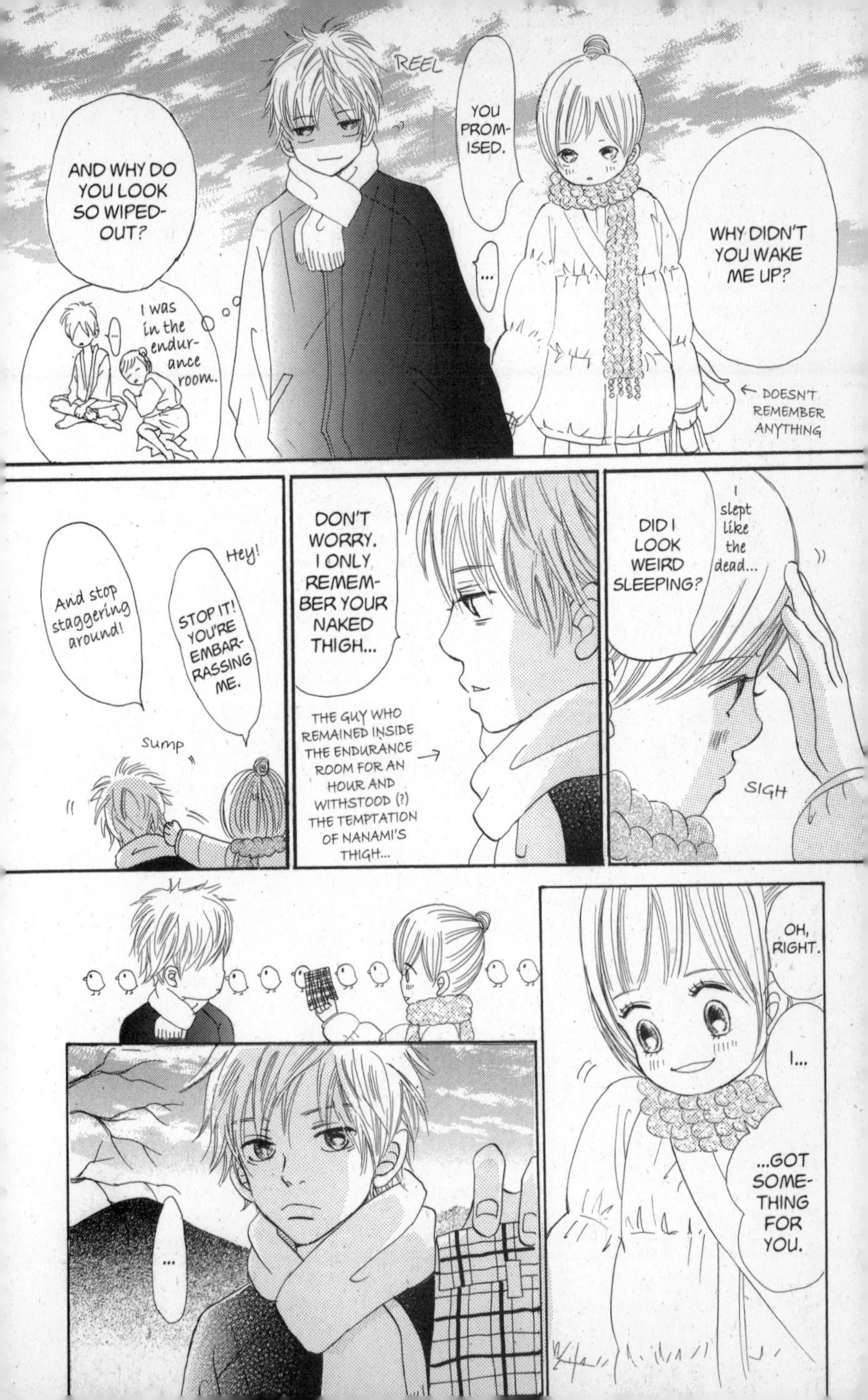
WHY DIDN'T YOU WAKE ME UP?
← DOESN'T REMEMBER ANYTHING
YOU PROMISED.
REEL
...
AND WHY DO YOU LOOK SO WIPED-OUT?
I was in the endurance room.
...
I slept like the dead...
DID I LOOK WEIRD SLEEPING?
SIGH
DON'T WORRY. I ONLY REMEMBER YOUR NAKED THIGH...
THE GUY WHO REMAINED INSIDE THE ENDURANCE ROOM FOR AN HOUR AND WITHSTOOD (?) THE TEMPTATION OF NANAMI'S THIGH... →
Hey!
STOP IT! YOU'RE EMBARRASSING ME.
And stop staggering around!
Sump
OH, RIGHT.
I...
...GOT SOMETHING FOR YOU.
...

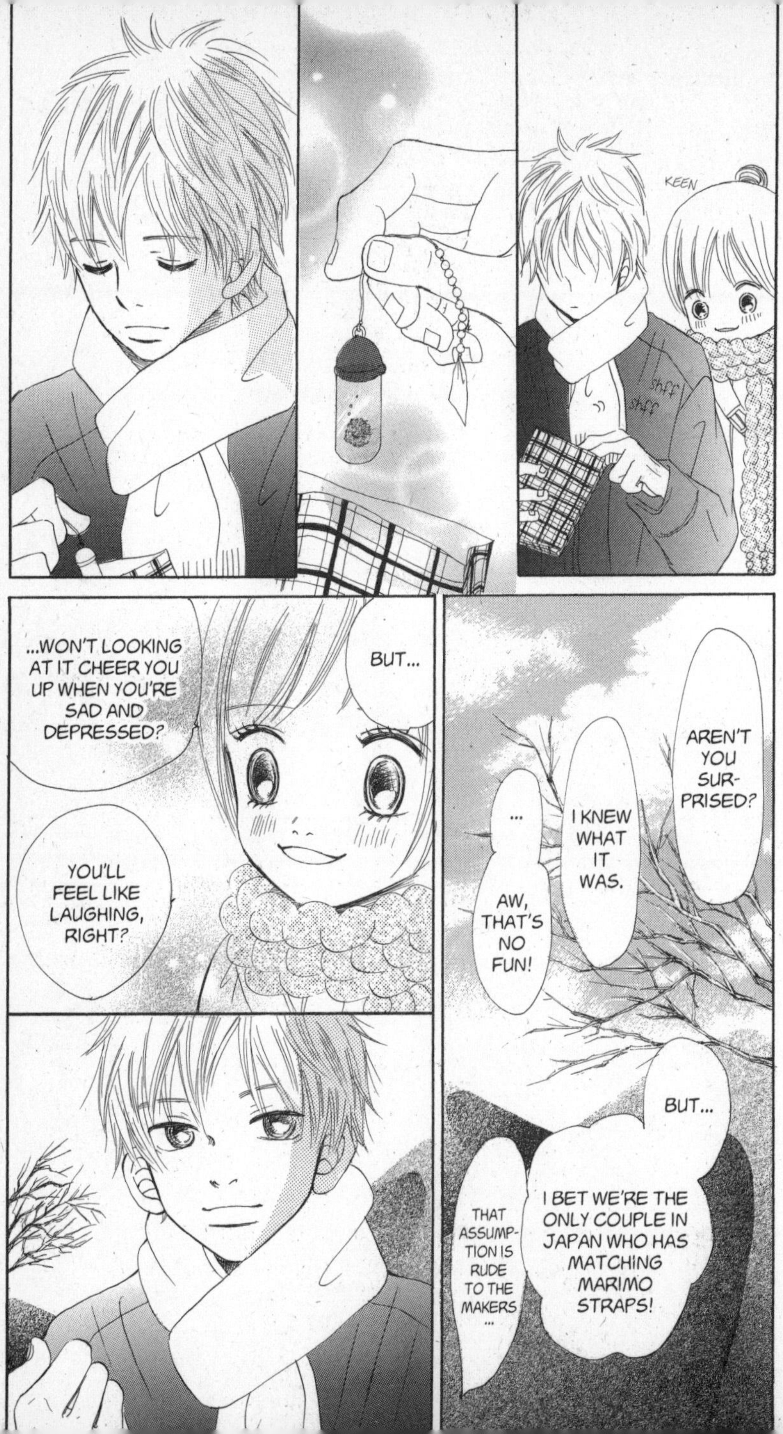
KEEN
shff
shff
AREN'T YOU SUR-PRISED?
I KNEW WHAT IT WAS.
...
AW, THAT'S NO FUN!
BUT...
I BET WE'RE THE ONLY COUPLE IN JAPAN WHO HAS MATCHING MARIMO STRAPS!
THAT ASSUMP-TION IS RUDE TO THE MAKERS ...
BUT...
...WON'T LOOKING AT IT CHEER YOU UP WHEN YOU'RE SAD AND DEPRESSED?
YOU'LL FEEL LIKE LAUGHING, RIGHT?

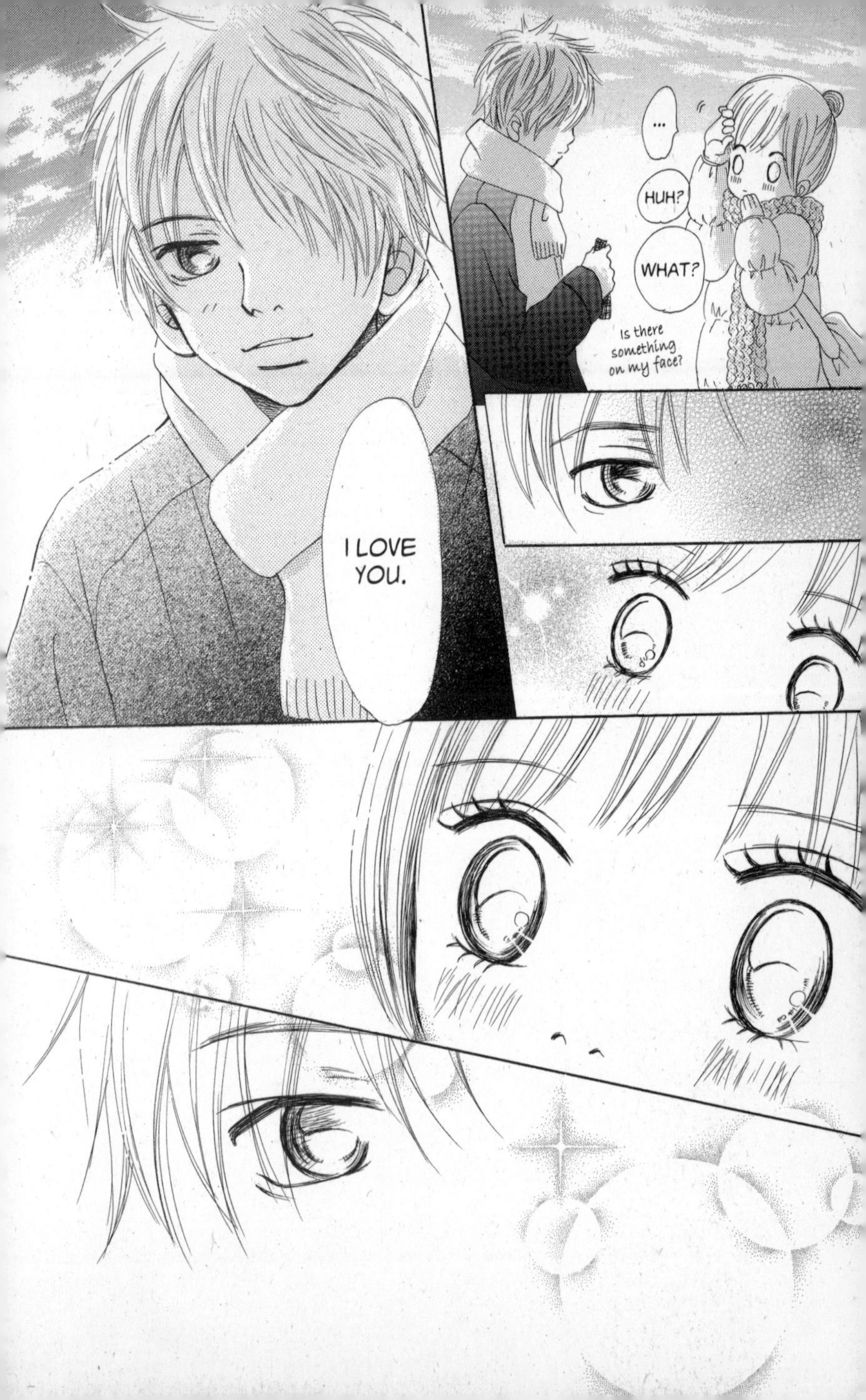
...
HUH?
WHAT?
Is there something on my face?
I LOVE YOU.

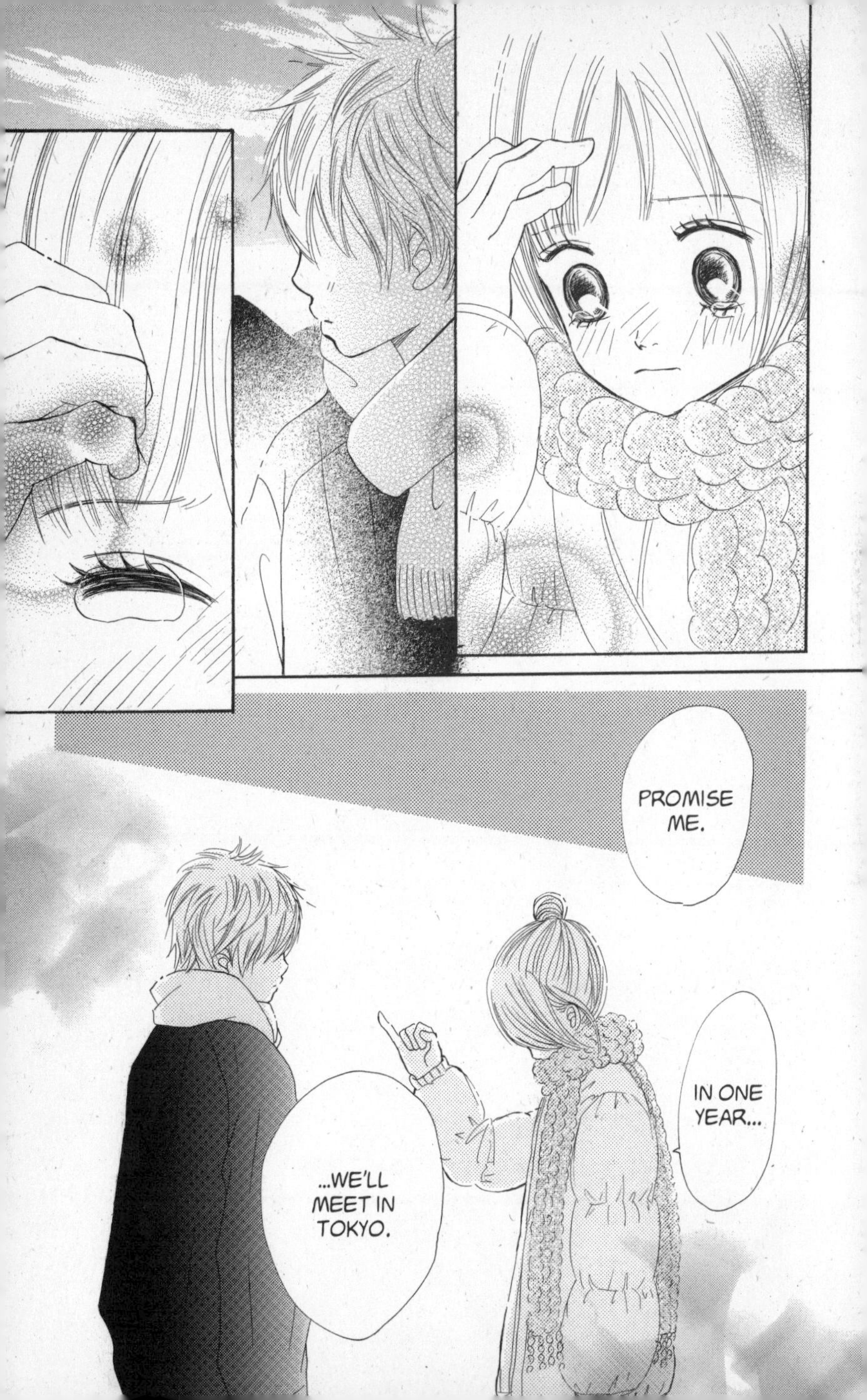
PROMISE ME.
IN ONE YEAR...
...WE'LL MEET IN TOKYO.

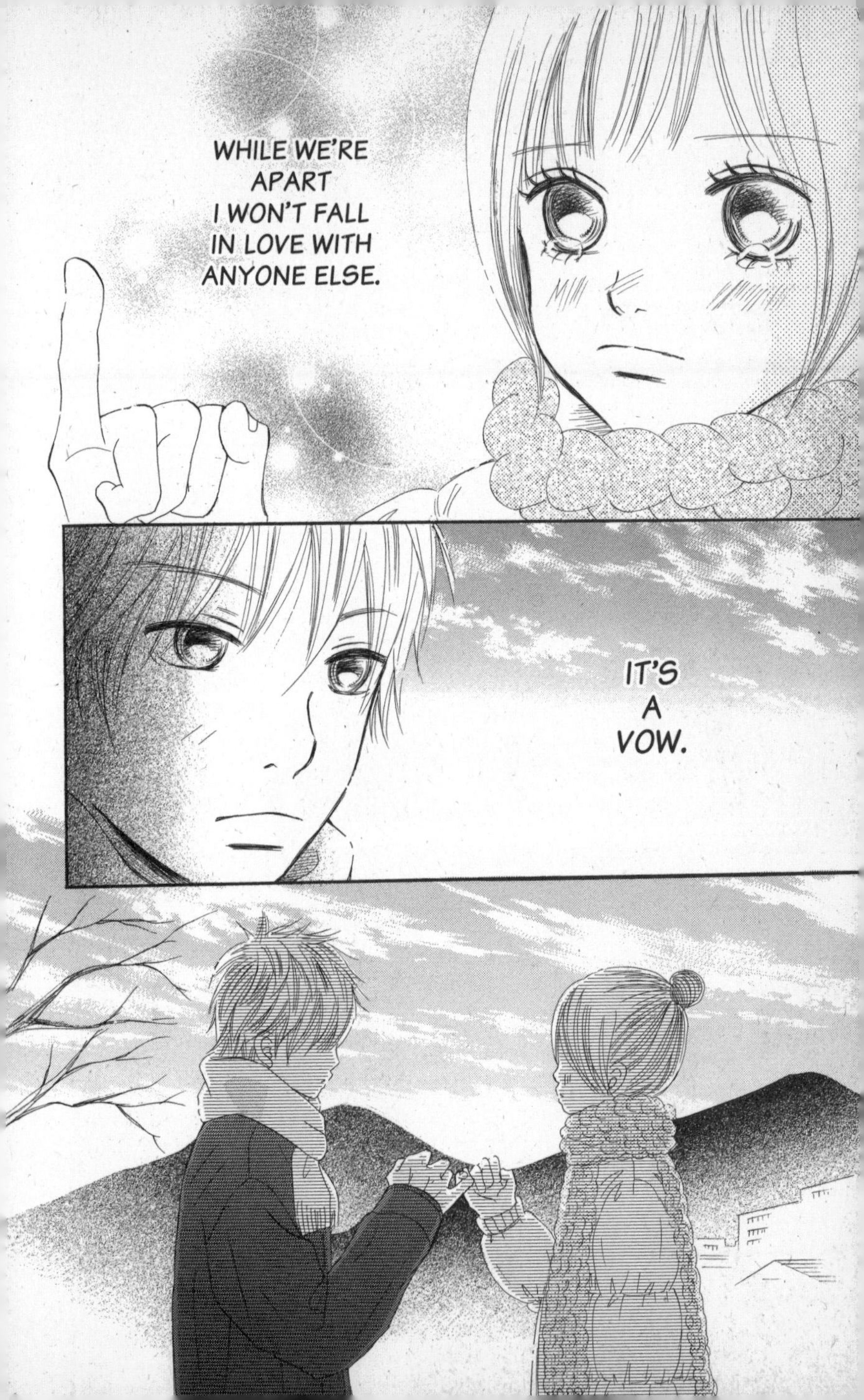
WHILE WE'RE APART I WON'T FALL IN LOVE WITH ANYONE ELSE.
IT'S A VOW.

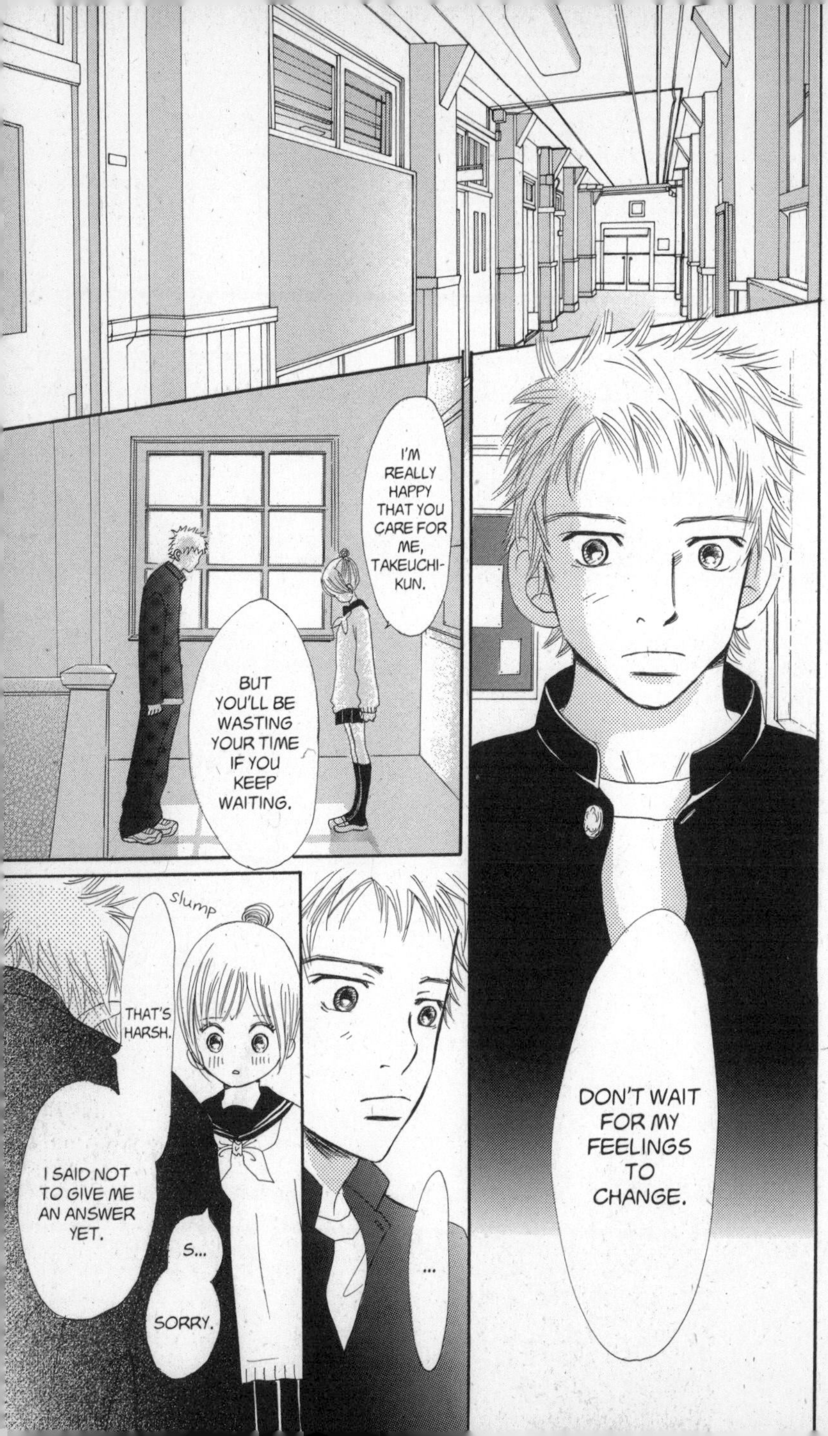
DON'T WAIT FOR MY FEELINGS TO CHANGE.
I'M REALLY HAPPY THAT YOU CARE FOR ME, TAKEUCHI-KUN.
BUT YOU'LL BE WASTING YOUR TIME IF YOU KEEP WAITING.
...
S...
SORRY.
I SAID NOT TO GIVE ME AN ANSWER YET.
slump
THAT'S HARSH.

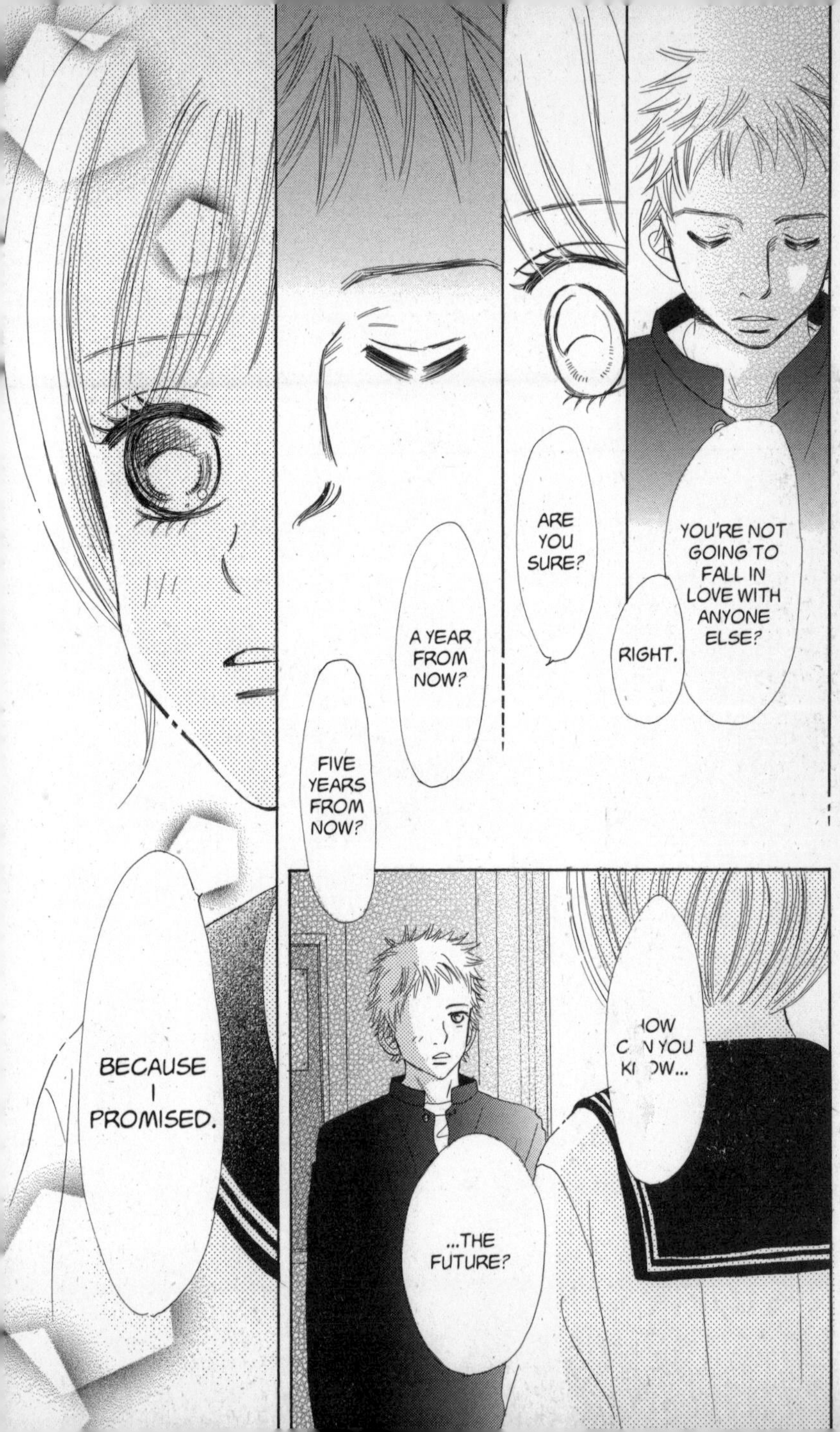
YOU'RE NOT GOING TO FALL IN LOVE WITH ANYONE ELSE?
RIGHT.
ARE YOU SURE?
A YEAR FROM NOW?
FIVE YEARS FROM NOW?
HOW CAN YOU KNOW...
...THE FUTURE?
BECAUSE I PROMISED.

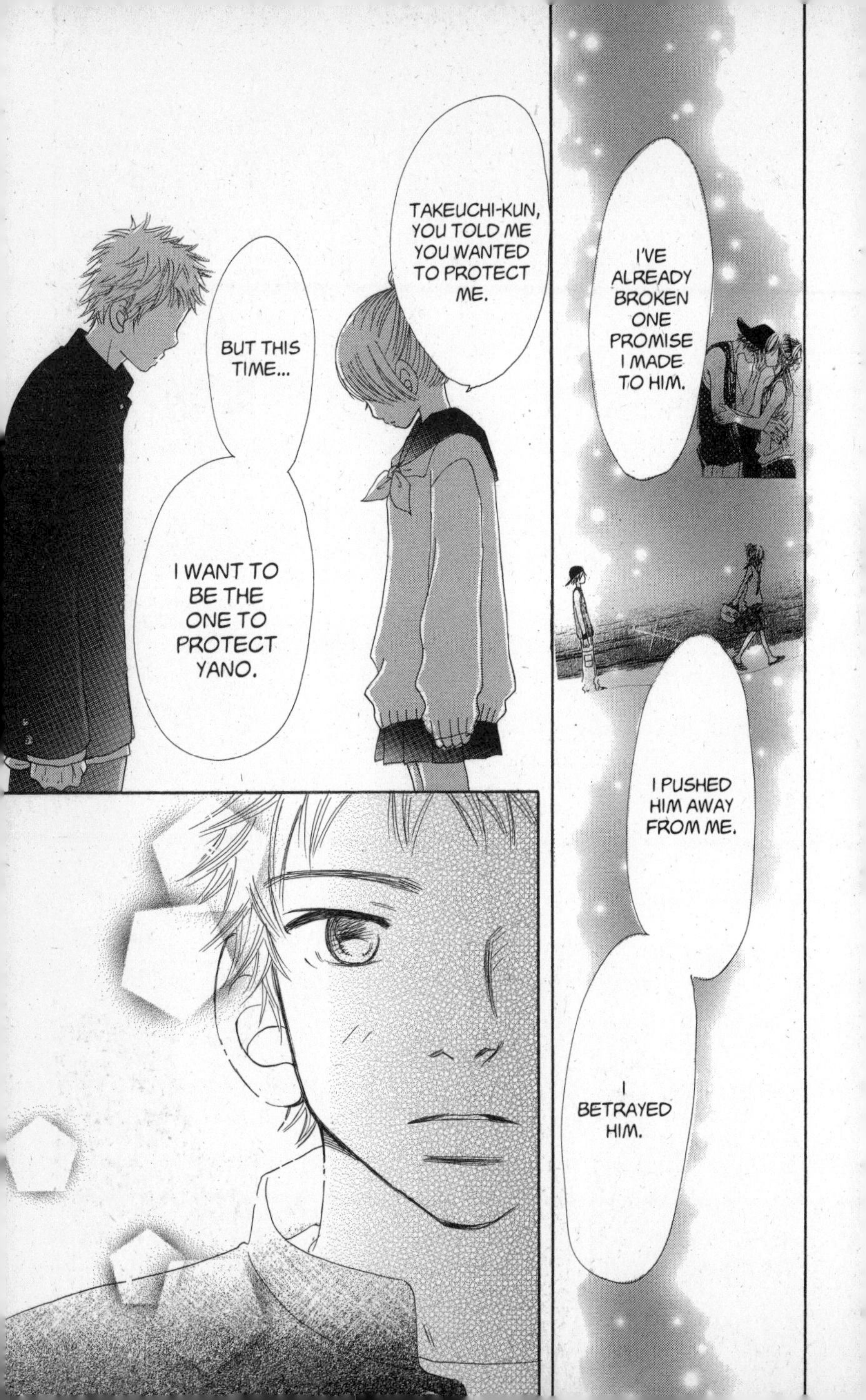
I'VE ALREADY BROKEN ONE PROMISE I MADE TO HIM.
I PUSHED HIM AWAY FROM ME.
I BETRAYED HIM.
TAKEUCHI-KUN, YOU TOLD ME YOU WANTED TO PROTECT ME.
BUT THIS TIME...
I WANT TO BE THE ONE TO PROTECT YANO.

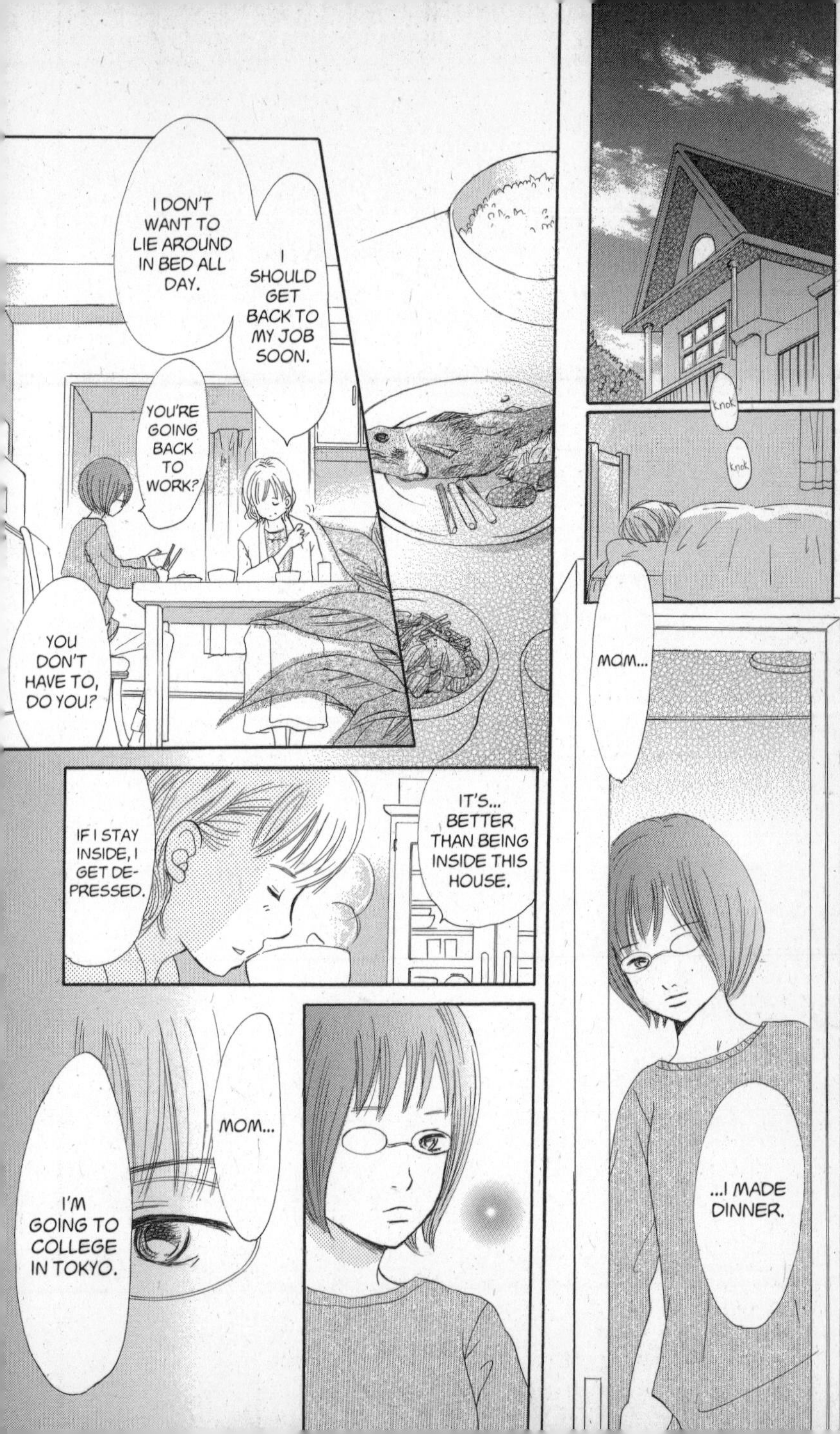
knok
knok
MOM...
...I MADE DINNER.
I SHOULD GET BACK TO MY JOB SOON.
YOU'RE GOING BACK TO WORK?
I DON'T WANT TO LIE AROUND IN BED ALL DAY.
YOU DON'T HAVE TO, DO YOU?
IT'S... BETTER THAN BEING INSIDE THIS HOUSE.
IF I STAY INSIDE, I GET DE-PRESSED.
MOM...
I'M GOING TO COLLEGE IN TOKYO.

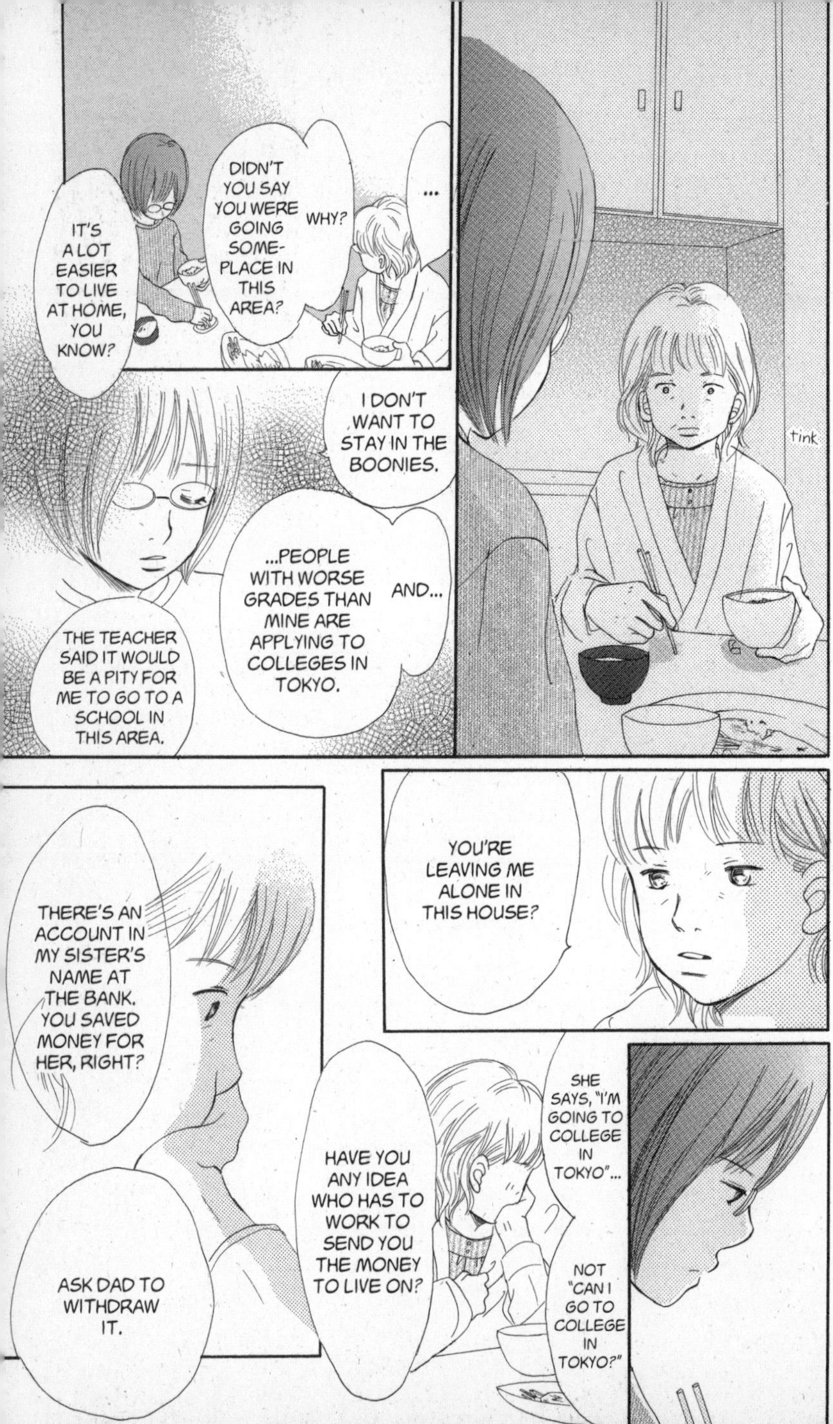
tink
...
WHY?
DIDN'T YOU SAY YOU WERE GOING SOME-PLACE IN THIS AREA?
IT'S A LOT EASIER TO LIVE AT HOME, YOU KNOW?
I DON'T WANT TO STAY IN THE BOONIES.
AND...
...PEOPLE WITH WORSE GRADES THAN MINE ARE APPLYING TO COLLEGES IN TOKYO.
THE TEACHER SAID IT WOULD BE A PITY FOR ME TO GO TO A SCHOOL IN THIS AREA.
YOU'RE LEAVING ME ALONE IN THIS HOUSE?
SHE SAYS, "I'M GOING TO COLLEGE IN TOKYO"...
NOT "CAN I GO TO COLLEGE IN TOKYO?"
HAVE YOU ANY IDEA WHO HAS TO WORK TO SEND YOU THE MONEY TO LIVE ON?
THERE'S AN ACCOUNT IN MY SISTER'S NAME AT THE BANK. YOU SAVED MONEY FOR HER, RIGHT?
ASK DAD TO WITHDRAW IT.

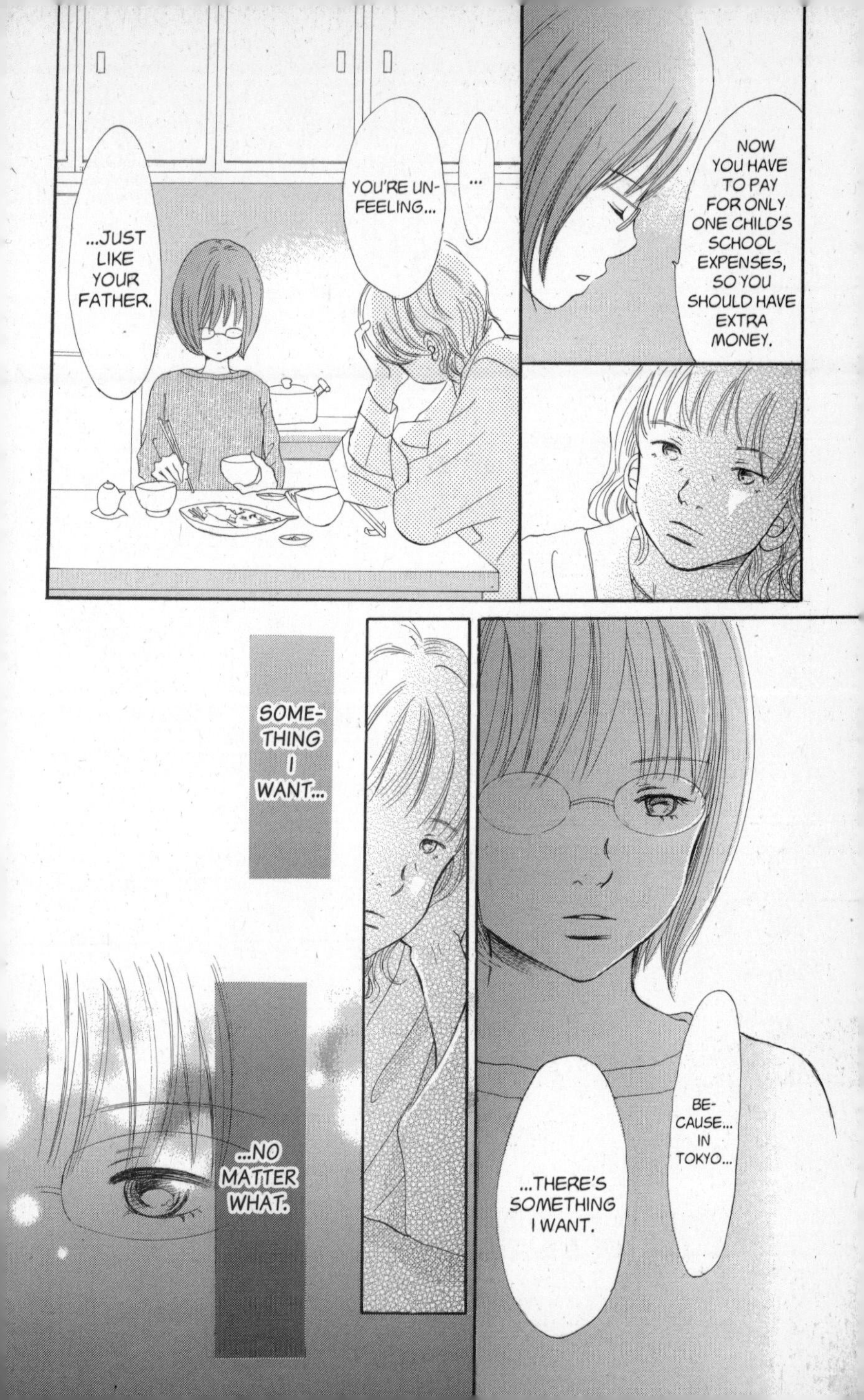
NOW YOU HAVE TO PAY FOR ONLY ONE CHILD'S SCHOOL EXPENSES, SO YOU SHOULD HAVE EXTRA MONEY.
...
YOU'RE UN-FEELING...
...JUST LIKE YOUR FATHER.
BE-CAUSE... IN TOKYO...
...THERE'S SOMETHING I WANT.
SOME-THING I WANT...
...NO MATTER WHAT.

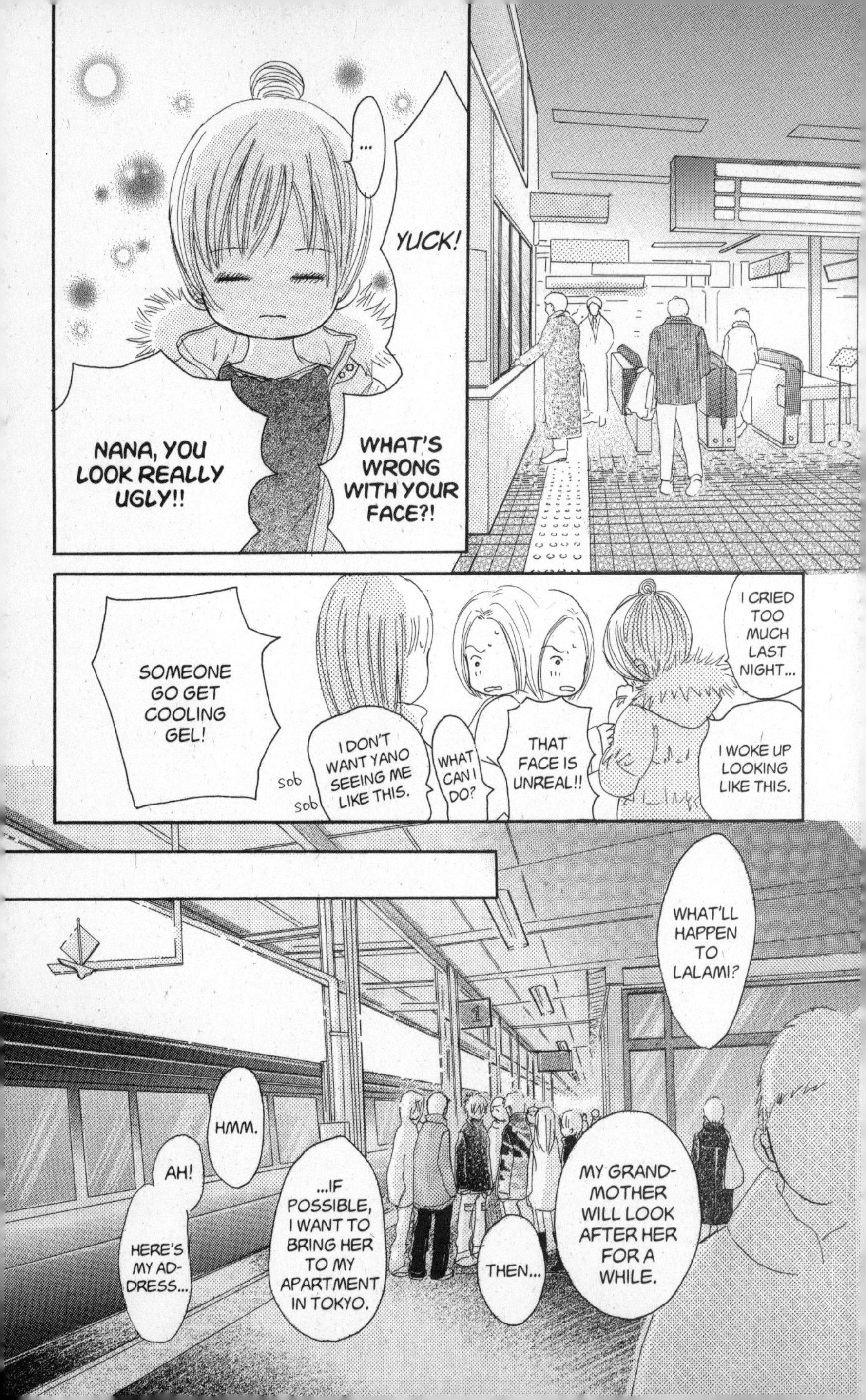
...
YUCK!
WHAT'S WRONG WITH YOUR FACE?!
NANA, YOU LOOK REALLY UGLY!!
I CRIED TOO MUCH LAST NIGHT...
I WOKE UP LOOKING LIKE THIS.
THAT FACE IS UNREAL!!
WHAT CAN I DO?
I DON'T WANT YANO SEEING ME LIKE THIS.
sob sob
SOMEONE GO GET COOLING GEL!
WHAT'LL HAPPEN TO LALAMI?
MY GRAND-MOTHER WILL LOOK AFTER HER FOR A WHILE.
THEN...
...IF POSSIBLE, I WANT TO BRING HER TO MY APARTMENT IN TOKYO.
HMM.
AH!
HERE'S MY AD-DRESS...

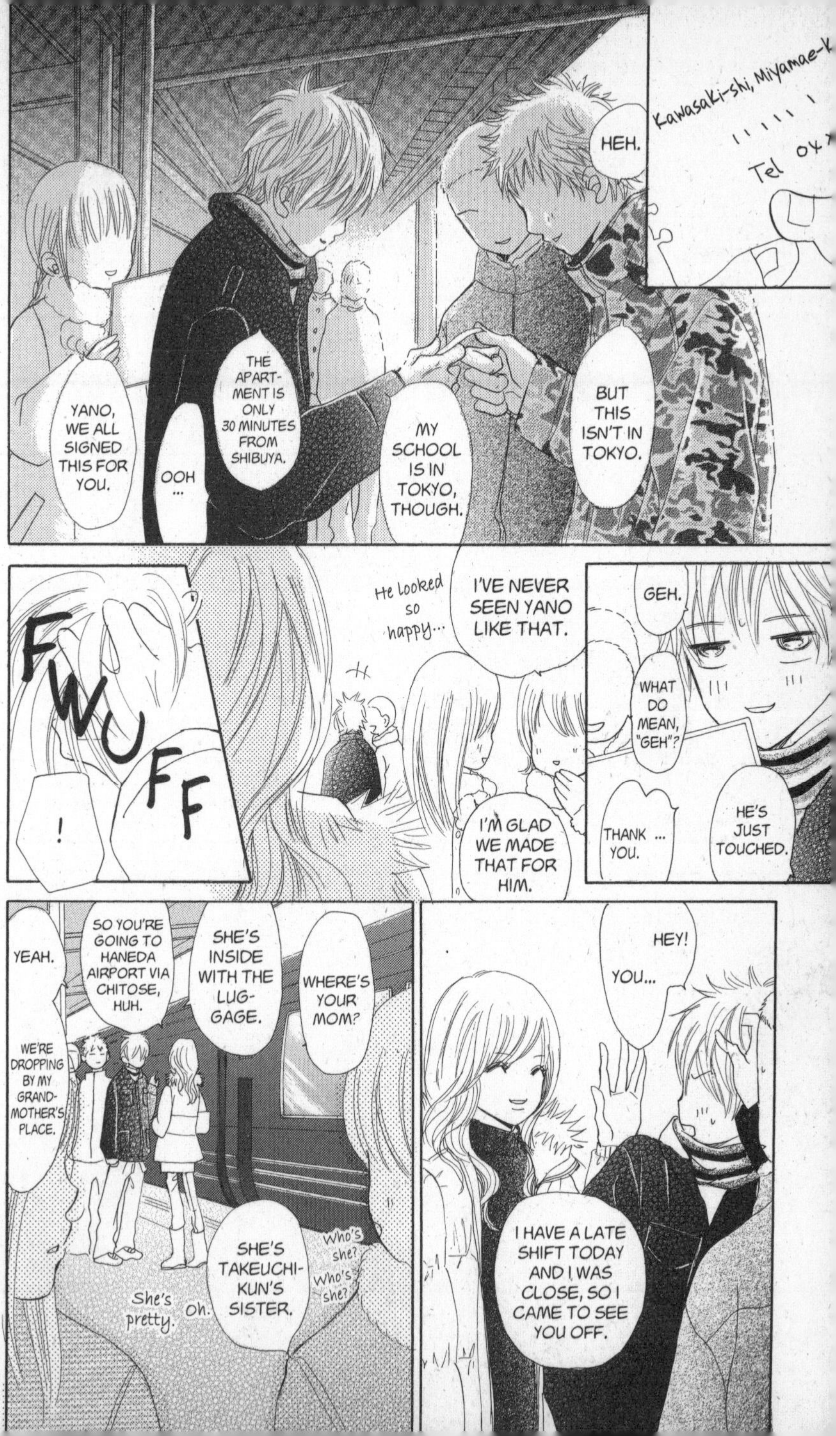
Kawasaki-shi, Miyamae-K
Tel 04
HEH.
BUT THIS ISN'T IN TOKYO.
MY SCHOOL IS IN TOKYO, THOUGH.
THE APARTMENT IS ONLY 30 MINUTES FROM SHIBUYA.
OOH...
YANO, WE ALL SIGNED THIS FOR YOU.
GEH.
WHAT DO MEAN, "GEH"?
HE'S JUST TOUCHED.
THANK... YOU.
I'VE NEVER SEEN YANO LIKE THAT.
He looked so happy...
I'M GLAD WE MADE THAT FOR HIM.
FWUFF
!
HEY! YOU...
I HAVE A LATE SHIFT TODAY AND I WAS CLOSE, SO I CAME TO SEE YOU OFF.
WHERE'S YOUR MOM?
SHE'S INSIDE WITH THE LUGGAGE.
SO YOU'RE GOING TO HANEDA AIRPORT VIA CHITOSE, HUH.
YEAH.
WE'RE DROPPING BY MY GRANDMOTHER'S PLACE.
Who's she? Who's she?
SHE'S TAKEUCHI-KUN'S SISTER.
Oh.
She's pretty.

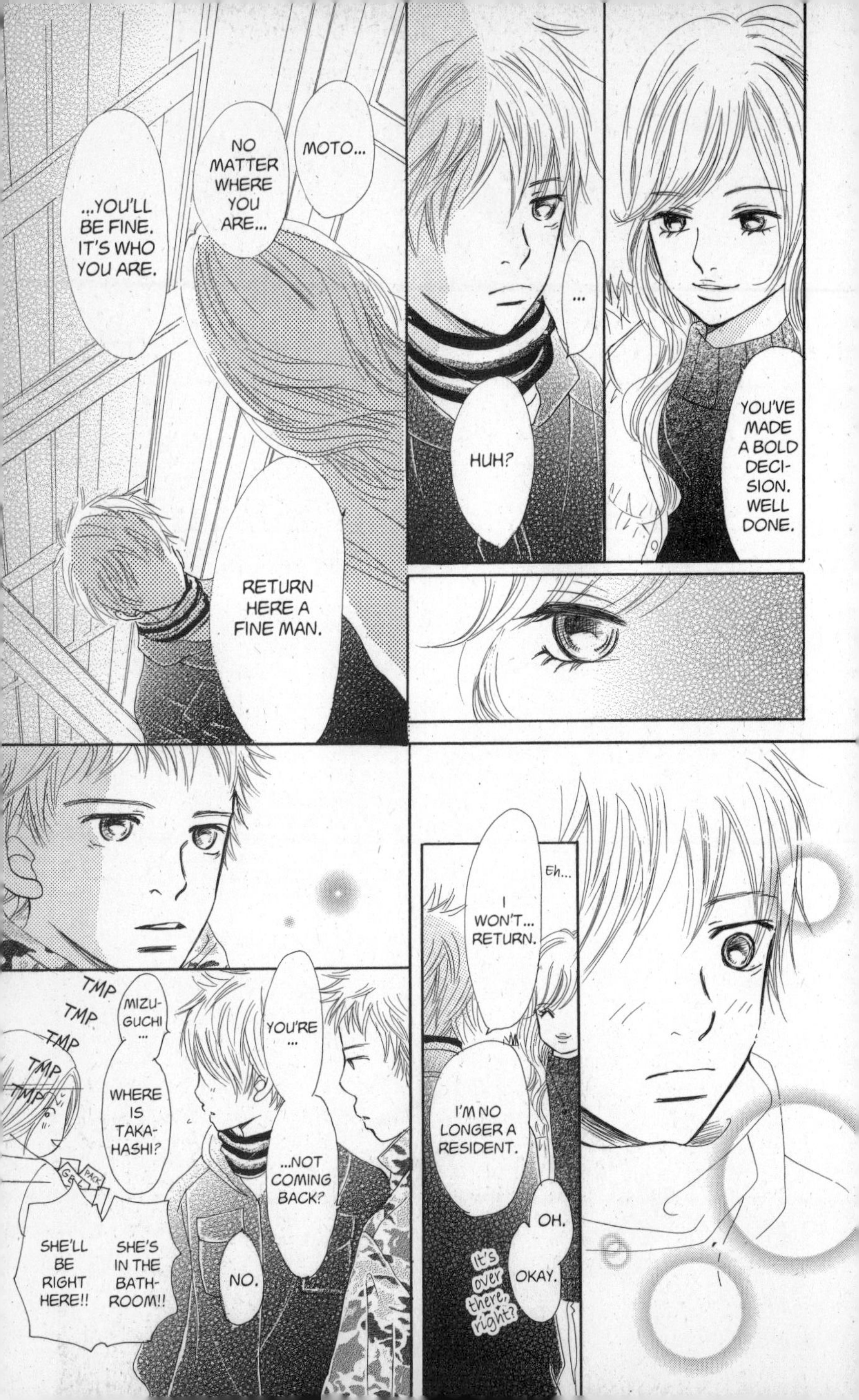
YOU'VE MADE A BOLD DECISION. WELL DONE.
...
HUH?
MOTO...
NO MATTER WHERE YOU ARE...
...YOU'LL BE FINE. IT'S WHO YOU ARE.
RETURN HERE A FINE MAN.
Eh...
I WON'T... RETURN.
I'M NO LONGER A RESIDENT.
OH.
OKAY.
It's over there, right?
YOU'RE ...
...NOT COMING BACK?
NO.
MIZUGUCHI ...
WHERE IS TAKAHASHI?
TMP
TMP
TMP
TMP
TMP
PACK
GEL
SHE'S IN THE BATHROOM!!
SHE'LL BE RIGHT HERE!!

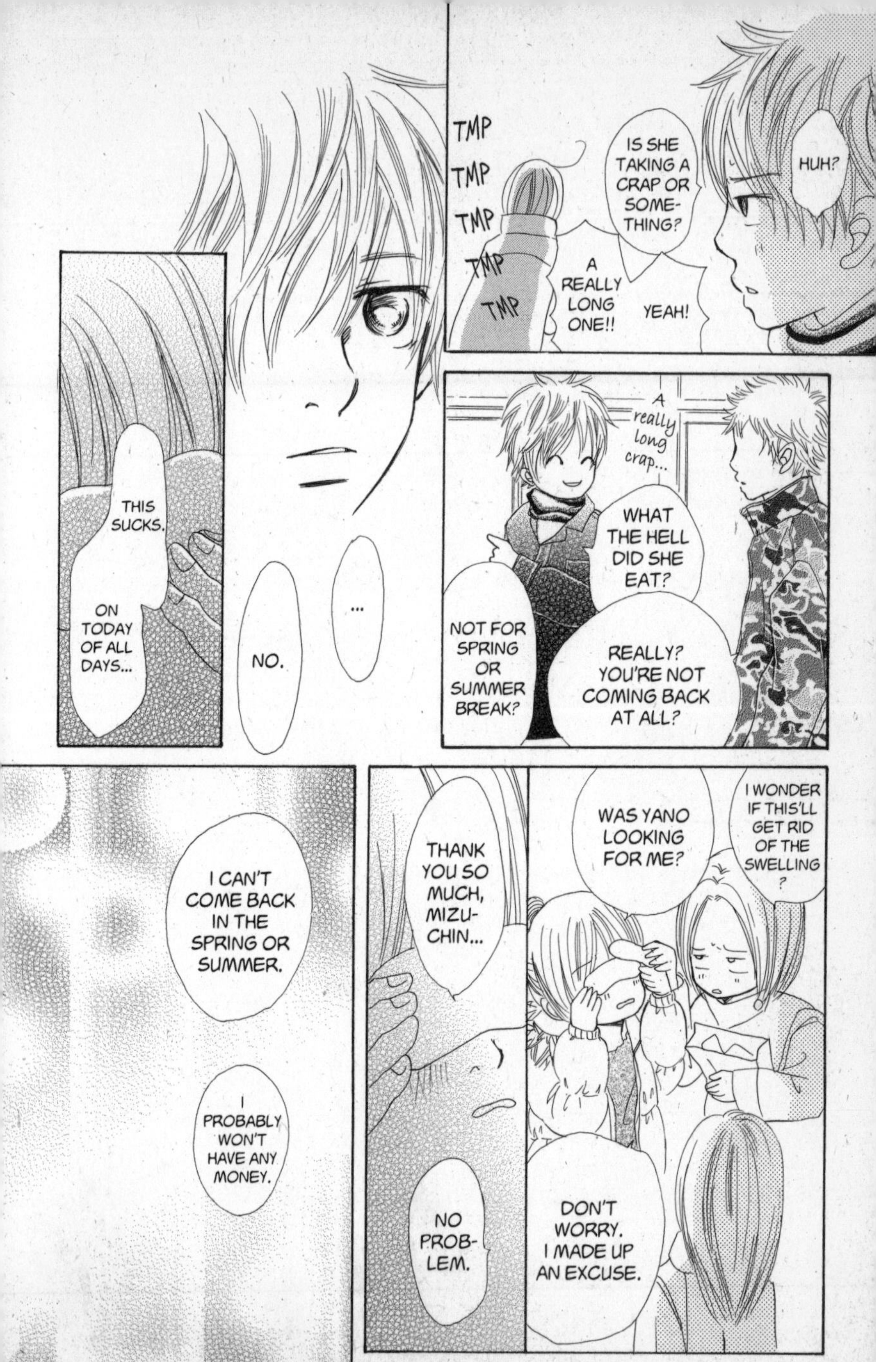
TMP TMP TMP TMP TMP
HUH?
IS SHE TAKING A CRAP OR SOMETHING?
YEAH!
A REALLY LONG ONE!!
A really long crap...
WHAT THE HELL DID SHE EAT?
REALLY? YOU'RE NOT COMING BACK AT ALL?
NOT FOR SPRING OR SUMMER BREAK?
...
NO.
THIS SUCKS.
ON TODAY OF ALL DAYS...
I WONDER IF THIS'LL GET RID OF THE SWELLING?
WAS YANO LOOKING FOR ME?
DON'T WORRY. I MADE UP AN EXCUSE.
THANK YOU SO MUCH, MIZU-CHIN...
NO PROBLEM.
I CAN'T COME BACK IN THE SPRING OR SUMMER.
I PROBABLY WON'T HAVE ANY MONEY.

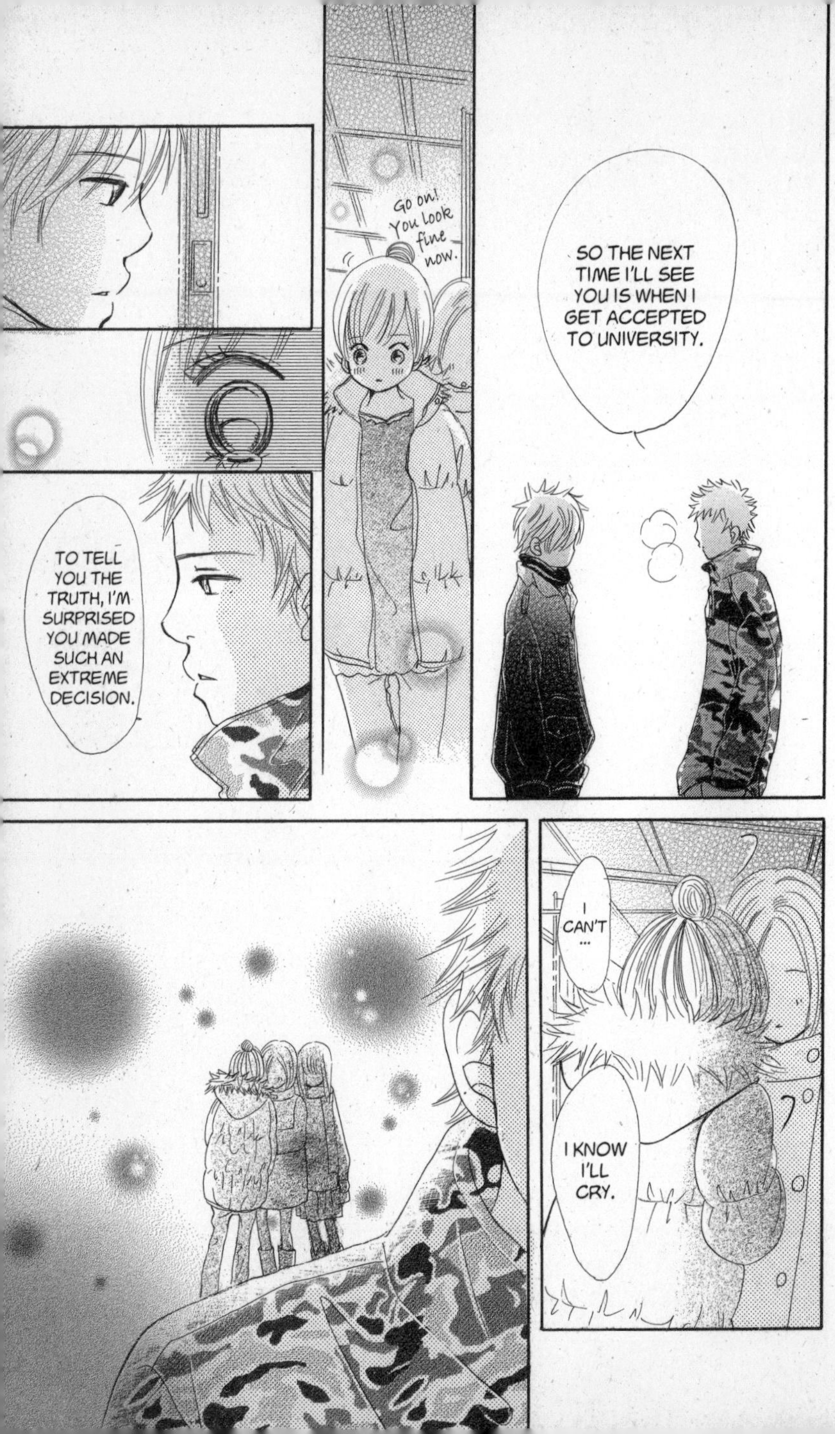
SO THE NEXT TIME I'LL SEE YOU IS WHEN I GET ACCEPTED TO UNIVERSITY.
Go on! You look fine now.
TO TELL YOU THE TRUTH, I'M SURPRISED YOU MADE SUCH AN EXTREME DECISION.
I CAN'T ...
I KNOW I'LL CRY.

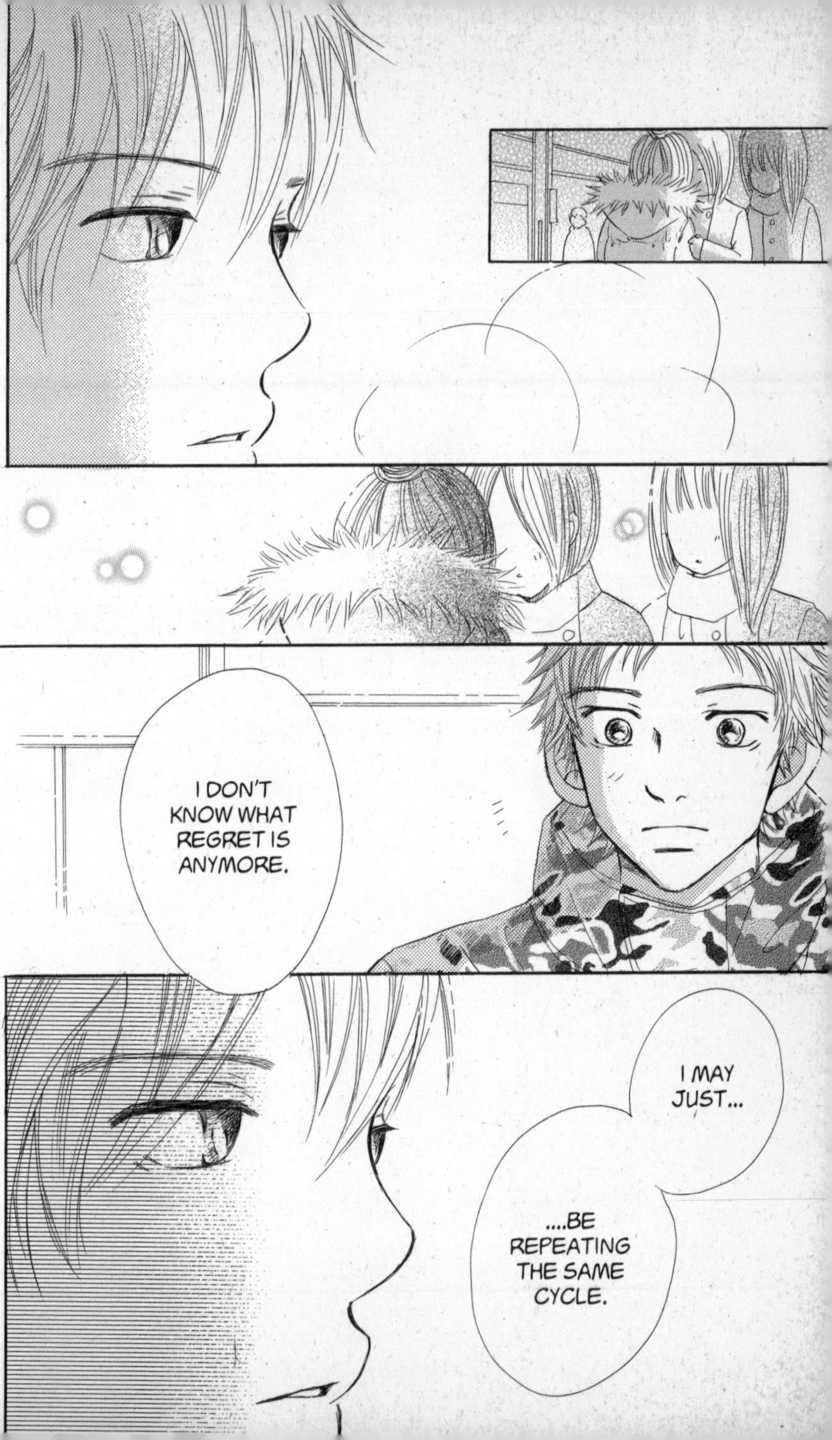
I DON'T KNOW WHAT REGRET IS ANYMORE.
I MAY JUST...
....BE REPEATING THE SAME CYCLE.

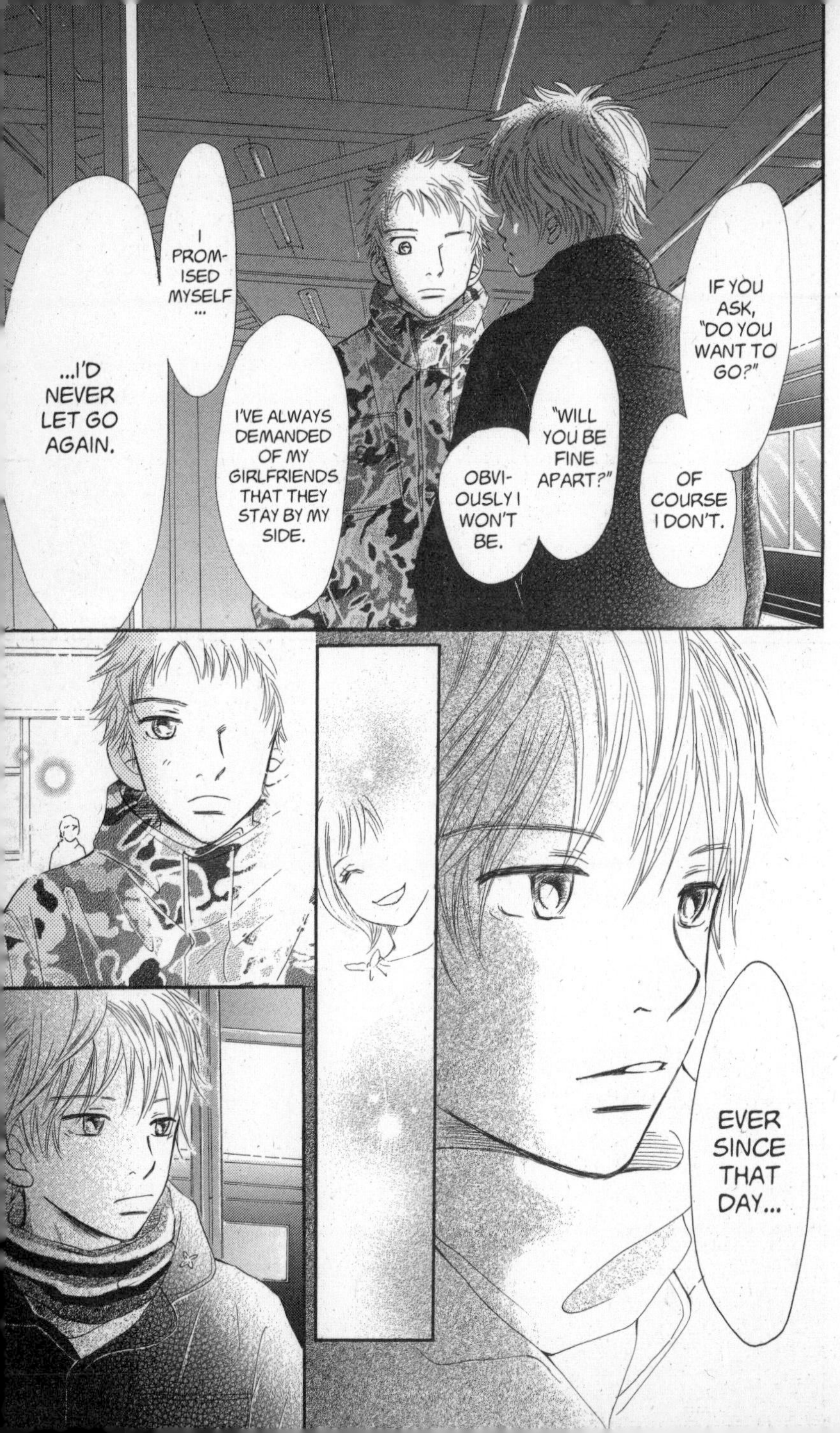
IF YOU ASK, "DO YOU WANT TO GO?"
OF COURSE I DON'T.
"WILL YOU BE FINE APART?"
OBVIOUSLY I WON'T BE.
I'VE ALWAYS DEMANDED OF MY GIRLFRIENDS THAT THEY STAY BY MY SIDE.
I PROMISED MYSELF...
...I'D NEVER LET GO AGAIN.
EVER SINCE THAT DAY...

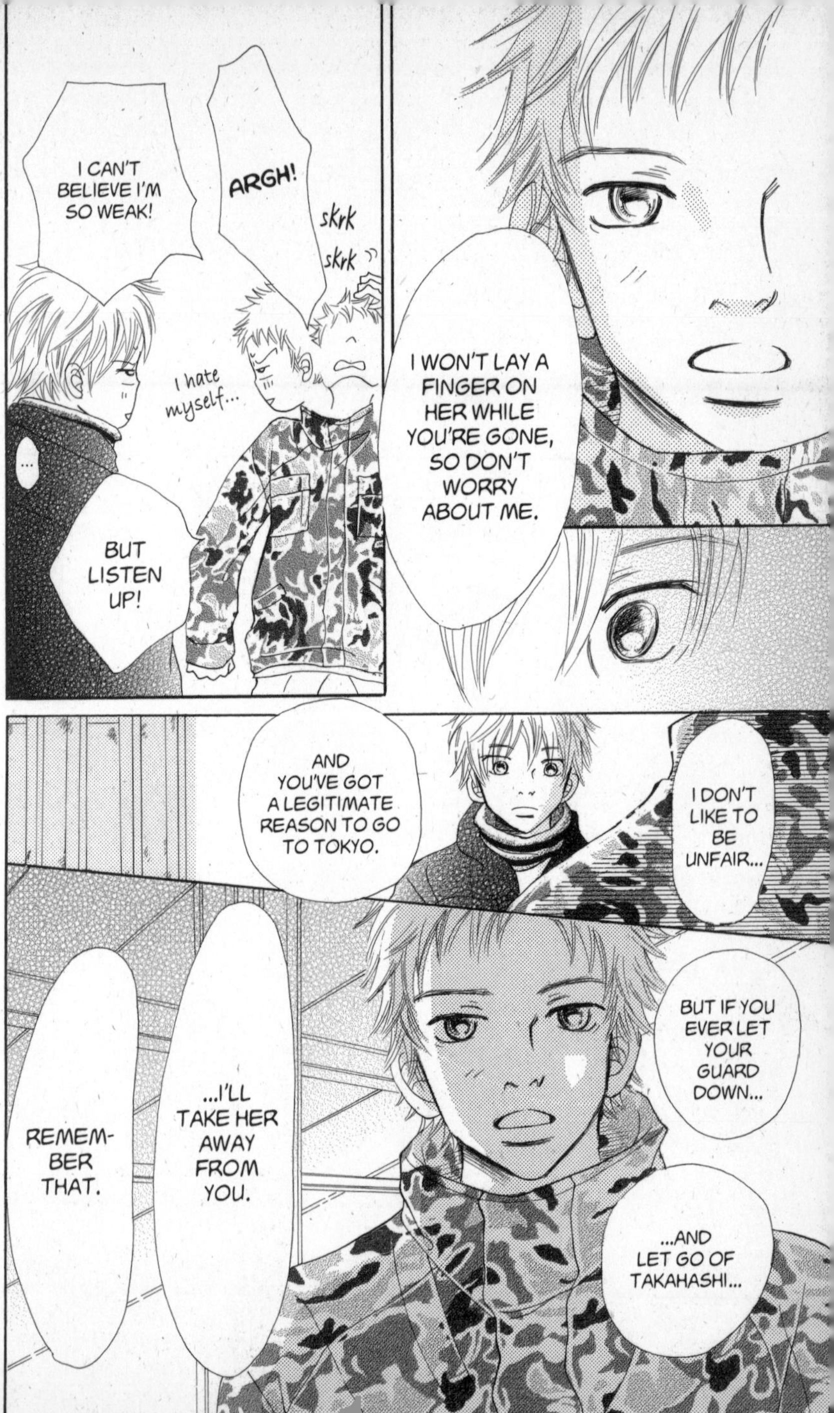
I WON'T LAY A FINGER ON HER WHILE YOU'RE GONE, SO DON'T WORRY ABOUT ME.
ARGH!
I CAN'T BELIEVE I'M SO WEAK!
skrk
skrk
I hate myself...
...
BUT LISTEN UP!
I DON'T LIKE TO BE UNFAIR...
AND YOU'VE GOT A LEGITIMATE REASON TO GO TO TOKYO.
BUT IF YOU EVER LET YOUR GUARD DOWN...
...AND LET GO OF TAKAHASHI...
...I'LL TAKE HER AWAY FROM YOU.
REMEM-BER THAT.

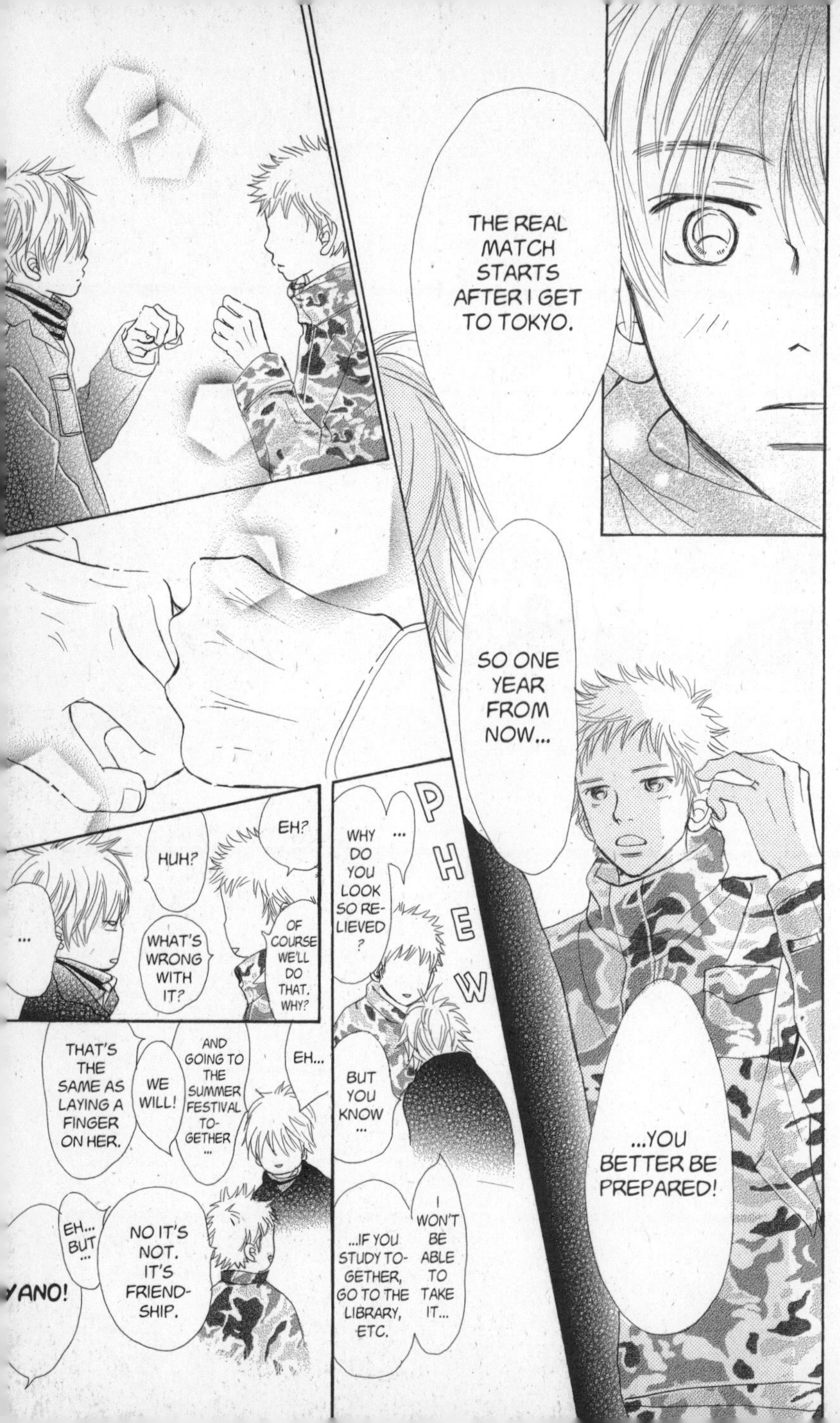

THE REAL MATCH STARTS AFTER I GET TO TOKYO.
SO ONE YEAR FROM NOW...
...YOU BETTER BE PREPARED!
...
WHY DO YOU LOOK SO RE-LIEVED?
PHEW
EH?
HUH?
OF COURSE WE'LL DO THAT. WHY?
WHAT'S WRONG WITH IT?
...
BUT YOU KNOW...
I WON'T BE ABLE TO TAKE IT...
...IF YOU STUDY TO-GETHER, GO TO THE LIBRARY, ETC.
EH...
AND GOING TO THE SUMMER FESTIVAL TO-GETHER...
WE WILL!
THAT'S THE SAME AS LAYING A FINGER ON HER.
NO IT'S NOT. IT'S FRIEND-SHIP.
EH... BUT...
YANO!

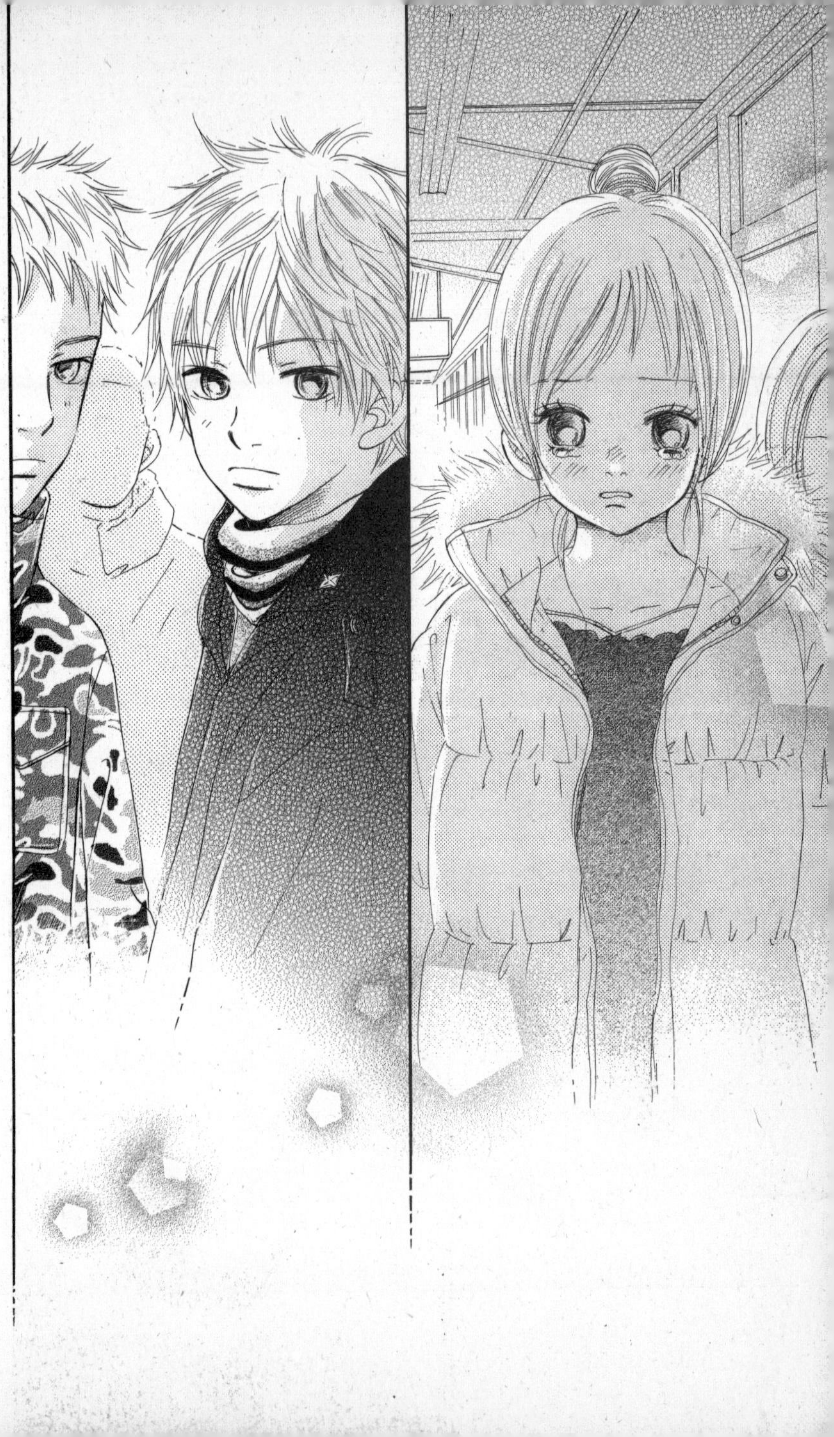

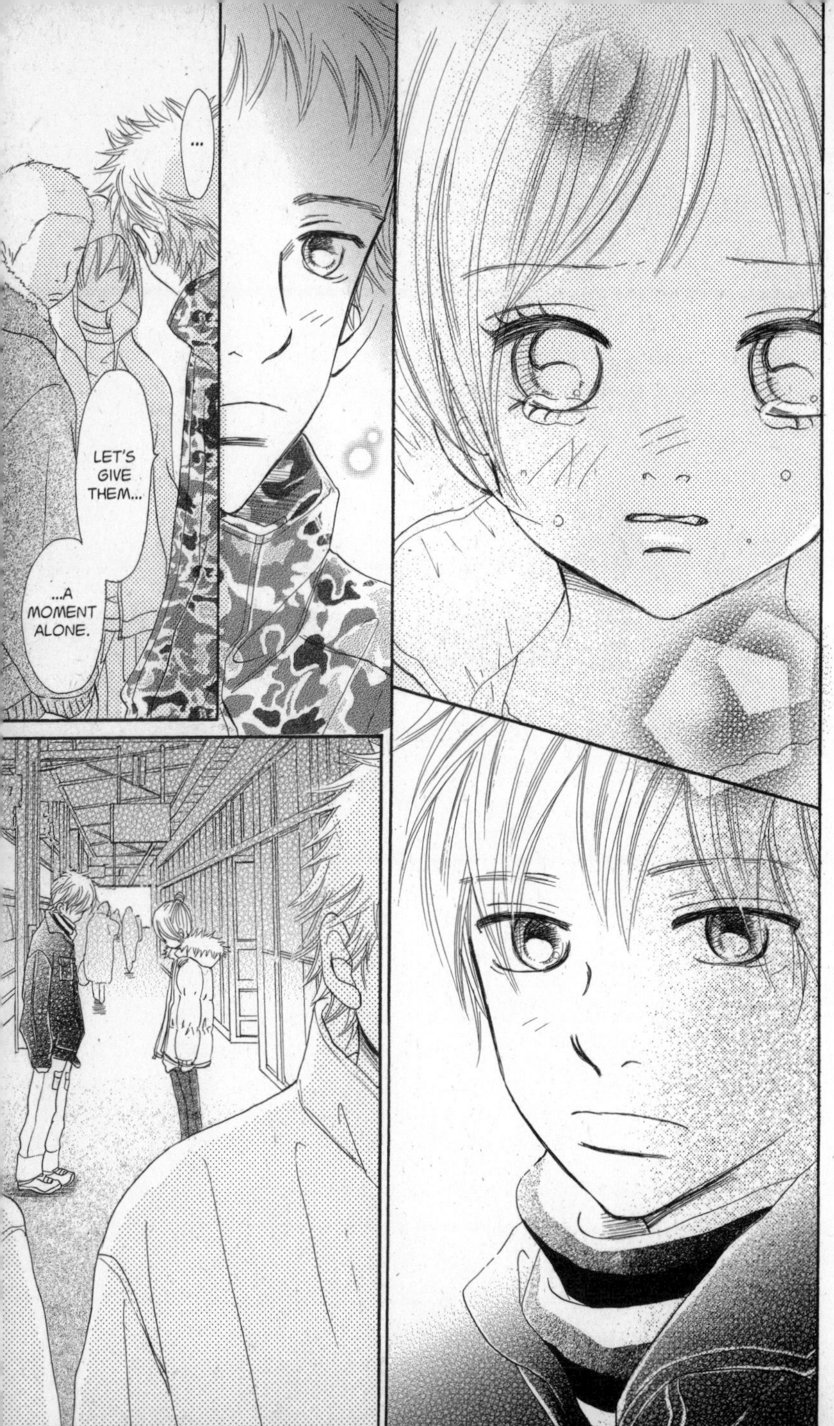
...
LET'S GIVE THEM...
...A MOMENT ALONE.

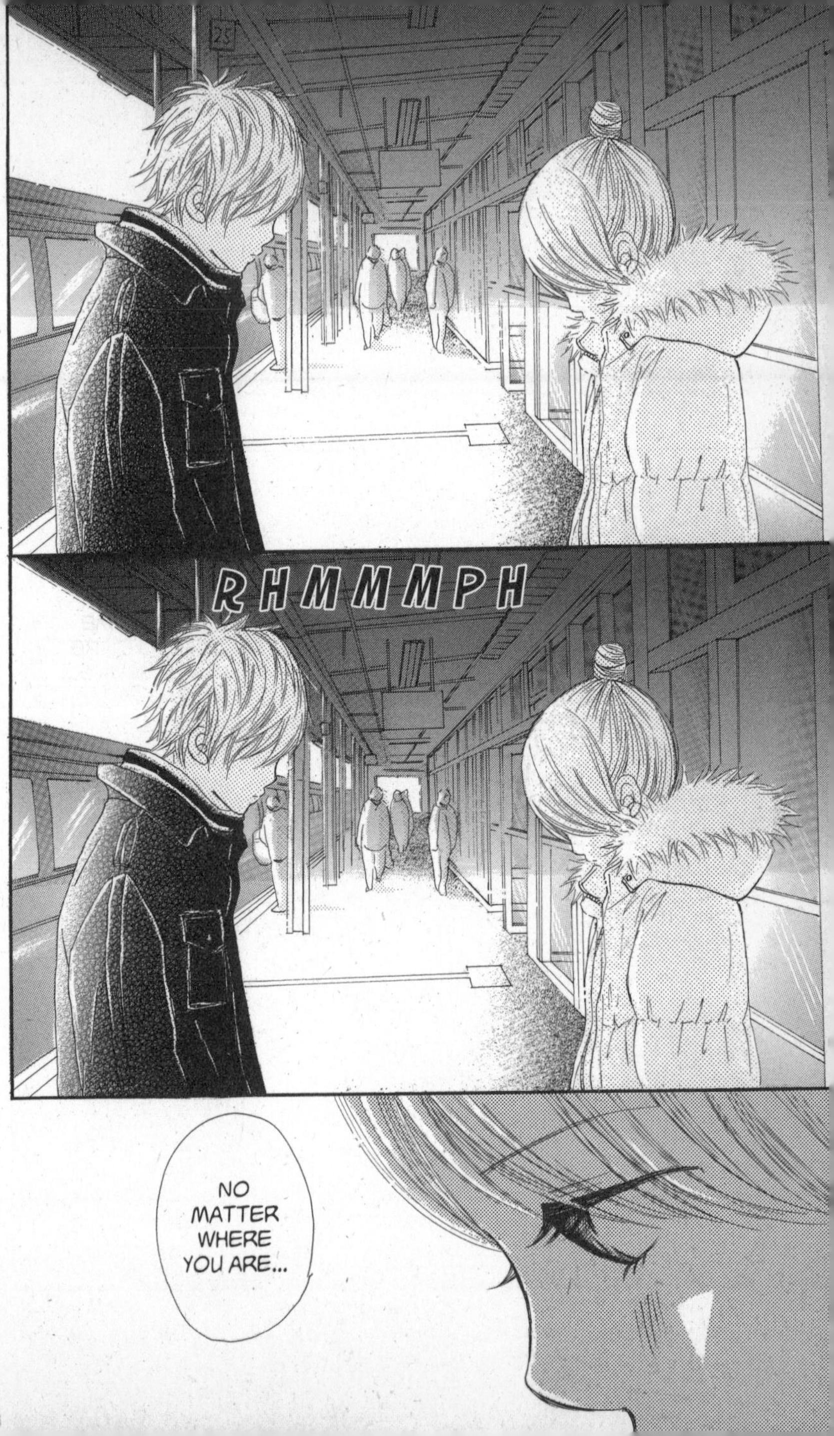
RHMMMPH
NO MATTER WHERE YOU ARE...

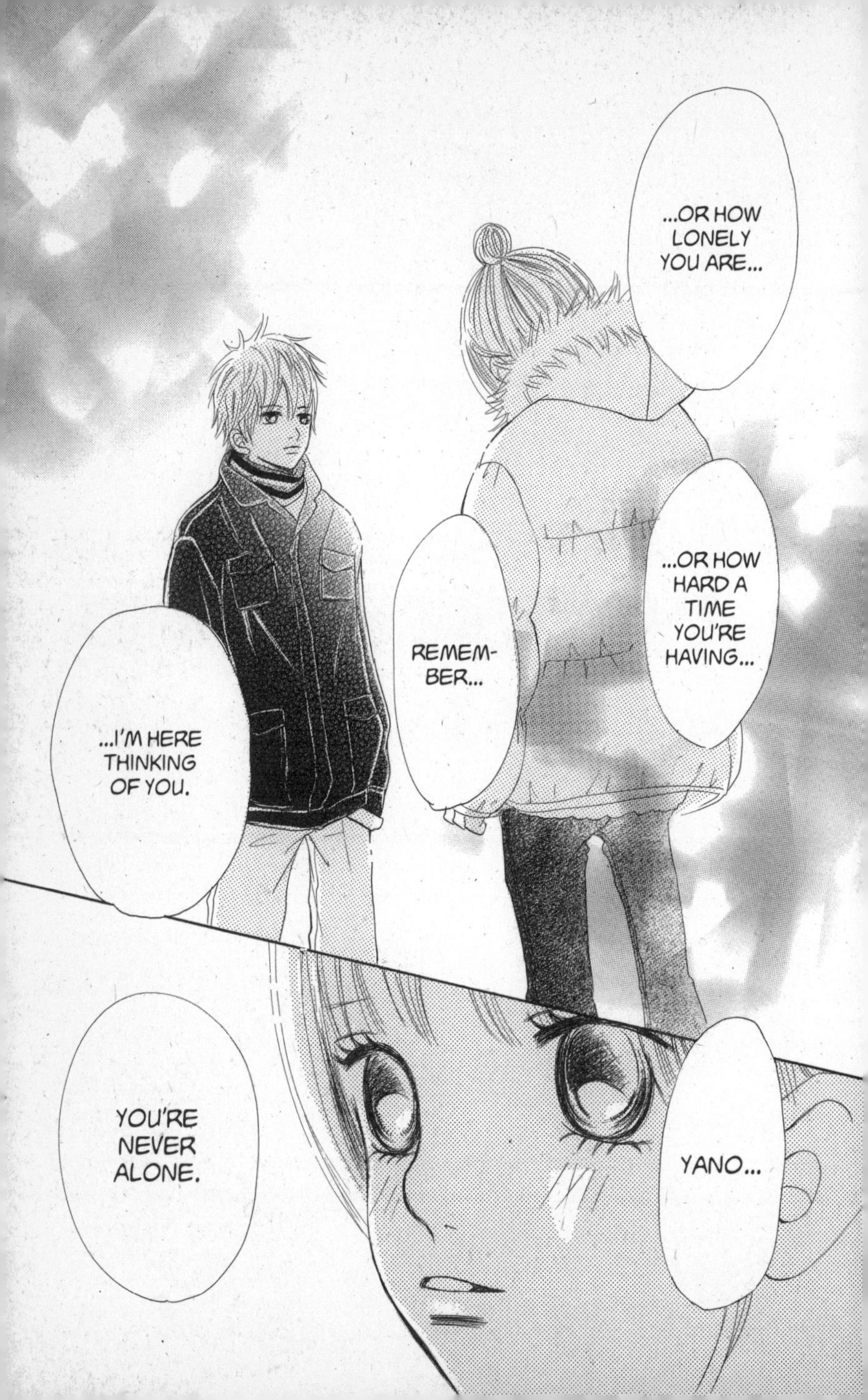
...OR HOW LONELY YOU ARE...
...OR HOW HARD A TIME YOU'RE HAVING...
REMEM-BER...
...I'M HERE THINKING OF YOU.
YANO...
YOU'RE NEVER ALONE.

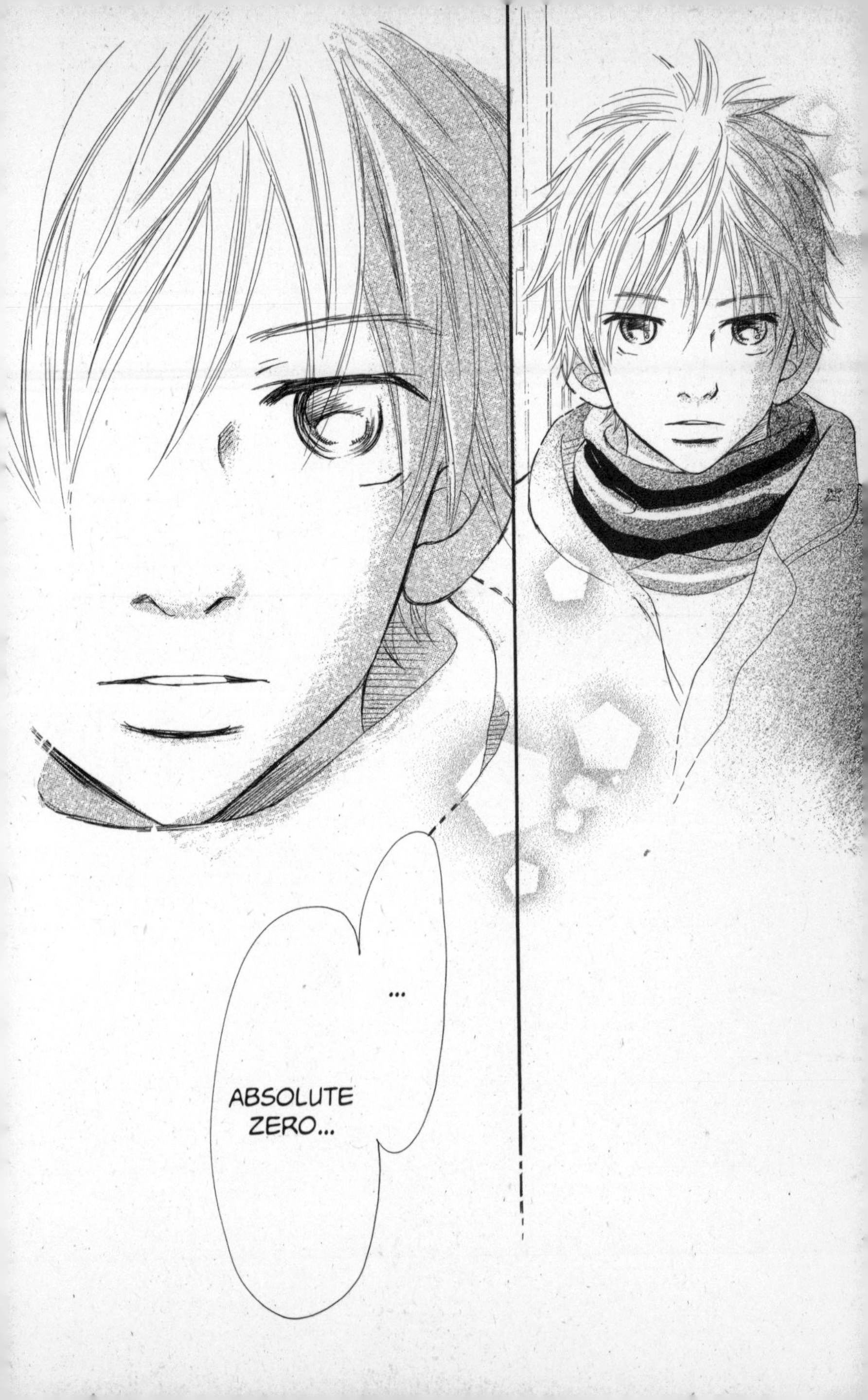
...
ABSOLUTE ZERO...

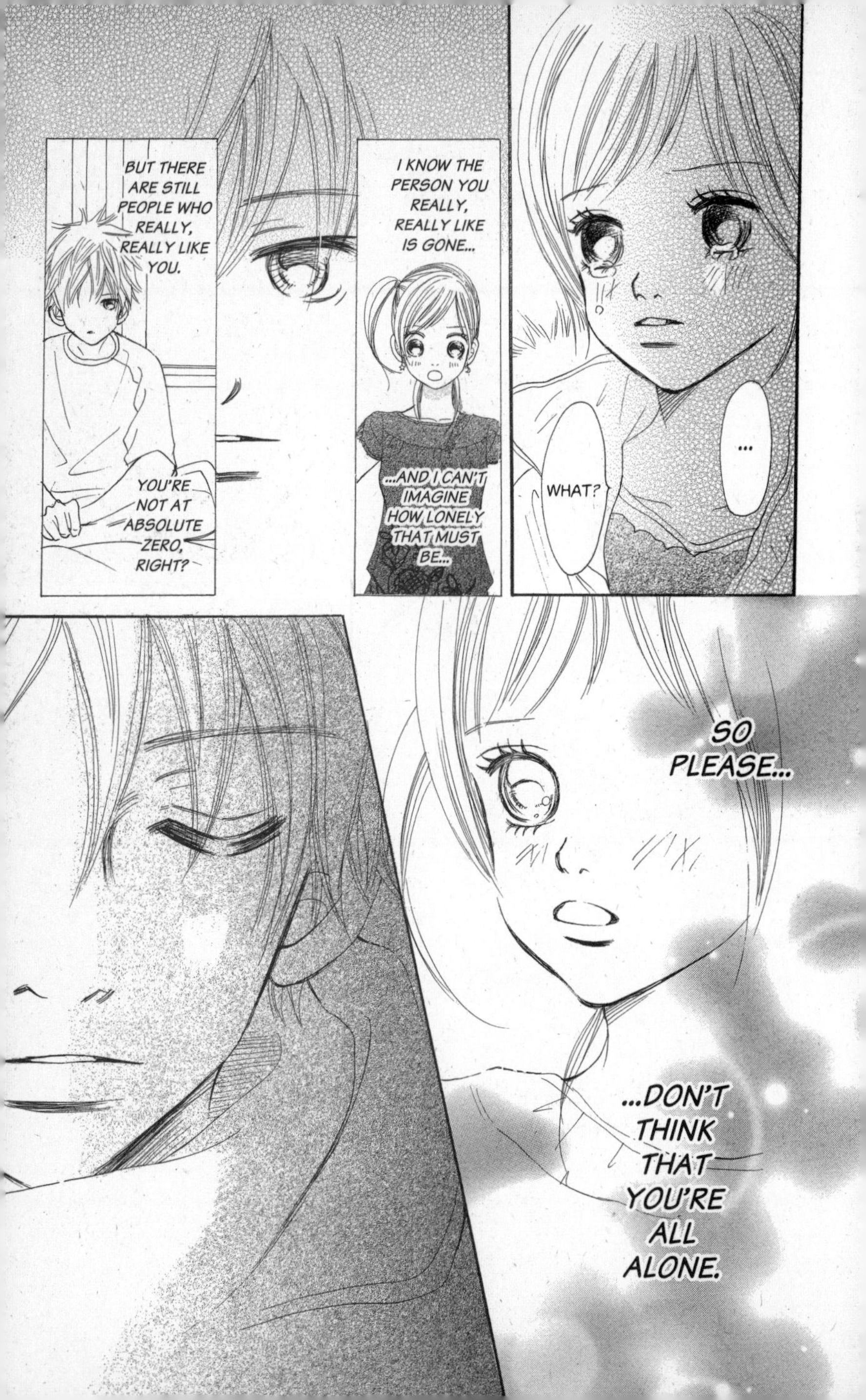
...
WHAT?
I KNOW THE PERSON YOU REALLY, REALLY LIKE IS GONE...
...AND I CAN'T IMAGINE HOW LONELY THAT MUST BE...
BUT THERE ARE STILL PEOPLE WHO REALLY, REALLY LIKE YOU.
YOU'RE NOT AT ABSOLUTE ZERO, RIGHT?
SO PLEASE...
...DON'T THINK THAT YOU'RE ALL ALONE.

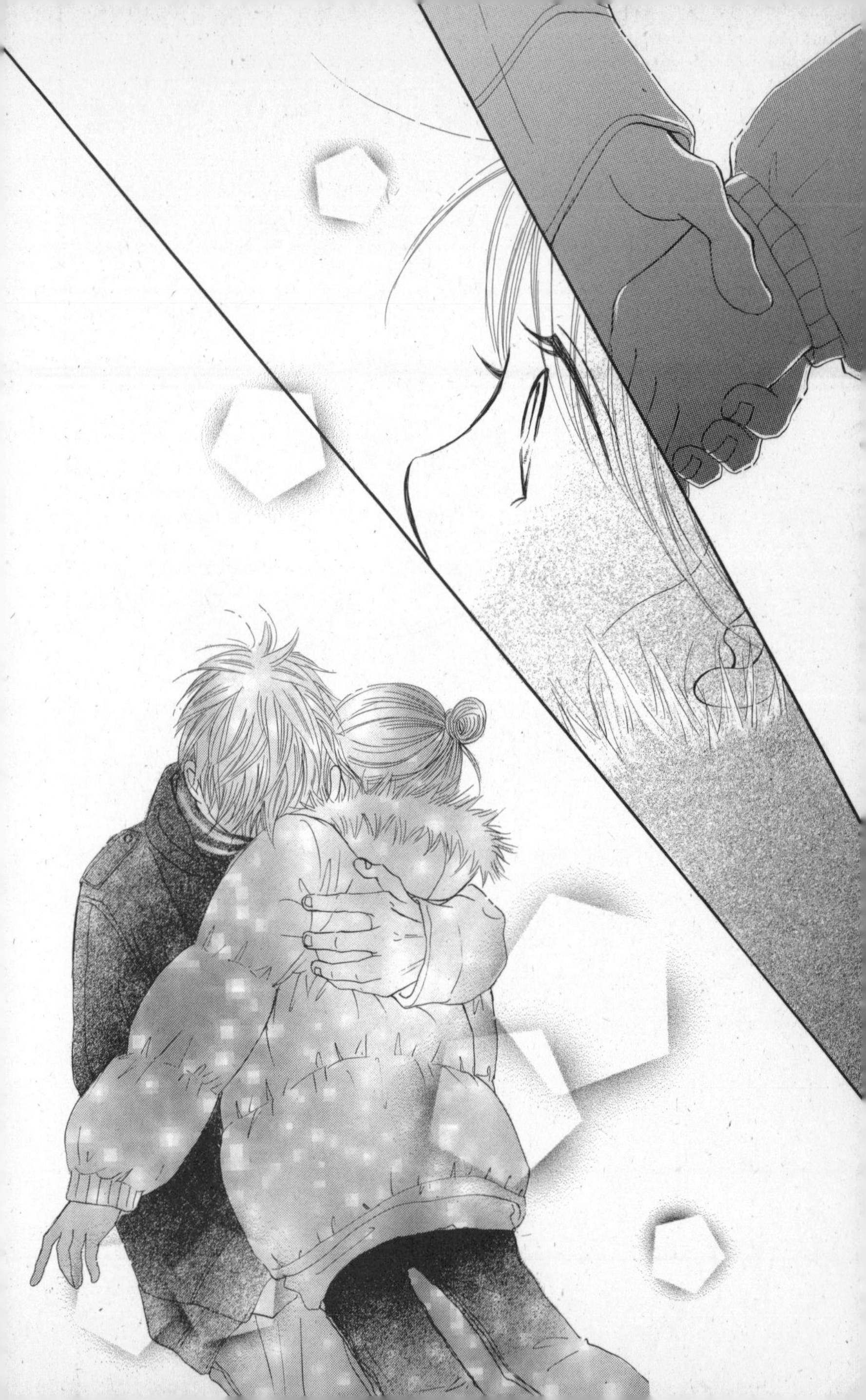

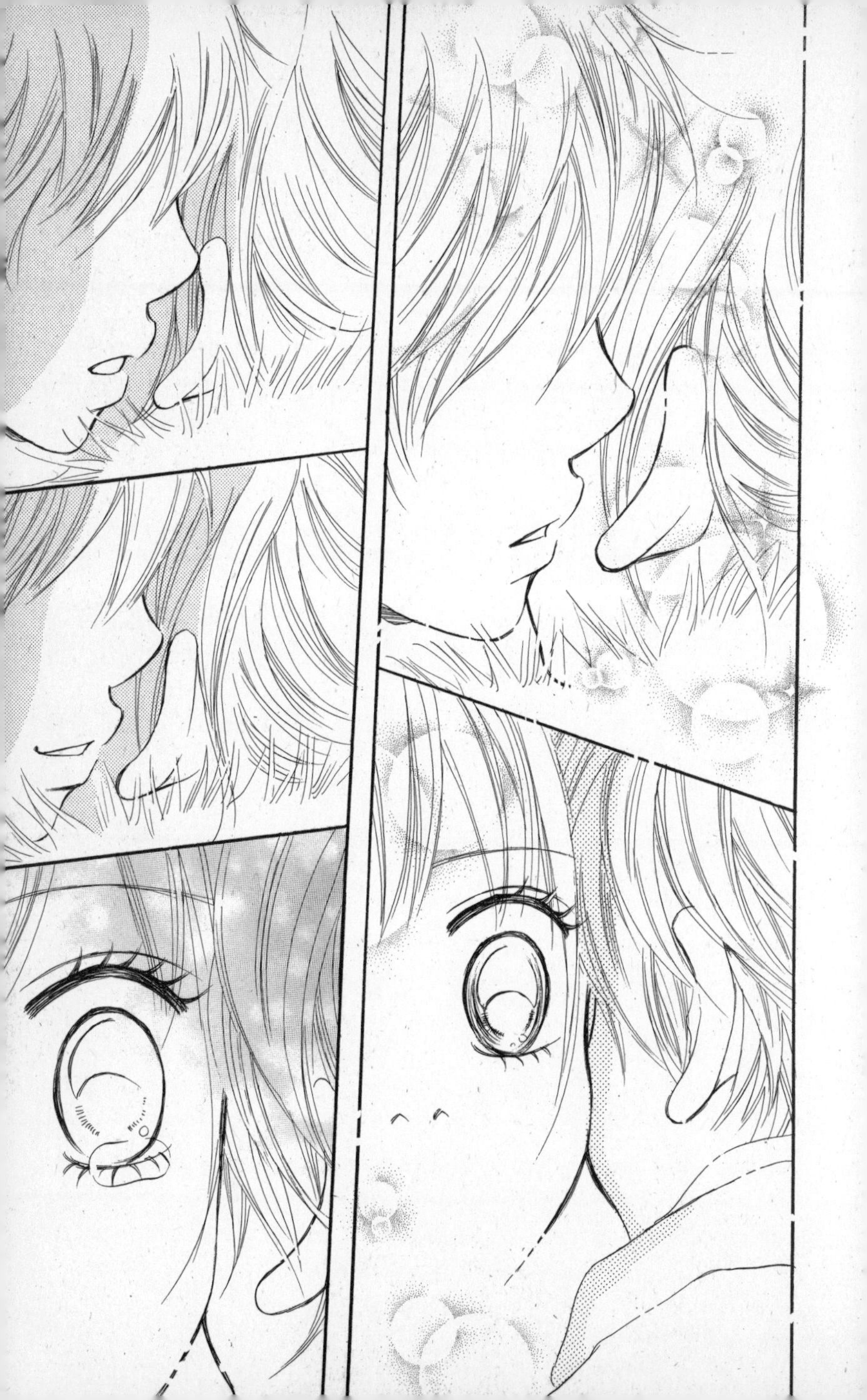

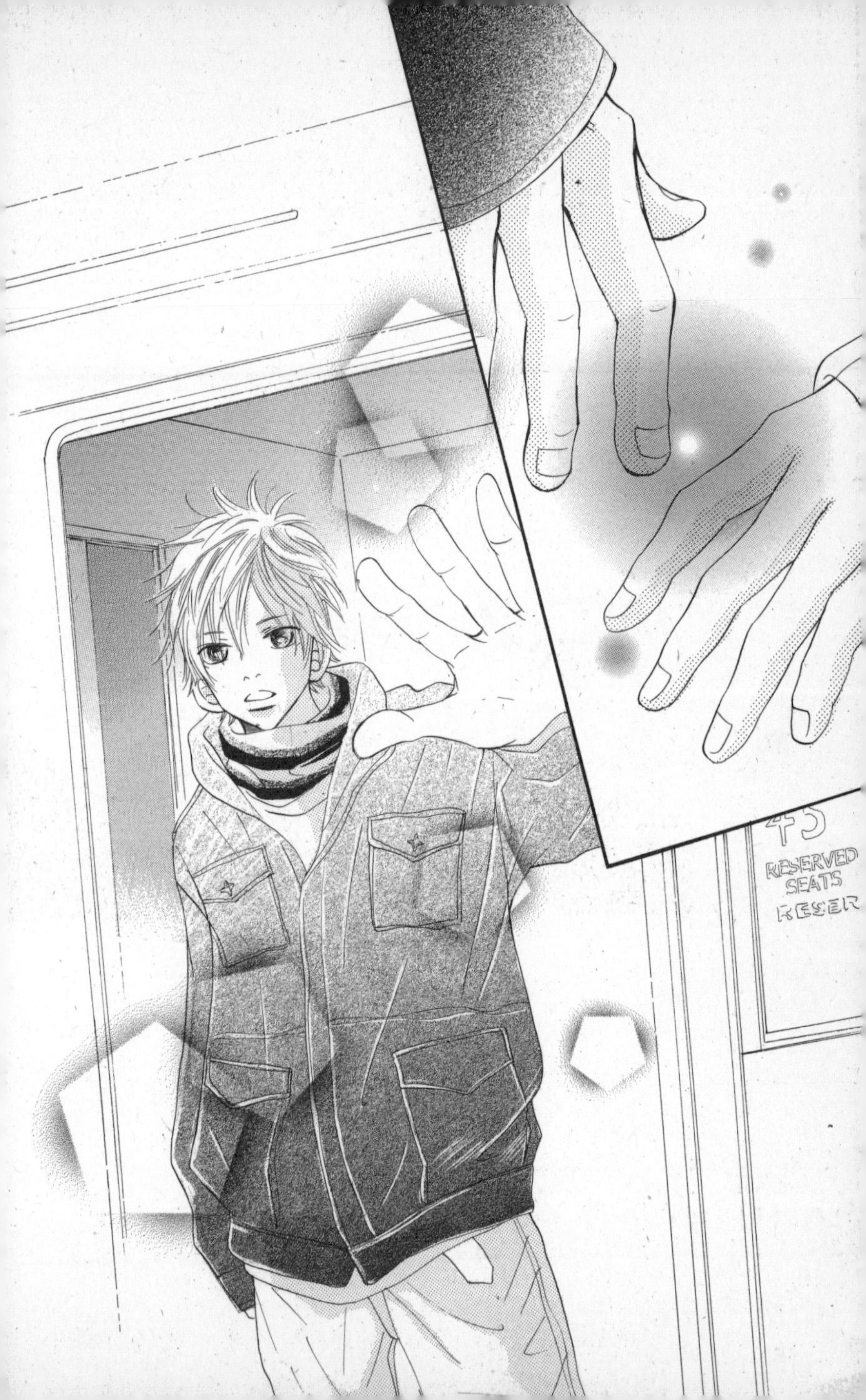
RESERVED
SEATS
RESER

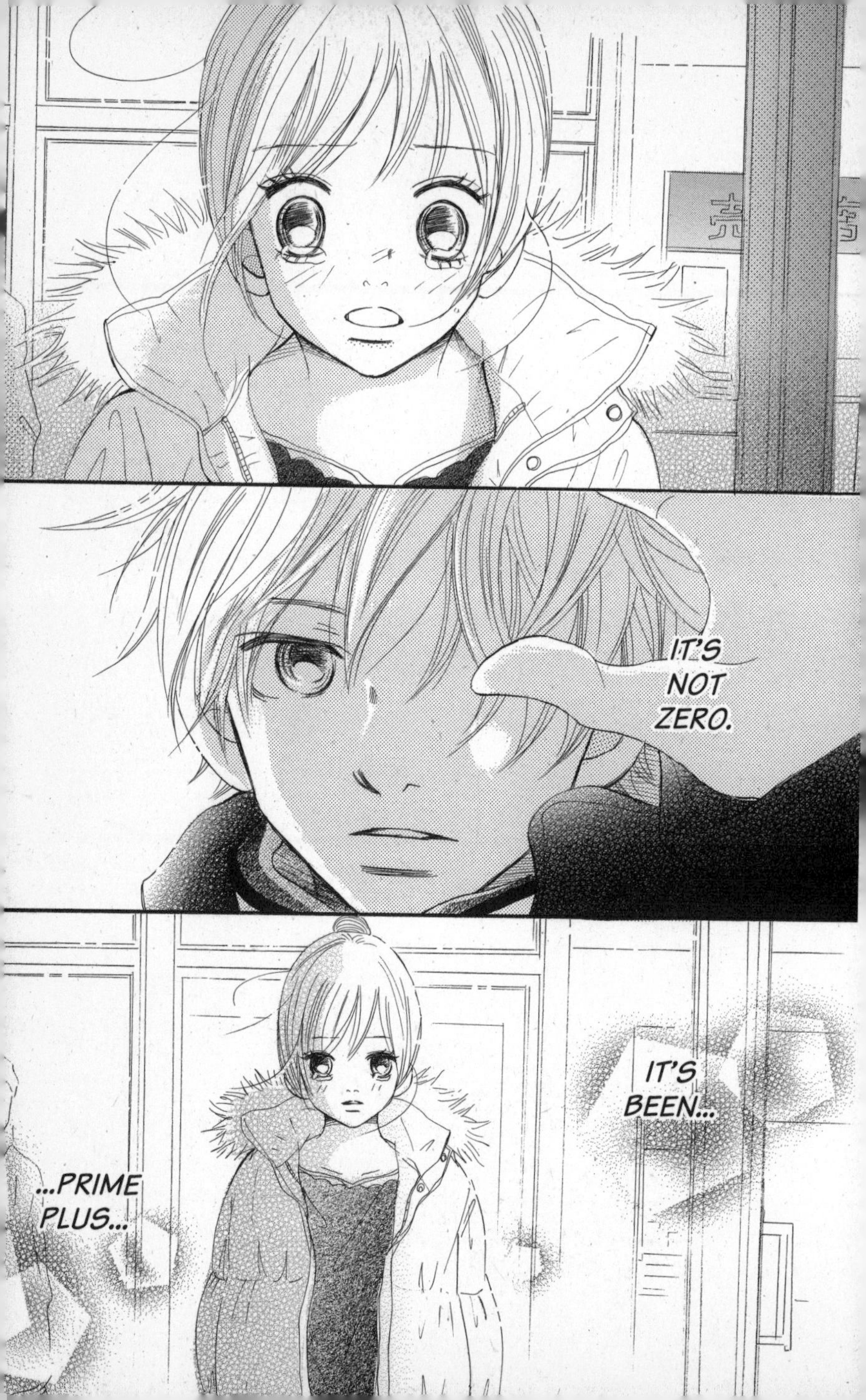
IT'S NOT ZERO.
IT'S BEEN...
...PRIME PLUS...

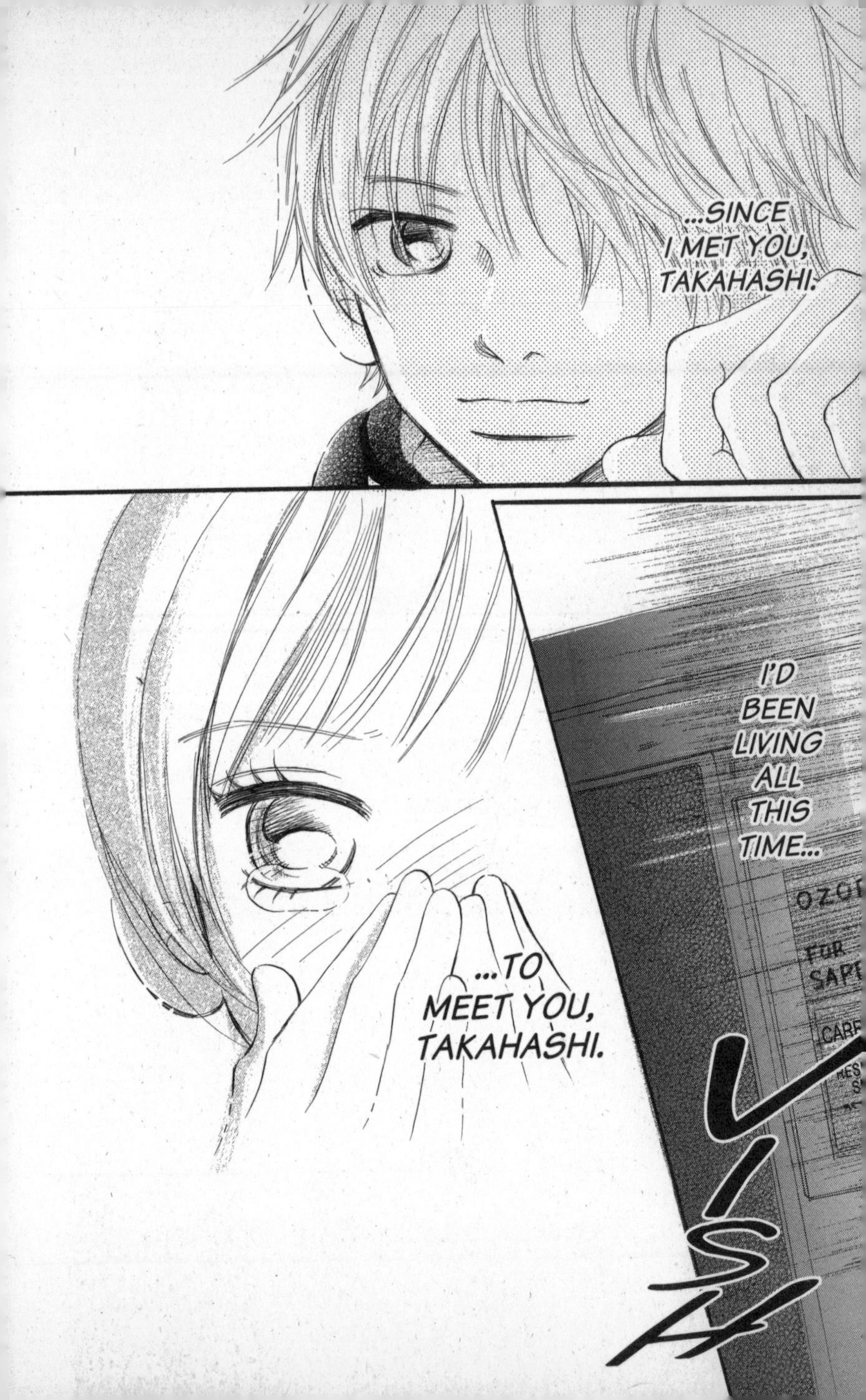
...SINCE I MET YOU, TAKAHASHI.
I'D BEEN LIVING ALL THIS TIME...
VISH
...TO MEET YOU, TAKAHASHI.

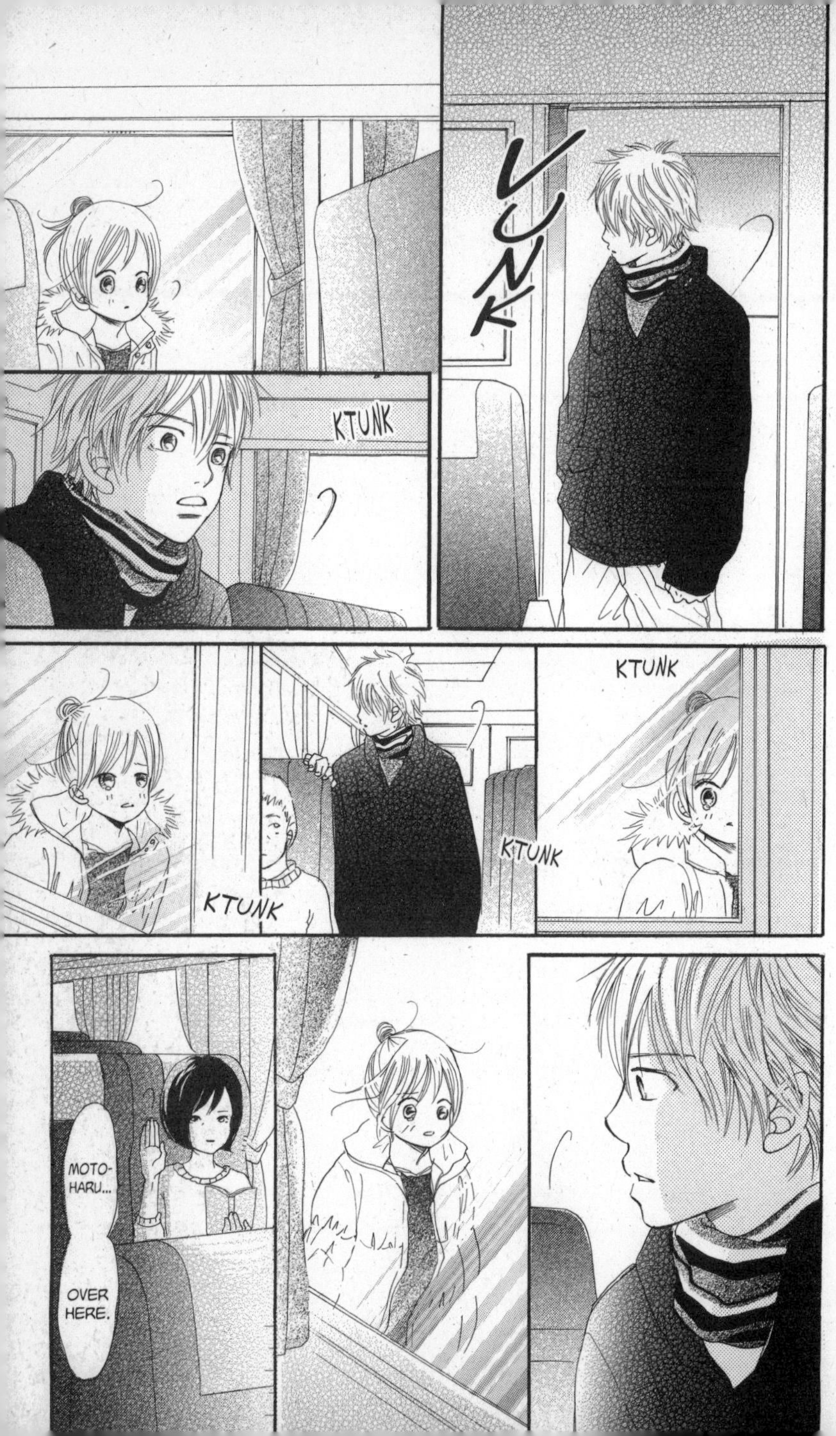
VUNK
KTUNK
KTUNK
KTUNK
KTUNK
MOTO-HARU...
OVER HERE.

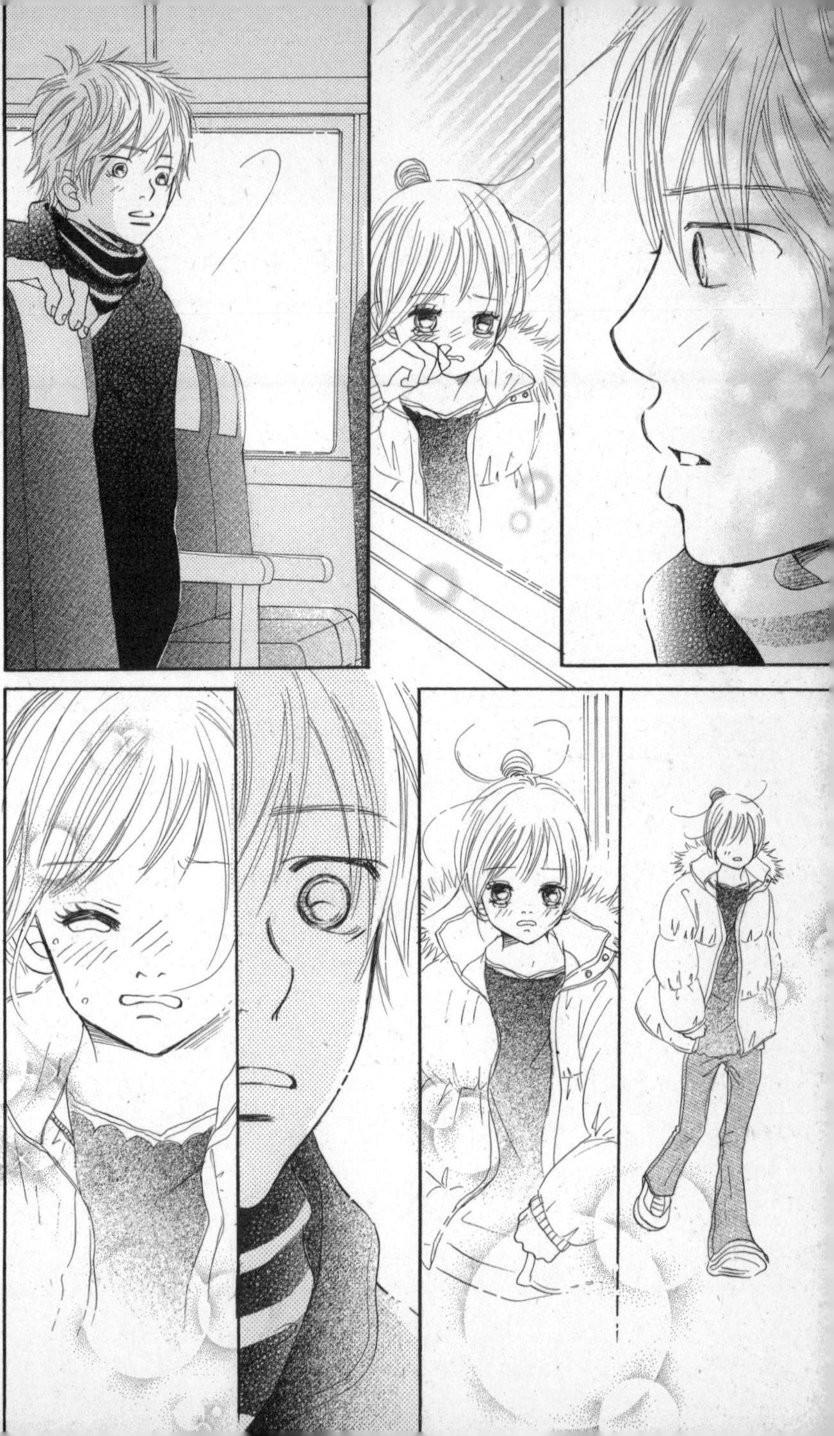

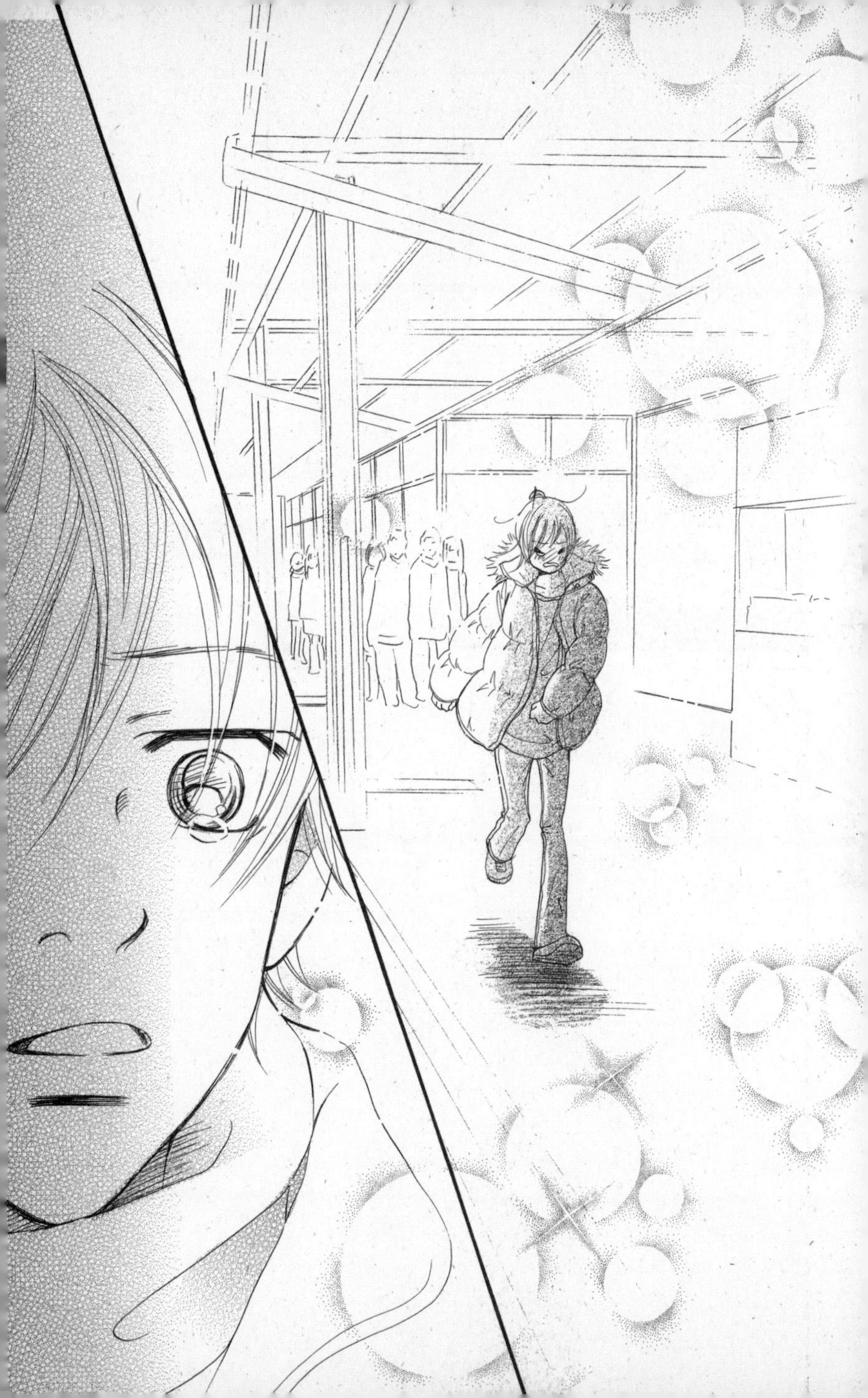

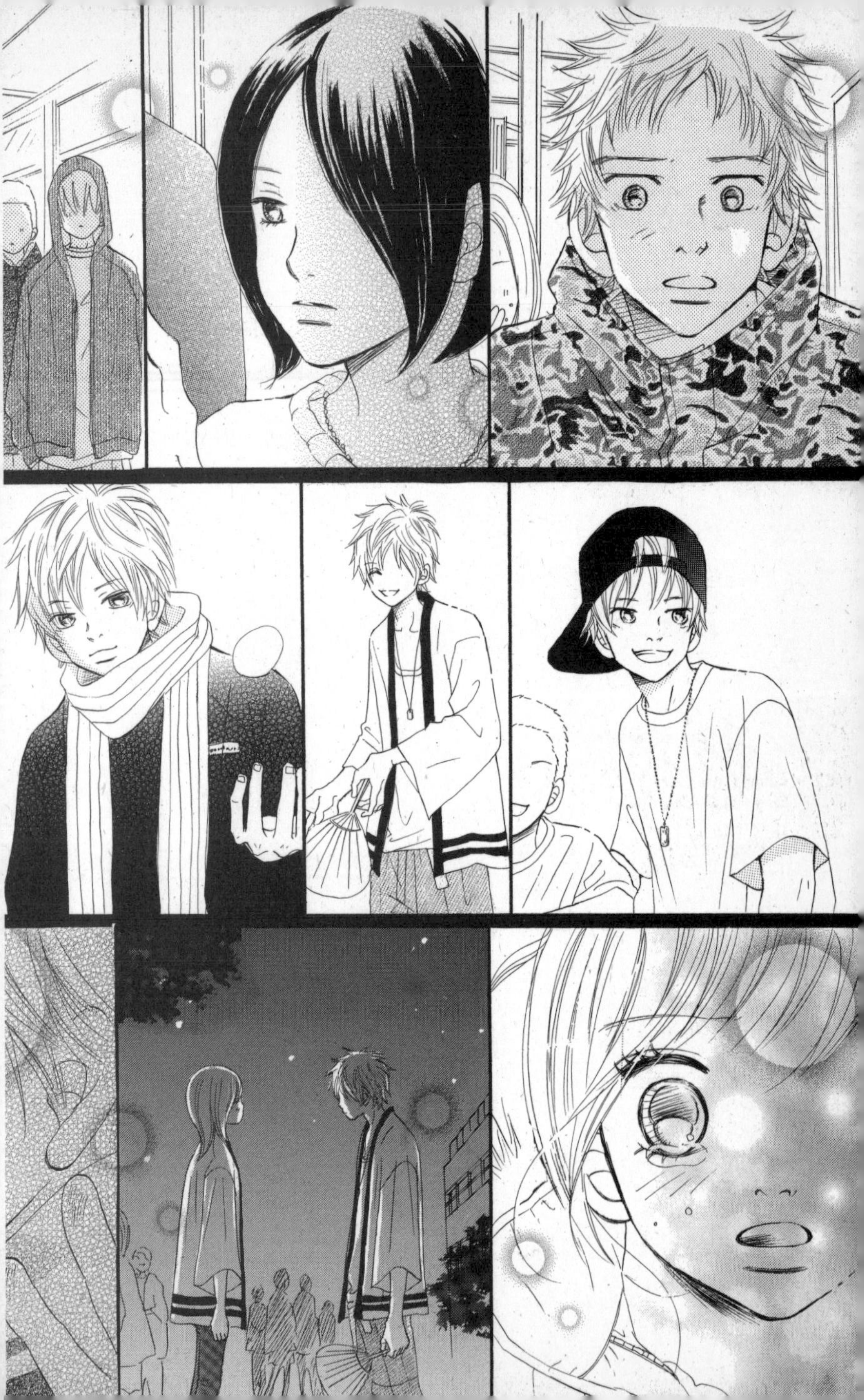

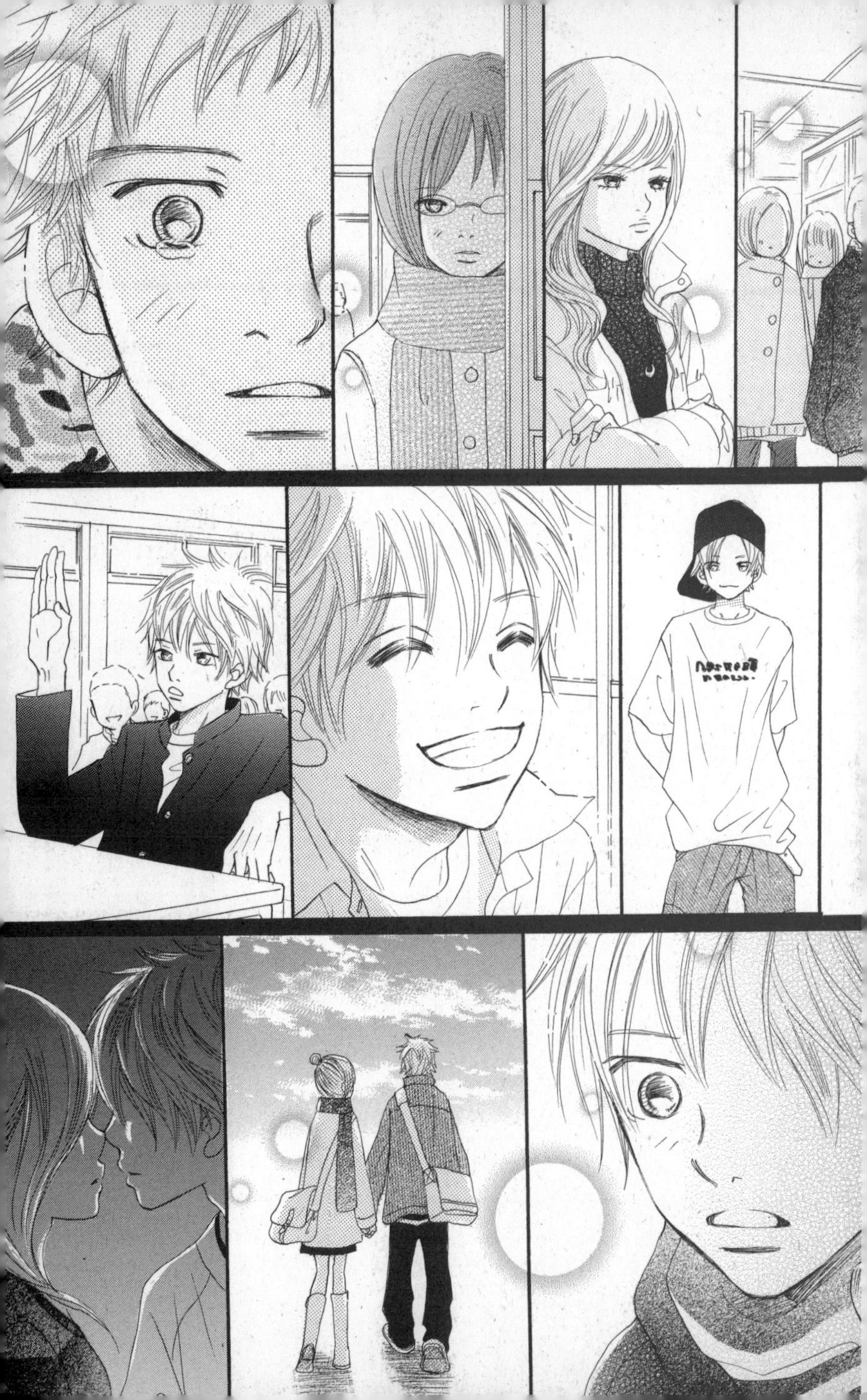

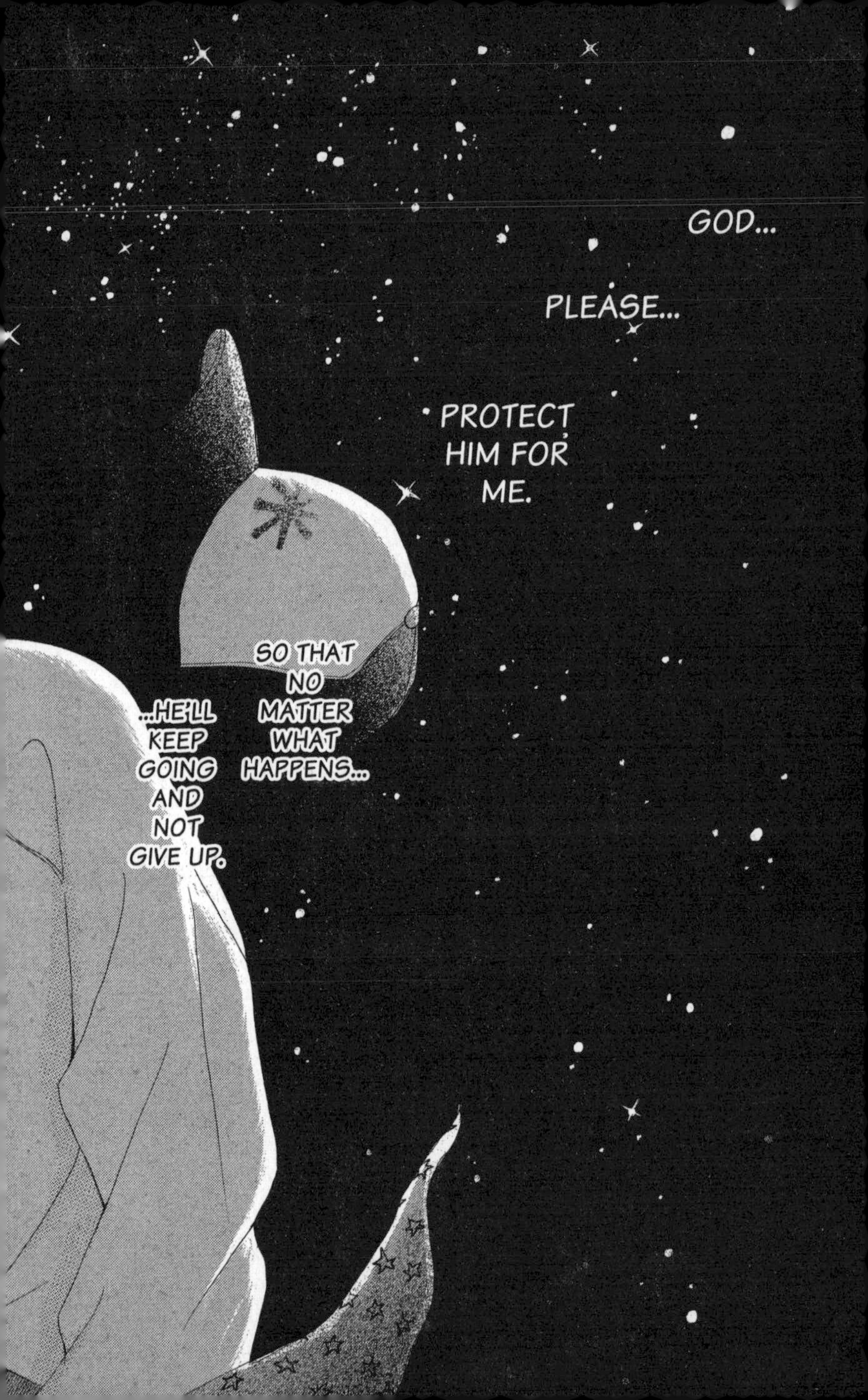
GOD...
PLEASE...
PROTECT HIM FOR ME.
SO THAT NO MATTER WHAT HAPPENS...
...HE'LL KEEP GOING AND NOT GIVE UP.

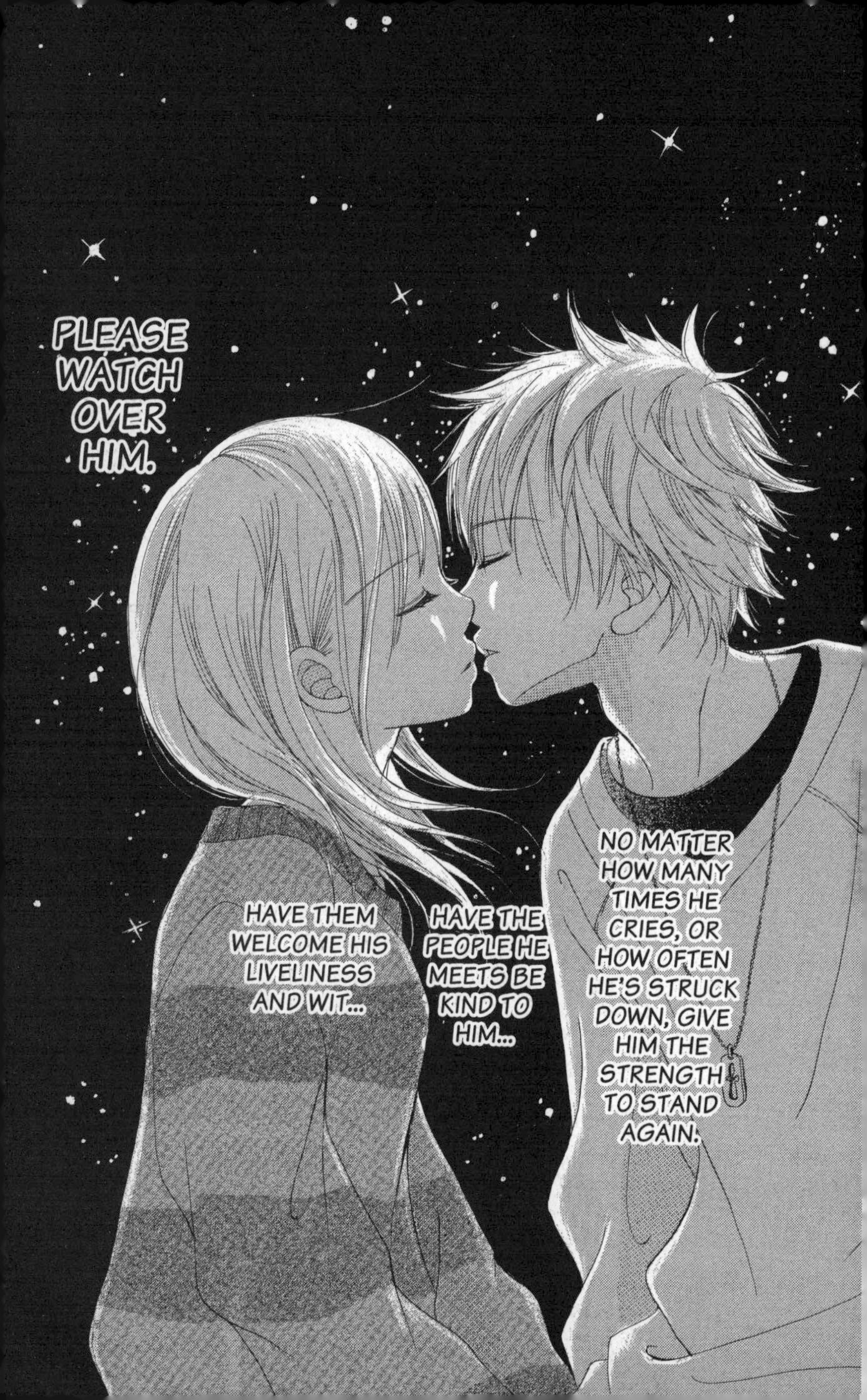
PLEASE WATCH OVER HIM.
NO MATTER HOW MANY TIMES HE CRIES, OR HOW OFTEN HE'S STRUCK DOWN, GIVE HIM THE STRENGTH TO STAND AGAIN.
HAVE THE PEOPLE HE MEETS BE KIND TO HIM...
HAVE THEM WELCOME HIS LIVELINESS AND WIT...

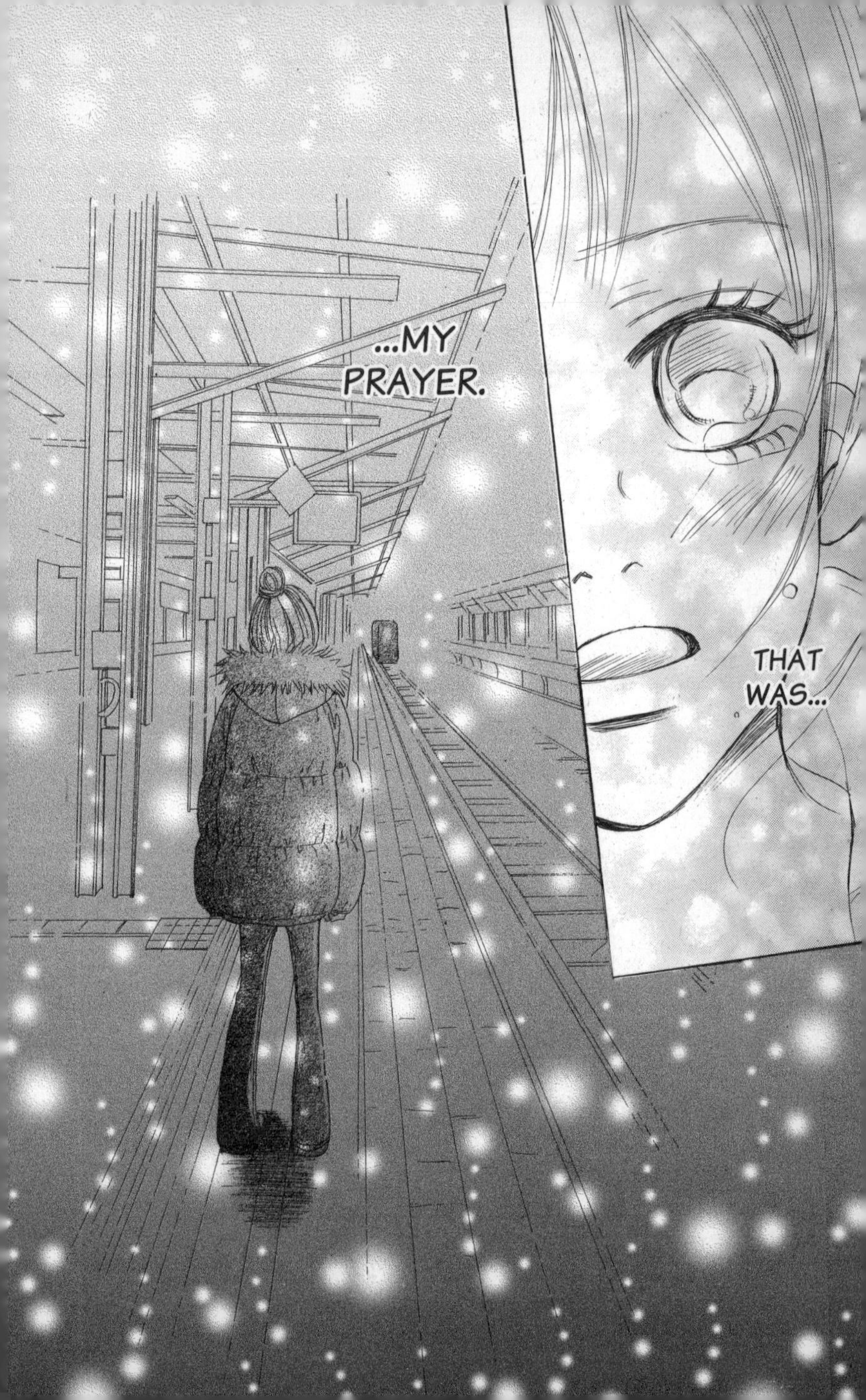
THAT WAS...
...MY PRAYER.

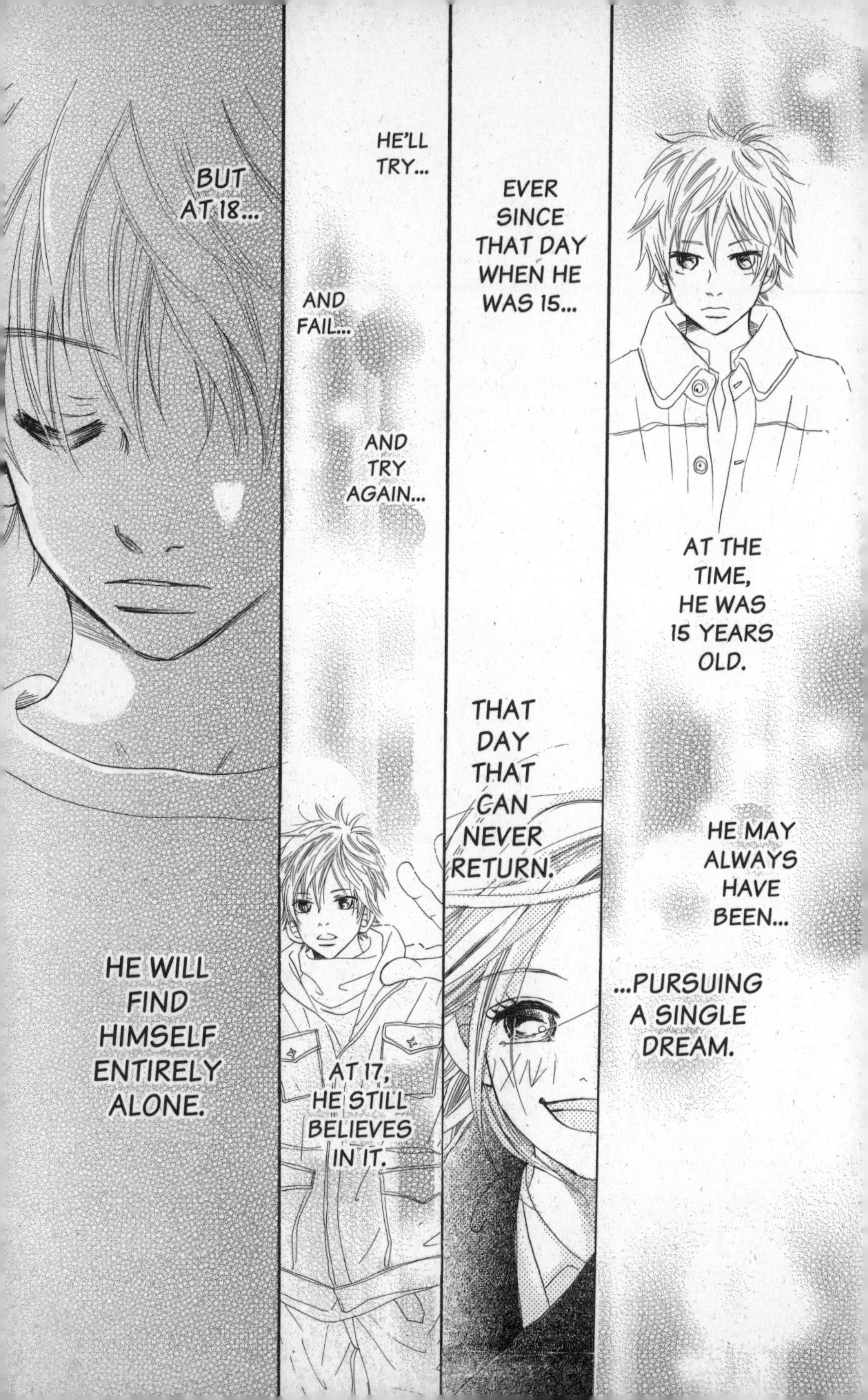
AT THE TIME, HE WAS 15 YEARS OLD.
HE MAY ALWAYS HAVE BEEN...
...PURSUING A SINGLE DREAM.
EVER SINCE THAT DAY WHEN HE WAS 15...
THAT DAY THAT CAN NEVER RETURN.
HE'LL TRY...
AND FAIL...
AND TRY AGAIN...
AT 17, HE STILL BELIEVES IN IT.
BUT AT 18...
HE WILL FIND HIMSELF ENTIRELY ALONE.

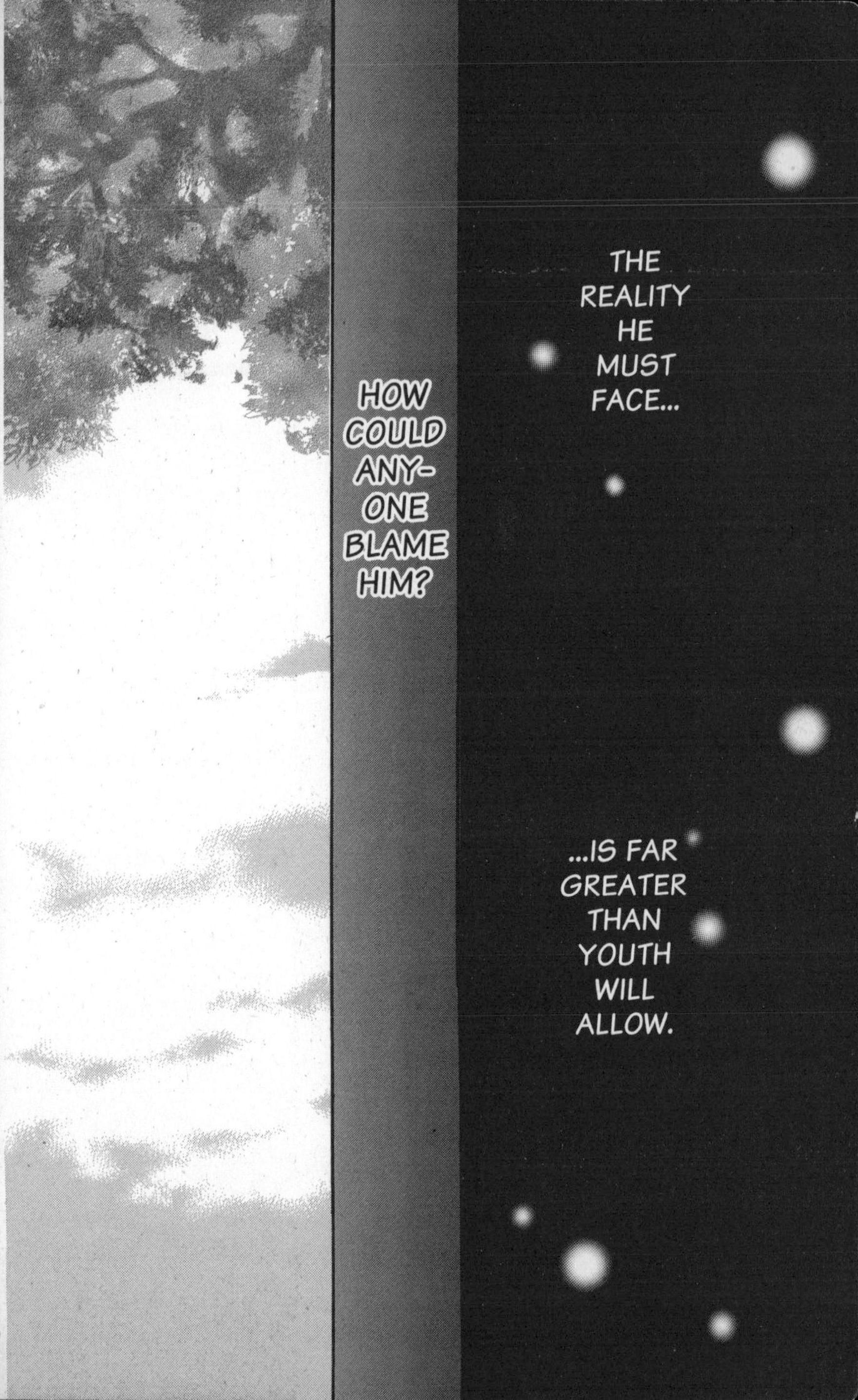
THE REALITY HE MUST FACE...
...IS FAR GREATER THAN YOUTH WILL ALLOW.
HOW COULD ANY-ONE BLAME HIM?

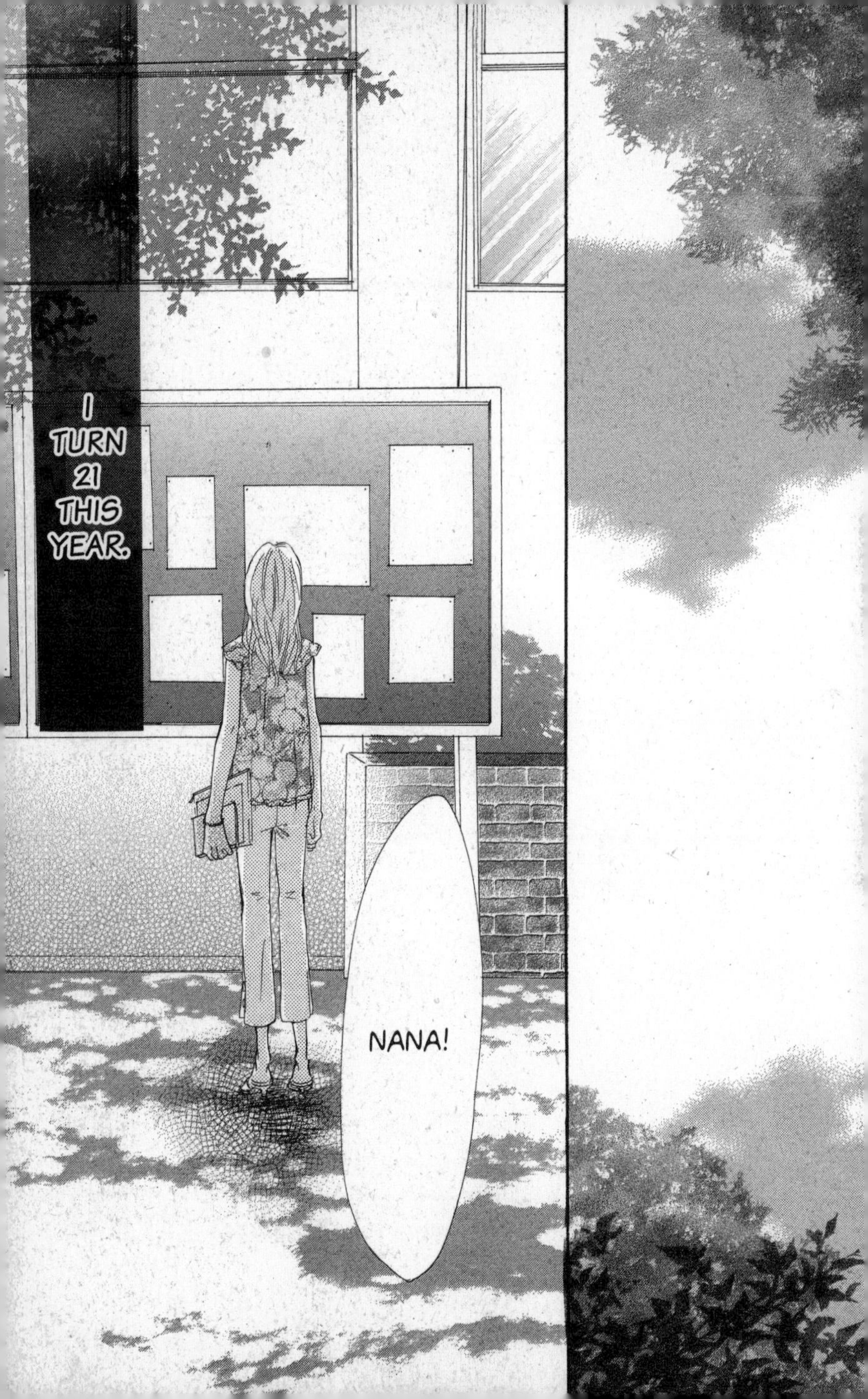
I TURN 21 THIS YEAR.
NANA!

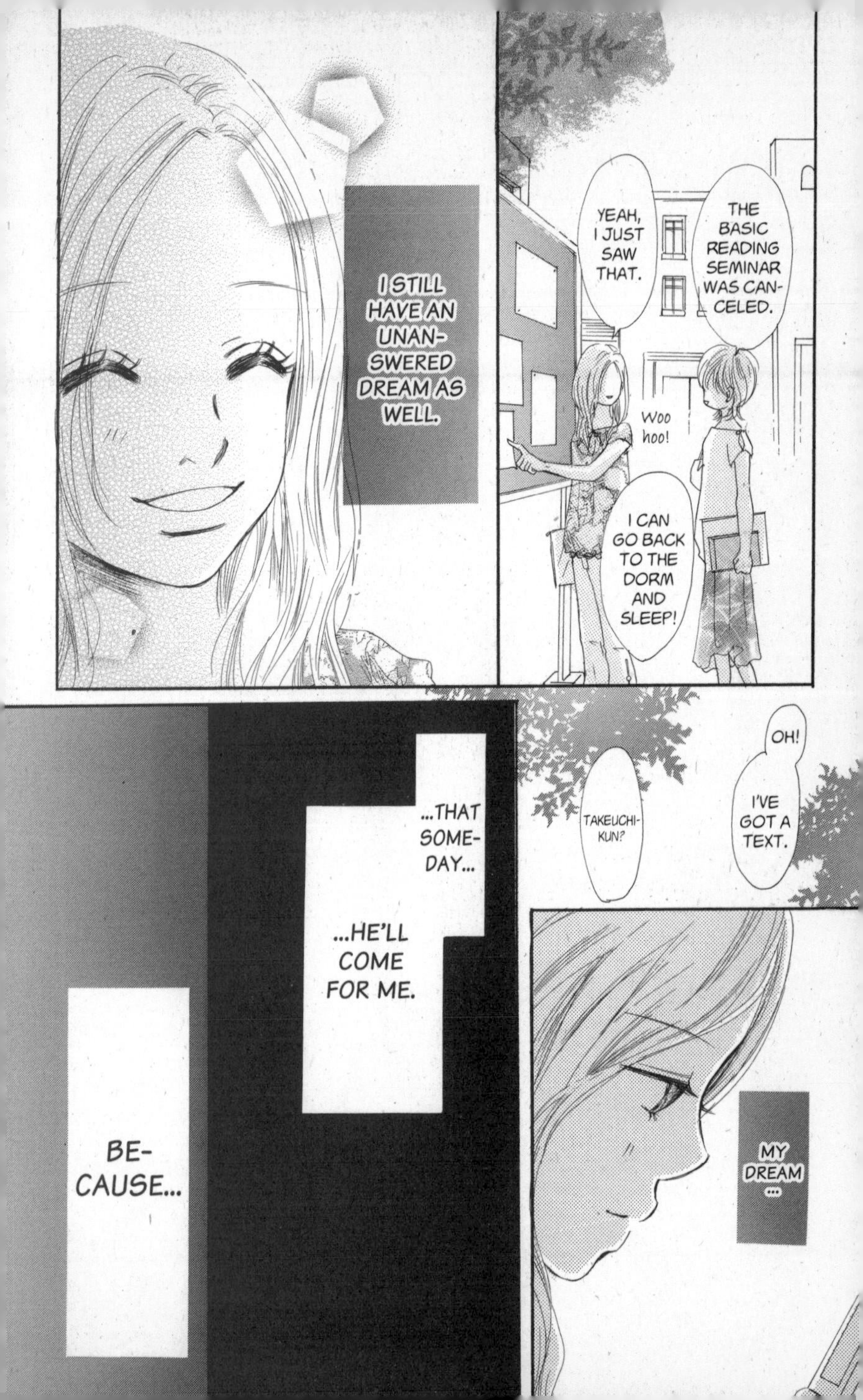
THE BASIC READING SEMINAR WAS CAN-CELED.
YEAH, I JUST SAW THAT.
Woo hoo!
I CAN GO BACK TO THE DORM AND SLEEP!
I STILL HAVE AN UNAN-SWERED DREAM AS WELL.
OH!
I'VE GOT A TEXT.
TAKEUCHI-KUN?
MY DREAM...
...THAT SOME-DAY...
...HE'LL COME FOR ME.
BE-CAUSE...

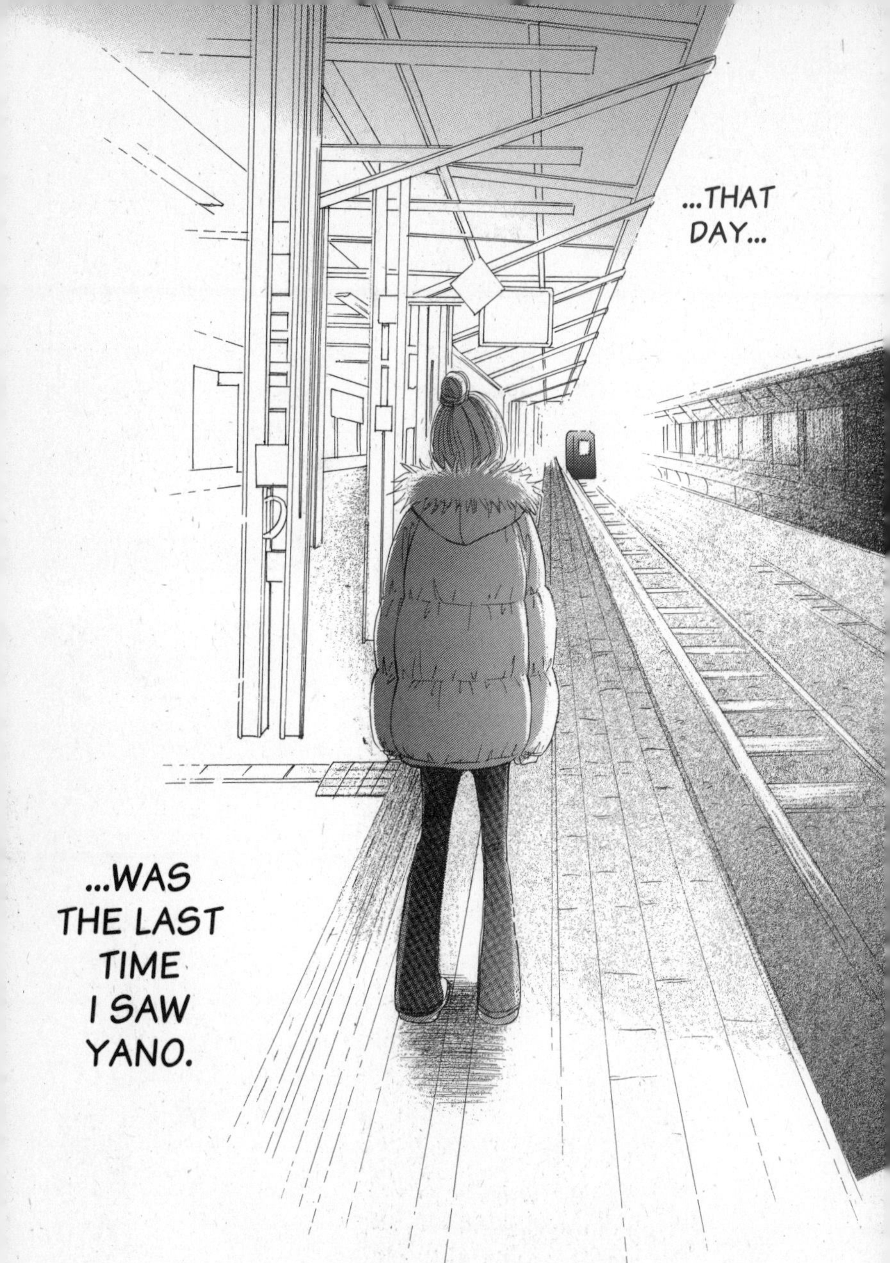
...THAT DAY...
...WAS THE LAST TIME I SAW YANO.

WE WERE THERE VOL. 8/END

Notes

Honorifics
In Japan, people are usually addressed by their name followed by a suffix.
The suffix shows familiarity or respect, depending on the relationship.
Male (familiar): first or last name + kun
Female (familiar): first or last name + chan
Adult (polite): last name + san
Upperclassman (polite): last name + senpai
Teacher or professional: last name + sensei
Close friends or lovers: first name only, no suffix

Nana-chan vs. Nana-san
Nanami's nickname is "Nana-chan." Yano's ex-girlfriend
was a year older, so she was known as "Nana-san."

Terms
Two hundred thousand yen is around two thousand U.S. dollars.
The "Doto area" refers to the eastern area of Hokkaido.

I'm currently discussing moving to the
south with a friend from my hometown.
Preferably somewhere I can see the sea.
–Yuki Obata

Yuki Obata's birthday is January 9. Her debut manga, *Raindrops*, won
the Shogakukan Shinjin Comics Taisho Kasaku Award in 1998. Her
current series, *We Were There* (*Bokura ga Ita*), won the 50th Shogakukan
Manga Award and was adapted into an animated television series. She
likes sweets, coffee, drinking with friends, and scary stories. Her hobby
is browsing in bookshops.

We Were There
Vol. 8
Shojo Beat Edition

STORY & ART BY
YUKI OBATA

Adaptation/Nancy Thistlethwaite
Translation/Tetsuichiro Miyaki
Touch-up Art & Lettering/Inori Fukuda Trant
Design/Courtney Utt
Editor/Nancy Thistlethwaite

VP, Production/Alvin Lu
VP, Sales & Product Marketing/Gonzalo Ferreyra
VP, Creative/Linda Espinosa
Publisher/Hyoe Narita

BOKURA GA ITA 8 by Yuuki OBATA © 2005 Yuuki OBATA
All rights reserved. Original Japanese edition
published in 2005 by Shogakukan Inc., Tokyo.

Printed in Canada

Published by VIZ Media, LLC
P.O. Box 77010
San Francisco, CA 94107

10 9 8 7 6 5 4 3 2 1
First printing, January 2010

www.viz.com

www.shojobeat.com